Basic Grammar in use

Self-study reference and practice for students of North American English

THIRD
EDITION

with answers

Raymond Murphy
with William R. Smalzer

CAMBRIDGE
UNIVERSITY PRESS

CAMBRIDGE
UNIVERSITY PRESS

University Printing House, Cambridge CB2 8BS, United Kingdom

One Liberty Plaza, 20th Floor, New York, NY 10006, USA

477 Williamstown Road, Port Melbourne, VIC 3207, Australia

4843/24, 2nd Floor, Ansari Road, Daryaganj, Delhi – 110002, India

79 Anson Road, #06–04/06, Singapore 079906

Cambridge University Press is part of the University of Cambridge.

It furthers the University's mission by disseminating knowledge in the pursuit of education, learning and research at the highest international levels of excellence.

www.cambridge.org
Information on this title: www.cambridge.org/9780521133340

© Cambridge University Press 1989, 2002, 2011

First published 1989
Second edition 2002
Third edition 2011
20 19 18

Printed in Malaysia by Vivar Printing

A catalog record for this publication is available from the British Library.

ISBN 978-0-521-13334-0 Student's Book with answers and CD-ROM
ISBN 978-0-521-13353-1 Student's Book with answers
ISBN 978-0-521-13337-1 Student's Book with CD-ROM
ISBN 978-0-521-13330-2 Workbook with answers

Book design and layout: Adventure House, NYC
Audio production: Richard LePage & Associates

Illustration credits: Carlos Castellanos, Richard Deverell, Travis Foster, Peter Hoey, Randy Jones, Gillian Martin, Sandy Nichols, Roger Penwill, Lisa Smith, Ian West, Simon Williams, and Tracy Wood

Contents

If you are not sure which units you need to study, use the **STUDY GUIDE** on page 263.

64 **myself/yourself/themselves**, etc.
65 **-'s** (**Kate's** camera / **my brother's** car, etc.)

A and *the*
66 **a/an**
67 **train**(s) **bus**(es) (singular and plural)
68 **a bottle** / **some water** (countable/uncountable 1)
69 **a cake** / **some cake** / **some cakes** (countable/uncountable 2)
70 **a/an** and **the**
71 **the . . .**
72 **go to work** **go home** **go to the movies**
73 **I like music** **I hate exams**
74 **the . . .** (names of places)

Determiners and pronouns
75 **this/that/these/those**
76 **one/ones**
77 **some** and **any**
78 **not + any** **no** **none**
79 **not + anybody/anyone/anything** **nobody/no one/nothing**
80 **somebody/anything/nowhere**, etc.
81 **every** and **all**
82 **all** **most** **some** **any** **no/none**
83 **both** **either** **neither**
84 **a lot** **much** **many**
85 **(a) little** **(a) few**

Adjectives and adverbs
86 **old/nice/interesting**, etc. (adjectives)
87 **quickly/badly/suddenly**, etc. (adverbs)
88 **old/older** **expensive** / **more expensive**
89 **older than . . .** **more expensive than . . .**
90 **not as . . . as**
91 **the oldest** **the most expensive**
92 **enough**
93 **too**

Word order
94 He **speaks English** very well. (word order 1)
95 **always/usually/often**, etc. (word order 2)
96 **still** **yet** **already**
97 **Give me that book!** **Give it to me!**

Conjunctions and clauses
98 **and** **but** **or** **so** **because**
99 **When . . .**
100 **If we go . . .** **If you see . . .**, etc.
101 **If I had . . .** **If we went . . .**, etc.
102 a person **who . . .** a thing **that/which** . . . (relative clauses 1)
103 the people **we met** the hotel **you stayed at** (relative clauses 2)

If you are not sure which units you need to study, use the **STUDY GUIDE** on page 263.

Prepositions

Phrasal verbs

To the Student

This is a grammar book for beginning to low-intermediate students of English. There are 116 units in the book, and each unit is about a different point of English grammar. There is a list of units at the beginning of the book (*Contents*).

Do not study all the units in order from beginning to end. It is better to choose the units that you *need* to do. For example, if you have a problem with the present perfect (*I have been, he has done,* etc.), study Units 16–21.

Use the *Contents* or the *Index* (at the back of the book) to find the unit (or units) that you need.

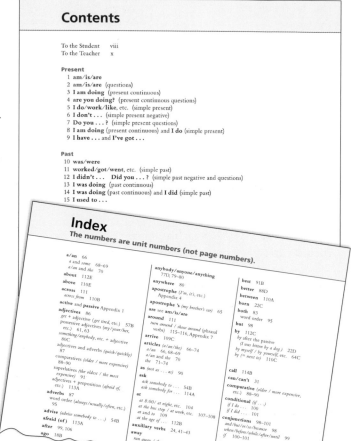

If you are not sure which units you need to study, use the *Study Guide* at the back of the book.

Study Guide (pages 263–275)

Each unit is two pages. The information is on the left-hand page and the exercises are on the right:

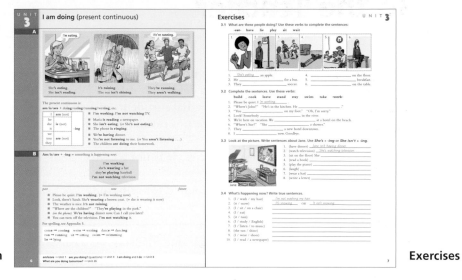

Information   **Exercises**

Study the left-hand page (information), and then do the exercises on the right-hand page.

Use the *Answer Key* to check your answers. The *Answer Key* is on pages 276–302.

Study the left-hand page again if necessary.

Don't forget the seven *Appendixes* at the back of the book (pages 235–243). These will give you information about active and passive forms, irregular verbs, short forms, spelling, and phrasal verbs.

There are also *Additional Exercises* at the back of the book (pages 244–262). There is a list of these exercises on page 244.

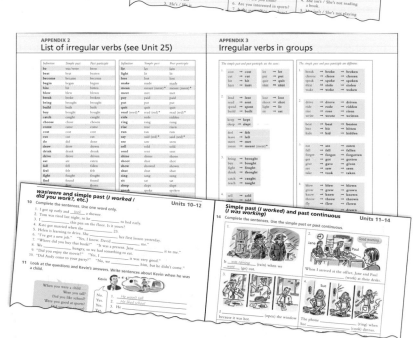

CD-ROM

This book is sold with or without a CD-ROM. On the CD-ROM, there are more exercises on all the units, and these are different from the exercises in the book. There are also more than 600 test questions.

To the Teacher

The most important features of this book are:
- It is a grammar book. It does not deal with other aspects of the language.
- It is for beginning to low-intermediate students of English. It does not cover areas of grammar which are not normally taught at the beginning to low-intermediate level.
- It is a reference book with exercises. It is not a course book and is not organized progressively.
- It is addressed to learners and intended for self-study.

Organization of the book

There are 116 units in the book, each one focusing on a particular area of grammar. The material is organized in grammatical categories, such as tenses, questions, and articles. Units are *not* ordered according to difficulty, and should therefore be selected and used in the order appropriate for the learner(s). The book should *not* be worked through from beginning to end. The units are listed in the *Contents*, and there is a comprehensive *Index* at the end of the book.

Each unit has the same format consisting of two facing pages. The grammar point is presented and explained on the left-hand page and the corresponding exercises are on the right. There are seven *Appendixes* (pages 235–243) dealing with active and passive forms, irregular verbs, short forms (contractions), spelling, and phrasal verbs. It might be useful for teachers to draw students' attention to these.

At the back of the book there is a set of *Additional Exercises* (pages 244–262). These exercises provide "mixed" practice bringing together grammar points from a number of different units (especially those concerning verb forms). There are 35 exercises in this section, and there is a full list on page 244.

Also at the back of the book there is a *Study Guide* to help students decide which units to study – see page 263.

Finally, there is an *Answer Key* (pages 276–302) for students to check their answers to all the exercises in the book. An edition without the *Study Guide* and *Answer Key* is available for teachers who would prefer it for their students.

Level

The book is for beginning learners, i.e., learners with very little English, but not for complete beginners. It is intended mainly for beginning students who are beyond the early stages of a beginners' course. It could also be used by low-intermediate learners whose grammar is weaker than other aspects of their English or who have problems with particular areas of basic grammar.

The explanations are addressed to the beginning learner and are therefore as simple and as short as possible. The vocabulary used in the examples and exercises has also been restricted so that the book can be used at this level.

Using the book

The book can be used by students working alone (see *To the Student*) or as supplementary course material. In either case the book can serve as a beginning grammar book.

When used as course material, the book can be used for immediate consolidation or for later revision or remedial work. It might be used by the whole class or by individual students needing extra help and practice.

In some cases it may be desirable to use the left-hand pages (presentation and explanation) in class, but it should be noted that these have been written for individual study and reference. In most cases, it would probably be better for teachers to present the grammar point in their preferred way with the exercises being done for homework. The left-hand page is then available for later reference by the student.

Some teachers may prefer to keep the book for revision and remedial work. In this case, individual students or groups of students can be directed to the appropriate units for self-study and practice.

CD-ROM

The book is sold with or without a CD-ROM. The CD-ROM contains further exercises on all the units in the book, as well as a bank of more than 600 test questions from which users can select to compile their own tests.

Basic Grammar in Use, *Third Edition*

This is a new edition of *Basic Grammar in Use*. The differences between this edition and the second edition are:

- The book has been redesigned with new color illustrations.
- There is reorganization, so some units have different numbers from the previous edition.
- There are many (usually minor) revisions to the explanations, examples, and exercises.
- There are two new pages of *Additional Exercises* (pages 244–262).
- There is a new CD-ROM with further exercises to accompany the book.

Basic Grammar
in use

am/is/are

A

I'm 22.

My name **is** Lisa.

I'm American. I'm from Chicago.

I'm a student.

My father **is** a doctor, and my mother **is** a journalist.

I'm **not** married.

My favorite color **is** blue.

My favorite sports **are** tennis and swimming.

I'm interested in art.

Lisa

B

Positive		
I	**am**	(I'**m**)
he she it	**is**	(he'**s**) (she'**s**) (it'**s**)
we you they	**are**	(we'**re**) (you'**re**) (they'**re**)

short forms

Negative				
I	**am not**	(I'**m not**)		
he she it	**is not**	(he'**s not** (she'**s not** (it'**s not**	*or* *or* *or*	he **isn't**) she **isn't**) it **isn't**)
we you they	**are not**	(we'**re not** (you'**re not** (they'**re not**	*or* *or* *or*	we **aren't**) you **aren't**) they **aren't**)

short forms

- I'**m** cold. Can you close the window, please?
- I'**m** 32 years old. My sister **is** 29.
- Steve **is** sick. He'**s** in bed.
- My brother **is** afraid of dogs.
- It'**s** 10:00. You'**re** late again.
- Ann and I **are** good friends.
- Your keys **are** on the table.

- I'**m** tired, but I'**m not** hungry.
- Tom **isn't** interested in politics. He'**s** interested in music.
- Jane **isn't** a teacher. She'**s** a student.
- Those people **aren't** Canadian. They'**re** Australian.
- It'**s** sunny today, but it **isn't** warm.

I'm afraid of dogs.

C

that'**s** = that **is**   there'**s** = there **is**   here'**s** = here **is**

- Thank you. That'**s** very nice of you.
- Look! There'**s** Chris.
- "Here'**s** your key."   "Thank you."

HOTEL

Here's your key.

Thank you.

am/is/are (questions) → Unit 2   **there is/are** → Unit 38   **a/an** → Unit 66   **short forms** → Appendix 4

Exercises

1.1 Write the short form (*she's* / *we aren't*, etc.).

1. she is ___she's___
2. they are _____
3. it is not _____
4. that is _____
5. I am not _____
6. you are not _____

1.2 Write *am*, *is*, or *are*.

1. The weather __is__ nice today.
2. I _____ not rich.
3. This bag _____ heavy.
4. These bags _____ heavy.
5. Look! There _____ Carol.
6. My brother and I _____ good tennis players.
7. Amy _____ at home. Her children _____ at school.
8. I _____ a taxi driver. My sister _____ a nurse.

1.3 Complete the sentences.

1. Steve is sick. ___He's___ in bed.
2. I'm not hungry, but _____ thirsty.
3. Mr. Thomas is a very old man. _____ 98.
4. These chairs aren't beautiful, but _____ comfortable.
5. The weather is nice today. _____ warm and sunny.
6. "_____ late." "No, I'm not. I'm early!"
7. Catherine isn't at home. _____ at work.
8. "_____ your coat." "Oh, thank you very much."

1.4 Look at Lisa's sentences in 1A. Now write sentences about yourself.

1. (name?) My _____
2. (from?) I _____
3. (age?) I _____
4. (job?) I _____
5. (favorite color or colors?) My _____
6. (interested in . . . ?) I _____

1.5 Write sentences for the pictures. Use:

afraid   angry   cold   hot   hungry   ~~thirsty~~

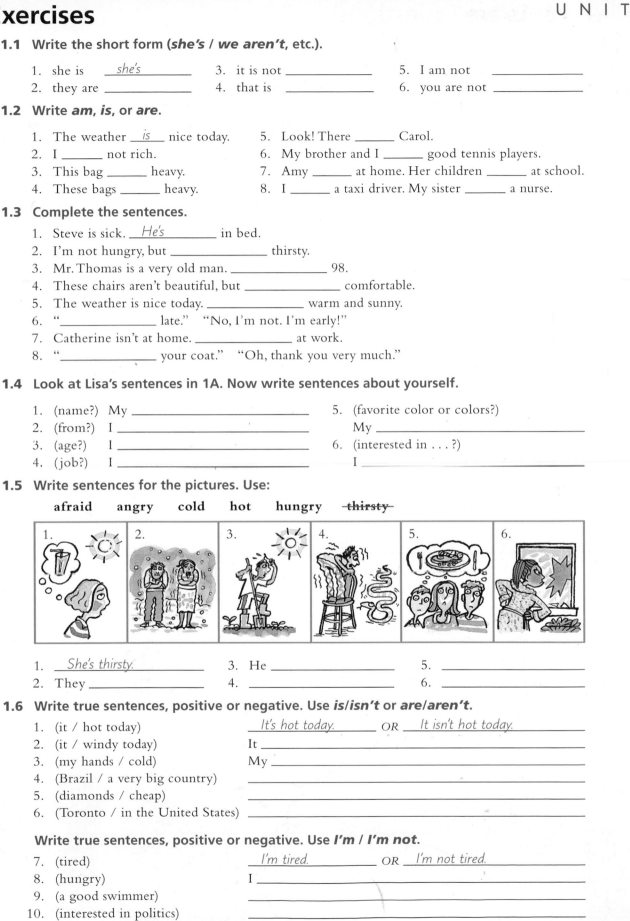

1. ___She's thirsty.___
2. They _____
3. He _____
4. _____
5. _____
6. _____

1.6 Write true sentences, positive or negative. Use *is/isn't* or *are/aren't*.

1. (it / hot today)   ___It's hot today.___ OR ___It isn't hot today.___
2. (it / windy today)   It _____
3. (my hands / cold)   My _____
4. (Brazil / a very big country)   _____
5. (diamonds / cheap)   _____
6. (Toronto / in the United States)   _____

Write true sentences, positive or negative. Use *I'm* / *I'm not*.

7. (tired)   ___I'm tired.___ OR ___I'm not tired.___
8. (hungry)   I _____
9. (a good swimmer)   _____
10. (interested in politics)   _____

am/is/are (questions)

A

Positive	
I	am
he she it	is
we you they	are

Question	
am	I?
is	he? she? it?
are	we? you? they?

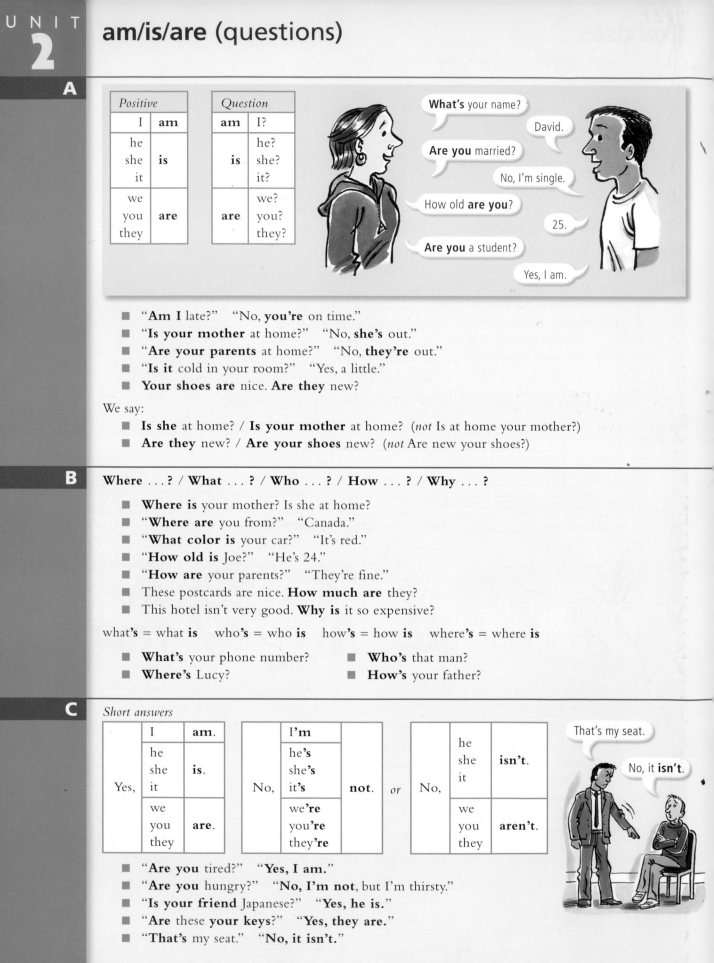

What's your name?

David.

Are you married?

No, I'm single.

How old are you?

25.

Are you a student?

Yes, I am.

- "**Am I** late?" "No, **you're** on time."
- "**Is your mother** at home?" "No, **she's** out."
- "**Are your parents** at home?" "No, **they're** out."
- "**Is it** cold in your room?" "Yes, a little."
- **Your shoes are** nice. **Are they** new?

We say:
- **Is she** at home? / **Is your mother** at home? (*not* Is at home your mother?)
- **Are they** new? / **Are your shoes** new? (*not* Are new your shoes?)

B

Where . . . ? / What . . . ? / Who . . . ? / How . . . ? / Why . . . ?

- **Where is** your mother? Is she at home?
- "**Where are** you from?" "Canada."
- "**What color is** your car?" "It's red."
- "**How old is** Joe?" "He's 24."
- "**How are** your parents?" "They're fine."
- These postcards are nice. **How much are** they?
- This hotel isn't very good. **Why is** it so expensive?

what**'s** = what **is**   who**'s** = who **is**   how**'s** = how **is**   where**'s** = where **is**

- **What's** your phone number?
- **Where's** Lucy?
- **Who's** that man?
- **How's** your father?

C

Short answers

Yes,	I	am.
	he she it	is.
	we you they	are.

No,	I'm	
	he's she's it's	not.
	we're you're they're	

or

No,	he she it	isn't.
	we you they	aren't.

That's my seat.

No, it **isn't**.

- "**Are you** tired?" "**Yes, I am.**"
- "**Are you** hungry?" "**No, I'm not**, but I'm thirsty."
- "**Is your friend** Japanese?" "**Yes, he is.**"
- "**Are** these **your keys**?" "**Yes, they are.**"
- "**That's** my seat." "**No, it isn't.**"

am/is/are → Unit 1   questions → Unit 45   what/which/how → Unit 48

Exercises

2.1 Find the right answers for the questions.

1.	Where's the camera?	a)	Toronto.	1. _g_
2.	Is your car blue?	b)	No, I'm not.	2. ____
3.	Is Linda from London?	c)	Yes, you are.	3. ____
4.	Am I late?	d)	My sister.	4. ____
5.	Where's Ann from?	e)	Black.	5. ____
6.	What color is your bag?	f)	No, it's black.	6. ____
7.	Are you hungry?	g)	In your bag.	7. ____
8.	How is George?	h)	No, she's American.	8. ____
9.	Who's that woman?	i)	Fine.	9. ____

2.2 Make questions with these words.

1. (is / at home / your mother) _Is your mother at home_____ ?
2. (your parents / are / how) _How are your parents_____ ?
3. (interesting / is / your job) _____ ?
4. (the stores / are / open today) _____ ?
5. (from / where / you / are) _____ ?
6. (interested in sports / you / are) _____ ?
7. (is / near here / the post office) _____ ?
8. (at school / are / your children) _____ ?
9. (you / are / late / why) _____ ?

2.3 Complete the questions. Use *What . . . / Who . . . / Where . . . / How . . . .*

1.	_____ _How are_ your children?	They're fine.
2.	_____ the bus stop?	At the end of the block.
3.	_____ your children?	Five, six, and ten.
4.	_____ these oranges?	$1.50 a pound.
5.	_____ your favorite sport?	Skiing.
6.	_____ the man in this photograph?	That's my father.
7.	_____ your new shoes?	Black.

2.4 Write the questions.

Paul

1.	(name?) _What's your name?_____	Paul.
2.	(Australian?) _____	No, I'm Canadian.
3.	(how old?) _____	I'm 30.
4.	(a teacher?) _____	No, I'm a lawyer.
5.	(married?) _____	Yes, I am.
6.	(wife a lawyer?) _____	No, she's a teacher.
7.	(from?) _____	She's from Mexico.
8.	(her name?) _____	Ana.
9.	(how old?) _____	She's 27.

2.5 Write short answers (*Yes, I am. / No, he isn't.*, etc.).

1. Are you married? _No, I'm not._____   4. Are your hands cold? _____
2. Are you thirsty? _____   5. Is it dark now? _____
3. Is it cold today? _____   6. Are you a teacher? _____

→ Additional exercises 1–2 (pages 244–245)

I am doing (present continuous)

She**'s eating**.
She **isn't reading**.

It**'s raining**.
The sun **isn't shining**.

They**'re running**.
They **aren't walking**.

The present continuous is:

am/is/are + do**ing**/eat**ing**/runn**ing**/writ**ing**, etc.

I	**am** (not)	
he she it	**is** (not)	**-ing**
we you they	**are** (not)	

- **I'm working. I'm not watching** TV.
- Maria **is reading** a newspaper.
- She **isn't eating**. (*or* She**'s not eating**.)
- The phone **is ringing**.
- We**'re having** dinner.
- You**'re not listening** to me. (*or* You **aren't listening** . . .)
- The children **are doing** their homework.

B   **Am/is/are** + **-ing** = something is happening *now*:

> **I'm working**
> she**'s wearing** a hat
> they**'re playing** baseball
> **I'm not watching** television

---

past   *now*   *future*

- Please be quiet. **I'm working**. (= I'm working now)
- Look, there's Sarah. She**'s wearing** a brown coat. (= she is wearing it now)
- The weather is nice. It**'s not raining**.
- "Where are the children?"   "They**'re playing** in the park."
- *(on the phone)* We**'re having** dinner now. Can I call you later?
- You can turn off the television. **I'm not watching** it.

For spelling, see Appendix 5.

come ➞ com**ing**   write ➞ writ**ing**   dance ➞ danc**ing** run ➞ ru**nn**ing   sit ➞ si**tt**ing   swim ➞ swi**mm**ing lie ➞ **ly**ing

am/is/are → Unit 1   **are you doing?** (questions) → Unit 4   **I am doing** and **I do** → Unit 8
What are you doing tomorrow? → Unit 26

Exercises

3.1 **What are these people doing? Use these verbs to complete the sentences:**

~~eat~~   have   lie   play   sit   wait

1. __She's eating__ an apple.
2. He _____ for a bus.
3. They _____ soccer.
4. _____ on the floor.
5. _____ breakfast.
6. _____ on the table.

3.2 **Complete the sentences. Use these verbs:**

build   cook   leave   stand   stay   swim   take   ~~work~~

1. Please be quiet. I __'m working__ .
2. "Where's John?"   "He's in the kitchen. He _____ ."
3. "You _____ on my foot."   "Oh, I'm sorry."
4. Look! Somebody _____ in the river.
5. We're here on vacation. We _____ at a hotel on the beach.
6. "Where's Sue?"   "She _____ a shower."
7. They _____ a new hotel downtown.
8. I _____ now. Goodbye.

3.3 **Look at the picture. Write sentences about Jane. Use *She's* + *-ing* or *She isn't* + *-ing*.**

Jane

1. (have dinner) __Jane isn't having dinner.__
2. (watch television) __She's watching television.__
3. (sit on the floor) She _____
4. (read a book) _____
5. (play the piano) _____
6. (laugh) _____
7. (wear a hat) _____
8. (write a letter) _____

3.4 **What's happening now? Write true sentences.**

1. (I / wash / my hair)   __I'm not washing my hair.__
2. (it / snow)   __It's snowing.__   OR   __It isn't snowing.__
3. (I / sit / on a chair)   _____
4. (I / eat)   _____
5. (it / rain)   _____
6. (I / study / English)   _____
7. (I / listen / to music)   _____
8. (the sun / shine)   _____
9. (I / wear / shoes)   _____
10. (I / read / a newspaper)   _____

are you doing? (present continuous questions)

A

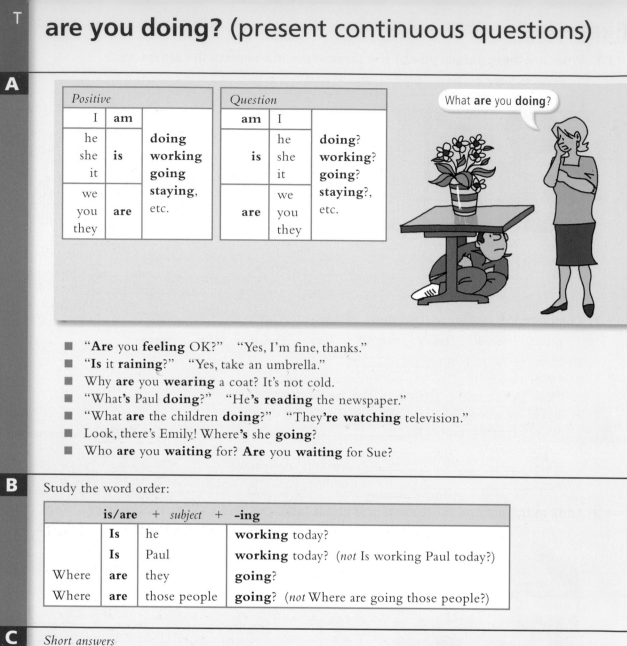

Positive		
I	am	
he she it	is	doing working going staying, etc.
we you they	are	

Question		
am	I	
is	he she it	doing? working? going? staying?, etc.
are	we you they	

What **are** you **doing**?

- "**Are** you **feeling** OK?"   "Yes, I'm fine, thanks."
- "**Is it raining**?"   "Yes, take an umbrella."
- Why **are** you **wearing** a coat? It's not cold.
- "**What's** Paul **doing**?"   "He**'s reading** the newspaper."
- "What **are** the children **doing**?"   "They**'re watching** television."
- Look, there's Emily! Where**'s** she **going**?
- Who **are** you **waiting** for? **Are** you **waiting** for Sue?

B

Study the word order:

	is/are	+ subject +	-ing
	Is	he	**working** today?
	Is	Paul	**working** today? (not Is working Paul today?)
Where	**are**	they	**going**?
Where	**are**	those people	**going**? (not Where are going those people?)

C

Short answers

Yes,	I	am.
	he she it	is.
	we you they	are.

No,	I'm	not.
	he's she's it's	
	we're you're they're	

or

No,	he she it	isn't.
	we you they	aren't.

- "**Are** you **leaving** now?"   "**Yes, I am.**"
- "**Is** Paul **working** today?"   "**Yes, he is.**"
- "**Is it raining**?"   "**No, it isn't.**"
- "**Are** your friends **staying** at a hotel?"   "**No, they aren't.** They're staying with me."

I am doing → Unit 3   **What are you doing tomorrow?** → Unit 26   questions → Units 45–48

Exercises

4.1 Look at the pictures and write the questions.

1. (you / watch / it?) _____
   Are you watching it?
   No, you can turn it off.

2. (you / leave / now?) _____
   Yes, see you tomorrow.

3. (it / rain?) _____
   No, not right now.

4. (you / enjoy / the movie?) _____
   Yes, it's very funny.

5. (that clock / work?) _____
   No, it's broken.

6. (you / wait / for a bus?) _____
   No, for a taxi.

4.2 Look at the pictures and complete the questions. Use:

cr̶y̶   e̶a̶t̶   g̶o̶   laugh   look at   r̶e̶a̶d̶

1. What __*are you*__ __*reading*__ ?

2. Where _____ she _____ ?

3. What _____ _____ ?

4. Why _____ ?

5. What _____ ?

6. Why _____ ?

4.3 Make questions with these words. Put the words in the right order.

1. (is / working / Paul / today) __*Is Paul working today*__ ?
2. (what / the children / are / doing) __*What are the children doing*__ ?
3. (you / are / listening / to me) _____ ?
4. (where / your friends / are / going) _____ ?
5. (are / watching / your parents / television) _____ ?
6. (what / Jessica / is / cooking) _____ ?
7. (why / you / are / looking / at me) _____ ?
8. (is / coming / the bus) _____ ?

4.4 Write short answers (*Yes, I am.* / *No, he isn't.*, etc.).

1. Are you watching TV? __*No, I'm not.*__
2. Are you wearing a watch? _____
3. Are you eating something? _____
4. Is it raining? _____
5. Are you sitting on the floor? _____
6. Are you feeling all right? _____

→ Additional exercise 3 (page 245)

I do/work/like, etc. (simple present)

We **read** a lot.

They're looking at their books.
They **read** a lot.

I **like** ice cream.

He's eating an ice cream cone.
He **likes** ice cream.

They **read** / he **likes** / I **work**, etc. = the *simple present*:

I/we/you/they	**read**	**like**	**work**	**live**	**watch**	**do**	**have**
he/she/it	**reads**	**likes**	**works**	**lives**	**watches**	**does**	**has**

Remember:

he work**s** / **she** live**s** / **it** rain**s**, etc.

- **I work** in an office. **My brother works** in a bank. (*not* My brother work)
- **Lucy lives** in Houston. **Her parents live** in Chicago.
- **It rains** a lot in the winter.

I **have** → he/she/it **has**:

- **John has** lunch at home every day.

For spelling, see Appendix 5.

-es after **-s** / **-sh** / **-ch**:	pass → pass**es**	finish → finish**es**	watch → watch**es**
-y → -ies:	stud**y** → stud**ies**	tr**y** → tr**ies**	
also:	do → do**es**	go → go**es**	

We use the simple present for things that are true in general, or for things that happen sometimes or all the time:

- I **like** big cities.
- Your English is good. You **speak** very well.
- Tim **works** very hard. He **starts** at 7:30 and **finishes** at 8:00 at night.
- The earth **goes** around the sun.
- We **do** a lot of different things in our free time.
- It **costs** a lot of money to build a hospital.

Always/never/often/usually/sometimes + simple present

- Sue **always gets** to work early. (*not* Sue gets always)
- I **never eat** breakfast. (*not* I eat never)
- We **often sleep** late on weekends.
- Mark **usually plays** tennis on Sundays.
- I **sometimes walk** to work, but not very often.

I don't . . . (negative) → Unit 6   **Do you** . . . ? (questions) → Unit 7   **I am doing** and **I do** → Unit 8
always/usually/often, etc. (word order) → Unit 95

Exercises

5.1 Write these verbs with *-s* or *-es*.

1. (read) she ___reads___
2. (think) he _____
3. (fly)   it _____
4. (dance) he _____
5. (have) she _____
6. (finish) it _____

5.2 Complete the sentences about the people in the pictures. Use:

eat   go   live   ~~play~~   play   sleep

1. ___He plays___ the piano.
2. They _____ in a very big house.
3. _____ a lot of fruit.
4. _____ tennis.
5. _____ to the movies a lot.
6. _____ seven hours a night.

5.3 Complete the sentences. Use:

boil   close   cost   cost   like   like   meet   open   ~~speak~~   teach   wash

1. Maria ___speaks___ four languages.
2. Banks usually _____ at 9:00 in the morning.
3. The art museum _____ at 5:00 in the afternoon.
4. Tina is a teacher. She _____ math to young children.
5. My job is very interesting. I _____ a lot of people.
6. Peter's car is always dirty. He never _____ it.
7. Food is expensive. It _____ a lot of money.
8. Shoes are expensive. They _____ a lot of money.
9. Water _____ at 100 degrees Celsius.
10. Julia and I are good friends. I _____ her, and she _____ me.

5.4 Write sentences from these words. Use the right form of the verb (*arrive* or *arrives*, etc.).

1. (always / early / Sue / arrive) ___Sue always arrives early.___
2. (to the movies / never / I / go) _____
3. (work / Martina / hard / always) _____
4. (like / chocolate / children / usually) _____
5. (Julia / parties / enjoy / always) _____
6. (often / people's names / I / forget) _____
7. (television / Tim / watch / never) _____
8. (usually / dinner / we / have / at 6:30) _____
9. (Jenny / always / nice clothes / wear) _____

5.5 Write sentences about yourself. Use *always/never/often/usually/sometimes*.

1. (watch TV in the evening) ___I usually watch TV in the evening.___
2. (read in bed) I _____
3. (get up before 7:00) _____
4. (go to work/school by bus) _____
5. (drink coffee in the morning) _____

I don't . . . (simple present negative)

The simple present negative is **don't/doesn't** + *verb*:

Coffee?

No, thanks. I **don't drink** coffee.

She **doesn't drink** coffee.

I **don't like** my job.

He **doesn't like** his job.

Positive			Negative		
I we you they	work like do have		I we you they	**don't** (**do not**)	**work like do have**
he she it	works likes does has		he she it	**doesn't** (**does not**)	

- I **drink** coffee, but I **don't drink** tea.
- Sue **drinks** tea, but she **doesn't drink** coffee.
- You **don't work** very hard.
- We **don't watch** television very often.
- The weather is usually nice. It **doesn't rain** very often.
- Gary and Nicole **don't know** many people.

Remember:

I/we/you/they	**don't** . . .
he/she/it	**doesn't** . . .

- **I don't** like football.
- **He doesn't** like football.

- **I don't** like Fred, and **Fred doesn't** like me. (*not* Fred don't like)
- **My car doesn't** use much gas. (*not* My car don't use)
- Sometimes he is late, but **it doesn't** happen very often.

We use **don't/doesn't** + *base form* (don't **like** / doesn't **speak** / doesn't **do**, etc.):
- I **don't like** to wash the car. I **don't do** it very often.
- Sarah **speaks** Spanish, but she **doesn't speak** Italian. (*not* doesn't speaks)
- Bill **doesn't do** his job very well. (*not* Bill doesn't his job)
- Paula **doesn't** usually **have** breakfast. (*not* doesn't . . . has)

I do/work/like, etc. (simple present) → Unit 5   Do you . . . ? (simple present questions) → Unit 7

Exercises

6.1 Write the negative.

1. I play the piano very well.   _I don't play the piano very well._
2. Jane plays the piano very well.   Jane _____
3. They know my phone number.   They _____
4. We work very hard.   _____
5. Mike has a car.   _____
6. You do the same thing every day.   _____

6.2 Study the information and write sentences with *like*.

Do you like . . . ?

Bill and Rose   Carol   You

	Bill and Rose	Carol	You
1. classical music?	yes	no	?
2. boxing?	no	yes	
3. horror movies?	yes	no	

1.   _Bill and Rose like classical music._
     Carol _____
     I _____ classical music.

2.   Bill and Rose _____
     Carol _____
     I _____

3.   _____
     _____
     _____

6.3 Write about yourself. Use:

I never . . .   or   I . . . a lot   or   I don't . . . very often.

1. (watch TV)   _I never watch TV._   OR   _I watch TV a lot._   OR
   I don't watch TV very often.
2. (go to the theater)   _____
3. (ride a bicycle)   _____
4. (eat in restaurants)   _____
5. (travel by train)   _____

6.4 Complete the sentences. All of them are negative. Use *don't/doesn't* + these verbs:

cost   go   know   ~~read~~   see   use   wear

1. I buy a newspaper every day, but sometimes I _don't read_ it.
2. Paul has a car, but he _____ it very often.
3. Paul and his friends like movies, but they _____ to the movie theater very often.
4. Amanda is married, but she _____ a ring.
5. I _____ much about politics. I'm not interested in it.
6. The Regent Hotel isn't expensive. It _____ much to stay there.
7. Brian lives near us, but we _____ him very often.

6.5 Put the verb into the correct form, positive or negative.

1. Margaret _speaks_ four languages – English, Japanese, Arabic, and Spanish. (speak)
2. I _don't like_ my job. It's very boring. (like)
3. "Where's Martin?"   "I'm sorry. I _____ ." (know)
4. Sue is a very quiet person. She _____ very much. (talk)
5. Andy _____ a lot of coffee. It's his favorite drink. (drink)
6. It's not true! I _____ it! (believe)
7. That's a very beautiful picture. I _____ it a lot. (like)
8. Mark is a vegetarian. He _____ meat. (eat)

Do you . . . ? (simple present questions)

We use **do/does** in simple present questions:

Positive			Question			
I	**work**			I		
we	**like**		**do**	we		
you	**do**			you		**work?**
they	**have**			they		**like?**
						do?
he	**works**			he		**have?**
she	**likes**		**does**	she		
it	**does**			it		
	has					

Do you **play** the guitar?

Study the word order:

do/does	+	*subject*	+	*infinitive*	
	Do	you	**work**	on Sundays?
	Do	your friends	**live**	near here?
	Does	Chris	**play**	tennis?
Where	**do**	your parents	**live?**	
How often	**do**	you	**wash**	your hair?
What	**does**	this word	**mean?**	
How much	**does**	it	**cost**	to fly to Puerto Rico?

Questions with **always/usually/ever**:

	Do	you	**always**	**have**	breakfast?
	Does	Chris	**ever**	**call**	you?
What	**do**	you	**usually**	**do**	on weekends?

What do you **do**? = What's your job?

- ■ "**What do** you **do**?" "I work in a bank."

Remember:

do I/we/you/they . . .
does he/she/it . . .

- ■ **Do they** like music?
- ■ **Does he** like music?

Short answers

Yes,	I/we/you/they **do**.
	he/she/it **does**.

No,	I/we/you/they **don't**.
	he/she/it **doesn't**.

- ■ "**Do you** play tennis?" "**No, I don't**."
- ■ "**Do your parents** speak English?" "**Yes, they do**."
- ■ "**Does Gary** work hard?" "**Yes, he does**."
- ■ "**Does your sister** live in Vancouver?" "**No, she doesn't**."

Exercises

7.1 Write questions with *Do . . . ?* and *Does . . . ?*

1. I like chocolate. How about you? <u>*Do you like chocolate*</u> ?
2. I play tennis. How about you? _____ you _____ ?
3. You live near here. How about Lucy? _____ Lucy _____ ?
4. Tom plays tennis. How about his friends? _____ ?
5. You speak English. How about your brother? _____ ?
6. I do yoga every morning. How about you? _____ ?
7. Sue often travels on business. How about Paul? _____ ?
8. I want to be famous. How about you? _____ ?
9. You work hard. How about Anna? _____ ?

7.2 Make questions from these words + *do/does*. Put the words in the right order.

1. (where / live / your parents) <u>*Where do your parents live*</u> ?
2. (you / early / always / get up) <u>*Do you always get up early*</u> ?
3. (how often / TV / you / watch) _____ ?
4. (you / want / what / for dinner) _____ ?
5. (like / you / football) _____ ?
6. (your brother / like / football) _____ ?
7. (what / you / do / in your free time) _____ ?
8. (your sister / work / where) _____ ?
9. (to the movies / ever / you / go) _____ ?
10. (what / mean / this word) _____ ?
11. (often / snow / it / here) _____ ?
12. (go / usually / to bed / what time / you)

   _____ ?

13. (how much / to call Mexico / it / cost)

   _____ ?

14. (you / for breakfast / have / usually / what)

   _____ ?

7.3 Complete the questions. Use these verbs:

~~do~~ do enjoy get like start teach work

1. What <u>*do you do*</u> ? — I work in a bookstore.
2. _____ it? — It's OK.
3. What time _____ in the morning? — At 9:00.
4. _____ on Saturdays? — Sometimes.
5. How _____ to work? — Usually by bus.
6. And your husband. What _____ ? — He's a teacher.
7. What _____ ? — Science.
8. _____ his job? — Yes, he loves it.

7.4 Write short answers (*Yes, he does. / No, I don't.*, etc.).

1. Do you watch TV a lot? <u>*No, I don't.*</u>   OR   <u>*Yes, I do.*</u>
2. Do you live in a big city? _____
3. Do you ever ride a bicycle? _____
4. Does it rain a lot where you live? _____
5. Do you play the piano? _____

→ Additional exercises 4–7 (pages 245–246)   15

I am doing (present continuous) and I do (simple present)

Jack is watching television.
He is *not* playing the guitar.

But Jack has a guitar.
He plays it a lot, and he plays very well.

Jack **plays** the guitar,
but he **is not playing** the guitar now.

Is he playing the guitar?	**No, he isn't.**	*(present continuous)*
Does he play the guitar?	**Yes, he does.**	*(simple present)*

Present continuous (**I am doing**) = now, at the time of speaking:

I'm doing

past   now   future

- Please be quiet. I**'m** work**ing**. (*not* I work)
- Tom **is** tak**ing** a shower at the moment. (*not* Tom takes)
- Take an umbrella with you. It**'s** rain**ing**.
- You can turn off the television. I**'m** not watch**ing** it.
- Why are you under the table? What **are** you do**ing**?

Simple present (**I do**) = in general, all the time, or sometimes:

I do

past   now   future

- I **work** every day from 9:00 to 5:30.
- Tom **takes** a shower every morning.
- It **rains** a lot in the winter.
- I **don't watch** television very often.
- What **do** you usually **do** on weekends?

We do *not* use these verbs in the present continuous (**I am -ing**):

like	**love**	**want**	**know**	**understand**	**remember**	**depend**
prefer	**hate**	**need**	**mean**	**believe**	**forget**	

Use only the simple present with these verbs (I **want** / **do you like?**, etc.):

- I'm tired. I **want** to go home. (*not* I'm wanting)
- "**Do you know** that girl?" "Yes, but I **don't remember** her name."
- I **don't understand**. What **do** you **mean**?

present continuous → **Units 3–4**   simple present → **Units 5–7**   present for the future → **Unit 26**

Exercises

8.1 Answer the questions about the pictures.

1. I'm a photographer.

   Does he take photographs? __Yes, he does.__
   Is he taking a photograph? __No, he isn't.__
   What is he doing?
   __He's taking a bath.__

2. I'm a bus driver.

   Is she driving a bus? _____
   Does she drive a bus? _____
   What is she doing?
   _____

3. I'm a window washer.

   Does he wash windows? _____
   Is he washing a window? _____
   What is he doing?
   _____

4. We are teachers.

   Are they teaching? _____
   Do they teach? _____
   What do they do?
   _____

8.2 Complete the sentences with *am/is/are* or *do/don't/does/doesn't*.

1. Excuse me, __do__ you speak English?
2. "Where's Kate?" "I _____ know."
3. What's so funny? Why _____ you laughing?
4. "What _____ your sister do?" "She's a dentist."
5. It _____ raining. I _____ want to go out in the rain.
6. "Where _____ you come from?" "Canada."
7. How much _____ it cost to send a letter to Canada?
8. Steve is a good tennis player, but he _____ play very often.

8.3 Put the verb in the present continuous (*I am doing*) or the simple present (*I do*).

1. Excuse me, __do you speak__ (you / speak) English?
2. "Where's Tom?" __"He's taking__ (he / take) a shower."
3. __I don't watch__ (I / not / watch) television very often.
4. Listen! Somebody _____ (sing).
5. Sandra is tired. _____ (she / want) to go home now.
6. How often _____ (you / read) a newspaper?
7. "Excuse me, but _____ (you / sit) in my seat." "Oh, I'm sorry."
8. I'm sorry, _____ (I / not / understand). Can you speak more slowly?
9. It's late. _____ (I / go) home now. _____ (you / come) with me?
10. What time _____ (your father / finish) work every day?
11. You can turn off the radio. _____ (I / not / listen) to it.
12. "Where's Paul?" "In the kitchen. _____ (he / cook) something."
13. Martin _____ (not / usually / drive) to work. He _____ (usually / walk).
14. Sue _____ (not / like) coffee. _____ (she / prefer) tea.

I have . . . and I've got . . .

A

You can say **I have** or **I've got**, **he has** or **he's got**:

I we you they	**have**	*or*	I we you they	**have got**	(I**'ve got**) (we**'ve got**) (you**'ve got**) (they**'ve got**)
he she it	**has**	*or*	he she it	**has got**	(he**'s got**) (she**'s got**) (it**'s got**)

short form

I've got a headache.

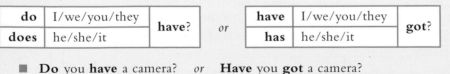

- I **have** blue eyes.   *or*   I**'ve got** blue eyes.
- Tim **has** two sisters.   *or*   Tim **has got** two sisters.
- Our car **has** four doors.   *or*   Our car **has got** four doors.
- Sarah isn't feeling well. She **has** a headache.   *or*   She**'s got** a headache.
- They like animals. They **have** a horse, three dogs, and six cats.   *or*   They**'ve got** a horse . . .

B

I **don't have** / I **haven't got**, etc. *(negative)*

You can say:

I/we/you/they	**don't**	**have**	*or*	I/we/you/they	**haven't**	**got**
he/she/it	**doesn't**			he/she/it	**hasn't**	

- I **have** a bike, but I **don't have** a car.   *or*   I**'ve got** a bike, but I **haven't got** a car.
- Mr. and Mrs. Harris **don't have** any children.   *or*   . . . **haven't got** any children.
- It's a nice house, but it **doesn't have** a garage.   *or*   . . . it **hasn't got** a garage.
- Mariko **doesn't have** a job.   *or*   Mariko **hasn't got** a job.

C

Do you **have** . . . ? / **Have** you **got** . . . ?, etc. *(questions)*

You can say:

do	I/we/you/they	**have**?	*or*	**have**	I/we/you/they	**got**?
does	he/she/it			**has**	he/she/it	

- **Do** you **have** a camera?   *or*   **Have** you **got** a camera?
- **Does** Helen **have** a car?   *or*   **Has** Helen **got** a car?
- What kind of car **does** she **have**?   *or*   What kind of car **has** she **got**?
- What **do** you **have** in your bag?   *or*   What **have** you **got** in your bag?

D

Short answers

- "**Do** you have a camera?"   "Yes, I **do**." / "No, I **don't**."   *or*
  "**Have** you got a camera?"   "Yes, I **have**." / "No, I **haven't**."
- "**Does** Anne have a car?"   "Yes, she **does**." / "No, she **doesn't**."   *or*
  "**Has** Anne got a car?"   "Yes, she **has**." / "No, she **hasn't**."

had / didn't have (past) → Units 11–12   **have breakfast / have a headache**, etc. → Unit 59   **some/any** → Unit 77

Exercises

9.1 Write the short form with *got* (*we've got / he hasn't got*, etc.).

1. we have got __we've got__
2. he has got _____
3. they have got _____
4. she has not got _____
5. it has got _____
6. I have not got _____

9.2 Read the questions and answers. Then write sentences about Mark.

1.	Have you got a car?	No.	1.	_He hasn't got a car._
2.	Have you got a computer?	Yes.	2.	He _____
3.	Have you got a dog?	No.	3.	_____
4.	Have you got a cell phone?	No.	4.	_____
5.	Have you got a watch?	Yes.	5.	_____
6.	Have you got any brothers or sisters?	Yes, two brothers and a sister.	6.	_____

Mark

What about you? Write sentences with *I've got* or *I haven't got*.

7. (a computer) _____
8. (a dog) _____
9. (a bike) _____
10. (brothers / sisters) _____

9.3 Write these sentences with *have/has* or *don't have / doesn't have*. The meaning is the same.

1. They have got two children.   _They have two children._
2. She hasn't got a key.   _She doesn't have a key._
3. He has got a new job.   _____
4. They haven't got much money.   _____
5. Have you got an umbrella?   _____
6. We have got a lot of work to do.   _____
7. I haven't got your phone number.   _____
8. Has your father got a car?   _____
9. How much money have we got?   _____

9.4 Complete the sentences with *do, doesn't, don't, got, has*, or *have*.

1. Sarah hasn't ___got___ a car. She goes everywhere by bicycle.
2. They like animals. They ___have___ three dogs and two cats.
3. Charles isn't happy. He _____ got a lot of problems.
4. They don't read much. They _____ have many books.
5. "What's wrong?"   "I've _____ something in my eye."
6. "Where's my pen?"   "I don't know. I don't _____ it."
7. Julia wants to go to the concert, but she _____ have a ticket.

9.5 Complete the sentences. Use *have/has* or *don't have / doesn't have* with:

> **a lot of friends**   **four wheels**   ~~a headache~~   **six legs**
> ~~a big yard~~   **much time**   **a key**

1. I'm not feeling well. I _have a headache._
2. It's a nice house, but it _doesn't have a big yard._
3. Most cars _____
4. Everybody likes Tom. He _____
5. I can't open the door. I _____
6. An insect _____
7. Hurry! We _____

→ Additional exercises 5–7 (page 246)

was/were

last night   *now*

Now Robert **is** at work.

At midnight last night,
he **wasn't** at work.

He **was** in bed.
He **was** asleep.

am/is (present) → **was** (past):

- I **am** tired. (now)   I **was** tired **last night**.
- Where **is** Kate? (now)   Where **was** Kate **yesterday**?
- The weather **is** nice today.   The weather **was** nice **last week**.

are (present) → **were** (past):

- You **are** late. (now)   You **were** late **yesterday**.
- They **aren't** here. (now)   They **weren't** here **last Sunday**.

Positive			Negative			Question		
I he she it	**was**		I he she it	**was not** (**wasn't**)			**was**	I? he? she? it?
we you they	**were**		we you they	**were not** (**weren't**)			**were**	we? you? they?

- Last year Rachel **was** 22, so she **is** 23 now.
- When I **was** a child, I **was** afraid of dogs.
- We **were** hungry after the trip, but we **weren't** tired.
- The hotel **was** comfortable, but it **wasn't** expensive.

- **Was** the weather nice when you **were** on vacation?
- Your shoes are nice. **Were** they expensive?
- Why **were** you late this morning?

Short answers

Yes,	I/he/she/it **was**.
	we/you/they **were**.

No,	I/he/she/it **wasn't**.
	we/you/they **weren't**.

- "**Were you** late?"   "**No, I wasn't**."
- "**Was Ted** at work yesterday?"   "**Yes, he was**."
- "**Were Sue and Steve** at the party?"   "**No, they weren't**."

am/is/are → Units 1–2   I was doing → Unit 13

Exercises

10.1 Where were these people at 3:00 yesterday afternoon?

1. __Gary was in bed.__
2. Jack and Kate _____
3. Sue _____
4. _____
5. _____
6. And you? I _____

10.2 Write *am/is/are* (present) or *was/were* (past).

1. Last year she __was__ 22, so she __is__ 23 now.
2. Today the weather _____ nice, but yesterday it _____ very cold.
3. I _____ hungry. Can I have something to eat?
4. I feel fine this morning, but I _____ very tired last night.
5. Where _____ you at 11:00 last Friday morning?
6. Don't buy those shoes. They _____ very expensive.
7. I like your new jacket. _____ it expensive?
8. This time last year I _____ in Paris.
9. "Where _____ the children?" "I don't know. They _____ here a few minutes ago."

10.3 Write *was/were* or *wasn't/weren't*.

1. We weren't happy with the hotel. Our room __was__ very small, and it __wasn't__ clean.
2. Mark _____ at work last week because he _____ sick. He's better now.
3. Yesterday _____ a holiday, so the banks _____ closed. They're open today.
4. "_____ Kate and Bill at the party?" "Kate _____ there, but Bill _____ ."
5. "Where are my keys?" "I don't know. They _____ on the table, but they're not there now."
6. You _____ at home last night. Where _____ you?

10.4 Write questions from these words + *was/were*. Put the words in the right order.

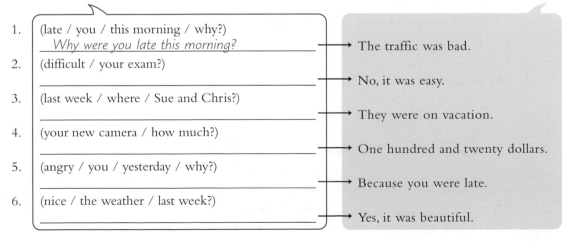

1. (late / you / this morning / why?)
   __Why were you late this morning?__ → The traffic was bad.
2. (difficult / your exam?)
   _____ → No, it was easy.
3. (last week / where / Sue and Chris?)
   _____ → They were on vacation.
4. (your new camera / how much?)
   _____ → One hundred and twenty dollars.
5. (angry / you / yesterday / why?)
   _____ → Because you were late.
6. (nice / the weather / last week?)
   _____ → Yes, it was beautiful.

worked/got/went, etc. (simple past)

A

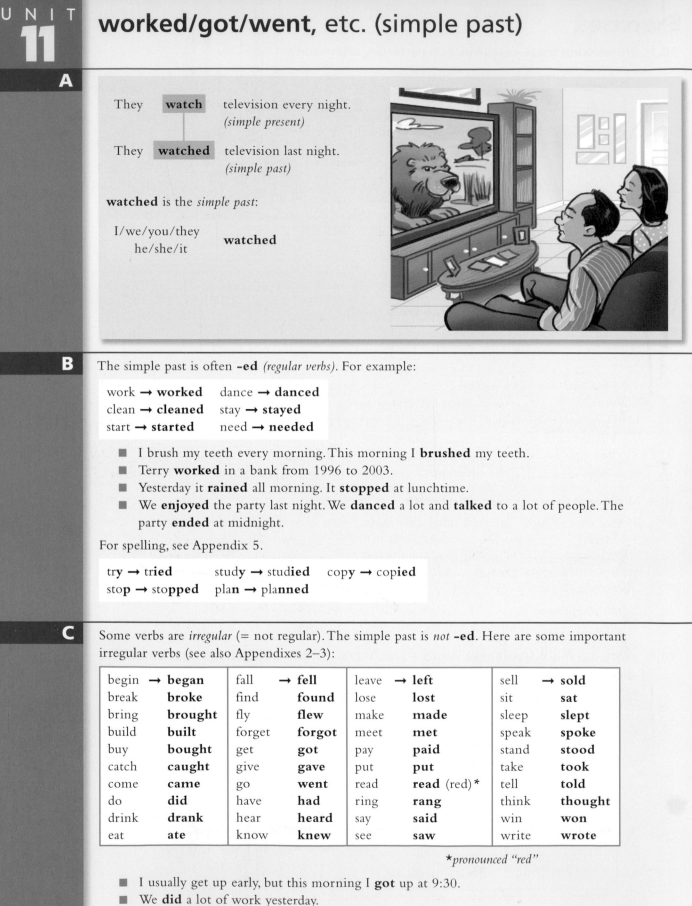

They **watch** television every night. *(simple present)*

They **watched** television last night. *(simple past)*

watched is the *simple past*:

I/we/you/they
he/she/it   **watched**

B

The simple past is often **-ed** *(regular verbs)*. For example:

work → **worked**   dance → **danced**
clean → **cleaned**   stay → **stayed**
start → **started**   need → **needed**

- I brush my teeth every morning. This morning I **brushed** my teeth.
- Terry **worked** in a bank from 1996 to 2003.
- Yesterday it **rained** all morning. It **stopped** at lunchtime.
- We **enjoyed** the party last night. We **danced** a lot and **talked** to a lot of people. The party **ended** at midnight.

For spelling, see Appendix 5.

try → tr**ied**   study → stud**ied**   copy → cop**ied**
sto**p** → sto**pped**   plan → pla**nned**

C

Some verbs are *irregular* (= not regular). The simple past is *not* **-ed**. Here are some important irregular verbs (see also Appendixes 2–3):

begin →	**began**	fall →	**fell**	leave →	**left**	sell →	**sold**
break	**broke**	find	**found**	lose	**lost**	sit	**sat**
bring	**brought**	fly	**flew**	make	**made**	sleep	**slept**
build	**built**	forget	**forgot**	meet	**met**	speak	**spoke**
buy	**bought**	get	**got**	pay	**paid**	stand	**stood**
catch	**caught**	give	**gave**	put	**put**	take	**took**
come	**came**	go	**went**	read	**read** (red)*	tell	**told**
do	**did**	have	**had**	ring	**rang**	think	**thought**
drink	**drank**	hear	**heard**	say	**said**	win	**won**
eat	**ate**	know	**knew**	see	**saw**	write	**wrote**

pronounced "red"

- I usually get up early, but this morning I **got** up at 9:30.
- We **did** a lot of work yesterday.
- Caroline **went** to the movies three times last week.
- James **came** into the room, **took** off his coat, and **sat** down.

Exercises

11.1 Complete the sentences. Use a verb from the box.

~~brush~~	die	end	enjoy	happen	open	rain	start	stay	want

1. I _brushed_ my teeth three times yesterday.
2. It was hot in the room, so I _____ the window.
3. The movie was very long. It _____ at 7:15 and _____ at 10:00.
4. When I was a child, I _____ to be a doctor.
5. The accident _____ last Sunday afternoon.
6. It's a nice day today, but yesterday it _____ all day.
7. We _____ our vacation last year. We _____ at a very nice place.
8. Anna's grandfather _____ when he was 90 years old.

11.2 Write the simple past of these verbs.

1. get _got_
2. see _____
3. play _____
4. pay _____
5. visit _____
6. buy _____
7. go _____
8. think _____
9. copy _____
10. know _____
11. put _____
12. speak _____

11.3 Read about Lisa's trip to Mexico City. Put the verbs in the correct form.

Last Tuesday, Lisa (1) _flew_ from Los Angeles to Mexico City. She (2) _____ up at 6:00 in the morning and (3) _____ a cup of coffee. At 7:15 she (4) _____ home and (5) _____ to the airport. When she (6) _____ there, she (7) _____ the car, (8) _____ to the terminal, and (9) _____ in. Then she (10) _____ breakfast at an airport café and (11) _____ for her flight. The plane (12) _____ on time and (13) _____ in Mexico City four hours later. Finally she (14) _____ a taxi from the airport to her hotel downtown.

fly
get, have
leave, drive
get, park
walk, check
have, wait
depart, arrive
take

11.4 Write sentences about the past (*yesterday / last week*, etc.).

1. James always goes to work by car. Yesterday _he went to work by car._
2. Rachel often loses her keys. She _____ last week.
3. Kate meets her friends every night. She _____ last night.
4. I usually buy two newspapers every day. Yesterday I _____
5. We often go to the movies on weekends. Last Sunday we _____
6. I eat an orange every day. Yesterday I _____
7. Tom always takes a shower in the morning. This morning he _____
8. Our friends often come to see us. They _____ last Friday.

11.5 Write sentences about what <u>you</u> did yesterday.

1. _I went to the theater._
2. _____
3. _____
4. _____
5. _____
6. _____

I didn't . . . Did you . . . ?
(simple past negative and questions)

A We use **did** in simple past negatives and questions:

Base Form	Positive		Negative			Question		
play	I	**played**	I		play		I	play?
start	we	**started**	we		start		we	start?
watch	you	**watched**	you		watch		you	watch?
have	they	**had**	they	**did not**	have	**did**	they	have?
see	he	**saw**	he	**(didn't)**	see		he	see?
do	she	**did**	she		do		she	do?
go	it	**went**	it		go		it	go?

B **Do/does** *(present)* → **did** *(past)*:

- I **don't** watch television very often.
  I **didn't** watch television **yesterday**.
- **Does** she go out often?
  Did she go out **last night**?

C We use **did/didn't** + *base form* (**watch/play/go**, etc.):

I **watched**	*but*	I **didn't watch**	*(not* I didn't watched*)*
they **went**		**did** they **go**?	*(not* did they went?*)*
he **had**		he **didn't have**	
you **did**		**did** you **do**?	

- I **played** tennis yesterday, but I **didn't win**.
- "**Did** you **do** your homework?" "No, I **didn't have** time."
- We **went** to the movies, but we **didn't enjoy** the film.

D Study the word order in questions:

	did + *subject*	+	*base form*	
	Did	your sister	**call**	you?
What	**did**	you	**do**	last night?
How	**did**	the accident	**happen**?	
Where	**did**	your parents	**go**	for vacation?

E *Short answers*

Yes,	I/we/you/they he/she/it	**did**.

No,	I/we/you/they he/she/it	**didn't**.

- "**Did you** see Joe yesterday?" "**No, I didn't.**"
- "**Did it** rain on Sunday?" "**Yes, it did.**"
- "**Did Helen** come to the party?" "**No, she didn't.**"
- "**Did your parents** have a good trip?" "**Yes, they did.**"

worked/got/went, etc. (simple past) → Unit 11

Exercises

12.1 Complete these sentences with the verb in the negative.

1. I saw Barbara, but I __*didn't see*__ Jane.
2. They worked on Monday, but they _____ on Tuesday.
3. We went to the post office, but we _____ to the bank.
4. She had a pen, but she _____ any paper.
5. Jack did some work in the yard, but he _____ any work in the house.

12.2 Write questions with *Did* . . . ?

1. I watched TV last night. How about you?   __*Did you watch TV last night*_____ ?
2. I enjoyed the party. How about you?   _____ ?
3. I had a nice vacation. How about you?   _____ ?
4. I finished work early. How about you?   _____ ?
5. I slept well last night. How about you?   _____ ?

12.3 What did you do yesterday? Write positive or negative sentences.

1. (watch TV)   __*I watched TV.*____   OR   __*I didn't watch TV.*_____
2. (get up before 7:00)   I _____
3. (take a shower)   _____
4. (buy a magazine)   _____
5. (eat meat)   _____
6. (go to bed before 10:30) _____

12.4 Write B's questions. Use:

cost   **get to work**   go   **go to bed late**   happen   **have a nice time**   ~~stay~~   win

1. *A:* We went to Chicago last month. *B:* Where __*did you stay*_____ ? *A:* With some friends.	5. *A:* We came home by taxi. *B:* How much _____ ? *A:* Twenty dollars.
2. *A:* I was late for the meeting. *B:* What time _____ ? *A:* Half past nine.	6. *A:* I'm tired this morning. *B:* _____ ? *A:* No, but I didn't sleep very well.
3. *A:* I played tennis this afternoon. *B:* _____ ? *A:* No, I lost.	7. *A:* We went to the beach yesterday. *B:* _____ ? *A:* Yes, it was great.
4. *A:* I had a nice vacation. *B:* Good. Where _____ ? *A:* To the mountains.	8. *A:* The window is broken. *B:* How _____ ? *A:* I don't know.

12.5 Put the verb in the correct form – positive, negative, or question.

1. We went to the movies, but the film wasn't very good. We __*didn't enjoy*___ it. (enjoy)
2. Tim _____ some new clothes yesterday – two shirts, a jacket, and a sweater. (buy)
3. "_____ yesterday?" "No, it was a nice day." (rain)
4. We were tired, so we _____ long at the party. (stay)
5. It was very warm in the room, so I _____ a window. (open)
6. "Did you call Chris this morning?" "No, I _____ time." (have)
7. "I cut my hand this morning." "How _____ that?" (do)
8. "Why weren't you at the meeting yesterday?" "I _____ about it." (know)

→ Additional exercises 10–13 (page 248)

I was doing (past continuous)

A

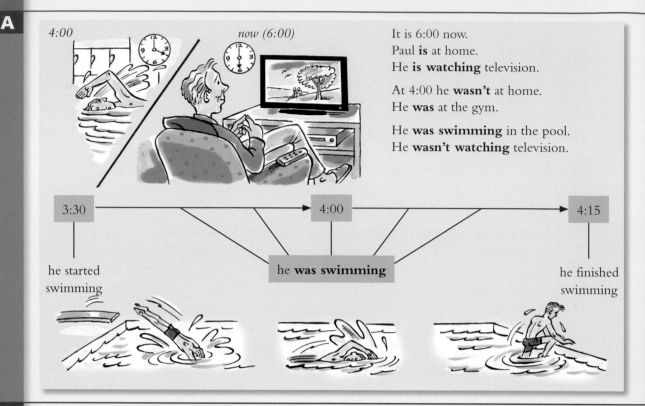

It is 6:00 now.
Paul **is** at home.
He **is watching** television.

At 4:00 he **wasn't** at home.
He **was** at the gym.

He **was swimming** in the pool.
He **wasn't watching** television.

4:00   now (6:00)

3:30 ——→ 4:00 ——→ 4:15

he started swimming   he **was swimming**   he finished swimming

B

Was/were + **-ing** is the *past continuous*:

Positive		
I he she it	**was**	**doing watching playing swimming living,** etc.
we you they	**were**	

Negative		
I he she it	**was not (wasn't)**	**doing watching playing swimming living,** etc.
we you they	**were not (weren't)**	

Question		
was	I he she it	**doing? watching? playing? swimming? living?,** etc.
were	we you they	

- What **were** you **doing** at 11:30 yesterday? **Were** you **working**?
- "What did he say?" "I don't know. I **wasn't listening**."
- It **was raining**, so we didn't go out.
- In 2001 we **were living** in Japan.
- Today she's wearing a skirt, but yesterday she **was wearing** pants.
- I woke up early yesterday. It was a beautiful morning. The sun **was shining**, and the birds **were singing**.

Spelling (liv**e** → liv**ing** / run → ru**nning** / li**e** → l**ying**, etc.) → Appendix 5

C

Am/is/are + **-ing** *(present)* → **was/were** + **-ing** *(past)*:

Present	Past
- I**'m working** (now).	- I **was working** at 10:30 last night.
- It **isn't raining** (now).	- It **wasn't raining** when we went out.
- What **are** you **doing** (now)?	- What **were** you **doing** at 3:00?

was/were → Unit 10   **I was doing** and **I did** (past continuous and simple past) → **Unit 14**

Exercises

13.1 Look at the pictures. Where were these people at 3:00 yesterday afternoon? And what were they doing? Write two sentences for each picture.

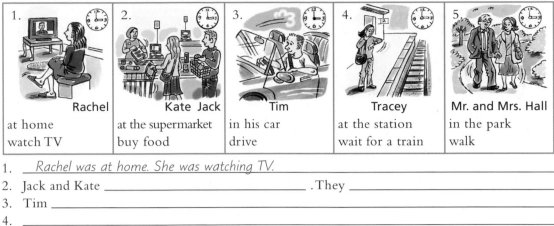

1. Rachel	2. Kate Jack	3. Tim	4. Tracey	5. Mr. and Mrs. Hall
at home	at the supermarket	in his car	at the station	in the park
watch TV	buy food	drive	wait for a train	walk

1. _Rachel was at home. She was watching TV._ _____
2. Jack and Kate _____. They _____
3. Tim _____
4. _____
5. _____
6. And you? I _____

13.2 Sarah did a lot of things yesterday. Look at the pictures and complete the sentences.

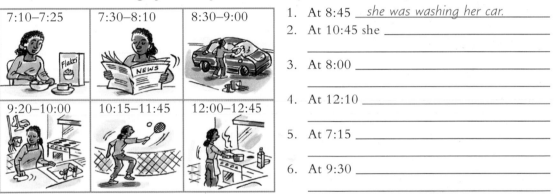

7:10–7:25	7:30–8:10	8:30–9:00
9:20–10:00	10:15–11:45	12:00–12:45

1. At 8:45 _she was washing her car._ _____
2. At 10:45 she _____
   _____
3. At 8:00 _____
   _____
4. At 12:10 _____
   _____
5. At 7:15 _____
6. At 9:30 _____
   _____

13.3 Complete the questions. Use *was/were -ing*. Use *what/where/why* if necessary.

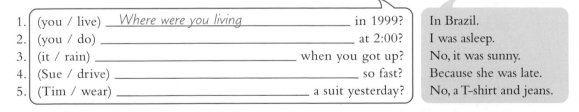

1. (you / live) _Where were you living_ _____ in 1999?   In Brazil.
2. (you / do) _____ at 2:00?   I was asleep.
3. (it / rain) _____ when you got up?   No, it was sunny.
4. (Sue / drive) _____ so fast?   Because she was late.
5. (Tim / wear) _____ a suit yesterday?   No, a T-shirt and jeans.

13.4 Look at the picture. You saw Joe in the street yesterday afternoon. What was he doing? Write positive or negative sentences.

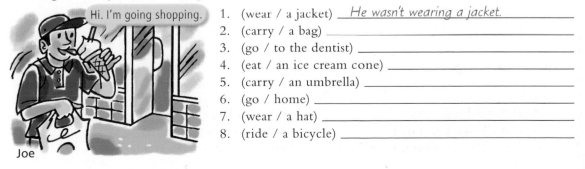

Hi. I'm going shopping.

Joe

1. (wear / a jacket) _He wasn't wearing a jacket._ _____
2. (carry / a bag) _____
3. (go / to the dentist) _____
4. (eat / an ice cream cone) _____
5. (carry / an umbrella) _____
6. (go / home) _____
7. (wear / a hat) _____
8. (ride / a bicycle) _____

I **was doing** (past continuous) and
I **did** (simple past)

A

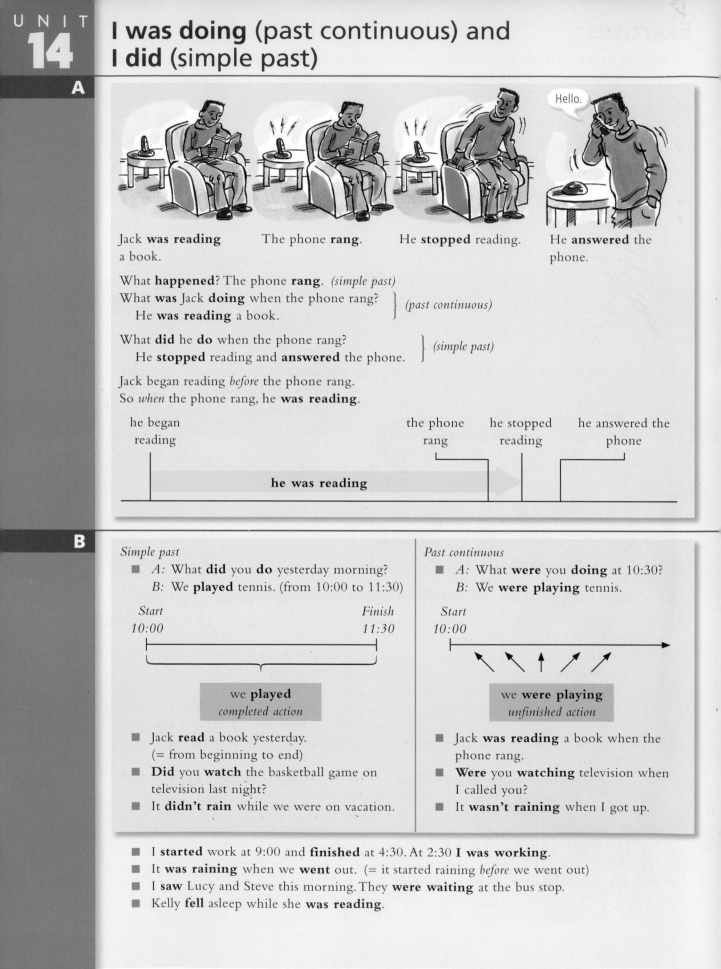

Jack **was reading** a book. | The phone **rang**. | He **stopped** reading. | He **answered** the phone.

What **happened**? The phone **rang**. *(simple past)*

What **was** Jack **doing** when the phone rang? ⎫
   He **was reading** a book. ⎬ *(past continuous)*

What **did** he **do** when the phone rang? ⎫
   He **stopped** reading and **answered** the phone. ⎬ *(simple past)*

Jack began reading *before* the phone rang.
So *when* the phone rang, he **was reading**.

he began reading | the phone rang | he stopped reading | he answered the phone

he was reading

B

Simple past

- *A:* What **did** you **do** yesterday morning?
  B: We **played** tennis. (from 10:00 to 11:30)

Start   *Finish*
10:00   11:30

we **played**
completed action

- Jack **read** a book yesterday.
  (= from beginning to end)
- **Did** you **watch** the basketball game on television last night?
- It **didn't rain** while we were on vacation.

Past continuous

- *A:* What **were** you **doing** at 10:30?
  B: We **were playing** tennis.

Start
10:00

we **were playing**
unfinished action

- Jack **was reading** a book when the phone rang.
- **Were** you **watching** television when I called you?
- It **wasn't raining** when I got up.

- I **started** work at 9:00 and **finished** at 4:30. At 2:30 **I was working**.
- It **was raining** when we **went** out. (= it started raining *before* we went out)
- I **saw** Lucy and Steve this morning. They **were waiting** at the bus stop.
- Kelly **fell** asleep while she **was reading**.

I **did** (simple past) → Units 11–12   I **was doing** (past continuous) → Unit 13   while → Unit 106

Exercises

14.1 Look at the pictures. Put the verbs in the correct form, past continuous or simple past.

1.

Lucy __*broke*__ (break) her arm last week.
It _____ (happen) when
she _____ (paint) her
room. She _____ (fall)
off the ladder.

2.

The train _____ (arrive)
at the station, and Paula _____
(get) off. Two friends of hers, Jon and Rachel,
_____ (wait) to
meet her.

3.

Yesterday Sue _____ (walk)
down the street when she _____ (meet)
James. He _____ (go)
to the station to catch a train, and he
_____ (carry) a bag.
They _____ (stop) to
talk for a few minutes.

14.2 Put the verb into the past continuous or simple past.

1. *A:* What __*were you doing*__ (you / do) when the phone __*rang*__ (ring)?
   B: I __*was watching*__ (watch) television.

2. *A:* Was Jane busy when you went to see her?
   B: Yes, she _____ (study).

3. *A:* What time _____ (the mail / arrive) this morning?
   B: It _____ (come) while I _____ (have) breakfast.

4. *A:* Was Tracey at work today?
   B: No, she _____ (not / go) to work. She was sick.

5. *A:* How fast _____ (you / drive) when the police
   _____ (stop) you?
   B: I'm not sure, but I _____ (not / drive) very fast.

6. *A:* _____ (your team / win) the baseball game yesterday?
   B: No, the weather was very bad, so we _____ (not / play).

7. *A:* How _____ (you / break) the window?
   B: We _____ (play) baseball. I _____ (hit) the ball
   and it _____ (break) the window.

8. *A:* _____ (you / see) Jenny last night?
   B: Yes, she _____ (wear) a very nice jacket.

9. *A:* What _____ (you / do) at 2:00 this morning?
   B: I was asleep.

10. *A:* I _____ (lose) my key last night.
    B: How _____ (you / get) into your apartment?
    A: I _____ (climb) in through a window.

→ Additional exercises 14–15 (pages 249–250)

I used to . . .

A

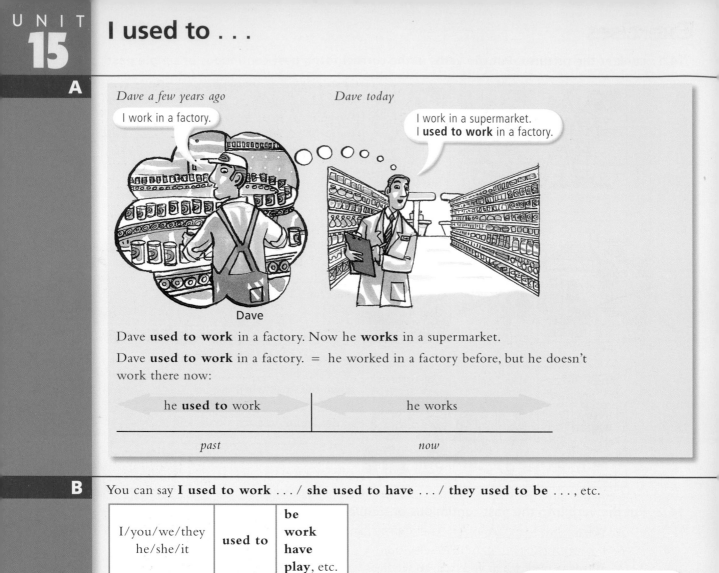

Dave a few years ago

I work in a factory.

Dave today

I work in a supermarket.
I **used to work** in a factory.

Dave

Dave **used to work** in a factory. Now he **works** in a supermarket.

Dave **used to work** in a factory. = he worked in a factory before, but he doesn't work there now:

he **used to** work	he works
past	*now*

B

You can say **I used to work** . . . / **she used to have** . . . / **they used to be** . . . , etc.

I/you/we/they he/she/it	**used to**	**be** **work** **have** **play**, etc.

I **used to have** very long hair.

- When I was a child, I **used to like** chocolate.
- I **used to read** a lot of books, but I don't read much these days.
- Liz has short hair now, but it **used to be** very long.
- They **used to live** on the same street as us, so we **used to see** them a lot. But we don't see them very often these days.
- Helen **used to have** a piano, but she sold it a few years ago.

The negative is **I didn't use to** . . . .

- When I was a child, I **didn't use to like** tomatoes.

The question is **did you use to** . . . ?

- Where **did** you **use to live** before you came here?

C

We use **used to** . . . only for the past. You cannot say "I use to . . ." for the present:

- I **used to play** tennis. These days I **play** golf. (*not* I use to play golf)
- We usually **get** up early. (*not* We use to get up early)

Exercises

15.1 Look at the pictures. Complete the sentences with *used to* . . . .

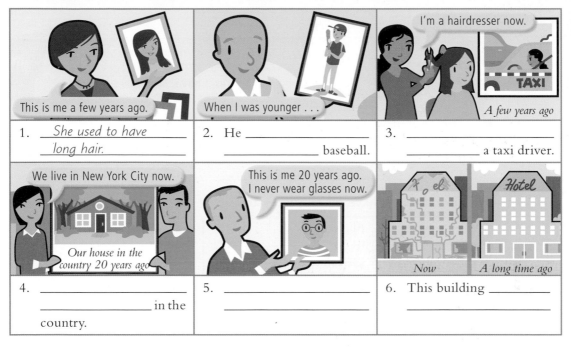

1. _She used to have long hair._
2. He _____ _____ baseball.
3. _____ _____ a taxi driver.
4. _____ _____ in the country.
5. _____ _____
6. This building _____

15.2 Karen works very hard and has very little free time. A few years ago, things were different.

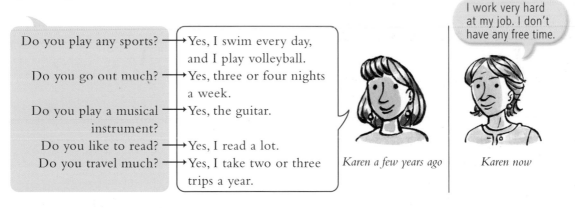

Karen a few years ago

Karen now

Write sentences about Karen with *used to* . . . .

1. _She used to swim every day._
2. She _____ volleyball.
3. _____
4. _____
5. _____
6. _____

15.3 Complete these sentences. Use *used to* or the simple present (*I play / he lives*, etc.).

1. I _used to play_ tennis. I stopped playing a few years ago.
2. "Do you play any sports?" "Yes, I _play_ basketball."
3. "Do you have a car?" "No, I _____ one, but I sold it."
4. George _____ a waiter. Now he's the manager of a hotel.
5. "Do you go to work by car?" "Sometimes, but most days I _____ by train."
6. When I was a child, I never _____ meat, but I eat it now.
7. Mary loves to watch TV. She _____ TV every night.
8. We _____ near the airport, but we moved downtown a few years ago.
9. Normally I start work at 7:00, so I _____ up very early.
10. What games _____ you _____ when you were a child?

Have you ever . . . ?

Have been / have driven / have played, etc., is the *present perfect* (**have** + *past participle*):

| I
we
you
they | **have ('ve)**
have not (haven't) | **played**
lived
visited
read | | **have** | I
we
you
they | **played?**
lived?
visited?
read? | } *regular verbs* |
| he
she
it | **has ('s)**
has not (hasn't) | **lost**
been
flown | | **has** | he
she
it | **lost?**
been?
flown? | } *irregular verbs* |

Regular verbs   The past participle is **-ed** (the same as the simple past):

> play → I have play**ed**   live → I have liv**ed**   visit → she has visit**ed**

Irregular verbs   The past participle is not **-ed**.
    Sometimes the past participle is the same as the simple past:

> buy → I **bought** / I have **bought**   have → he **had** / he has **had**

Sometimes the past participle is different (see Appendixes 2–3).

> break → I **broke** / I have **broken**   see → you **saw** / you have **seen**

We use the present perfect when we talk about a time from the past until now, for example, a person's life.

> | **Have you ever been to Japan?** |
> | *———————— time from the past until now ————————* |

past   *now*

■ "**Have** you **been** to France?"   "No, I **haven't**."
■ We**'ve been** to Canada, but we **haven't been** to Alaska.
■ Mary is an interesting person. She **has had** many different jobs and **has lived**
  in many places.
■ I**'ve seen** that woman before, but I can't remember where.
■ How many times **has** Brazil **won** the World Cup?
■ "**Have** you **read** this book?"   "Yes, I**'ve read** it twice." (**twice** = two times)

Present perfect + **ever** (in questions) and **never**:

■ "**Has** Ann **ever been** to Australia?"   "Yes, once." (**once** = one time)
■ "**Have** you **ever played** golf?"   "Yes, I play a lot."
■ My sister **has never traveled** by plane.
■ I**'ve never ridden** a horse.
■ "Who is that man?"   "I don't know. I**'ve never seen him** before."

present perfect → **Units 17–18**   present perfect and simple past → **Units 19–21**   irregular verbs → **Appendixes 2–3**

Exercises

16.1 You are asking Helen questions beginning with *Have you ever* . . . ?
Write the questions.

Helen

1. (Montreal?)
2. (play / golf?)
3. (South Korea?)
4. (lose / your passport?)
5. (fly / in a helicopter?)
6. (win / a race?)
7. (Peru?)
8. (drive / a bus?)
9. (break / your leg?)

Have you ever been to Montreal?
Have you ever played golf?
Have _____
_____
_____
_____
_____
_____
_____

No, never.
Yes, many times.
Yes, once.
No, never.
Yes, a few times.
No, never.
Yes, twice.
No, never.
Yes, once.

16.2 Write sentences about Helen. (Look at her answers in Exercise 16.1.)

1. (Peru) *She's been to Peru twice.* _____
2. (South Korea) She _____
3. (win / a race) _____
4. (fly / in a helicopter) _____

Now write about yourself. How often have you done these things?

5. (New York) I _____
6. (play / tennis) _____
7. (drive / a truck) _____
8. (be / late for work or school) _____

16.3 Mary is 65 years old. She has had an interesting life. What has she done?

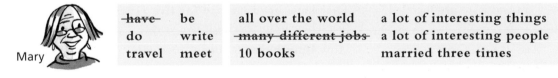

~~have~~	be	all over the world	a lot of interesting things
do	write	~~many different jobs~~	a lot of interesting people
travel	meet	10 books	married three times

Mary

1. *She has had many different jobs.* _____
2. She _____
3. _____
4. _____
5. _____
6. _____

16.4 Put the verbs in the present perfect.

1. *I've seen* (I / see) that woman before, but I can't remember her name.
2. " *Have you ever played* (you / ever / play) golf?"   "Yes, I play golf a lot."
3. "_____ (you / ever / write) a poem?"   "Yes, in high school."
4. "Does Emma know Sam?"   "No, _____ (she / never / meet) him."
5. Ann and Eli have lots of books, and _____ (they / read) all of them.
6. _____ (I / never / be) to Australia, but _____
    (my brother / be) there twice.
7. Joy's favorite movie is *Howard and Belinda*. _____ (she / see) it five
    times, but _____ (I / never / see) it.
8. _____ (I / travel) by plane, bus, and train. Someday, I want to take a
    trip by boat.

→ Additional exercises 16–18 (pages 250–251)

How long have you . . . ?

Jane is on vacation in Brazil.
She is there now.

She arrived in Brazil on Monday.
Today is Thursday.

How long **has she been** in Brazil?

She **has been** in Brazil { **since Monday.**
for three days.

How long **have you been** in Brazil?

Since Monday.

Compare **is** and **has been**:

She is in Brazil
now.

is = *present*

She **has been** in Brazil { **since Monday.**
for three days.

has been = *present perfect*

Monday

now
Thursday

Compare:

Simple present	*Present perfect* (**have been** / **have lived** / **have known**, etc.)
Dan and Kate **are** married.	They **have been** married **for five years**. (*not* They are married for five years.)
Are you married?	**How long have** you **been** married? (*not* How long are you married?)
Do you **know** Lisa?	**How long have** you **known** her? (*not* How long do you know her?)
I **know** Lisa.	I**'ve known** her **for a long time**. (*not* I know her for . . .)
Vera **lives** in Brasília.	**How long has** she **lived** in Brasília? She **has lived** there **all her life**.
I **have** a car.	**How long have** you **had** your car? I**'ve had** it **since April**.

Present continuous	*Present perfect continuous* (**have been** + **–ing**)
I**'m studying** German.	**How long have** you **been studying** German? (*not* How long are you studying German?) I**'ve been studying** German **for two years**.
David **is watching** TV.	**How long has** he **been watching** TV? He**'s been** (= He **has been**) watching TV **since 5:00**.
It**'s raining**.	It**'s been** (= It **has been**) **raining all day**.

for and **since** → Units 18, 105

Exercises

17.1 Complete these sentences.

1. Jane is in Brazil. She ___*has been*___ there since Monday.
2. I know Lisa. I ___*have known*___ her for a long time.
3. Sarah and Andy are married. They ___have been___ married since 1999.
4. Brian is sick. He ___has been___ sick for the last few days.
5. We live on Main Street. We ___have lived___ there for a long time.
6. Catherine works in a bank. She ___has worked___ in a bank for five years.
7. Alan has a headache. He ___has had___ a headache since he got up this morning.
8. I'm studying English. I ___have been studying___ English for six months.

17.2 Make questions with *How long* . . . ?

1. Jane is on vacation.
2. Scott and Judy are in Brazil.
3. I know Amy.
4. Diana is studying Italian.
5. My brother lives in Seattle.
6. I'm a teacher.
7. It is raining.

1. *How long has she been on vacation* ?
2. How long ___have Scott & Judy been in Brazil___ ?
3. How long ___have___ you ___known Amy___ ?
4. ___How long has Diana been studying Italian___ ?
5. ___How long has your brother lived in Seattle___ ?
6. ___How long have you been a teacher___ ?
7. ___How long has it been raining___ ?

17.3

1. We're married.
2. I live in South Korea.
3. We're on vacation.
4. The sun is shining.
5. I'm waiting.
6. I have a beard.

Look at the pictures and complete the sentences with:

for 10 minutes	all day	all her life
~~for 10 years~~	since he was 20	since Sunday

1. ___They have been married for 10 years.___
2. She ___has lived in South Korea all her life___
3. They ___have been on vacation since Sunday___ .
4. The sun ___has been shining all day___ .
5. She ___has been waiting for the bus for 10 min___ .
6. He ___has had a beard since he was 20___

17.4 Which is right?

1. Mark ~~lives~~ / has lived in Canada since April. (*has lived* is right)
2. Jane and I are friends. I know / I've known her very well.
3. Jane and I are friends. ~~I know~~ / I've known her for a long time.
4. *A:* Sorry I'm late. How long ~~are you waiting~~ / have you been waiting?
   B: Not long. Only five minutes.
5. Martin works / ~~has worked~~ in a hotel now. He likes his job a lot.
6. Ruth is reading the newspaper. ~~She is reading~~ / She has been reading it for two hours.
7. "How long ~~do you live~~ / have you lived in this house?" "About 10 years."
8. "Is that a new coat?" "No, ~~I have~~ / I've had this coat for a long time."
9. Tom is / ~~has been~~ in Seattle right now. ~~He is~~ / He has been there for the last three days.

→ **Additional exercises 16–18 (pages 250–251)**

for since ago

A

For and **since**

We use **for** and **since** to say *how long*:

■ Jane **is** in Brazil. She **has been** there ⎰ **for three days**.
⎱ **since Monday**.

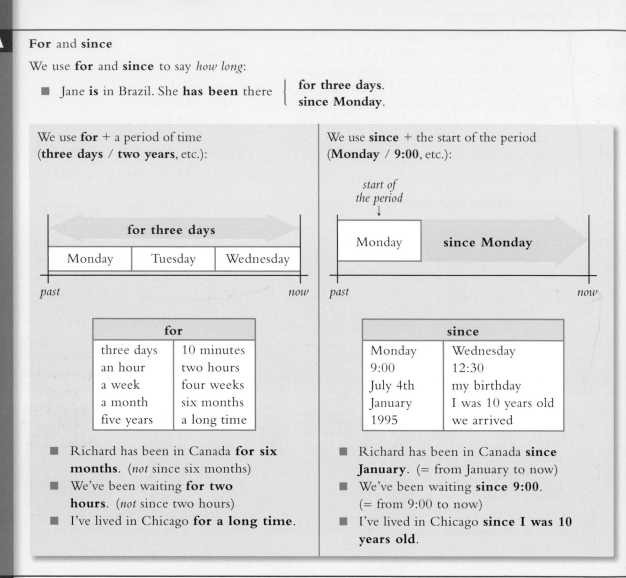

We use **for** + a period of time
(**three days** / **two years**, etc.):

for	
three days	10 minutes
an hour	two hours
a week	four weeks
a month	six months
five years	a long time

■ Richard has been in Canada **for six months**. (*not* since six months)
■ We've been waiting **for two hours**. (*not* since two hours)
■ I've lived in Chicago **for a long time**.

We use **since** + the start of the period
(**Monday** / **9:00**, etc.):

since	
Monday	Wednesday
9:00	12:30
July 4th	my birthday
January	I was 10 years old
1995	we arrived

■ Richard has been in Canada **since January**. (= from January to now)
■ We've been waiting **since 9:00**. (= from 9:00 to now)
■ I've lived in Chicago **since I was 10 years old**.

B

Ago

ago = before now:
■ Susan started her new job **three weeks ago**. (= three weeks before now)
■ "When did Tom leave?" "**Ten minutes ago**." (= ten minutes before now)
■ I had dinner **an hour ago**.
■ Life was very different **a hundred years ago**.

We use **ago** with the *past* (**started/did/had/was**, etc.).

Compare **ago** and **for**:
■ **When did** Jane **arrive** in Brazil?
She **arrived** in Brazil **three days ago**.
■ **How long has** she **been** in Brazil?
She **has been** in Brazil **for three days**.

present perfect + **for/since** → Unit 17 **from/until/since/for** → Unit 105 **for** and **during** → Unit 106

Exercises

18.1 Write *for* or *since*.

1. Jane has been in Brazil __since__ Monday.
2. Jane has been in Brazil __for__ three days.
3. My aunt has lived in Australia _____ 15 years.
4. Jennifer is in her office. She has been there _____ 7:00.
5. Mexico has been an independent country _____ 1821.
6. The bus is late. We've been waiting _____ 20 minutes.
7. Nobody lives in those houses. They have been empty _____ many years.
8. Michael has been sick _____ a long time. He has been in the hospital _____ October.

18.2 Answer these questions. Use *ago*.

1. When was the last time you ate?   _Three hours ago._____
2. When was the last time you were sick?   _____
3. When was the last time you went to the movies? _____
4. When was the last time you were in a car?   _____
5. When was the last time you went on vacation? _____

18.3 Complete the sentences. Use *for* or *ago* with these words.

1. Jane arrived in Brazil __three days ago._____ (three days)
2. Jane has been in Brazil __for three days._____ (three days)
3. Lynn and Mark have been married _____ (20 years)
4. Lynn and Mark got married _____ (20 years)
5. Dan arrived _____ (an hour)
6. I bought these shoes _____ (a few days)
7. Silvia has been studying English _____ (six months)
8. Have you known Lisa _____ ? (a long time)

18.4 Complete the sentences with *for* or *since*.

1. (Jane is in Brazil – she arrived there three days ago)
   _Jane has been in Brazil for three days._____
2. (Jack is here – he arrived on Tuesday)
   Jack has _____
3. (It's raining – it started an hour ago)
   It's been _____
4. (I know Sue – I met her in 2002)
   I've _____
5. (Claire and Matthew are married – they got married six months ago)
   Claire and Matthew have _____
6. (Liz is studying medicine at the university – she started three years ago)
   Liz has _____
7. (David plays the piano – he started when he was seven years old)
   David has _____

18.5 Write sentences about yourself. Begin your sentences with:

   I've lived . . .   I've been . . .   I've been studying . . .   I've known . . .   I've had . . .

1. _I've lived in this town for three years._____
2. _____
3. _____
4. _____
5. _____

→ Additional exercises 16–18 (pages 250–251)

I have done and I did
(present perfect and simple past 1)

They are at home.

He is washing his car.

He **has washed** his car.
(= his car is clean *now*)

His car is dirty.

They are going out.

They **have gone** out.
(= they are not at home *now*)

B

We use the present perfect for *an action in the past* with a result *now*:

- **I've lost** my passport. (= I can't find my passport *now*)
- "Where's Rebecca?" "She**'s gone** to bed." (= she is in bed *now*)
- We**'ve bought** a new car. (= we have a new car *now*)
- It's Rachel's birthday tomorrow, and I **haven't bought** her a present.
  (= I don't have a present for her *now*)
- "Bob is away on vacation." "Oh, where **has** he **gone**?" (= where is he *now*?)
- **Have** you **met** my brother, or should I introduce you?
- I was a very slow typist in college, but I**'ve gotten** faster.

Usually you can also use the simple past (he **washed** / I **lost**, etc.) in these situations. So you can say:

- "Where's your key?" "I**'ve lost** it." *or* "I **lost** it."
- "Is Peter here?" "No, he**'s gone** home." *or* "He **went** home."
- We**'ve bought** a new car. *or* We **bought** a new car.

C

We use only the simple past (not the present perfect) with a *finished* time (**yesterday**, **last week**, etc.).

- I **lost** my key **yesterday**. (*not* I have lost)
- We **bought** a new car **last week**. (*not* we have bought)

simple past → **Units 11–12**   present perfect → **Units 16–18**   present perfect and simple past → **Units 20–21**

Exercises

19.1 Look at the pictures. What has happened? Use the present perfect. Choose from:

go to bed   ~~wash her car~~   stop raining   close the door   fall down   take a shower

before → *now*

1. _She has washed her car._

2. He _____ .

3. They _____ .

4. It _____ .

5. He _____ .

6. The _____ .

19.2 Rewrite the sentences that have <u>underlined</u> verbs. Use the present perfect.

1. Lee Ming isn't here. He <u>went</u> home. _He has gone home._
2. I don't need to call them. I <u>wrote</u> them a letter. _____
3. Karen's not coming to the party. She <u>broke</u> her arm. _____
4. My brother and his wife don't live here any more. They <u>moved</u> to Seattle.
   _____
5. I <u>made</u> a big mistake. _____
6. I <u>lost</u> my wallet. _____
   <u>Did</u> you <u>see</u> it anywhere? _____
7. <u>Did</u> you <u>hear</u>? _____
   Mark <u>got</u> married. _____

Now rewrite these present perfect sentences in the simple past.

8. I'<u>ve done</u> the shopping. _I did the shopping._
9. Brian <u>has taken</u> my bike again without asking. _____
10. <u>Have</u> you <u>told</u> your friends the good news? _____
11. We <u>haven't paid</u> the electric bill. _____

just, already, and yet
(present perfect and simple past 2)

A

Just = a short time ago

We use **just** with the *present perfect* or the *simple past*.

■ A: Are Diane and Paul here?
B: Yes, they**'ve just arrived**. *or*
Yes, **they just** arrived.

■ A: Are you hungry?
B: No, I**'ve just had** dinner. *or*
I **just had** dinner.

■ A: Is Tom here?
B: No, sorry, he**'s just left**. *or*
He **just left**.

Hi! Come in.

They **have just arrived**.

B

Already = before you expected / before I expected

We use **already** with the *present perfect* or the *simple past*.

■ A: What time are Diane and Paul coming?
B: They**'ve already arrived**. *or*
They **already arrived**.

■ It's only 9:00 and Anna **has already gone** to bed.
or . . . Anna **already went** to bed.
(= before I expected)

■ A: Jon, this is Emma.
B: Yes, I know. We**'ve already met**. *or*
We **already met**.

Jon, this is Emma.

Yes, I know. We**'ve already met**.

C

Yet = until now

We use **yet** with the *present perfect* or the *simple past*. We use **yet** in negative sentences and questions. **Yet** is usually at the end.

yet in *negative sentences*

■ A: Are Diane and Paul here?
B: No, they **haven't arrived yet**. *or*
. . . they **didn't arrive yet**.
(but B expects Diane and Paul to arrive soon)

■ A: Does James know that you're going away?
B: No, I **haven't told** him **yet**. *or*
. . . I **didn't tell** him **yet**.
(but B is going to tell him soon)

■ Silvia has bought a new dress, but she **hasn't worn** it **yet**. *or* . . . she **didn't wear** it **yet**.

The film **hasn't started yet**.

yet in *questions*

■ A: **Have** Diane and Paul **arrived yet**? *or*
Did Diane and Paul **arrive yet**?
B: No, not yet. We're still waiting for them.

■ A: **Has** Nicole **started** her new job **yet**? *or*
Did Nicole **start** her new job **yet**?
B: No, she's starting next week.

■ A: This is my new dress.
B: Oh, it's nice. **Have** you **worn** it **yet**? *or*
Did you **wear** it **yet**?

This is my new dress.

Oh, it's nice. **Have** you **worn** it **yet**?

present perfect → Units 16–18   present perfect and simple past → Units 19, 21   still, yet, and already → Unit 96

Exercises

20.1 Write a sentence with *just* for each picture.

1. _They've just arrived._   3. They _____
2. He _____   4. The race _____

20.2 Complete the sentences. Use *already* + present perfect.

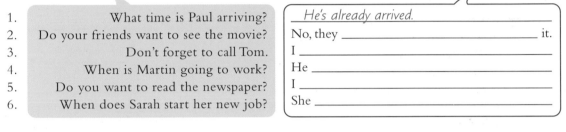

1. What time is Paul arriving?   _He's already arrived._ _____
2. Do your friends want to see the movie?   No, they _____ it.
3. Don't forget to call Tom.   I _____
4. When is Martin going to work?   He _____
5. Do you want to read the newspaper?   I _____
6. When does Sarah start her new job?   She _____

20.3 Rewrite these sentences. Use the present perfect.

1. <u>Did Sarah start</u> her new job yet? _Has Sarah started her new job yet?_ _____
2. <u>Did you tell</u> your father about the accident yet? _____
3. <u>I just ate</u> a big dinner, so I'm not hungry. _____
4. Jenny can watch TV because <u>she already</u> did her homework. _____
5. You can't go to bed – <u>you didn't brush</u> your teeth yet. _____
6. You can't talk to Pete because <u>he just went</u> home. _____
7. <u>Nicole just got out</u> of the hospital, so she can't go to work. _____

Now rewrite these sentences in the simple past.

8. <u>Have you given</u> the post office our new address yet?
   Did you give the post office our new address yet? _____
9. <u>The mail carrier hasn't come</u> yet. _____
10. <u>I've just spoken</u> to your sister. _____
11. <u>Has Mario bought</u> a new computer yet? _____
12. <u>Ted and Alice haven't told</u> anyone they're getting married yet.

    _____

13. <u>We've already done</u> our packing for our trip. _____
14. <u>I've just swum</u> a mile. I feel great! _____

20.4 Write questions with the present perfect and *yet*.

1. Your friend has a new job. Perhaps she has started it. You ask her:
   Have you started your new job yet? _____
2. Your friend has some new neighbors. Maybe he has met them. You ask him:
   _____ you _____ ?
3. Your friend has to pay her phone bill. Perhaps she has paid it. You ask her:

   _____ ?

4. Tom was trying to sell his car. Maybe he has sold it. You ask a friend about Tom.

   _____ ?

I've lost my key. I lost my key last week.
(present perfect and simple past 3)

A

Sometimes you can use the *present perfect* (I **have lost** / he **has gone**, etc.) or the *simple past* (I **lost** / he **went**, etc.).

■ "Is Peter here?"   "No, he**'s gone** home."   *or*   "No, he **went** home."

But with a finished time (**yesterday** / **last week**, etc.), we use only the simple past (not the present perfect).

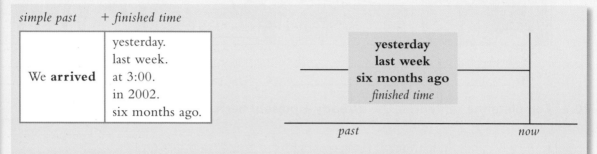

simple past	*+ finished time*
We **arrived**	yesterday. last week. at 3:00. in 2002. six months ago.

Do *not* use the present perfect (**have arrived** / **have done** / **have been**, etc.) with a finished time:

■ I **saw** Paula **yesterday**. (*not* I have seen)
■ Where **were** you **on Sunday afternoon**? (*not* Where have you been)
■ We **didn't take** a vacation **last year**. (*not* We haven't taken)
■ "What **did** you **do last night**?"   "I **stayed** at home."
■ William Shakespeare **lived from 1564 to 1616**. He **was** a writer. He **wrote** many plays and poems.

Use the simple past to ask **When . . . ?** or **What time . . . ?**

■ **When did** you **buy** your computer? (*not* When have you bought?)
■ **What time did** Andy **go** out? (*not* What time has Andy gone out?)

B

Compare:

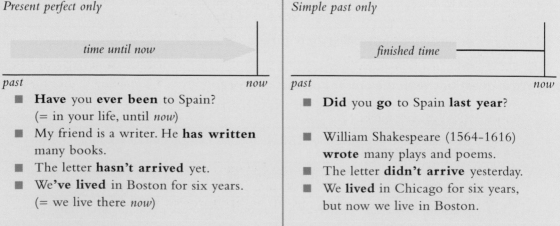

Present perfect or simple past

■ I **have lost** my key.   *or*   I **lost** my key. (= I can't find it *now*)
■ Ben **has gone** home.   *or*   Ben **went** home. (= he isn't here *now*)
■ **Have** you **had** lunch?   *or*   **Did** you **have** lunch?
■ The letter **hasn't arrived** yet.   *or*   The letter **didn't arrive** yet.

Present perfect only	*Simple past only*
■ **Have** you **ever been** to Spain? (= in your life, until *now*)	■ **Did** you **go** to Spain **last year**?
■ My friend is a writer. He **has written** many books.	■ William Shakespeare (1564-1616) **wrote** many plays and poems.
■ The letter **hasn't arrived** yet.	■ The letter **didn't arrive** yesterday.
■ We**'ve lived** in Boston for six years. (= we live there *now*)	■ We **lived** in Chicago for six years, but now we live in Boston.

present perfect → Units 16–18   present perfect and simple past → Units 19–20

Exercises

21.1 Complete the answers to the questions.

1.	Have you had lunch?	Yes, _I had it_ _____ an hour ago.
2.	Have you started your new job?	Yes, I _____ last week.
3.	Have your friends arrived?	Yes, they _____ on Friday.
4.	Has Sarah gone out?	Yes, _____ at 5:00.
5.	Have you worn your new suit?	Yes, _____ yesterday.

21.2 Are these sentences OK? Correct the verbs that are wrong. (The verbs are <u>underlined</u>.)

1. <u>I've lost</u> my key. I can't find it.   _OK_ _____
2. <u>Have you seen</u> Kate yesterday?   _Did you see_ _____
3. <u>I've finished</u> my work at 2:00.   _____
4. I'm ready now. <u>I've finished</u> my work.   _____
5. What time <u>have you finished</u> your work?   _____
6. Sue isn't here. <u>She's gone</u> out.   _____
7. Steve's grandmother <u>has died</u> two years ago.   _____
8. Where <u>have you been</u> last night?   _____

21.3 Put the verb in the present perfect or past.

1. My friend is a writer. He _has written_ (write) many books.
2. We _didn't take_ (not / take) a vacation last year.
3. I _____ (play) tennis yesterday afternoon.
4. What time _____ (you / go) to bed last night?
5. _____ (you / ever / meet) a famous person?
6. The weather _____ (not / be) very good yesterday.
7. Kathy travels a lot. She _____ (visit) many countries.
8. I _____ (turn) off the light before leaving this morning.
9. I live in New York now, but I _____ (live) in Mexico for many years.
10. "What's Peru like? Is it beautiful?"   "I don't know. I _____ (not / be) there."

21.4 Put the verb in the present perfect or past.

1. A: _Have you ever been_ (you / ever / be) to Florida?
   B: Yes, we _went_ (go) there on vacation two years ago.
   A: _____ (you / have) a good time?
   B: Yes, it _____ (be) great.

2. A: What does your friend do?
   B: She's a painter. She _____ (win) many prizes for her paintings.
   A: _____ (you / see) any of her paintings?
   B: Yes, I _____ (see) some of her work last week.

3. Rose works in a factory, but she _____ (have) a lot of different jobs.
   Five years ago she _____ (be) a waitress in a restaurant. After that, she
   _____ (work) on a ranch, but she _____
   (not / enjoy) it very much.

4. A: Do you know Martin's sister?
   B: I _____ (see) her a few times, but I _____
   (never / speak) to her. _____ (you / ever / speak) to her?
   A: Yes. I _____ (meet) her at a party last week. She's very nice.

→ Additional exercises 19–23, 29–31 (pages 252–254, 257–259)

is done   was done (passive 1)

A

The office is **cleaned** every day.

The office was **cleaned** yesterday.

Compare active and passive:

Somebody **cleans** the office every day.   (active)

The office **is cleaned** every day.   (passive)

Somebody **cleaned** the office yesterday.   (active)

The office **was cleaned** yesterday.   (passive)

B

The passive is:

				past participle	
simple present	**am/is/are**	(not)	+	**cleaned**	**done**
simple past	**was/were**			**invented**	**built**
				injured	**taken**, etc.

The past participle of regular verbs is **-ed** (clean**ed**/damag**ed**, etc.).

For a list of irregular past participles (**done/built/taken**, etc.), see Appendixes 2–3.

- Butter **is made** from milk.
- Oranges **are imported** into Canada.
- How often **are** these rooms **cleaned**?
- I **am** never **invited** to parties.

- This house **was built** 100 years ago.
- These houses **were built** 100 years ago.
- When **was** the telephone **invented**?
- We **weren't invited** to the party last week.
- "**Was** anybody **injured** in the accident?"
  "Yes, two people **were taken** to the hospital."

C

Was/were born

- I **was born** in Colombia in 1989. (*not* I am born)
- "Where **were** you **born**?"   "In Cairo."

D

Passive + **by**

- The telephone was invented **by Alexander Graham Bell** in 1876.
  (= Alexander Graham Bell invented it)
- I was bitten **by a dog** a few days ago.
- Do you like these paintings? They were painted **by a friend of mine**.

is being done / has been done → Unit 23   irregular verbs → Unit 25, Appendixes 2–3   **by** → Unit 112
active and passive → Appendix 1

Exercises

22.1 Write sentences from these words. Some of the sentences are questions. Sentences 1–7 are present.

1. (the office / clean / every day) _The office is cleaned every day._
2. (these rooms / clean / every day?) _Are these rooms cleaned every day?_
3. (glass / make / from sand) Glass _____
4. (stamps / sell / in a post office) _____
5. (this word / not / use / very often) _____
6. (we / allow / to park here?) _____
7. (how / this word / pronounce?) _____

Sentences 8–15 are past.

8. (the office / clean / yesterday) _The office was cleaned yesterday._
9. (the house / paint / last month) The house _____
10. (my phone / steal / a few days ago) _____
11. (three people / injure / in the accident) _____
12. (when / this bridge / build?) _____
13. (I / not / wake up / by the noise) _____
14. (how / these windows / break?) _____
15. (you / invite / to Jon's party last week?) _____
_____

22.2 These sentences are not correct. Correct them.

1. (This house built) 100 years ago. _This house was built 100 years ago._
2. Soccer plays in most countries of the world. _____
3. Why did the letter send to the wrong address? _____
4. A garage is a place where cars repair. _____
5. Where are you born? _____
6. How many languages are speaking in Switzerland? _____
7. Somebody broke into our house, but nothing stolen. _____
8. When was invented the bicycle? _____

22.3 Complete the sentences. Use the passive (present or past) of these verbs:

~~clean~~   damage   find   give   invite   make   make   show   steal   ~~take~~

1. The room _is cleaned_ every day.
2. I saw an accident yesterday. Two people _were taken_ to the hospital.
3. Paper _____ from wood.
4. There was a fire at the hotel last week. Two of the rooms _____ .
5. "Where did you get this picture?" "It _____ to me by a friend of mine."
6. Many British programs _____ on American television.
7. "Did Jim and Sue go to the wedding?" "No. They _____ , but they didn't go."
8. "How old is this movie?" "It _____ in 1965."
9. My car _____ last week, but the next day it _____
by the police.

22.4 Where were they born?

1. (Makoto / Tokyo)   _Makoto was born in Tokyo._
2. (Isabel / São Paulo)   Isabel _____
3. (her parents / Rio de Janeiro) Her _____
4. (you / ???)   I _____
5. (your mother / ???)   _____

is being done   has been done (passive 2)

Is/are being . . . *(present continuous passive)*

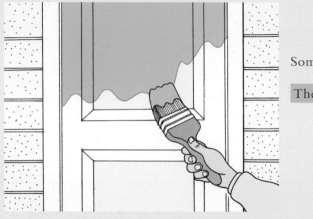

Somebody **is painting** the door . *(active)*

The door **is being painted**.   *(passive)*

- My car is at the garage. It **is being repaired**. (= somebody is repairing it)
- Some new houses **are being built** across from the park. (= somebody is building them)

Compare the present continuous passive and simple present passive:
- The office **is being cleaned** right now. *(present continuous passive)*
  The office **is cleaned** every day. *(simple present passive)*
- In the United States, football games **are** usually **played** on weekends, but no big games **are being played** next weekend.

For the present continuous and simple present, see Units 8 and 26.

Has/have been . . . *(present perfect passive)*

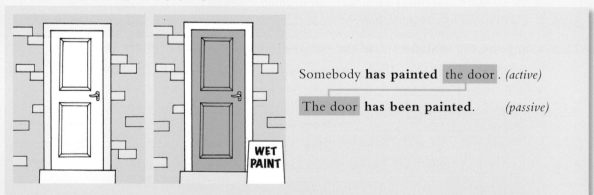

Somebody **has painted** the door . *(active)*

The door **has been painted**.   *(passive)*

- My key **has been stolen**. (= somebody has stolen it)
- My keys **have been stolen**. (= somebody has stolen them)
- I'm not going to the party. I **haven't been invited**. (= nobody has invited me)
- **Has** this shirt **been washed**? (= has somebody washed it?)

Compare the present perfect and simple past:
- The room isn't dirty any more. It **has been cleaned**. *(present perfect passive)*
  The room **was cleaned** yesterday. *(simple past passive)*
- I can't find my keys. I think they**'ve been stolen**. *(present perfect passive)*
  My keys **were stolen** last week. *(simple past passive)*

For the present perfect and simple past, see Units 19–21.

is done / was done → Unit 22   active and passive → **Appendix 1**

Exercises

23.1 What's happening?

1. The car _is being repaired._
2. A bridge _____
3. The windows _____
4. The grass _____

23.2 Look at the pictures. What is happening or what has happened? Use the present continuous (*is/are being* . . .) or the present perfect (*has/have been* . . .).

1. (the office / clean) _The office is being cleaned._
2. (the shirts / iron) _The shirts have been ironed._
3. (the window / break) The window _____
4. (the roof / repair) The roof _____
5. (the car / damage) _____
6. (the houses / tear / down) _____
7. (the trees / cut / down) _____
8. (they / invite / to a party) _____

23.3 Complete the sentences. (Study Unit 22 before you do this exercise.)

1. I can't use my office right now. _It is being painted_____ (paint).
2. We didn't go to the party. We _weren't invited_____ (not / invite).
3. The washing machine was broken, but it's OK now. It _____ (repair).
4. The washing machine _____ (repair) yesterday afternoon.
5. A factory is a place where things _____ (make).
6. How old are these houses? When _____ (they / build)?
7. *A:* _____ (the computer / use) at the moment?
   B: Yes, Steve is using it.
8. I've never seen these flowers before. What _____ (they / call)?
9. My sunglasses _____ (steal) at the beach yesterday.
10. The bridge is closed. It _____ (damage) last week, and it
    _____ (not / repair) yet.

→ Additional exercises 24–27 (pages 255–256)

UNIT 24

be/have/do in present and past tenses

A

Be (= **am/is/are/was/were**) + **-ing** (**cleaning/working**, etc.)

am/is/are + **-ing** *(present continuous)* → Units 3–4 and 26

- Please be quiet. I**'m working**.
- It **isn't raining** right now.
- What **are** you **doing** tonight?

was/were + **-ing** *(past continuous)* → Unit 13

- I **was working** when she arrived.
- It **wasn't raining**, so we didn't need an umbrella.
- What **were** you **doing** at 3:00?

B

Be + *past participle* (**cleaned/made/eaten**, etc.)

am/is/are + *past participle* *(simple present passive)* → Unit 22

- I**'m** never **invited** to parties.
- Butter **is made** from milk.
- These offices **aren't cleaned** every day.

was/were + *past participle* *(simple past passive)* → Unit 22

- The office **was cleaned** yesterday.
- These houses **were built** 100 years ago.
- How **was** the window **broken**?
- Where **were** you **born**?

C

Have/has + *past participle* (**cleaned/lost/eaten/been**, etc.)

have/has + *past participle* *(present perfect)* → Units 16–17, 19–21

- I**'ve lived** in this house for 10 years.
- Tom **has never ridden** a horse.
- Kate **hasn't been** to South America.
- Where **have** Paul and Nicole **gone**?

D

Do/does/did + *base form* (**clean/like/eat/go**, etc.)

do/does + *base form* *(simple present negative and questions)* → Units 6–7

- I like coffee, but I **don't like** tea.
- Chris **doesn't go** out very often.
- What **do** you usually **do** on weekends?
- **Does** Silvia **live** alone?

did + *base form* *(simple past negative and questions)* → Unit 12

- I **didn't watch** TV yesterday.
- It **didn't rain** last week.
- What time **did** Paul and Nicole **go** out?

irregular verbs → Unit 25, Appendixes 2–3

Exercises

24.1 Write *is/are* or *do/does*.

1. __Do__ you work at night?
2. Where __are__ they going?
3. Why _____ you looking at me?
4. _____ Bill live near you?
5. _____ you like to cook?
6. _____ the sun shining?
7. What time _____ the stores close?
8. _____ Maria working today?
9. What _____ this word mean?
10. _____ you feeling all right?

24.2 Write *am not/isn't/aren't* or *don't/doesn't*. All these sentences are negative.

1. Tom __doesn't__ work at night.
2. I'm very tired. I _____ want to go out tonight.
3. I'm very tired. I _____ going out tonight.
4. Gary _____ working this week. He's on vacation.
5. My parents are usually at home. They _____ go out very often.
6. Nicole has traveled a lot, but she _____ speak any foreign languages.
7. You can turn off the television. I _____ watching it.
8. Liz has invited us to her party next week, but we _____ going.

24.3 Write *was/were/did/have/has*.

1. Where __were__ your shoes made?
2. _____ you go out last night?
3. What _____ you doing at 10:30?
4. Where _____ your mother born?
5. _____ Barbara gone home?
6. What time _____ she go?
7. When _____ these houses built?
8. _____ Steve arrived yet?
9. Why _____ you go home early?
10. How long _____ they been married?

24.4 Write *is/are/was/were/have/has*.

1. Joe __has__ lost his passport.
2. This bridge _____ built 10 years ago.
3. _____ you finished your work yet?
4. This town is always clean. The streets _____ cleaned every day.
5. Where _____ you born?
6. I _____ just made some coffee. Would you like some?
7. Glass _____ made from sand.
8. This is a very old photograph. It _____ taken a long time ago.
9. David _____ bought a new car.

24.5 Complete the sentences. Choose from the box and put the verb into the correct form.

damage	~~rain~~	enjoy	~~go~~	pronounce	eat
listen	use	open	go	understand	

1. I'm going to take an umbrella with me. It's __raining__ .
2. Why are you so tired? Did you __go__ to bed late last night?
3. Where are the chocolates? Have you _____ all of them?
4. How is your new job? Are you _____ it?
5. My car was badly _____ in the accident, but I was OK.
6. Chris has a car, but she doesn't _____ it very often.
7. Mary isn't at home. She has _____ away for a few days.
8. I don't _____ the problem. Can you explain it again?
9. Martin is in his room. He's _____ to music.
10. I don't know how to say this word. How is it _____ ?
11. How do you _____ this window? Can you show me?

Regular and irregular verbs

Regular verbs

The *simple past* and *past participle* of regular verbs is **-ed**:
clean → clean**ed**   live → liv**ed**   paint → paint**ed**   study → stud**ied**

Simple past (→ Unit 11)
- ■ I **cleaned** my room yesterday.
- ■ Charlie **studied** engineering in college.

Past participle
have/has + *past participle* (present perfect → Units 16–17, 19–21):
- ■ I **have cleaned** my room.
- ■ Tina **has lived** in Miami for 10 years.

be (**is/are/were/has been**, etc.) + *past participle* (passive → Units 22–23):
- ■ These rooms **are cleaned** every day.
- ■ My car **has been repaired**.

Irregular verbs

The simple past and past participle of irregular verbs do *not* end in **-ed**:

	make	break	cut
simple past	**made**	**broke**	**cut**
past participle	**made**	**broken**	**cut**

Sometimes the simple past and past participle are the same. For example:

	make	find	buy	cut
simple past *past participle*	**made**	**found**	**bought**	**cut**

- ■ I **made** a cake yesterday. *(simple past)*
- ■ I **have made** some coffee. *(past participle – present perfect)*
- ■ Butter **is made** from milk. *(past participle – present passive)*

Sometimes the simple past and past participle are different. For example:

	break	know	begin	go
simple past	**broke**	**knew**	**began**	**went**
past participle	**broken**	**known**	**begun**	**gone**

- ■ Somebody **broke** this window last night. *(simple past)*
- ■ Somebody **has broken** this window. *(past participle – present perfect)*
- ■ This window **was broken** last night. *(past participle – past passive)*

Exercises

25.1 Write the simple past / past participle of these verbs. (The simple past and past participle are the same for all the verbs in this exercise.)

1. make   _made_
2. cut   _cut_
3. say   _____
4. bring   _____
5. pay   _____

6. enjoy   _____
7. buy   _____
8. sit   _____
9. leave   _____
10. happen   _____

11. hear   _____
12. put   _____
13. catch   _____
14. watch   _____
15. understand   _____

25.2 Write the simple past and past participle of these verbs.

1. break   _broke_   _broken_
2. begin   _____   _____
3. eat   _____   _____
4. drink   _____   _____
5. drive   _____   _____
6. speak   _____   _____
7. write   _____   _____

8. come   _____   _____
9. know   _____   _____
10. take   _____   _____
11. go   _____   _____
12. give   _____   _____
13. throw   _____   _____
14. get   _____   _____

25.3 Put the verb in the right form.

1. I _washed_ my hands because they were dirty. (wash)
2. Somebody has _broken_ this window. (break)
3. I feel good. I _____ very well last night. (sleep)
4. We _____ a really good movie yesterday. (see)
5. It _____ a lot while we were on vacation. (rain)
6. I've _____ my bag. (lose) Have you _____ it? (see)
7. Rosa's bicycle was _____ last week. (steal)
8. I _____ to bed early because I was tired. (go)
9. Have you _____ your work yet? (finish)
10. The shopping mall was _____ about 20 years ago. (build)
11. Anna _____ to drive when she was 16. (learn)
12. I've never _____ a horse. (ride)
13. Julia is a good friend of mine. I've _____ her for a long time. (know)
14. Yesterday I _____ and _____ my leg. (fall / hurt)
15. My brother _____ in the Boston Marathon last year. Have you ever _____ in a marathon? (run / run)

25.4 Complete the sentences. Choose from the box and put the verb into the correct form.

cost	drive	fly	~~make~~	meet	sell
speak	swim	tell	think	wake up	win

1. I have _made_ some coffee. Would you like some?
2. Have you _____ John about your new job?
3. We played basketball on Sunday. We didn't play very well, but we _____ the game.
4. I know Gary, but I've never _____ his wife.
5. We were _____ by loud music in the middle of the night.
6. Stephanie jumped into the river and _____ to the other side.
7. "Did you like the movie?" "Yes, I _____ it was very good."
8. Many different languages are _____ in the Philippines.
9. Our vacation _____ a lot of money because we stayed in an expensive hotel.
10. Have you ever _____ a very fast car?
11. All the tickets for the concert were _____ very quickly.
12. A bird _____ in through the open window while we were having our dinner.

What are you doing tomorrow?

A

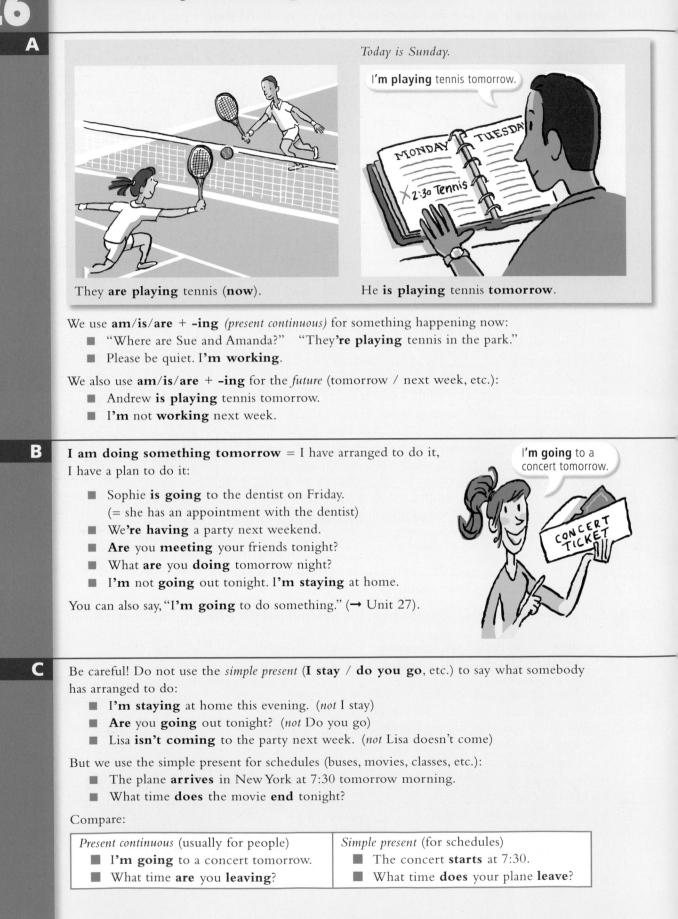

Today is Sunday.

I**'m playing** tennis tomorrow.

MONDAY   TUESDAY

X 2:30 Tennis

They **are playing** tennis (**now**).   He **is playing** tennis **tomorrow**.

We use **am/is/are** + **–ing** *(present continuous)* for something happening now:
- "Where are Sue and Amanda?"   "They**'re playing** tennis in the park."
- Please be quiet. I**'m working**.

We also use **am/is/are** + **–ing** for the *future* (tomorrow / next week, etc.):
- Andrew **is playing** tennis tomorrow.
- I**'m** not **working** next week.

B

I am doing something tomorrow = I have arranged to do it,
I have a plan to do it:

- Sophie **is going** to the dentist on Friday.
  (= she has an appointment with the dentist)
- We**'re having** a party next weekend.
- **Are** you **meeting** your friends tonight?
- What **are** you **doing** tomorrow night?
- I**'m** not **going** out tonight. I**'m staying** at home.

You can also say, "I**'m going** to do something." (→ Unit 27).

I**'m going** to a concert tomorrow.

CONCERT TICKET

C

Be careful! Do not use the *simple present* (**I stay / do you go**, etc.) to say what somebody
has arranged to do:
- I**'m staying** at home this evening. (*not* I stay)
- **Are** you **going** out tonight? (*not* Do you go)
- Lisa **isn't coming** to the party next week. (*not* Lisa doesn't come)

But we use the simple present for schedules (buses, movies, classes, etc.):
- The plane **arrives** in New York at 7:30 tomorrow morning.
- What time **does** the movie **end** tonight?

Compare:

Present continuous (usually for people)	*Simple present* (for schedules)
■ I**'m going** to a concert tomorrow.	■ The concert **starts** at 7:30.
■ What time **are** you **leaving**?	■ What time **does** your plane **leave**?

present continuous → Units 3–4   simple present → Units 5–7   I'm going to . . . → Unit 27

Exercises

26.1 Look at the pictures. What are these people doing next Friday?

1.	2.	3.	4.	5.
Andrew	Richard	Rachel	Karen	Tom and Sue

1. _Andrew is playing tennis on Friday._
2. Richard _____ to the movies.
3. Rachel _____
4. _____ lunch with Ken.
5. _____

26.2 Write questions. All the sentences are future.

1. (you / go / out / tonight?)   _Are you going out tonight?_ _____
2. (you / work / next week?)   _____
3. (what / you / do / tomorrow night?) _____
4. (what time / your friends / come?) _____
5. (when / Liz / go / on vacation?)   _____

26.3 Write sentences about yourself. What are you doing in the next few days?

1. _I'm staying at home tonight._ _____
2. _I'm going to the theater on Monday._ _____
3. _____
4. _____
5. _____
6. _____

26.4 Put the verb in the present continuous (*he is leaving*, etc.) or simple present (*the train leaves*, etc.).

1. "_Are you going_ (you / go) out tonight?" "No, I'm too tired."
2. _We're going_ (we / go) to a concert tonight. _It starts_ (it / start) at 7:30.
3. Listen to this! _____ (Karen / get) married next month!
4. *A:* My parents _____ (go) on vacation next week.
    B: Oh, that's nice. Where _____ (they / go)?
5. Silvia is taking an English course this semester. The course _____
    (end) on Friday.
6. There's a party tomorrow night, but _____ (I / not / go).
7. _____ (I / go) out with some friends tonight. Why don't you
    come, too? _____ (we / meet) at John's house at 8:00.
8. *A:* How _____ (you / get) home after the party tomorrow? By taxi?
    B: No, I can go by bus. The last bus _____ (leave) at midnight.
9. *A:* Do you want to go to the movies tonight?
    B: Yes, what time _____ (the movie / begin)?
10. *A:* What _____ (you / do) tomorrow afternoon?
    B: _____ (I / work).

I'm going to . . .

A

I'm going to do something

I'm going to watch TV tonight.

morning   *tonight*

She **is going to watch** TV tonight.

We use **am/is/are going to . . .** for the *future*:

I **am** he/she/it **is** we/you/they **are**	(not) **going to**	do . . . drink . . . watch . . .

am I **is** he/she/it **are** we/you/they	**going to**	buy . . . ? eat . . . ? wear . . . ?

B

I am going to do something = I have decided to do it; my intention is to do it:

I decided to do it ⟶ **I'm going to do it**

past   *now*   *future*

- **I'm going to buy** some books tomorrow.
- Sarah **is going to sell** her car.
- **I'm not going to have** breakfast this morning. I'm not hungry.
- What **are** you **going to wear** to the wedding next week?
- "Your hands are dirty."   "Yes, I know. **I'm going to wash** them."
- **Are** you **going to invite** Martin to your party?

We also use the present continuous (**I am doing**) for the future, usually for arrangements (→ Unit 26):

- I **am playing** tennis with Julia tomorrow.

C

Something **is going to happen**

Something **is going to happen** = we can see *now* that it is sure to happen:

- Look at the sky! It's **going to rain**.
  (black clouds *now* → rain)
- Oh, no! It's 9:00, and I'm not ready.
  I'm going to be late.
  (9:00 *now* and not ready → late)

It's going to rain.

present for the future → **Unit 26**   will → **Units 28–29**

Exercises

27.1 **What are these people saying?**

1. I'm going to watch TV.
2. I _____
3. I _____
4. We _____

27.2 **Complete the sentences. Use *going to* + these verbs:**

do   eat   give   lie down   stay   walk   ~~wash~~   watch   ~~wear~~

1. My hands are dirty. _I'm going to wash_ them.
2. What _are you going to wear_ to the party tonight?
3. It's a nice day. I don't want to take the bus. I _____ .
4. Steve is going to San Diego next week. He _____ with some friends.
5. I'm hungry. I _____ this sandwich.
6. It's Sharon's birthday next week. We _____ her a present.
7. Sue says she's feeling very tired. She _____ for an hour.
8. The president's speech is on television tonight. _____ you _____ it?
9. What _____ Rachel _____ when she finishes school?

27.3 **Look at the pictures. What is going to happen?**

1. _It's going to rain._
2. The shelf _____
3. The car _____
4. He _____

27.4 **What are you going to do today or tomorrow? Write three sentences.**

1. I'm _____
2. _____
3. _____

A

Sarah

Sarah goes to work every day. She is always there from 8:30 until 4:30.

It is 11:00 now. Sarah **is** at work.

At 11:00 yesterday, she **was** at work.

At 11:00 tomorrow, she **will be** at work.

will + *base form* (**will be** / **will win** / **will come**, etc.):

I/we/you/they he/she/it	**will** (**'ll**) **will not** (**won't**)	**be win eat come**, etc.

will	I/we/you/they he/she/it	**be**? **win**? **eat**? **come**?, etc.

'll = **will**: I**'ll** (I will) / you**'ll** / she**'ll**, etc.

won't = **will not**: I **won't** (= I will not) / you **won't** / she **won't**, etc.

B

We use **will** for the *future* (tomorrow / next week, etc.):
- Sue travels a lot. Today she is in Los Angeles. Tomorrow she**'ll be** in Mexico City. Next week she**'ll be** in New York.
- You can call me tonight. I**'ll be** at home.
- Leave the old bread in the yard. The birds **will eat** it.
- We**'ll** probably **go** out tonight.
- **Will** you **be** at home tonight?

- I **won't be** here tomorrow. (= I will not be here)
- Don't drink coffee before you go to bed. You **won't sleep**.

We often say **I think . . . will . . .** :
- **I think** Kelly **will pass** her driver's test.
- **I don't think** it **will rain** this afternoon.
- **Do you think** the test **will be** difficult?

C

We do *not* use **will** for things we have already arranged or decided to do (→ Units 26–27):
- We**'re going** to the movies on Saturday. Do you want to come with us? (*not* We will go)
- I**'m** not **working** tomorrow. (*not* I won't work)
- **Are** you **going to take** your driver's test tomorrow? (*not* Will you take)

Exercises

28.1 Helen is traveling in South America. Complete the sentences with *she was*, *she's*, or *she'll be*.

Helen

1. Yesterday _she was_ in Rio de Janeiro.
2. Tomorrow _____ in Bogotá.
3. Last week _____ in Santiago.
4. Next week _____ in Caracas.
5. Right now _____ in Lima.
6. Three days ago _____ in Buenos Aires.
7. At the end of her trip _____ very tired.

28.2 Where will you be? Write sentences about yourself. Use:
I'll be . . . or *I'll probably be . . .* or *I don't know where I'll be.*

1. (at 10:00 tomorrow) _I'll be at work._ OR _I'll probably be at the beach._
2. (one hour from now) _____
3. (at midnight tonight) _____
4. (at 3:00 tomorrow afternoon) _____
5. (two years from now) _____

28.3 Put in *will ('ll)* or *won't*.

1. Don't drink coffee before you go to bed. You _won't_ sleep.
2. "Are you ready yet?" "Not yet. I _____ be ready in five minutes."
3. I'm going away for a few days. I'm leaving tonight, so I _____ be at home tomorrow.
4. It _____ rain, so you don't need to take an umbrella.
5. *A:* I don't feel very well tonight.
   B: Well, go to bed early, and you _____ feel better in the morning.
6. It's Bill's birthday next Monday. He _____ be 25.
7. I'm sorry I was late this morning. It _____ happen again.

28.4 Write sentences with *I think . . .* or *I don't think . . . .*

1. (Kelly will pass the driver's test) _I think Kelly will pass the driver's test._
2. (Kelly won't pass the driver's test) _I don't think Kelly will pass the driver's test._
3. (we'll win the game) I _____
4. (I won't be here tomorrow) _____
5. (Sue will like her present) _____
6. (they won't get married) _____
7. (you won't like the movie) _____

28.5 Which is right? (Study Unit 26 before you do this exercise.)

1. ~~We'll go~~ / We're going to the theater tonight. We've got tickets. (*We're going* is right)
2. "What will you do / are you doing tomorrow night?" "Nothing. I'm free."
3. They'll leave / They're leaving tomorrow morning. Their train is at 8:40.
4. I'm sure your aunt will lend / is lending us some money. She's very rich.
5. "Why are you putting on your coat?" "I'll go / I'm going out."
6. Do you think Claire will call / is calling us tonight?
7. Steve can't meet us on Saturday. He'll work / He's working.
8. Let's fly to Miami instead of driving. It won't take / isn't taking as long.
9. *A:* What are your plans for the weekend?
   B: Some friends will come / are coming to stay with us.

will 2

A

You can use **I'll . . .** (**I will**) when you offer something or decide to do something:
- ■ "My suitcase is very heavy." "**I'll carry** it for you."
- ■ "**I'll call** you tomorrow, OK?" "OK, bye."

We often say **I think I'll . . .** / **I don't think I'll . . .** when we decide to do something:
- ■ I'm tired. **I think I'll go** to bed early tonight.
- ■ It's a nice day. **I think I'll sit** outside.
- ■ It's raining. **I don't think I'll go** out.

Do not use the simple present (**I go** / **I call**, etc.) in sentences like these:
- ■ **I'll call** you tomorrow, OK? (*not* I call you)
- ■ I think **I'll go** to bed early. (*not* I go to bed)

B

Do not use **I'll . . .** for something you decided before (→ Units 26–27):
- ■ **I'm working** tomorrow. (*not* I'll work)
- ■ There's a good program on TV tonight. **I'm going to watch** it. (*not* I'll watch)
- ■ What **are** you **doing** this weekend? (*not* What will you do)

C

Shall I . . . ? Shall we . . . ?

Shall I answer the phone?

No, that's OK. I'll answer it.

Shall I / **Shall we . . . ?** = Do you think this is a good thing to do? Do you think this is a good idea?
- ■ It's very warm in this room. **Shall I open** the window?
- ■ "**Shall I call** you tonight?" "OK."
- ■ It's a nice day. **Shall we go** for a walk?
- ■ What **shall we have** for dinner?

We use **should** in the same way.
- ■ "**Should I call** you tonight?" "OK."
- ■ It's a nice day. **Should we go** for a walk?
- ■ What **should we have** for dinner?

What are you doing tomorrow? → Unit 26   **I'm going to . . .** → Unit 27   **will** 1 → Unit 28   **should** → Unit 33

Exercises

29.1 Complete the sentences. Use *I'll (I will)* + these verbs:

~~carry~~   do   eat   send   show   sit   stay

1. My suitcase is very heavy.   *I'll carry* _____ it for you.
2. Enjoy your vacation.   Thank you. _____ you a postcard.
3. I don't want this banana.   Well, I'm hungry. _____ it.
4. Do you want a chair?   No, it's OK. _____ on the floor.
5. Did you call Jenny?   Oh no, I forgot. _____ it now.
6. Are you coming with me?   No, I don't think so. _____ here.
7. How do you use this camera?   Give it to me and _____ you.

29.2 Complete the sentences. Use *I think I'll . . .* or *I don't think I'll . . .* + these verbs:

buy   **buy**   ~~go~~   **have**   **play**

1. It's cold today. __*I don't think I'll go*_____ out.
2. I'm hungry. I _____ something to eat.
3. I feel very tired. _____ tennis.
4. I like this hat. _____ it.
5. This camera is too expensive. _____ it.

29.3 Which is right?

1. ~~I call~~ / I'll call you tomorrow, OK? (*I'll call* is right)
2. I haven't done the shopping yet. I do / I'll do it later.
3. I like sports. I watch / I'll watch a lot of sports on TV.
4. I need some exercise. I think I go / I'll go for a walk.
5. Gerry is going to buy / will buy a new car. He told me last week.
6. "This letter is for Rose." "OK. I give / I'll give / I'm going to give it to her."
7. *A:* Are you doing / Will you do anything this evening?
   B: Yes, I'm going / I'll go out with some friends.
8. I can't go out with you tomorrow night. I work / I'm working / I'll work.
9. I like this hat. I think I buy / I'll buy it.

29.4 What does Anne say to Kathy? Find the right answers.

 Kathy

 Anne

1. It's very warm in this room.   _d_   a) If you want. Where should we go?
2. This TV program isn't very good.   ____   b) Yes, who shall we invite?
3. Should we have a party?   ____   c) No, shall I go and get some?
4. It's dark in this room.   ____   d) Shall I open the window?
5. Should I go to the store?   ____   e) Should I turn on the light?
6. Shall we go out?   ____   f) OK, how many shall we buy?
7. Shall I wait here?   ____   g) Should I turn it off?
8. Do we have any bread?   ____   h) No, come with me.
9. Should we get some lottery tickets?   ____   i) No, it's OK. I'll go.

→ Additional exercises 28–31 (pages 256–259)

might

A

He **might go** to Costa Rica.
(= it is possible that he will go to Costa Rica)

It **might rain**.
(= it is possible that it will rain)

might + *base form* (**might go** / **might be** / **might rain**, etc.):

I/we/you/they he/she/it	**might** (not)	**be** **go** **play** **come**, etc.

B

I might = it is possible that I will:

- I **might go** to the movies tonight, but I'm not sure. (= it is possible that I will go)
- *A:* When is Rebecca going to call you?
  B: I don't know. She **might call** this afternoon.
- Take an umbrella with you. It **might rain**.
- Buy a lottery ticket. You **might be** lucky. (= perhaps you will be lucky)
- "Are you going out tonight?" "**I might**." (= I might go out)

Study the difference:

- **I'm playing** tennis tomorrow. *(sure)*
  I **might play** tennis tomorrow. *(possible)*
- Rebecca **is going to call** later. *(sure)*
  Rebecca **might call** later. *(possible)*

C

I might not = it is possible that I will not:

- I **might not go** to work tomorrow. (= it is possible that I will not go)
- Sue **might not come** to the party. (= it is possible that she will not come)

D

May

You can use **may** in the same way. **I may** = **I might**:

- I **may go** to the movies tonight. (= I might go)
- Sue **may not come** to the party. (= Sue might not come)

May I . . . ? = Is it OK to . . . ? / Can I . . . ?:

- **May I** ask a question? (= is it OK to ask / can I ask?)
- "**May I** sit here?" "Sure."

Exercises

30.1 Write sentences with *might*.

1. (it's possible that I'll go to the movies) *I might go to the movies.*
2. (it's possible that I'll see you tomorrow) I _____
3. (it's possible that Sarah will forget to call) _____
4. (it's possible that it will snow today) _____
5. (it's possible that I'll be late tonight) _____

Write sentences with *might not*.

6. (it's possible that Mark will not be here next week) _____
7. (it's possible that I won't have time to go out) _____

30.2 Somebody is asking you about your plans. You have some ideas, but you are not sure. Choose from the list and write sentences with *I might*.

    fish   ~~**Italy**~~   **Monday**   **a new car**   **take a trip**   **take a taxi**

1. Where are you going for your vacation?   I'm not sure. *I might go to Italy.*
2. What are you doing this weekend?   I don't know. I _____
3. When will you see Kate again?   I'm not sure. _____
4. What are you going to have for dinner?   I don't know. _____
5. How are you going to get home tonight?   I'm not sure. _____
6. I hear you won some money. What are you going to do with it?   I haven't decided yet. _____

30.3 You ask Bill questions about his plans for tomorrow. Sometimes he is sure, but usually he is not sure.

1. Are you playing tennis tomorrow?   Yes, in the afternoon.
2. Are you going out tomorrow evening?   Possibly.
3. Are you going to get up early?   Maybe.
4. Are you working tomorrow?   No, I'm not.
5. Will you be at home tomorrow morning?   Maybe.
6. Are you going to watch television?   I might.
7. Are you going out in the afternoon?   Yes, I am.
8. Are you going shopping?   Perhaps. I'm not sure.

Bill

Now write about Bill. Use *might* where necessary.

1. *He's playing tennis tomorrow afternoon.*
2. *He might go out tomorrow evening.*
3. He _____
4. _____
5. _____
6. _____
7. _____
8. _____

30.4 Write three things that you might do tomorrow.

1. _____
2. _____
3. _____

can and could

"I **can play** the piano."

"**Could** you **open** the door, please?"

EXIT

He **can play** the piano.

can + *base form* (**can do** / **can play** / **can come**, etc.):

I/we/you/they he/she/it	**can** **can't (cannot)**	**do** **play** **see** **come**, etc.

can	I/we/you/they he/she/it	**do**? **play**? **see**? **come**?, etc.

I can do something = I *know how* to do it, or *it is possible* for me to do it:

- I **can play** the piano. My brother **can play** the piano, too.
- Sarah **can speak** Italian, but she **can't speak** Spanish.
- "**Can** you **swim**?"   "Yes, but I'm not a very good swimmer."
- "**Can** you **change** a twenty-dollar bill?"   "I'm sorry, I **can't**."
- I'm having a party next week, but Paul and Rachel **can't come**.

For the *past* (**yesterday** / **last week**, etc.), we use **could/couldn't**:

- When I was young, I **could run** very fast.
- Before Maria came to the United States, she **couldn't understand** much English.
  Now she **can understand** everything.
- I was tired last night, but I **couldn't sleep**.
- I had a party last week, but Paul and Rachel **couldn't come**.

Can you . . . ?   Could you . . . ?   Can I . . . ?   Could I . . . ?

We use **Can you . . . ?** or **Could you . . . ?** when we ask people to do things:

- **Can you** open the door, please?   *or*   **Could you** open the door, please?
- **Can you** wait a minute, please?   *or*   **Could you** wait . . . ?

We use **Can I have . . . ?** or **Could I have . . . ?** to ask for something:

- *(in a store)* **Can I have** change for a dollar, please?   *or*   **Could I have** . . . ?

Can I . . . ? or **Could I . . . ?** = is it OK to do something?:

- Tom, **can I** borrow your umbrella?   *or*   Tom, **could I** borrow your umbrella?
- *(on the phone)* Hello, **can I** speak to Gary, please?   *or*   . . . **could I** speak . . . ?

May I . . . ? → Unit 30

Exercises

31.1 Ask Steve if he can do these things:

1. _Can you swim?_
2. _____
3. _____
4. _____
5. _____
6. _____

Can you do these things? Write sentences about yourself. Use _I can_ or _I can't_.

7. I _____ 10. _____
8. _____ 11. _____
9. _____ 12. _____

31.2 Complete these sentences. Use _can_ or _can't_ + one of these verbs:

~~come~~   find   hear   see   speak

1. I'm sorry, but we _can't come_ to your party next Saturday.
2. I like this hotel room. You _____ the mountains from the window.
3. You are speaking very quietly. I _____ you.
4. Have you seen my suitcase? I _____ it.
5. Catherine got the job because she _____ five languages.

31.3 Complete these sentences. Use _can't_ or _couldn't_ + one of these verbs:

decide   eat   find   go   go   ~~sleep~~

1. I was tired, but I _couldn't sleep_ .
2. I wasn't hungry yesterday. I _____ my dinner.
3. Kate doesn't know what to do. She _____ .
4. I wanted to speak to Martin yesterday, but I _____ him.
5. James _____ to the concert next Saturday. He has to work.
6. Paula _____ to the meeting last week. She was sick.

31.4 What do you say in these situations? Use _can_ or _could_.

1. (open)   _Could you open the door, please?_
2. (pass)
3. (turn down)
4. (have)
5. (look)
6. (use)

must

She **must be** sick = I am sure she is sick; it is clear that she is sick.

must + base form (**must be** / **must know**, etc.):

I/we/you/they he/she/it	must (not)	be know have live, etc.

We use **must** when we believe that something is true.

- You worked 10 hours today. You **must be** tired.
- My brother has worked at your company for years. You **must know** him.
- My friends have the same zip code as you. They **must live** near you.
- *(on the telephone)* This isn't the Smiths'? I'm sorry. I **must have** the wrong number.

We use **must not** when we believe that something is *not* true.

- The phone rang eight times and Karen didn't answer. She **must not be** at home.
- Carlos takes the bus everywhere. He **must not have** a car.
- The Silvas are always home on Fridays. They **must not work** then.

Must has another meaning. You **must do** something = it is necessary to do it.

- You **must be** careful with this knife. It's very sharp.
- Workers **must wear** safety glasses at this machine.
- In the United States, you **must be** 18 to vote.

For the *past* (**yesterday**, **last week**, etc.), we use **had to** . . . (*not* must).

- They were in a dangerous situation. They **had to be** careful. (*not* They must be careful.)
- We **had to wear** safety glasses when we visited the factory last week. (*not* We must wear)

You **must not do** something = it is necessary *not* to do it; it is the wrong thing to do.

- Bicyclists **must not ride** on the sidewalk. (= they must ride in the street)
- You **must not be** late for school again!

Exercises

32.1 Complete the sentences. Use *must be* + these words or phrases:

for you   good   hungry   in the kitchen   ~~tired~~   very happy

1. Silvia worked 10 hours today. She __*must be tired*__ .
2. It's evening, and you haven't eaten anything all day. You _____ .
3. It's the most popular restaurant in town, so the food _____ .
4. "I got the job."   "You did? You _____ ."
5. The phone's ringing. I know it's not for me. It _____ .
6. My keys aren't in the living room, so they _____ .

32.2 Complete the sentences. Use *must* + these verbs:

drink   have   ~~know~~   like   work

1. My brother has worked at your company for years. You __*must know*__ him.
2. Marilyn wears something blue every day. She _____ the color blue.
3. The Hills have six children and three dogs. They _____ a big house.
4. Mrs. Lee bought three gallons of milk at the store. Her children _____ a lot of milk.
5. I know Mrs. Romo has a job, but she's always home during the day. She _____ at night.

32.3 Write *must* or *must not*.

1. *(on the telephone)* This isn't the Smiths'? I __*must*__ have the wrong number.
2. Carlos takes the bus everywhere. He __*must not*__ have a car.
3. Brandon is very thin. He _____ eat very much.
4. I never see my neighbor in the morning. He _____ leave for work very early.
5. I always have to repeat things when I talk to Kelly. She _____ hear very well.
6. Jim wears the same clothes every day. He _____ have many clothes.
7. You have a cold and a fever? Poor thing! You _____ feel awful.

32.4 Complete the sentences. Use *must* + these verbs:

~~be~~   be   get   know   take   wear

1. In most of the United States, you __*must be*__ at least 16 to get a driver's license.
2. For this job, you _____ both Spanish and German.
3. People in the front seat of a car _____ a seat belt.
4. High school students who want to go to college _____ good grades.
5. This highway is closed. Drivers _____ another road.
6. A tennis player _____ very good to play professionally.

32.5 Write *must*, *mustn't*, or *had to*.

1. We __*mustn't*__ forget to send Sam a birthday card.
2. We __*had to*__ wear safety glasses when we visited the factory.
3. I _____ hurry or I'll be late.
4. "Why were you so late?"   "I _____ wait half an hour for the bus."
5. Keep these papers in a safe place. You _____ lose them.
6. Bicyclists _____ follow the same traffic rules as drivers.
7. We _____ forget to turn off the lights when we leave.
8. I don't usually work on Saturdays, but last Saturday I _____ work.

should

You **shouldn't watch** TV so much.

should + *base form*
(**should do** / **should watch**, etc.):

		do
I/we/you/they	**should**	stop
he/she/it	**shouldn't**	go
		watch, etc.

You **should do** something = it is a good thing to do; it is the right thing to do:
- Tom doesn't study enough. He **should study** harder.
- It's a good movie. You **should go** and see it.
- When you play tennis, you **should** always **watch** the ball.

Should I/we **do** something? = is it a good thing to do?
- **Should** I **invite** Karen to dinner?
- **Should** we **make** something special for dinner?

You **shouldn't do** something = it is not a good thing to do (**shouldn't** = should not):
- Tom **shouldn't go** to bed so late.
- You watch TV all the time. You **shouldn't watch** TV so much.

We often say **I think . . . should . . .** :
- **I think** Lisa **should buy** some new clothes.
  (= I think it is a good idea.)
- It's late. **I think** I **should go** home now.
- *A:* Shall I buy this coat?
  B: Yes, **I think** you **should**.

I don't think . . . should . . . :
- **I don't think** you **should work** so hard.
  (= I don't think it is a good idea.)
- **I don't think** we **should go** yet. It's too early.

Do you think . . . should . . . ? :
- **Do you think** I **should buy** this hat?
- What time **do you think** we **should go** home?

Do you think I **should buy** this hat?

Should is different from **have to**.
- I **should** study tonight, but I think I'll go to the movies.
- I **have to** study tonight. I can't go to the movies.

Another way to say **should** is **ought to**:
- I **ought to study** tonight, but I think I'll go to the movies. (= I should study)
- I think Lisa **ought to buy** some new clothes. (= Lisa should buy)

shall/should → Unit 29   must → Unit 32   have to → Unit 34

Exercises

33.1 Complete the sentences. Use *you should* + these verbs:

    eat   go   read   visit   ~~watch~~   wear

1. When you play tennis, ___*you should watch*___ the ball.
2. It's late, and you're very tired. _____ to bed.
3. _____ plenty of fruit and vegetables.
4. If you have time, _____ the Science Museum. It's very interesting.
5. When you're driving, _____ a seat belt.
6. It's a very good book. _____ it.

33.2 Write about the people in the pictures. Use *He/She shouldn't . . . so . . . .*

1. ___*She shouldn't watch TV so much.*___
2. He _____
3. _____ hard.
4. _____

33.3 You are not sure what to do, so you ask a friend. Write questions with *Do you think I should . . . ?*

1. You are in a store. You are trying on a jacket. (buy?)
   You ask your friend: ___*Do you think I should buy this jacket?*___
2. You can't drive. (learn?)
   You ask your friend: Do you think _____
3. You don't like your job. (get another job?)
   You ask your friend: _____
4. You are going to have a party. (invite Gary?)
   You ask your friend: _____

33.4 Write sentences with *I think . . . should . . .* or *I don't think . . . should . . . .*

1. We have to get up early tomorrow. (go home now) ___*I think we should go home now.*___
2. That coat is too big for you. (buy it) ___*I don't think you should buy it.*___
3. You don't need your car. (sell it) _____
4. Karen needs a change. (take a trip) _____
5. Sally and Dan are too young. (get married) _____
6. You're still sick. (go to work) _____
7. James isn't feeling well today. (go to the doctor) _____
8. The hotel is too expensive for us. (stay there) _____

33.5 What do **you** think? Write sentences with *should*.

1. I think ___*everybody should learn another language.*___
2. I think everybody _____
3. I think _____
4. I don't think _____
5. I think I _____

I have to . . .

A

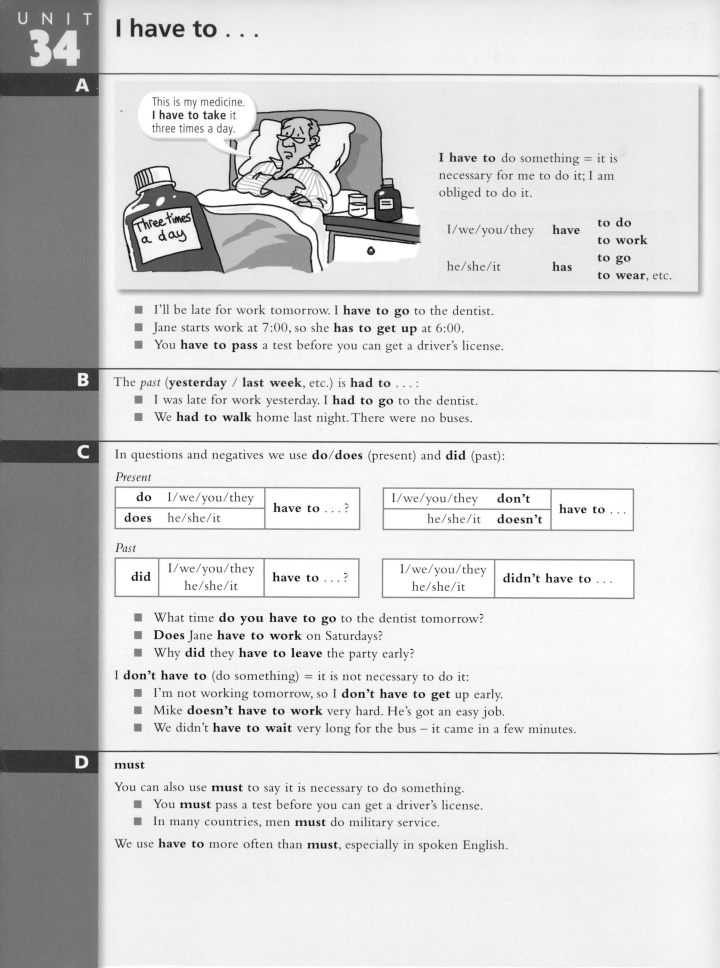

This is my medicine. **I have to take** it three times a day.

I have to do something = it is necessary for me to do it; I am obliged to do it.

I/we/you/they	**have**	**to do**
		to work
he/she/it	**has**	**to go**
		to wear, etc.

- I'll be late for work tomorrow. I **have to go** to the dentist.
- Jane starts work at 7:00, so she **has to get up** at 6:00.
- You **have to pass** a test before you can get a driver's license.

B

The *past* (**yesterday** / **last week**, etc.) is **had to** . . . :

- I was late for work yesterday. I **had to go** to the dentist.
- We **had to walk** home last night. There were no buses.

C

In questions and negatives we use **do/does** (present) and **did** (past):

Present

do	I/we/you/they	**have to . . . ?**
does	he/she/it	

I/we/you/they	**don't**	**have to . . .**
he/she/it	**doesn't**	

Past

did	I/we/you/they he/she/it	**have to . . . ?**

I/we/you/they he/she/it	**didn't have to . . .**

- What time **do you have to go** to the dentist tomorrow?
- **Does** Jane **have to work** on Saturdays?
- Why **did** they **have to leave** the party early?

I **don't have to** (do something) = it is not necessary to do it:

- I'm not working tomorrow, so I **don't have to get** up early.
- Mike **doesn't have to work** very hard. He's got an easy job.
- We didn't **have to wait** very long for the bus – it came in a few minutes.

D **must**

You can also use **must** to say it is necessary to do something.

- You **must** pass a test before you can get a driver's license.
- In many countries, men **must** do military service.

We use **have to** more often than **must**, especially in spoken English.

must → Unit 32

Exercises

34.1 Complete the sentences. Use *have to* or *has to* + these verbs:

hit   read   speak   take   travel   ~~wear~~

1. My eyes are not very good. I ___*have to wear*___ glasses.
2. At the end of the course all the students _____ a test.
3. Sarah is studying literature. She _____ a lot of books.
4. Alberto doesn't understand much English. You _____ very slowly to him.
5. Kate is not at home much. She _____ a lot for her job.
6. In tennis you _____ the ball over the net.

34.2 Complete the sentences. Use *have to* or *had to* + these verbs:

answer   buy   change   go   take   wake   ~~walk~~

1. We ___*had to walk*___ home last night. There were no buses.
2. It's late. I _____ now. I'll see you tomorrow.
3. I went to the store after work yesterday. I _____ some food.
4. This train doesn't go all the way downtown. You _____ at First Avenue.
5. We took a test yesterday. We _____ six questions out of ten.
6. I'm going to bed. I _____ up early tomorrow.
7. Amy and her cousin can't go out with us tonight. They _____ care of Amy's little brother.

34.3 Complete the questions. Some are present and some are past.

1.	I have to get up early tomorrow.	What time ___*do you have to get up*___ ?
2.	George had to wait a long time.	How long _____ ?
3.	Liz has to go somewhere.	Where _____ ?
4.	We had to pay a lot of money.	How much _____ ?
5.	I have to do some work.	What exactly _____ ?
6.	They had to leave early.	Why _____ ?
7.	Paul has to go to Moscow.	When _____ ?

34.4 Write sentences with *don't/doesn't/didn't have to* . . . .

1. Why are you going out? You ___*don't have to go*___ out.
2. Why is Sue waiting? She _____ .
3. Why did you get up early? You _____ .
4. Why is Paul working so hard? He _____ .
5. Why do you want to leave now? We _____ .
6. Why did they tell me something I already know? They _____ .

34.5 Write some things that you (or your friends or family) *have to do* or *had to do*.

1. (every day) ___*I have to drive 50 miles to work every day.*___
2. (every day) _____
3. (yesterday) _____
4. (tomorrow) _____
5. (last week) _____
6. (when I was younger) _____

Would you like . . . ?   I'd like . . .

Would you like . . . ? = Do you want . . . ?

We use **Would you like . . . ?** to offer things:
- ■ *A:* **Would you like** some coffee?
  B: No, thank you.
- ■ *A:* **Would you like** a piece of candy?
  B: Yes, thanks.
- ■ *A:* Which **would you like**, tea or coffee?
  B: Tea, please.

Would you like a piece of candy?

Yes, thanks.

We use **Would you like to . . . ?** to invite somebody:
- ■ **Would you like to go** for a walk?
- ■ *A:* **Would you like to have** dinner with us on Sunday?
  B: Yes, **I'd love to**. (= I would love to have dinner with you)
- ■ What **would you like to do** tonight?

I'd like . . . is a polite way to say "I want." (**I'd** like = **I would** like)
- ■ I'm thirsty. **I'd like** a drink.
- ■ *(in a tourist office)* **I'd like** some information about hotels, please.
- ■ I'm feeling tired. **I'd like to stay** home tonight.

Would you like . . . ? and **Do you like . . . ?**

Would you like . . . ? / I'd like . . .

Would you like some coffee?

Yes, please.

Would you like some coffee? = Do you want some coffee?
- ■ *A:* **Would you like** to go to the movies tonight?
  (= do you want to go *tonight*?)
  B: Yes, I'd love to.
- ■ **I'd like** an orange, please.
  (= can I have an orange?)
- ■ What **would you like** to do next weekend?

Do you like . . . ? / I like . . .

Do you like coffee?

Yes, I do.

Would you like some now?

No, thank you. Not now.

Do you like coffee? = Do you think coffee is good?
- ■ *A:* **Do you like** to go to the movies?
  (in general)
  B: Yes, I go to the movies a lot.
- ■ **I like** oranges. *(in general)*
- ■ What **do you like** to do on weekends?

like to do and **like -ing** → Unit 53   **I would do** something **if . . .** → Unit 101

Exercises

35.1 What are the people in the pictures saying? Use *Would you like . . . ?*

1. Would you like a piece of candy?
2.
3.
4.
5.
6.

35.2 What do you ask Sue in these situations? Use *Would you like to . . . ?*

1. You want to go to the movies tonight. Perhaps Sue will go with you. (go)
   You ask: _Would you like to go to the movies tonight?_
2. You want to play tennis tomorrow. Perhaps Sue will play, too. (play)
   You ask: _____
3. You have an extra ticket for a concert next week. Perhaps Sue will come. (come)
   You ask: _____
4. It's raining and Sue is going out. She doesn't have an umbrella, but you have one. (borrow)
   You ask: _____

35.3 Which is right?

1. "~~Do you like~~ / Would you like a piece of candy?"   "Yes, thanks." (*Would you like* is right)
2. "Do you like / Would you like bananas?"   "Yes, I love them."
3. "Do you like / Would you like some ice cream?"   "No, thank you."
4. "What do you like / would you like to drink?"   "A glass of water, please."
5. "Do you like / Would you like to go out for a walk?"   "Not now. Maybe later."
6. I like / I'd like tomatoes, but I don't eat them very often.
7. What time do you like / would you like to have dinner tonight?
8. "Do you like / Would you like something to eat?"   "No, thanks. I'm not hungry."
9. "Do you like / Would you like your new job?"   "Yes, I'm enjoying it."
10. I'm tired. I like / I'd like to go to bed now.
11. "I like / I'd like a sandwich, please."   "Sure. What kind of sandwich?"
12. "What kind of music do you like / would you like?"   "All kinds."

I'd rather . . .

Would you like to sit here?

No, thanks. **I'd rather** sit on the floor.

Ann likes to sit on the floor. She doesn't want to sit on a chair. So she says:

I'd rather sit on the floor. (= I would prefer to sit on the floor.)

I'd rather . . . = I **would** rather . . .

I **would rather** do something = I would prefer to do something:

Positive	
I'd rather (I **would rather**)	do stay have be

Negative	
I'd rather not (I **would rather not**)	do stay have be

Question	
would you **rather**	do . . . ? stay . . . ? have . . . ? be . . . ?

- I don't really want to go out. **I'd rather stay** home. (= I'd prefer to stay home)
- "Should we go now?"   "No, not yet. **I'd rather wait** until later."
- I'd like to go now, but Tom **would rather wait** until later.
- I don't like to be late. **I'd rather be** early.

- I'm feeling tired. **I'd rather not go out** tonight. (= I'd prefer not to go out)
- Sue is feeling tired. She**'d rather not go out** tonight.
- We're not hungry. We**'d rather not eat** yet.
- "Would you like to go out tonight?"   "**I'd rather not**." (= I'd rather not go out)

- "**Would** you **rather have** milk or juice?"   "Juice, please."
- Which **would** you **rather do** – go to the movies or watch a DVD at home?

We say "**I'd rather do** something" (*not* to do something):
- **I'd rather sit** on the floor. (*not* I'd rather to sit)
- Sue **would rather** not **go** out. (*not* would rather not to go)

But we say "**I'd prefer to do** something":
- **I'd prefer to sit** on the floor.
- Sue **would prefer** not **to go** out.

You can say "**I'd rather** . . . **than** . . . ":
- **I'd rather** go out **than** stay home.
- **I'd rather** have a dog **than** a cat.
- We**'d rather** go to the movies **than** watch a DVD at home.
- **I'd rather** be at home right now **than** here.

Exercises

36.1 Look at the pictures and complete B's sentences. Use *I'd rather* . . . .

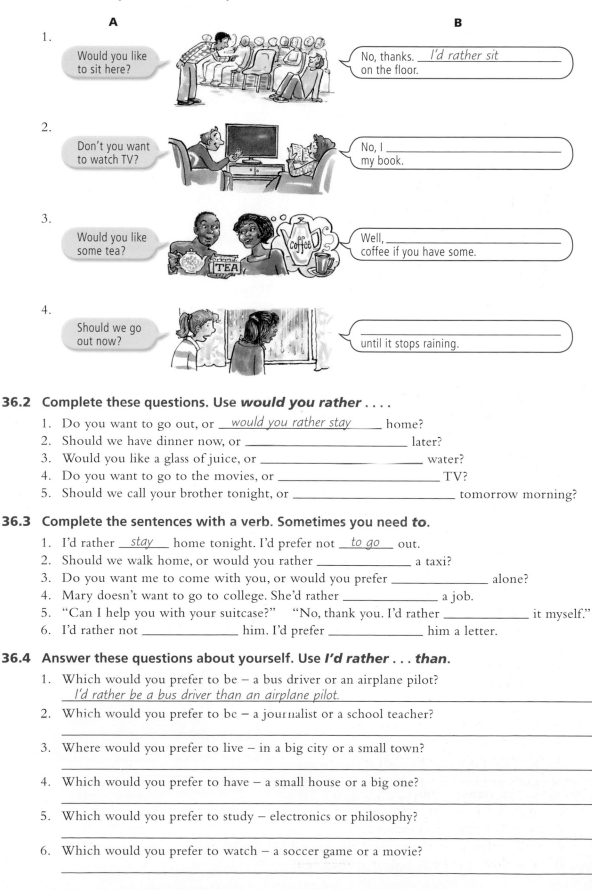

A

1. Would you like to sit here?

   B: No, thanks. *I'd rather sit* on the floor.

2. Don't you want to watch TV?

   B: No, I _____ my book.

3. Would you like some tea?

   B: Well, _____ coffee if you have some.

4. Should we go out now?

   B: _____ until it stops raining.

36.2 Complete these questions. Use *would you rather* . . . .

1. Do you want to go out, or __*would you rather stay*__ home?
2. Should we have dinner now, or _____ later?
3. Would you like a glass of juice, or _____ water?
4. Do you want to go to the movies, or _____ TV?
5. Should we call your brother tonight, or _____ tomorrow morning?

36.3 Complete the sentences with a verb. Sometimes you need *to*.

1. I'd rather __*stay*__ home tonight. I'd prefer not __*to go*__ out.
2. Should we walk home, or would you rather _____ a taxi?
3. Do you want me to come with you, or would you prefer _____ alone?
4. Mary doesn't want to go to college. She'd rather _____ a job.
5. "Can I help you with your suitcase?" "No, thank you. I'd rather _____ it myself."
6. I'd rather not _____ him. I'd prefer _____ him a letter.

36.4 Answer these questions about yourself. Use *I'd rather . . . than*.

1. Which would you prefer to be – a bus driver or an airplane pilot?
   I'd rather be a bus driver than an airplane pilot.

2. Which would you prefer to be – a journalist or a school teacher?
   _____

3. Where would you prefer to live – in a big city or a small town?
   _____

4. Which would you prefer to have – a small house or a big one?
   _____

5. Which would you prefer to study – electronics or philosophy?
   _____

6. Which would you prefer to watch – a soccer game or a movie?
   _____

Do this! Don't do that! Let's do this!

We use **come/look/go/wait/do/be**, etc., when we tell somebody to do something:

- "**Come** here and **look** at this." "What is it?"
- I don't want to talk to you. **Go** away!
- I'm not ready yet. Please **wait** for me.
- Please **be** quiet. I'm working.

also

- Bye! **Have** a good trip! / **Have** a nice time! / **Have** a good flight! / **Have** fun!
  (= I hope you have a good trip, etc.)
- "**Have** some candy." "Oh, thanks."
  (= would you like some candy?)

We use **don't** . . . when we tell somebody not to do something:

- Be careful! **Don't fall**.
- Please **don't go**. Stay here with me.
- Be here on time. **Don't be** late.

You can say **Let's** . . . when you want people to do things with you. (**let's** = let us)

- It's a nice day. **Let's go** out.
  (= you and I can go out)
- Come on! **Let's dance.**
  (= you and I can dance)
- Are you ready? **Let's go**.

- **Let's have** fish for dinner tonight.
- *A:* Should we go out tonight?
- *B:* No, I'm tired. **Let's stay** home.

The negative is **Let's not** . . . :

- It's cold. **Let's not** go out. Let's stay home.
- **Let's not** have fish for dinner tonight. Let's have chicken.
- I'm tired of arguing. **Let's not** do it anymore.

Exercises

37.1 Look at the pictures. What are the people saying? Some sentences are positive
(*buy*/*come*, etc.) and some are negative (*don't buy* / *don't come*, etc.). Use
these verbs:

be   buy   ~~come~~   ~~drink~~   drop   forget   have   sit   sleep   smile

1. _Come_ in!
2. _Don't drink_ the water.
3. It's too expensive. _____ it.   USED CAR $ 25,000
4. OK, are you ready? _____ !
5. _____ on the cat!
6. Bye! _____ a nice time.
7. _____ to call me.   Don't worry. I won't.
8. I'm going to bed now.   OK. _____ well.
9. _____ careful with that vase. _____ it!

37.2 Complete the sentences. Use *let's* with:

~~go for a swim~~   go to a restaurant   take the bus   wait a little   watch TV

1. Would you like to play tennis?   No, _let's go for a swim_ .
2. Do you want to walk home?   No, _____ .
3. Shall I put a CD on?   No, _____ .
4. Should we have dinner at home?   No, _____ .
5. Would you like to go now?   No, _____ .

37.3 Answer with *No, don't . . .* or *No, let's not . . . .*

1. Shall I wait for you?   _No, don't wait for me._
2. Should we go home now?   _No, let's not go home yet._
3. Shall we go out?   _____
4. Do you want me to close the window?   _____
5. Should I call you tonight?   _____
6. Do you think we should wait for Andy?   _____
7. Do you want me to turn on the light?   _____
8. Should we take a taxi?   _____

there is   there are

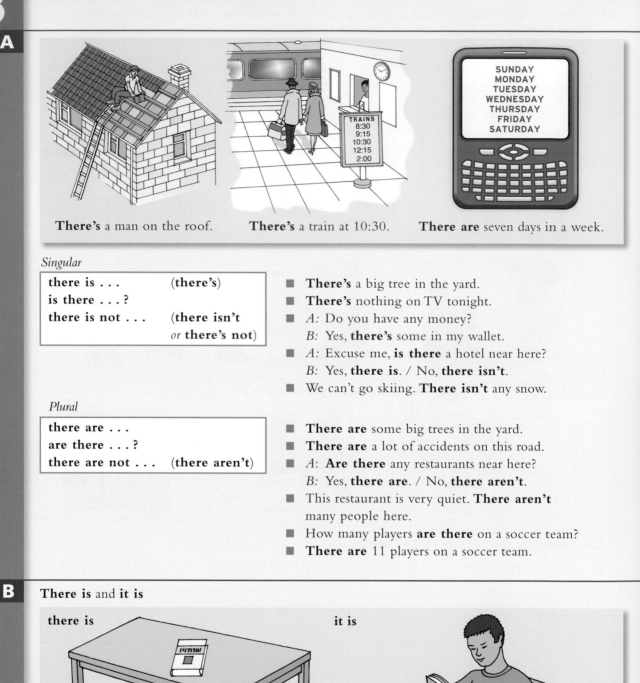

There's a man on the roof.   **There's** a train at 10:30.   **There are** seven days in a week.

Singular

there is . . .	(there's)
is there . . . ?	
there is not . . .	(there isn't
	or there's not)

- **There's** a big tree in the yard.
- **There's** nothing on TV tonight.
- *A:* Do you have any money?
  B: Yes, **there's** some in my wallet.
- *A:* Excuse me, **is there** a hotel near here?
  B: Yes, **there is**. / No, **there isn't**.
- We can't go skiing. **There isn't** any snow.

Plural

there are . . .	
are there . . . ?	
there are not . . .	(there aren't)

- **There are** some big trees in the yard.
- **There are** a lot of accidents on this road.
- *A:* **Are there** any restaurants near here?
  B: Yes, **there are**. / No, **there aren't**.
- This restaurant is very quiet. **There aren't** many people here.
- How many players **are there** on a soccer team?
- **There are** 11 players on a soccer team.

There is and **it is**

there is

There's a book on the table.
(*not* It's a book on the table.)

it is

I like this book . **It's** interesting.
(**it** = this book)

Compare:

- "What's **that noise**?"   "**It's** a train." (**It** = that noise)
  There's a train at 10:30. **It's** a fast train. (**It** = the 10:30 train)

- **There's** a lot of salt in this soup.
  I don't like **this soup**. **It's** too salty. (**It** = this soup)

there was / were / has been, etc. → Unit 39   **it and there** → Unit 40   **some and any** → Unit 77

Exercises

38.1 Springfield is a small town. Look at the information in the box and write sentences about Springfield with *There is/are* or *There isn't/aren't*.

1.	a golf course?	No
2.	any restaurants?	Yes (a lot)
3.	a hospital?	Yes
4.	a swimming pool?	No
5.	any movie theaters?	Yes (two)
6.	a university?	No
7.	any big hotels?	No

1. _There isn't a golf course._
2. _There are a lot of restaurants._
3. _____
4. _____
5. _____
6. _____
7. _____

38.2 Write sentences about your town (or a town that you know). Use *There is/are* or *There isn't/aren't*.

1. _There are a few restaurants._
2. _There's a big park._
3. _____
4. _____
5. _____
6. _____

38.3 Write *there is / there isn't / is there* or *there are / there aren't / are there*.

1. Springfield isn't an old town. _There aren't_ any old buildings.
2. Look! _____ a photograph of your brother in the newspaper!
3. "Excuse me, _____ a bank near here?"   "Yes, at the end of the block."
4. _____ five people in my family: my parents, my two sisters, and me.
5. "How many students _____ in the class?"   "Twenty."
6. The road is usually very quiet. _____ much traffic.
7. "_____ a bus from downtown to the airport?"   "Yes, every 20 minutes."
8. "_____ any problems?"   "No, everything is OK."
9. _____ nowhere to sit down. _____ any chairs.

38.4 Write sentences with *There are . . . .* Choose from the boxes.

five	twenty-six	letters	~~days~~	September	the solar system
~~seven~~	thirty	players	days	the United States	~~a week~~
eight	fifty	planets	states	a basketball team	the English alphabet

1. _There are seven days in a week._
2. _____
3. _____
4. _____
5. _____
6. _____

38.5 Write *there's / is there* or *it's / is it*.

1. "_There's_ a flight at 10:30."   "_Is it_ a nonstop flight?"
2. I'm not going to buy this shirt. _____ too expensive.
3. "What's wrong?"   "_____ something in my eye."
4. _____ a red car outside your house. _____ yours?
5. "_____ anything good on TV tonight?"   "Yes, _____ a movie at 8:00."
6. "What's that building?"   "_____ a school."
7. "_____ a restaurant in this hotel?"   "No, I'm afraid not."

there was/were   there has/have been
there will be

A   There was / there were (past)

There is a train every hour.

The time now is 11:15.
There was a train at 11:00.

Compare:

there is/are (present)	**there was/were** (past)
■ **There is** a good nature program on TV tonight.	■ **There was** a good nature program on TV last night.
■ We are staying at a very big hotel. **There are** 1,250 rooms.	■ We stayed at a very big hotel. **There were** 1,250 rooms.
■ **Are there** any phone messages for me this morning?	■ **Were there** any phone messages for me yesterday?
■ I'm hungry, but **there isn't** anything to eat.	■ I was hungry when I got home, but **there wasn't** anything to eat.

B   There has been / there have been (present perfect)

There's been
an accident.

■ Look! **There's been** an accident.
(**there's been** = there **has** been)
■ This road is very dangerous. **There have been** many accidents on it.

Compare **there was** (past):

■ **There was** an accident **last night**.
(*not* There has been an accident last night.)

For simple past and present perfect, see Units 19–21.

C   There will be

There will be rain
tomorrow afternoon.

■ Do you think **there will be** a lot of people at the party on Saturday?
■ The manager of the company is leaving, so **there will be** a new manager soon.
■ I'm going out of town tomorrow. I'm packing my things today because **there won't be** time tomorrow.
(**there won't be** = there **will not** be)

---

was/were → Unit 10   has/have been → Units 16–17   will → Unit 28   there is/are → Unit 38
there and it → Units 38, 40   some and any → Unit 77

Exercises

39.1 Look at the two pictures. Now the room is empty, but what was in the room last week? Choose from the box and write sentences with *There was . . .* or *There were . . . .*

an armchair	a carpet	some flowers	a sofa
some books	~~a clock~~	three pictures	a small table

last week　　　　　　　　　　　　　　　　*now*

1. ___There was a clock_____ on the wall near the window.
2. _____ on the floor.
3. _____ on the wall near the door.
4. _____ in the middle of the room.
5. _____ on the table.
6. _____ on the shelves.
7. _____ in the corner near the door.
8. _____ opposite the armchair.

39.2 Write *there was / there wasn't / was there* or *there were / there weren't / were there*.

1. I was hungry, but __there wasn't____ anything to eat.
2. __Were there____ any phone messages for me yesterday?
3. I opened the envelope, but it was empty. _____ nothing in it.
4. "We stayed at a very nice hotel." "Really? _____ a swimming pool?"
5. "Did you buy any cherries?" "No, _____ any at the store."
6. The wallet was empty. _____ any money in it.
7. "_____ many people at the meeting?" "No, very few."
8. We didn't visit the museum. _____ enough time.
9. I'm sorry I'm late. _____ a lot of traffic.
10. Twenty years ago _____ many tourists here. Now there are a lot.

39.3 Write *there + is / are / was / were / has been / have been / will be*.

1. __There was____ a good program on TV last night.
2. _____ 24 hours in a day.
3. _____ a party at work last Friday, but I didn't go.
4. "Where can I buy a newspaper?" "_____ a drugstore at the end of the block."
5. "Why are the police outside the bank?" "_____ a robbery."
6. When we got to the theater, _____ a long line outside.
7. When you arrive tomorrow, _____ somebody at the airport to meet you.
8. Ten years ago _____ 500 children in the school. Now _____ more than a thousand.
9. Last week I went back to the town where I was born. It's very different now. _____ a lot of changes.
10. I think everything will be OK. I don't think _____ any problems.

It . . .

A

We use **it** for time/day/distance/weather:

time

- What time is **it**?
- **It**'s half past 10.
- **It**'s late.
- **It**'s time to go home.

day

THURSDAY
MARCH
16th

- What day is **it**?
- **It**'s Thursday.
- **It**'s March 16th.
- **It** was my birthday yesterday.

distance

**2
miles**

- **It**'s two miles from our house to downtown.
- How far is **it** from New York to Los Angeles?
- **It**'s a long way from here to the airport.
- We can walk home. **It** isn't far.

We use **far** in questions (**is it far?**) and negatives (**it isn't far**).
In positive sentences, we use **a long way** (**it's a long way**).

weather

- **It**'s raining.   **It** isn't raining.   **Is** it snowing?
- **It** rains a lot here.   **It** didn't rain yesterday.
  Does **it** snow very often?
- **It**'s warm/hot/cold/nice/cloudy/windy/sunny/clear/dry/
  humid/foggy/dark, etc.
- **It**'s a nice day today.

Compare **it** and **there**:
- **It rains** a lot in the winter.
  It's very **rainy** in the winter.
  There is **a lot of rain** in the winter.
- **It** was very **windy** yesterday.
  There was **a strong wind** yesterday.

B

It's nice to . . . , etc.

It's	easy / difficult / impossible / dangerous / safe expensive / interesting / nice / wonderful / terrible, etc.	to . . .

- **It**'s nice **to see you again**.
- **It**'s impossible **to understand her**.
- **It** wasn't easy **to find your house**.

C

Don't forget **it**:
- **It**'s raining again. (*not* Is raining again)
- Is **it** true that you're moving to Dallas? (*not* Is true that . . .)

there is → Units 38–39

Exercises

40.1 Write about the weather in the pictures. Use *It's* . . . .

1. _It's raining._
2. _____
3. _____

4. _____
5. _____
6. _____

40.2 Write *it is* (*it's*) or *is it*.

1. What time _is it_ ?
2. We have to go now. _____ very late.
3. _____ true that Bill can fly a helicopter?
4. "What day _____ today? Tuesday?"   "No, _____ Wednesday."
5. _____ 10 kilometers from downtown to the airport.
6. _____ OK to call you at the office?
7. "Do you want to walk to the hotel?"   "I don't know. How far _____ ?"
8. _____ Lisa's birthday today. She's 27.
9. I don't believe it! _____ impossible.

40.3 Write questions with *How far* . . . ?

1. (here / the station)   _How far is it from here to the station?_
2. (the hotel / the beach)   _How_
3. (New York / Washington)   _____
4. (your house / the airport) _____

40.4 Write *it* or *there*.

1. The weather isn't so nice today. _It_ 's cloudy.
2. _There_ was a strong wind yesterday.
3. _____ 's hot in this room. Open a window.
4. _____ was a nice day yesterday. _____ was warm and sunny.
5. _____ was a storm last night. Did you hear it?
6. I was afraid because _____ was very dark.
7. _____ 's often cold here, but _____ isn't much rain.
8. _____ 's a long way from here to the nearest gas station.

40.5 Complete the sentences. Choose from the boxes.

it's	easy ~~difficult~~ impossible	dangerous nice interesting	to	work in this office visit different places see you again	~~get up early~~ go out alone make friends

1. If you go to bed late, _it's difficult to get up early_ in the morning.
2. Hello, Jane. _____ . How are you?
3. _____ . There is too much noise.
4. Everybody is very nice at work. _____ .
5. I like traveling. _____ .
6. Some cities are not safe. _____ at night.

I am, I don't, etc.

A

I'm not tired.

I am.

Do you like tea?

No, **I don't**.

Yes, I do.

She isn't tired, but **he is**.
(**he is** = he is tired)

He likes tea, but **she doesn't**.
(**she doesn't** = she doesn't like tea)

In these examples, it is not necessary to repeat some words ("he is *tired*," "she doesn't *like tea*").

You can use these verbs in the same way:

| am/is/are |
| was/were |
| have/has |
| do/does/did |
| can |
| will |
| might |
| should |

- ■ I haven't seen the movie, but my sister **has**. (= my sister has seen the movie)
- ■ *A:* Please help me.
  B: I'm sorry. I **can't**. (= I can't help you)
- ■ *A:* Are you tired?
  B: I **was**, but **I'm not** now. (= I was tired, but I'm not tired now)
- ■ *A:* Do you think Jane will call tonight?`
  B: She **might**. (= she might call)
- ■ *A:* Are you going to study tonight?
  B: I **should**, but I probably **won't**. (= I should study, but I probably won't study)

You *cannot* use **'m/'s/'ve**, etc. *(short forms)*, in this way. You must use **am/is/have**, etc.:

- ■ She isn't tired, but he **is**. (*not* . . . but he's)

But you *can* use **isn't / haven't / won't**, etc. *(negative short forms)*:

- ■ My sister has seen the movie, but I **haven't**.
- ■ "Are you and Jane working tomorrow?" "I am, but Jane **isn't**."

B

You can use **I am / I'm not**, etc., after **Yes** and **No**:

- ■ "Are you tired?" "Yes, I **am**. / No, **I'm not**."
- ■ "Will Bill be here tomorrow?" "Yes, he **will**. / No, he **won't**."
- ■ "Is there a bus to the airport?" "Yes, there **is**. / No, there **isn't**."

C

We use **do/does** for the *simple present* (see Units 6–7):

- ■ I don't like hot weather, but Sue **does**. (= Sue likes hot weather)
- ■ Sue works hard, but I **don't**. (= I don't work hard)
- ■ "Do you enjoy your work?" "Yes, I **do**."

We use **did** for the *simple past* (see Unit 12):

- ■ *A:* Did you and Chris like the movie?
- ■ *B:* I **did**, but Chris **didn't**. (= I liked it, but Chris didn't like it)
- ■ "I had a good time." "I **did**, too." (= I had a good time, too)
- ■ "Did it rain yesterday?" "No, it **didn't**."

You have? / Have you?, etc. → Unit 42   so am I / neither do I, etc. → Unit 43

Exercises

41.1 **Complete these sentences. Use only one verb (*is*/*have*/*can*, etc.) each time.**

1. Kate wasn't hungry, but we __were__ .
2. I'm not married, but my brother _____ .
3. Bill can't help you, but I _____ .
4. I haven't read the book, but Tom _____ .
5. Karen won't be here, but Chris _____ .
6. You weren't late, but I _____ .

41.2 **Complete these sentences with a negative verb (*isn't*/*haven't*/*can't*, etc.).**

1. My sister can play the piano, but I __can't__ .
2. Sam is working today, but I _____ .
3. I was working, but my friends _____ .
4. Mark has been to China, but I _____ .
5. I'm ready to go, but Tom _____ .
6. I've seen the movie, but Kim _____ .

41.3 **Complete these sentences with *do*/*does*/*did* or *don't*/*doesn't*/*didn't*.**

1. I don't like hot weather, but Sue __does__ .
2. Sue likes hot weather, but I __don't__ .
3. My mother wears glasses, but my father _____ .
4. You don't know Paul very well, but I _____ .
5. I didn't enjoy the party, but my friends _____ .
6. I don't watch TV much, but Peter _____ .
7. Kate lives in Canada, but her parents _____ .
8. You had breakfast this morning, but I _____ .

41.4 **Complete the sentences. Write about yourself and other people.**

1. I didn't __go out last night, but my friends did.__
2. I like _____ , but _____
3. I don't _____ , but _____
4. I'm _____
5. I haven't _____

41.5 **Put in a verb, positive or negative.**

1. "Are you tired?" "I __was__ earlier, but I'm not now."
2. Steve is happy today, but he _____ yesterday.
3. The stores aren't open yet, but the post office _____ .
4. I don't have a telescope, but I know somebody who _____ .
5. I would like to help you, but I'm sorry I _____ .
6. I don't usually drive to work, but I _____ yesterday.
7. *A:* Have you ever been to Costa Rica?
   B: No, but Sandra _____ . She went there on vacation last year.
8. "Do you and Luke watch TV a lot?" "I _____ , but Luke doesn't."
9. I've been invited to Sam's wedding, but Kate _____ .
10. "Do you think Sarah will pass her driving test?" "Yes, I'm sure she _____ ."
11. "Are you going out tonight?" "I _____ . I don't know for sure."

41.6 **Answer these questions about yourself. Use *Yes, I have.* / *No, I'm not.*, etc.**

1. Are you Brazilian?   __No, I'm not.__
2. Do you have a car?   _____
3. Do you feel OK?   _____
4. Is it snowing?   _____
5. Are you hungry?   _____
6. Do you like classical music?   _____
7. Will you be in Boston tomorrow?   _____
8. Have you ever broken your arm?   _____
9. Did you buy anything yesterday?   _____
10. Were you asleep at 3:00 a.m.?   _____

You have? Have you? You are? Are you?, etc.

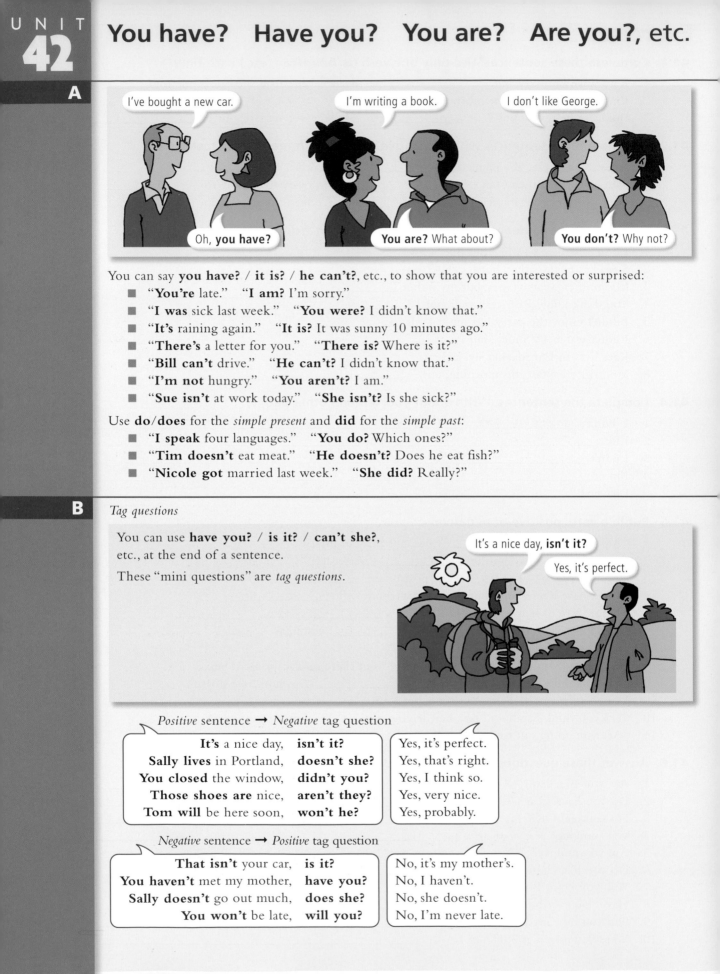

I've bought a new car.

Oh, **you have?**

I'm writing a book.

You are? What about?

I don't like George.

You don't? Why not?

You can say **you have? / it is? / he can't?**, etc., to show that you are interested or surprised:

■ "**You're** late." "**I am?** I'm sorry."
■ "**I was** sick last week." "**You were?** I didn't know that."
■ "**It's** raining again." "**It is?** It was sunny 10 minutes ago."
■ "**There's** a letter for you." "**There is?** Where is it?"
■ "**Bill can't** drive." "**He can't?** I didn't know that."
■ "**I'm not** hungry." "**You aren't?** I am."
■ "**Sue isn't** at work today." "**She isn't?** Is she sick?"

Use **do/does** for the *simple present* and **did** for the *simple past*:

■ "**I speak** four languages." "**You do?** Which ones?"
■ "**Tim doesn't** eat meat." "**He doesn't?** Does he eat fish?"
■ "**Nicole got** married last week." "**She did?** Really?"

Tag questions

You can use **have you? / is it? / can't she?**, etc., at the end of a sentence.

These "mini questions" are *tag questions*.

It's a nice day, **isn't it?**

Yes, it's perfect.

Positive sentence ➡ *Negative* tag question

It's a nice day,	**isn't it?**	Yes, it's perfect.
Sally lives in Portland,	**doesn't she?**	Yes, that's right.
You closed the window,	**didn't you?**	Yes, I think so.
Those shoes are nice,	**aren't they?**	Yes, very nice.
Tom will be here soon,	**won't he?**	Yes, probably.

Negative sentence ➡ *Positive* tag question

That isn't your car,	**is it?**	No, it's my mother's.
You haven't met my mother,	**have you?**	No, I haven't.
Sally doesn't go out much,	**does she?**	No, she doesn't.
You won't be late,	**will you?**	No, I'm never late.

I am, I don't, etc. → Unit 41

Exercises

42.1 Answer with *You do?* / *She doesn't?* / *They did?*, etc.

1. I speak four languages. _____You do_____ ? Which ones?
2. I work in a bank. _____ ? I work in a bank, too.
3. I didn't go to work yesterday. _____ ? Were you sick?
4. Jane doesn't like me. _____ ? Why not?
5. You look tired. _____ ? I feel fine.
6. Kate called me last night. _____ ? What did she say?

42.2 Answer with *You have?* / *You haven't?* / *She did?* / *She didn't?*, etc.

1. I've bought a new car. _____You have_____ ? What kind is it?
2. Tim doesn't eat meat. _____He doesn't_____ ? Does he eat fish?
3. I've lost my key. _____ ? When did you have it last?
4. Sue can't drive. _____ ? She should learn.
5. I was born in Italy. _____ ? I didn't know that.
6. I didn't sleep well last night. _____ ? Was the bed uncomfortable?
7. There's a football game on TV tonight. _____ ? Are you going to watch it?
8. I'm not happy. _____ ? Why not?
9. I saw Paula last week. _____ ? How is she?
10. Maria works in a factory. _____ ? What kind of factory?
11. I won't be here next week. _____ ? Where will you be?
12. The clock isn't working. _____ ? It was working yesterday.

42.3 Complete these sentences with a tag question (*isn't it?* / *haven't you?*, etc.).

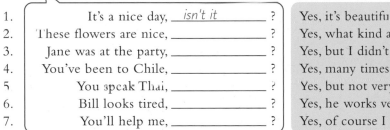

1. It's a nice day, _____isn't it_____ ? Yes, it's beautiful.
2. These flowers are nice, _____ ? Yes, what kind are they?
3. Jane was at the party, _____ ? Yes, but I didn't speak to her.
4. You've been to Chile, _____ ? Yes, many times.
5. You speak Thai, _____ ? Yes, but not very well.
6. Bill looks tired, _____ ? Yes, he works very hard.
7. You'll help me, _____ ? Yes, of course I will.

42.4 Complete these sentences with a tag question, positive (*is it?* / *do you?*, etc.) or negative (*isn't it?* / *don't you?*, etc.).

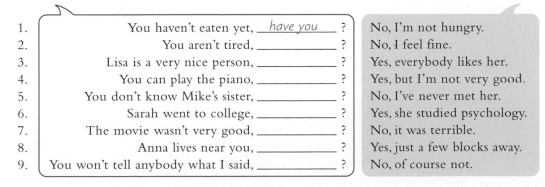

1. You haven't eaten yet, _____have you_____ ? No, I'm not hungry.
2. You aren't tired, _____ ? No, I feel fine.
3. Lisa is a very nice person, _____ ? Yes, everybody likes her.
4. You can play the piano, _____ ? Yes, but I'm not very good.
5. You don't know Mike's sister, _____ ? No, I've never met her.
6. Sarah went to college, _____ ? Yes, she studied psychology.
7. The movie wasn't very good, _____ ? No, it was terrible.
8. Anna lives near you, _____ ? Yes, just a few blocks away.
9. You won't tell anybody what I said, _____ ? No, of course not.

too/either so am I / neither do I, etc.

A

Too and either

We use **too** and **either** at the end of a sentence.

We use **too** after a *positive* verb:
- A: I'm happy.
  B: I'm happy, **too**.
- A: I liked the movie.
  B: I **liked** it, **too**.
- Jane is a doctor. Her husband **is** a doctor, **too**.

We use **either** after a *negative* verb:
- A: I'm not happy.
  B: I'm not happy, **either**.
  (*not* I'm not . . ., too.)
- A: I can't cook.
  B: I **can't**, **either**. (*not* I can't, too)
- Bill doesn't watch TV. He **doesn't** read newspapers, **either**.

B

so am I / neither do I, etc.

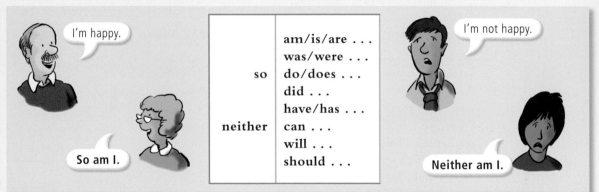

so	am/is/are . . . was/were . . . do/does . . . did . . . have/has . . .
neither	can . . . will . . . should . . .

so am I = I am, too
so have I = I have, too (etc.):
- A: **I'm** working.
  B: **So am I.** (= I'm working, too)
- A: **I was** late for work today.
  B: **So was Sam.** (= Sam was late, too)
- A: **I work** in a bank.
  B: **So do I.**
- A: **We went** to the movies last night.
  B: You did? **So did we.**
- A: **I'd** like to go to Australia.
  B: **So would I.**

neither am I = I'm not, either
neither can I = I can't, either (etc.):
- A: **I haven't** been to China.
  B: **Neither have I.** (= I haven't, either)
- A: **Kate can't** cook.
  B: **Neither can Tom.**
  (= Tom can't, either)
- A: **I won't** (= will not) be here tomorrow.
  B: **Neither will I.**
- A: **I never go** to the movies.
  B: **Neither do I.**

Remember: So **am** I (*not* So I am), Neither **have** I (*not* Neither I have).

I am, I don't, etc. → Unit 41

Exercises

43.1 Write *too* or *either*.

1. I'm happy.   I'm happy, __too__ .
2. I'm not hungry.   I'm not hungry, _____ .
3. I'm going out.   I'm going out, _____ .
4. It rained on Saturday.   It rained on Sunday, _____ .
5. Jenny can't drive a car.   She can't ride a bicycle, _____ .
6. I don't like to go shopping.   I don't like to go shopping, _____ .
7. Linda's mother is a teacher.   Her father is a teacher, _____ .

43.2 Answer with *So . . . I* (*So am I* / *So do I* / *So can I*, etc.).

1. I went to bed late last night.   __So did I.__
2. I'm thirsty.   _____
3. I've already read this book.   _____
4. I need a vacation.   _____
5. I'll be late tomorrow.   _____
6. I was very tired this morning.   _____

Answer with *Neither . . . I.*

7. I can't go to the party.   _____
8. I didn't call Alex last night.   _____
9. I haven't eaten lunch yet.   _____
10. I'm not going out tonight.   _____
11. I don't know what to do.   _____

43.3 You are talking to Maria. Write sentences about yourself. Where possible, use *So . . . I* or *Neither . . . I*. Look at these examples carefully:

I'm tired today.   You can answer: __So am I.__ OR __I'm not.__

I don't work hard.   You can answer: __Neither do I.__ OR __I do.__

Maria   You

1. I'm studying English.   _____
2. I can ride a bicycle.   _____
3. I'm not American.   _____
4. I like to cook.   _____
5. I don't like cold weather.   _____
6. I slept well last night.   _____
7. I've never been to India.   _____
8. I don't use my phone much.   _____
9. I'm going out tomorrow night.   _____
10. I wasn't sick last week.   _____
11. I didn't watch TV last night.   _____
12. I go to the movies a lot.   _____

isn't, haven't, don't, etc. (negatives)

We use **not** (**n't**) in negative sentences:

Positive → *Negative*

am	**am not** ('m not)
is	**is not** (isn't *or* 's not)
are	**are not** (aren't *or* 're not)
was	**was not** (wasn't)
were	**were not** (weren't)
have	**have not** (haven't)
has	**has not** (hasn't)
will	**will not** (won't)
can	**cannot** (can't)
could	**could not** (couldn't)
should	**should not** (shouldn't)
would	**would not** (wouldn't)
must	**must not**

- I**'m not** tired.
- It **isn't** (*or* It**'s not**) raining.
- They **aren't** (*or* They**'re not**) here.
- Brian **wasn't** hungry.
- The stores **weren't** open.
- I **haven't** finished my work.
- Sue **hasn't** been to Mexico.
- We **won't** be here tomorrow.
- George **can't** drive.
- I **couldn't** sleep last night.
- You **shouldn't** work so hard.
- I **wouldn't** like to be an actor.
- They **must not** have a car.

don't / doesn't / didn't

Simple present negative	I/we/you/they	**do not** (**don't**)	**work/live/go**, etc.
	he/she/it	**does not** (**doesn't**)	
Simple past negative	I/they/he/she, etc.	**did not** (**didn't**)	

Positive → *Negative*

I **want** to go out.	→	I **don't want** to go out.
They **work** hard.	→	They **don't work** hard.
Liz **plays** the guitar.	→	Liz **doesn't play** the guitar.
My father **likes** his job.	→	My father **doesn't like** his job.
I **got** up early this morning.	→	I **didn't get** up early this morning.
They **worked** hard yesterday.	→	They **didn't work** hard yesterday.
We **played** tennis.	→	We **didn't play** tennis.
Diane **had** dinner with us.	→	Diane **didn't have** dinner with us.

Don't . . .

Look!	→	**Don't look!**
Wait for me.	→	**Don't wait** for me.

Sometimes **do** is the main verb (**don't do / doesn't do / didn't do**):

Do something!	→	**Don't do** anything!
Sue **does** a lot on weekends.	→	Sue **doesn't do** much on weekends.
I **did** what you said.	→	I **didn't do** what you said.

simple present negative → **Unit 6**   simple past negative → **Unit 12**   **don't look / don't wait**, etc. → **Unit 37**
Why isn't/don't . . . ? → **Unit 45**

Exercises

44.1 Make these sentences negative.

1. He's gone out. _He hasn't gone out._
2. They're married. _____
3. I've had dinner. _____
4. It's cold today. _____
5. We'll be late. _____
6. You should go. _____

44.2 Make these sentences negative. Use *don't/doesn't/didn't*.

1. She saw me. _She didn't see me._
2. I like cheese. _____
3. They understood. _____
4. He lives here. _____
5. Go away! _____
6. I did the dishes. _____

44.3 Make these sentences negative.

1. She can swim. _She can't swim._
2. They've arrived. _____
3. I went to the bank. _____
4. He speaks Japanese. _____
5. We were angry. _____
6. He'll be happy. _____
7. Call me tonight. _____
8. It rained yesterday. _____
9. I could hear them. _____
10. I believe you. _____

44.4 Complete these sentences with a negative verb (*isn't/haven't/don't*, etc.).

1. They aren't rich. They _don't_ have much money.
2. "Would you like something to eat?" "No, thank you. I _____ hungry."
3. I _____ find my glasses. Have you seen them?
4. Steve _____ use e-mail much. He'd rather talk on the phone.
5. We can walk to the station from here. It _____ very far.
6. "Where's Jane?" "I _____ know. I _____ seen her today."
7. Be careful! _____ fall!
8. We went to the movies last night. I _____ like the movie very much.
9. I've been to Japan many times, but I _____ been to South Korea.
10. Julia _____ be here tomorrow. She'll be out of town.
11. "Who broke that window?" "Not me. I _____ do it."
12. We didn't see what happened. We _____ looking at the time.
13. Lisa bought a new coat a few days ago, but she _____ worn it yet.
14. You _____ drive so fast. It's dangerous.

44.5 You ask Gary some questions. He answers "Yes" or "No." Write sentences about Gary, positive or negative.

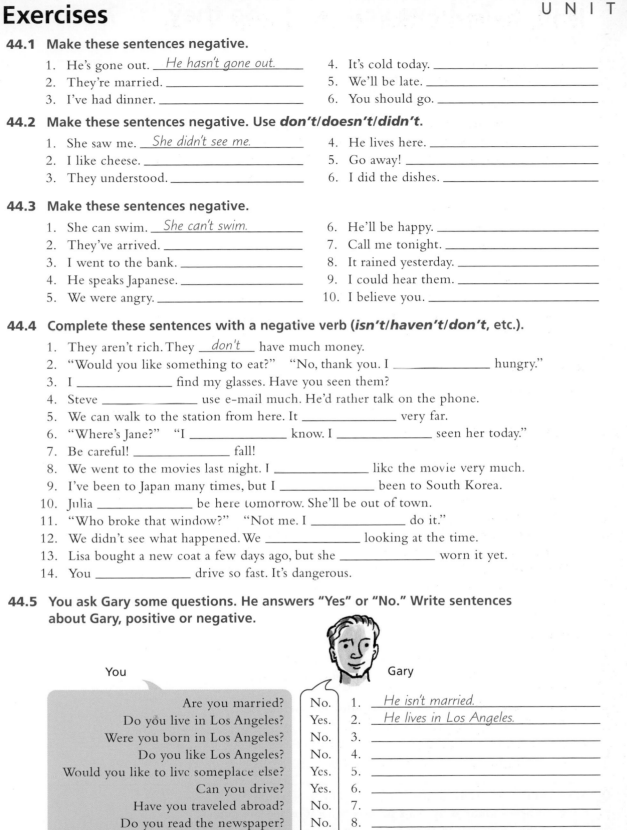

You	Gary	
Are you married?	No.	1. _He isn't married._
Do you live in Los Angeles?	Yes.	2. _He lives in Los Angeles._
Were you born in Los Angeles?	No.	3. _____
Do you like Los Angeles?	No.	4. _____
Would you like to live someplace else?	Yes.	5. _____
Can you drive?	Yes.	6. _____
Have you traveled abroad?	No.	7. _____
Do you read the newspaper?	No.	8. _____
Are you interested in politics?	No.	9. _____
Do you usually watch TV at night?	Yes.	10. _____
Did you watch TV last night?	No.	11. _____
Did you go out last night?	Yes.	12. _____

is it . . . ? have you . . . ? do they . . . ?, etc. (questions 1)

A

Positive	you	are		**You are** eating.	
Question	are	you		**Are you** eating?	What **are you** eating?

In questions, the first verb (**is/are/have**, etc.) is before the subject:

Positive			Question	
subject + verb			verb + subject	
I	**am** late.	→	**Am**	**I** late?
That seat	**is** free.	→	**Is**	**that seat** free?
She	**was** angry.	→	Why **was**	**she** angry?
David	**has** gone.	→	Where **has**	**David** gone?
You	**have** been to Japan.	→	**Have**	**you** been to Japan?
They	**will** be here soon.	→	When **will**	**they** be here?
Paula	**can** swim.	→	**Can**	**Paula** swim?

Remember: the subject is after the first verb.

■ Where **has David** gone? (*not* Where has gone David?)
■ **Are those people** waiting for something? (*not* Are waiting . . . ?)
■ When **was the telephone** invented? (*not* When was invented . . . ?)

B

do . . . ? / does . . . ? / did . . . ?

Simple present questions	**do** **does**	I/we/you/they he/she/it	**work/live/go**, etc. . . . ?
Simple past questions	**did**	I/they/he/she, etc.	

Positive		Question
They **work** hard.	→	**Do** they **work** hard?
You **watch** television.	→	How often **do** you **watch** television?
Chris **has** a car.	→	**Does** Chris **have** a car?
She **gets up** early.	→	What time **does** she **get** up?
They **worked** hard.	→	**Did** they **work** hard?
You **had** dinner.	→	What **did** you **have** for dinner?
She **got** up early.	→	What time **did** she **get** up?

Sometimes **do** is the main verb (do you **do** / did he **do**, etc.):

■ What **do** you usually **do** on weekends?
■ "What **does** your brother **do**?" "He works in a bank."
■ "I broke my finger last week." "How **did** you **do** that?" (*not* How did you that?)

C

Why isn't . . . ? / Why don't . . . ?, etc. (**Why** + *negative*):

■ Where's John? **Why isn't he** here? (*not* Why he isn't here?)
■ **Why can't Paula** come to the meeting tomorrow? (*not* Why Paula can't . . . ?)
■ **Why didn't you** call me last night?

simple present questions → Unit 7   simple past questions → Unit 12   questions 2–3 → Units 46–47
what/which/how → Units 48–49

Exercises

45.1 Write questions.

1.	I can swim.	(and you?)	_Can you swim?_
2.	I work hard.	(and Jack?)	_Does Jack work hard?_
3.	I was late this morning.	(and you?)	_____
4.	I've seen that movie.	(and Kate?)	_____
5.	I'll be here tomorrow.	(and you?)	_____
6.	I'm going out tonight.	(and Paul?)	_____
7.	I like my job.	(and you?)	_____
8.	I live near here.	(and Nicole?)	_____
9.	I enjoyed the movie.	(and you?)	_____
10.	I had a good vacation.	(and you?)	_____

45.2 You are talking to a friend about driving. Write the full questions.

You

1.	(have / a car?) _Do you have a car?_____	Yes, I do.
2.	(use / a lot?) _____ it _____	Yes, almost every day.
3.	(use / yesterday?) _____	Yes, to go to work.
4.	(enjoy driving?) _____	Not very much.
5.	(a good driver?) _____	I think I am.
6.	(ever / have / an accident?) _____	No, never.

45.3 Make questions with these words. Put the words in the right order.

1. (has / gone / where / David?) _Where has David gone?_____
2. (working / Rachel / is / today?) _Is Rachel working today?_____
3. (the children / what / are / doing?) What _____
4. (made / is / how / cheese?) _____
5. (to the party / coming / is / your sister?) _____
6. (you / the truth / tell / don't / why?) _____
7. (your guests / have / yet / arrived?) _____
8. (leave / what time / your plane / does?) _____
9. (to work / Jenny / why / go / didn't?) _____
10. (your car / in the accident / was / damaged?) _____

45.4 Complete the questions.

1.	I want to go out.	Where _do you want to go?_
2.	Kate and Paul aren't going to the party.	Why _aren't they going?_
3.	I'm reading.	What _____
4.	Sue went to bed early.	What time _____
5.	My parents are going on vacation.	When _____
6.	I saw Tom a few days ago.	Where _____
7.	I can't come to the party.	Why _____
8.	Tina has moved.	Where _____
9.	I need some money.	How much _____
10.	Angela doesn't like me.	Why _____
11.	It rains sometimes.	How often _____
12.	I did the shopping.	When _____

Who saw you?   Who did you see?
(questions 2)

A

Sylvia

Paul

Sylvia saw Paul.

Who **saw** Paul?
    Sylvia. (Sylvia saw him.)

Who **did** Sylvia **see**?
    Paul. (She saw Paul.)

Sylvia saw Paul

Subject   *Object*

Somebody saw Paul.   Sylvia saw somebody .

Who saw Paul?   Who did Sylvia see?

Sylvia. (Sylvia saw him.)   Paul. (She saw Paul.)

who is the *subject*   **who** is the *object*
Paul is the *object*   **Sylvia** is the *subject*

B

In these questions, **who**/**what** is the *subject*:
- **Who lives** in this house? (= somebody lives in it – who?)
  (*not* Who does live?)
- **What happened**? (= something happened – what?)
  (*not* What did happen?)
- **What's happening**? (What's = What **is**)
- **Who's got** my keys? (Who's = Who **has**)

In these questions, **who**/**what** is the *object*:
- Who did **you** meet yesterday? (= **you** met somebody – who?)
- What did **Paul** say? (= **Paul** said something – what?)
- Who are **you** calling?
- What was **Sylvia** wearing?

Compare:
- George likes oranges.   → **Who likes** oranges? – George.
                              What does George like? – Oranges.
- Jane won a new car.   → **Who won** a new car? – Jane.
                              What did Jane win? – A new car.

C

Use **who** for people (somebody). Use **what** for things, ideas, etc. (something):
- **Who** is your favorite **singer**?
- **What** is your favorite **song**?

questions → Units 45, 47   what/which/how → Unit 48

Exercises

46.1 Make questions with *who* or *what*. In these questions, *who*/*what* is the subject.

1. Somebody broke the window.
2. Something fell off the shelf.
3. Somebody wants to see you.
4. Somebody took my umbrella.
5. Something made me sick.
6. Somebody is coming.

Who broke the window?
What _____
_____ me?
_____
_____
_____

46.2 Make questions with *who* or *what* (subject or object).

1. I bought something.
2. Somebody lives in this house.
3. I called somebody.
4. Something happened last night.
5. Somebody knows the answer.
6. Somebody did the dishes.
7. Jane did something.
8. Something woke me up.
9. Somebody saw the accident.
10. I saw somebody.
11. Somebody has my pen.
12. This word means something.

What did you buy?
Who lives in this house?
_____
_____
_____
_____
_____
_____
_____
_____
_____
_____

46.3 You want the missing information (XXXXX). Write questions with *who* or *what*.

1. I lost **XXXXX** yesterday, but fortunately **XXXXX** found it and gave it back to me.

2. **XXXXX** called me last night. She wanted **XXXXX**.

3. I needed some advice, so I asked **XXXXX**. He said **XXXXX**.

4. I hear that **XXXXX** got married last week. **XXXXX** told me.

5. I met **XXXXX** on my way home tonight. She told me **XXXXX**.

6. Steve and I played tennis yesterday. **XXXXX** won. After the game, we **XXXXX**.

7. It was my birthday last week, and I got some presents. **XXXXX** gave me a book, and Catherine gave me **XXXXX**.

What did you lose?
Who found it?
Who _____
What _____
_____
_____
_____
_____
_____
_____
_____
_____
_____
_____
_____

Who is she talking to?   What is it like?
(questions 3)

Julia

Julia is talking to somebody.

Who is she talking to?

In questions beginning **Who** . . . ? / **What** . . . ? / **Where** . . . ? / **Which** . . . ?, prepositions
(**to**/**from**/**with**, etc.) usually go at the end:

- "**Where** are you **from**?"   "I'm from Thailand."
- "Jack was afraid."   "**What** was he afraid **of**?"
- "**Who** do these books belong **to**?"   "They're mine."
- "Tom's father is in the hospital."   "**Which hospital** is he **in**?"
- "Kate is going on vacation."   "**Who with**?" / "**Who** is she going **with**?"
- "Can we talk?"   "Sure. **What** do you want to talk **about**?"

What's it like? / **What are they like?**, etc.

What's your new
house like?

It's very big.

What**'s** it like? = What **is** it like?

What's it like? = tell me
something about it – is it good or bad,
big or small, old or new, etc.?

When we say "**What is it like?**," **like** is a *preposition*. It is not the verb **like** (**Do** you **like**
your new house?).

- *A:* There's a new restaurant near my house.
  B: **What's** it **like**? Is it good?
  A: I don't know. I haven't eaten there yet.

- *A:* **What's** your new teacher **like**?
  B: She's very good. We learn a lot.

- *A:* I met Nicole's parents yesterday.
  B: You did? **What** are they **like**?
  A: They're very nice.

- *A:* Did you have a good vacation? **What** was the weather **like**?
  B: It was great. It was sunny every day.

questions → Units 45–46   what/which/how → Unit 48   prepositions → Units 104–114

Exercises

47.1 You want the missing information (XXXXX). Write questions with *who* or *what*.

1. The letter is from **XXXXX**.
2. I'm looking for a **XXXXX**.
3. I went to the movies with **XXXXX**.
4. The movie was about **XXXXX**.
5. I gave the money to **XXXXX**.
6. The book was written by **XXXXX**.

Who is the letter from? _____
What _____ you _____
_____
_____
_____
_____

47.2 Write questions about the people in the pictures. Use these verbs + a preposition:

go   listen   look   ~~talk~~   talk   wait

1. _Who is she talking to?_ _____
2. What _____
3. Which restaurant _____
4. What _____
5. What _____
6. Which bus _____

47.3 Write questions with *Which . . . ?*

1. Tom's father is in the hospital.
2. We stayed at a hotel.
3. Jack plays for a football team.
4. I went to school in this town.

Which hospital is he in? _____
_____ you _____
_____
_____

47.4 You want some information about another country. You ask somebody who has been there. Ask questions with *What is/are . . . like?*

1. (the roads) _What are the roads like?_ _____
2. (the food) _____
3. (the people) _____
4. (the weather) _____

47.5 Ask questions with *What was/were . . . like?*

1. Your friend has just come back from a trip. Ask about the weather.
   What was the weather like? _____
2. Your friend has just come back from the movies. Ask about the movie.
   _____
3. Your friend has just finished a computer course. Ask about the classes.
   _____
4. Your friend has just come back from a business trip. Ask about the hotel.
   _____

What . . . ? Which . . . ? How . . . ?
(questions 4)

A

What + *noun* (**What color** . . . ? / **What kind** . . . ?, etc.)

- ■ **What color** is your car?   ■ **What color** are your eyes?
- ■ **What size** is this shirt?   ■ **What nationality** is she?
- ■ **What time** is it?   ■ **What day** is it today?
- ■ **What kind** of job do you want? (*or* **What type** of job . . . ? / **What sort** of job . . . ?)

What without a noun:

- ■ **What's** your favorite color?
- ■ **What** do you want to do tonight?

B

Which + *noun* (things or people):

- ■ **Which train** did you catch – the 9:50 or the 10:30?
- ■ **Which doctor** did you see – Doctor Lopez, Doctor Gray, or Doctor Hill?

We use **which** without a noun for things, not people:

- ■ **Which** is bigger – Canada or Australia?

We use **who** for people (without a noun):

- ■ **Who** is taller – Joe or Gary? (*not* Which is taller?)

C

What or **which**?

We use **which** when we are thinking about a small number of possibilities (perhaps 2, 3, or 4):

- ■ We can go this way or that way.
  Which way should we go?
- ■ There are four umbrellas here.
  Which is yours?

? or ? or ? or ?

WHICH?

What is more general:

- ■ **What's** the capital of Argentina? (of all the cities in Argentina)
- ■ **What kind** of music do you like? (of all kinds of music)

Compare:

- ■ **What color** are his eyes? (*not* Which color?)
  Which color do you prefer, **pink or yellow**?
- ■ **What** is the longest river in the world?
  Which is the longest river – **the Mississippi, the Amazon, or the Nile**?

D

How . . . ?

- ■ "**How** was the party last night?" "It was great."
- ■ "**How** do you get to work?" "By bus."

You can use **how** + *adjective/adverb* (**how tall** / **how old** / **how often**, etc.):

	tall are you?" "I'm five feet 10." (5 feet 10 inches *or* 1.78 meters)	
	big is the house?" "Not very big."	
	old is your mother?" "She's 45."	
"**How**	**far** is it from here to the airport?" "Ten miles." (about 16 kilometers)	
	often do you use your car?" "Every day."	
	long have they been married?" "Ten years."	
	much was the taxi?" "Ten dollars."	

questions → Units 45–47   How long does it take . . . ? → Unit 49   which one(s) → Unit 76

Exercises

48.1 Write questions with *What . . . ?*

1.	This shirt is nice.	(size?)	_What size is it?_
2.	I want a job.	(kind?)	_What kind of job do you want?_
3.	I have a new sweater.	(color?)	What _____
4.	I got up early this morning.	(time?)	_____ get up?
5.	I like music.	(type?)	_____
6.	I want to buy a car.	(kind?)	_____

48.2 Complete the questions. Use *Which . . . ?*

1. _Which way_ should we go? — Kendall Sq. Cambridge Storrow Dr.
3. _____ do you want to see? — THEATER 1 / THEATER 2
2. _____ is yours?
4. _____ goes downtown? — 10 25 32

48.3 Write *What/Which/Who*.

1. ___What___ is that man's name?
2. ___Which___ way should we go? Left or right?
3. You can have tea or coffee. _____ do you prefer?
4. "_____ day is it today?" "Friday."
5. _____ is your favorite sport?
6. This is a nice office. _____ desk is yours?
7. _____ is more expensive, meat or fish?
8. _____ is older, Liz or Steve?
9. _____ kind of camera do you have?
10. *A:* I've got three cameras.
    B: _____ camera do you use most?

48.4 Complete the questions with *How* + adjective or adverb (*high/long*, etc.).

1.	_How high_ is Mount Everest?	Over 29,000 feet.
2.	_____ is it to the station?	Almost two miles.
3.	_____ is Helen?	She's 26.
4.	_____ do the buses run?	Every 10 minutes.
5.	_____ is the water in the pool?	Seven feet.
6.	_____ have you lived here?	Almost three years.

48.5 Write questions with *How . . . ?*

1. Are you five feet nine? Five feet 10? Five feet 11? _How tall are you?_
2. Is this box one kilogram? Two? Three? _____
3. Are you 20 years old? 22? 25? _____
4. Did you spend $20? $30? $50? _____
5. Do you watch TV every day? Once a week? Never?

   _____
6. Is it 2,000 miles from New York to Los Angeles? 2,500? 3,000?

   _____

How long does it take . . . ?

A

How long **does it take to get** from . . . to . . . ?

New York

1 hour

Washington, D.C.

How long **does it take to get** from New York to Washington, D.C., by plane?

It takes an hour.

- How long **does it take to get from** Los Angeles to New York by train?
- **It takes** several days **to get from** Los Angeles to New York by train.
- How long **does it take to get from** your house to the airport by car?
- **It takes** ten minutes **to get from** my house to the airport by car.

B

How long does it take to do something?

How long	does did will	it take to . . . ?

It	takes took will take	a week a long time three hours	to . . .
	doesn't didn't won't	take	long	

- How long **does it take to cross** the Atlantic by ship?
- "I came by train."   "You did? How long **did it take** (**to get** here)?"
- How long **will it take to get** from here to the hotel?

- **It takes** a long time **to learn** a language.
- **It doesn't take** long **to make** an omelet.
- **It won't take** long **to fix** the computer.

C

How long does it take you to do something?

Day 1   *Day 2*   *Day 3*

How long	does did will	it take	you Tom them	to . . . ?

It	takes took will take	me Tom them	a week a long time three hours	to . . .

I started reading the book on Monday.
I finished it on Wednesday evening.

It **took me** three days **to read** it.

- How long **will it take me to learn** to drive?
- **It takes Tom** 20 minutes **to get** to work in the morning.
- **It took us** an hour **to do** the shopping.
- **Did it take you** a long time **to find** a job?
- **It will take me** an hour **to cook** dinner.

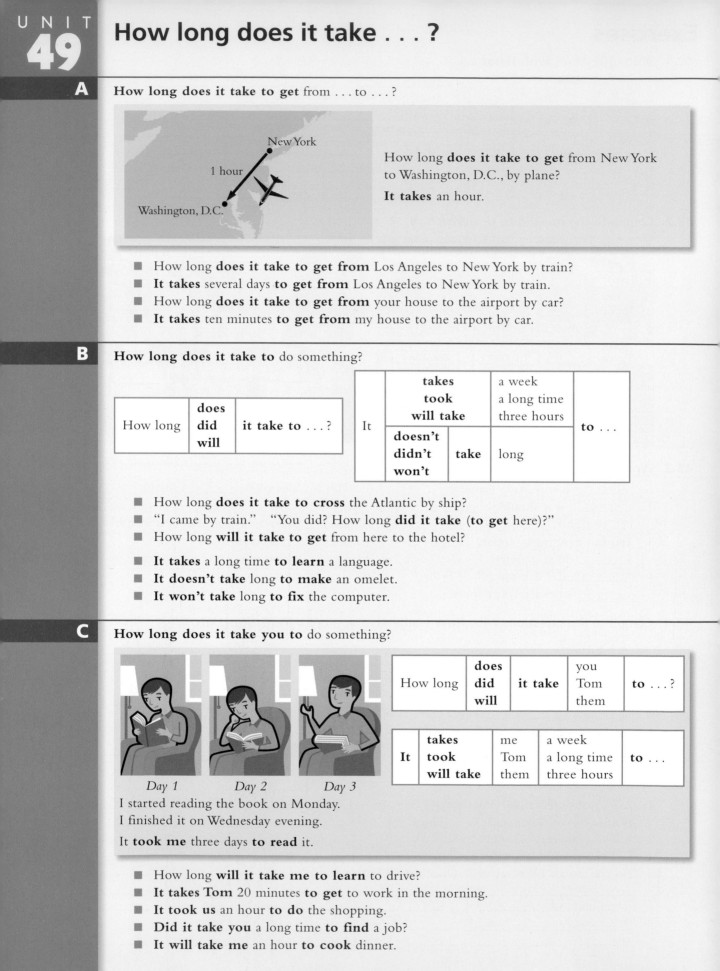

Exercises

49.1 Look at the pictures and write questions with **How long . . . ?**

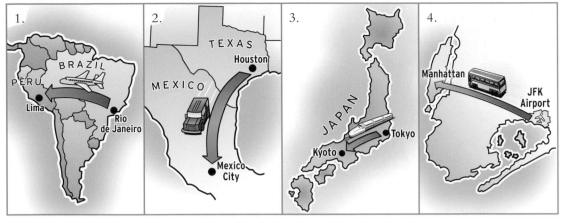

1. _____How long does it take to get from Rio de Janeiro to Lima by plane?_____
2. _____
3. _____
4. _____

49.2 How long does it take to do these things? Write full sentences.

1. fly from your city/country to Los Angeles
   _____It takes about 11 hours to fly from Seoul to Los Angeles._____

2. fly from your city/country to Australia

   _____

3. become a doctor in your country

   _____

4. walk from your home to the nearest supermarket

   _____

5. get from your house to the nearest airport

   _____

49.3 Write questions with **How long did it take . . . ?**

1. (Jane found a job.)   _____How long did it take her to find a job?_____
2. (I walked to the station.)   _____ you _____
3. (Tom painted the bathroom.) _____
4. (I learned to ski.)   _____
5. (They repaired the computer.) _____

49.4 Read the situations and write sentences with **It took . . . .**

1. I read a book last week. I started reading it on Monday. I finished it three days later.
   _____It took me three days to read the book._____

2. We walked home last night. We left at 10:00, and we got home at 10:20.

   _____

3. I learned to drive last year. I had my first driving lesson in January. I passed my driving test
   six months later.

   _____

4. Mark drove to Houston yesterday. He left home at 7:00 and got to Houston at 10:00.

   _____

5. Lisa began looking for a job a long time ago. She got a job last week.

   _____

6. *Write a sentence about yourself.*

   _____

Do you know where . . . ?
I don't know what . . . , etc.

A

Do you know where Paula **is**?

We say: Where **is Paula**?

but   **Do you know** where **Paula is** ?
(*not* Do you know where is Paula?)

In the same way we say:

I know
I don't know } where **Paula is**.

Can you tell me where **Paula is**?

Compare:

Who **are those people**?	*but*	**Do you know** / **Can you tell me**	who **those people are** / how old **Nicole is** / what time **it is** / where **I can** go	?

Who **are those people**?
How old **is Nicole**?
What time **is it**?
Where **can I** go?

How much **is this camera**?
When **are you** leaving town?
Where **have they** gone?
What **was Jenny** wearing?

but

Do you know **Can you tell me**	who **those people are** how old **Nicole is** what time **it is** where **I can** go	?
I know **I don't know** **I don't remember**	how much **this camera is** when **you're** leaving town where **they have** gone what **Jenny was** wearing	.

B

Questions with **do/does/did** (*simple present and simple past*)

Where **does he live** ?

but   **Do you know** where **he lives** ? (*not* Do you know where does he live?)

Compare:

How **do airplanes** fly?
What **does Jane** want?
Why **did she** go home?
Where **did I** put the key?

but

Do you know **I don't know** **I don't remember** **I know**	how **airplanes fly** what **Jane wants** why **she went** home where **I put** the key	? .

C

Questions beginning **Is . . . ?** / **Do . . . ?** / **Can . . . ?**, etc. (yes/no questions)

Compare:

Is Jack at home?
Have they got a car?
Can Brian swim?
Do they live near here?
Did anybody see you?

but

Do you know **I don't know**	**if** *or* **whether**	**Jack is** at home **they've got** a car **Brian can** swim **they live** near here **anybody saw** you	? .

You can use **if** *or* **whether** in these sentences:

- Do you know **if** they've got a car?   *or*   Do you know **whether** they've got a car?
- I don't know **if** anybody saw me.   *or*   I don't know **whether** anybody saw me.

Exercises

50.1 Answer these questions with *I don't know where/when/why . . .* , etc.

1.	Have your friends gone home?	(where) _I don't know where they've gone._
2.	Is Sue in her office?	(where) I don't know _____
3.	Is the building very old?	(how old) _____
4.	Will Paul be here soon?	(when) _____
5.	Was he angry because I was late?	(why) _____
6.	Has Donna lived here a long time?	(how long) _____

50.2 Complete the sentences.

1. (How do airplanes fly?) Do you know _how airplanes fly_____ ?
2. (Where does Susan work?) I don't know _____ .
3. (What did Peter say?) Do you remember _____ ?
4. (Why did he go home early?) I don't know _____ .
5. (What time does the meeting begin?) Do you know _____ ?
6. (How did the accident happen?) I don't remember _____ .

50.3 Which is right?

1. Do you know what time ~~is it~~ / it is? (*it is* is right)
2. Why are you / you are leaving?
3. I don't know where are they / they are going.
4. Can you tell me where is the museum / the museum is?
5. Where do you want / you want to go for vacation?
6. Do you know what do elephants eat / elephants eat?
7. I don't know how far is it / it is from the hotel to the station.

50.4 Write questions with *Do you know if/whether . . . ?*

1. (Do they have a car?) _Do you know if/whether they have a car?_
2. (Are they married?) Do you know _____
3. (Does Sue know Bill?) _____
4. (Will Gary be here tomorrow?) _____
5. (Did he pass his exam?) _____

50.5 Write questions beginning *Do you know . . . ?*

1. (What does Laura want?) _Do you know what Laura wants?_
2. (Where is Paula?) Do _____
3. (Is she working today?) _____
4. (What time does she start work?) _____
5. (Are the banks open tomorrow?) _____
6. (Where do Sarah and Tim live?) _____
7. (Did they go to Jane's party?) _____

50.6 Use your own ideas to complete these sentences.

1. Do you know why _the bus was late_____ ?
2. Do you know what time _____ ?
3. Excuse me, can you tell me where _____ ?
4. I don't know what _____ .
5. Do you know if _____ ?
6. Do you know how much _____ ?

She said that . . . He told me that . . .

A

Last week you went to a party. A lot of your friends were there. Here are some things they said to you:

Today you meet Paul. You tell him about the party. You tell Paul what your friends said:

	Present	Past	
Diane — **I'm** enjoying my new job.	am is	→ was	■ Diane said that **she was** enjoying her new job.
My father isn't very happy.			■ She said that **her father wasn't** very happy.
Sarah Tim — **We're** going to buy a house.	are	→ were	■ Sarah and Tim said that **they were** going to buy a house.
Peter — **I have** to leave early.	have has	→ had	■ Peter said that **he had** to leave early.
My sister has gone to Australia.			■ He said that **his sister had** gone to Australia.
Kate — **I can't** find a job.	can	→ could	■ Kate said that **she couldn't** find a job.
Steve — **I'll** call you.	will	→ would	■ Steve said that **he would** call me.
Rachel — **I don't** like my job.	do does	→ did	■ Rachel said that **she didn't** like her job.
My son doesn't like school.			■ She said that **her son didn't** like school.
Mike — **You look** tired.	look feel etc.	→ looked felt etc.	■ Mike said that **I looked** tired.
You — **I feel** fine.			■ I said that **I felt** fine.

B

say and **tell**

say (→ said)
- ■ He **said** that he was tired.
  (*not* He said me)
- ■ What did she **say to** you?
  (*not* say you)

We say **he said to me, I said to Ann**, etc.
but not "he said me," "I said Ann."

tell (→ told)
- ■ He **told me** that he was tired.
  (*not* He told that)
- ■ What did she **tell you**?
  (*not* tell to you)

We say **he told me, I told Ann**, etc.
but not "he told to me," "I told to Ann."

C

You can say:
- ■ He said **that** he was tired. *or* He said he was tired. (*without* that)
- ■ Kate told me **that** she couldn't find a job. *or* Kate told me she couldn't find a job.

Exercises

51.1 Read what these people say and write sentences with *He/She/They said (that)* . . . .

1. I've lost my watch.

   He said he had lost his watch.

2. I'm very busy.

   _____

3. I can't go to the party.

   _____

4. I have to go out.

   _____

5. I'm learning Russian.

   _____

6. I don't feel very well.

   _____

7. We'll be home late.

   _____

8. I've just gotten back from vacation.

   _____

9. I'm going to buy a new computer.

   _____

10. We don't have a key.

    _____

51.2 Use the pictures to complete the sentences.

1. I'm enjoying my new job. — Diane
2. I'm not hungry. — Emily
3. I need it. — Mike
4. I don't want to go. — Hannah — INVITATION
5. Sharon — You can have it.
6. Mark — I'll send you a postcard.
7. Where's Robert? / He's gone home. — Linda
8. I want to watch TV. — David
9. I'm going to the movies. — Mary

1. I met Diane last week. She said _she was enjoying her new job_ .
2. Emily didn't want anything to eat. She said _____ .
3. I wanted to borrow Mike's ladder, but he said _____ .
4. Hannah was invited to the party, but she said _____ .
5. Sharon told me she didn't want the picture. She said _____ .
6. Mark just left on vacation. He said _____ .
7. I was looking for Robert. Linda said _____ .
8. "Why did David stay at home?" "He said _____ ."
9. "Has Mary gone out?" "I think so. She said _____ ."

51.3 Write *say/said* or *tell/told*.

1. He __said__ he was tired.
2. What did she __tell__ you?
3. Anna _____ she didn't like Peter.
4. Jack _____ me that you were sick.
5. Please don't _____ Dan what happened.
6. Did Lucy _____ she would be late?
7. The woman _____ she was a reporter.
8. The woman _____ us she was a reporter.
9. They asked me a lot of questions, but I didn't _____ them anything.
10. They asked me a lot of questions, but I didn't _____ anything.

work/working   go/going   do/doing

A

Work/go/be, etc. *(base form)*

We use the base form with **will/can/must**, etc.:

| will |
| shall |
| might |
| may |
| can |
| could |
| must |
| should |
| would |

- Anna **will be** here soon.
- **Shall** I **open** the window? } → Units 28–29

- I **might call** you later.
- **May** I **sit** here? } → Unit 30

- I **can't meet** you tomorrow.
- **Could** you **pass** the salt, please? } → Unit 31

- It's late. You **must be** tired. → Unit 32
- You **shouldn't work** so hard. → Unit 33
- **Would** you **like** some coffee? → Unit 35

We use the base form with **do/does/did**:

| do/does |
| *(simple present)* |
| |
| |
| did |
| *(simple past)* |

- **Do** you **work**? → Units 6–7
- They **don't work** very hard.
- Helen **doesn't know** many people.
- How much **does** it **cost**?

- What time **did** the train **leave**? → Unit 12
- We **didn't sleep** well.

B

to work / to go / to be, etc. *(infinitive)*

| (I'm) **going to** . . . |
| |
| (I) **have to** . . . |
| |
| (I) **want to** . . . |
| |
| (I) **would like to** . . . |
| |
| (I) **used to** . . . |

- I'm **going to play** tennis tomorrow. → Unit 27
- What **are** you **going to do**?

- I **have to go** now. → Unit 34
- Everybody **has to eat**.

- Do you **want to go** out? → Unit 53
- They don't **want to come** with us.

- I'**d like to talk** to you. → Unit 35
- **Would** you **like to go** out?

- Dave **used to work** in a factory. → Unit 15

C

working/going/playing, etc.

| am/is/are + -ing |
| *(present continuous)* |
| |
| |
| was/were + -ing |
| *(past continuous)* |

- Please be quiet. I'**m working**. → Units 3–4, 8, 26
- Tom **isn't working** today.
- What time **are** you **going** out?

- It **was raining**, so we didn't go out. → Units 13–14
- What **were** you **doing** when the phone rang?

verbs + **to** . . . and **-ing** (I want to do / I enjoy doing) → Unit 53   go + **-ing** → Unit 56

Exercises

52.1 Complete the sentences. Write: . . . *call Paul* or . . . *to call Paul*.

1. I'll __call Paul_____ .
2. I'm going __to call Paul_____ .
3. Can you _____ Paul?
4. Shall I _____ ?
5. I'd like _____ .
6. Do you have _____ ?
7. You should _____ .
8. I want _____ .
9. I might _____ .
10. Could you _____ ?

52.2 Complete the sentences with a verb from the box. Sometimes you need the base form (*work/go*, etc.) and sometimes you need *-ing* (*working/going*, etc.).

do/doing	eat/eating	fly/flying	get/getting
go/going	listen/listening	~~sleep/sleeping~~	stay/staying
wait/waiting	watch/watching	wear/wearing	~~work/working~~

1. Please be quiet. I'm __working____ .
2. I feel tired today. I didn't __sleep___ very well last night.
3. What time do you usually _____ up in the morning?
4. "Where are you _____ ?" "To the bank."
5. Did you _____ television last night?
6. Look at that plane! It's _____ very low.
7. You can turn off the radio. I'm not _____ to it.
8. They didn't _____ anything because they weren't hungry.
9. My friends were _____ for me when I arrived.
10. "Does Susan always _____ glasses?" "No, only for reading."
11. "What are you _____ tonight?" "I'm _____ home."

52.3 Put the verb in the correct form. Choose from:

> the base form (*work/go*, etc.) or
> the infinitive (*to work/to go*, etc.) or
> *-ing* (*working/going*, etc.)

1. Should I __open___ the window? (open)
2. It's late. I have __to go___ now. (go)
3. Amanda isn't __working____ this week. She's on vacation. (work)
4. I'm tired. I don't want _____ out. (go)
5. It might _____ , so take an umbrella with you. (rain)
6. What time do you have _____ tomorrow morning? (leave)
7. I'm sorry I can't _____ you. (help)
8. My brother is a student. He's _____ physics. (study)
9. Would you like _____ on a trip around the world? (go)
10. When you saw Maria, what was she _____ ? (wear)
11. When you go to London, where are you going _____ ? (stay)
12. "Where's Gary?" "He's _____ a bath." (take)
13. I used _____ a car, but I sold it last year. (have)
14. He spoke very quietly. I couldn't _____ him. (hear)
15. You don't look well. I don't think you should _____ to work today. (go)
16. I don't know what he said. I wasn't _____ to him. (listen)
17. I'm sorry I'm late. I had _____ a phone call. (make)
18. I want _____ a doctor. (be) Medical students must _____ courses in biology and chemistry. (take)
19. May I please _____ your phone? (use)

to . . . (I want to do) and -ing (I enjoy doing)

A

verbs + **to . . .** (**I want to do**)

want	plan	decide	try
hope	expect	offer	forget
need	promise	refuse	learn

+ **to . . .** (**to do / to work / to be**, etc.)

- What do you **want to do** tonight?
- It's not very late. We don't **need to go** home yet.
- Tina has **decided to sell** her car.
- You **forgot to turn** off the light when you went out.
- My brother is **learning to drive**.
- I **tried to read** my book, but I was too tired.

B

verbs + **-ing** (**I enjoy doing**)

enjoy	stop	
mind	finish	suggest

+ **-ing** (**doing/working/being**, etc.)

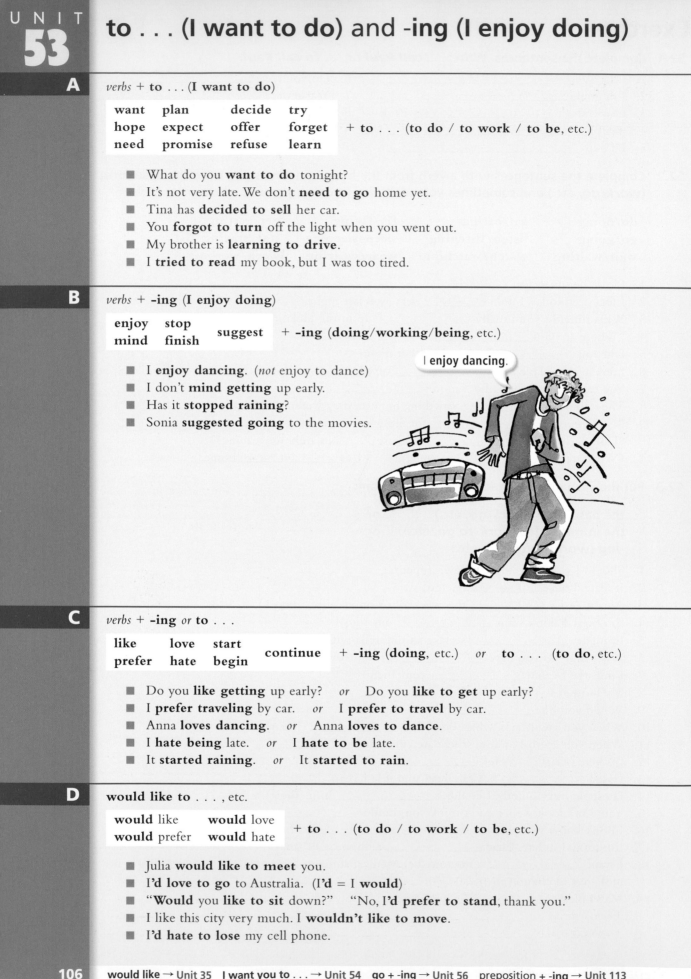

I enjoy dancing.

- I **enjoy dancing**. (*not* enjoy to dance)
- I don't **mind getting** up early.
- Has it **stopped raining**?
- Sonia **suggested going** to the movies.

C

verbs + **-ing** *or* **to . . .**

like	love	start	
prefer	hate	begin	continue

+ **-ing** (**doing**, etc.) *or* **to . . .** (**to do**, etc.)

- Do you **like getting** up early? *or* Do you **like to get** up early?
- I **prefer traveling** by car. *or* I **prefer to travel** by car.
- Anna **loves dancing**. *or* Anna **loves to dance**.
- I **hate being** late. *or* I **hate to be** late.
- It **started raining**. *or* It **started to rain**.

D

would like to . . . , etc.

would like	**would** love
would prefer	**would** hate

+ **to . . .** (**to do / to work / to be**, etc.)

- Julia **would like to meet** you.
- I**'d love to go** to Australia. (**I'd** = I would)
- "**Would** you **like to sit** down?" "No, I**'d prefer to stand**, thank you."
- I like this city very much. I **wouldn't like to move**.
- I**'d hate to lose** my cell phone.

 would like → Unit 35 **I want you to . . .** → Unit 54 **go + -ing** → Unit 56 **preposition + -ing** → Unit 113

Exercises

53.1 Put the verb in the right form, *to . . .* or *-ing*.

1. I enjoy ___dancing___ . (dance)
2. What do you want __to do__ tonight? (do)
3. Goodbye! I hope _____ you again soon. (see)
4. I learned _____ when I was five years old. (swim)
5. Have you finished _____ the kitchen? (clean)
6. Where's Anna? I need _____ her something. (ask)
7. Do you enjoy _____ other countries? (visit)
8. The weather was nice, so I suggested _____ for a walk by the river. (go)
9. Where's Bill? He promised _____ here on time. (be)
10. I'm not in a hurry. I don't mind _____ . (wait)
11. What have you decided _____ ? (do)
12. Gary was very angry and refused _____ to me. (speak)
13. I'm tired. I want _____ to bed. (go)
14. I was very upset and started _____ . (cry)
15. I'm trying _____ . (work) Please stop _____ . (talk)

53.2 Complete the sentences using *to . . .* or *-ing*. Use these verbs:

~~go~~   go   help   lose   rain   read   see   send   wait   watch

1. "Have you ever been to Australia?" "No, but I'd love __to go__ ."
2. Jane had a lot to do, so I offered _____ her.
3. I'm surprised that you're here. I didn't expect _____ you.
4. Nicole has a lot of books. She enjoys _____ .
5. This ring was my grandmother's. I'd hate _____ it.
6. Don't forget _____ us a postcard when you're on vacation.
7. I'm not going out until it stops _____ .
8. What should we do this afternoon? Would you like _____ to the beach?
9. When I'm tired in the evening, I like _____ television.
10. "Do you want to go now?" "No, I'd prefer _____ a few minutes."

53.3 Complete the answers to the questions.

1. Do you usually get up early?
2. Do you ever go to museums?
3. Would you like to go to a museum now?
4. Do you write e-mails often?
5. Have you ever been to Rome?
6. Do you ever travel by train?
7. Do you want to walk home or take a taxi?

Yes, I like __to get up early__ .
Yes, I love _____ .
No, I'm hungry. I'd prefer _____ to a restaurant.
No, I don't like _____ .
No, but I'd love _____ one day.
Yes, I enjoy _____ .
I don't mind _____ , but a taxi would be quicker.

53.4 Complete these sentences. Write about yourself. Use *to . . .* or *-ing*.

1. I enjoy _____
2. I don't like _____
3. If it's a nice day tomorrow, I'd like _____
4. When I'm on vacation, I like _____
5. I don't mind _____ , but _____
6. I wouldn't like _____

→ Additional exercise 32 (page 260)

I want you to . . .   I told you to . . .

A   **I want you to**

I'm leaving.

Please don't leave.

The woman **wants to leave**.

The man **doesn't want** the woman to leave.
He **wants** her **to stay**.

We say:

I want	you somebody Sarah	**to do** something

■ I **want you to be** happy. (*not* I want that you are happy)
■ They didn't **want anybody to know** their secret.
■ Do you **want me to lend** you some money?

We use **would like** in the same way:
■ **Would** you **like me to lend** you some money?

B   We also use this structure (*verb* + somebody + **to** . . .) with:

ask		*verb*	+	somebody +	**to** . . .	
ask	Sue	**asked**		a friend	**to lend**	her some money.
tell	I	**told**		you	**to be**	careful.
advise	What do you	**advise**		me	**to do**?	
expect	I didn't	**expect**		them	**to be**	here.
persuade	We	**persuaded**		Gary	**to come**	with us.
teach	I	**am teaching**		my brother	**to swim**.	

C   **I told** you **to** . . . / **I told** you **not to** . . .

Wait for me.

Don't wait for me.

Jane   Me   Paul   Sue

→ Jane **told** me **to wait** for her.   → Paul **told** Sue **not to wait** for him.

D   **make** and **let**

After **make** and **let**, we do *not* use **to**:
■ He's very funny. He **makes** me **laugh**. (*not* makes me to laugh)
■ At school our teacher **made** us **work** very hard.
■ Sue **let** me **use** her computer because mine wasn't working. (*not* let me to use)

You can say **Let's** . . . (= **Let us**) when you want people to do things with you:
■ Come on! **Let's dance**.
■ "Do you want to go out tonight?"   "No, I'm tired. **Let's stay** home."

Let's . . . → Unit 37   He told me that . . . → Unit 51

Exercises

54.1 Write sentences beginning *I want you . . . / I don't want you . . . / Do you want me . . . ?*

1. (you have to come with me) <u>I want you to come with me.</u>
2. (listen carefully) I want _____
3. (please don't be angry) I don't _____
4. (should I wait for you?) Do you _____
5. (don't call me tonight) _____
6. (you should meet Sarah) _____

54.2 Look at the pictures and complete the sentences.

1. Dan persuaded <u>me to go to the movies.</u>
2. I wanted to get to the station. A woman told _____
3. Brian was sick. I advised _____
4. Linda had a lot of luggage. She asked _____
5. I was too busy to talk to Tom. I told _____
6. I wanted to make a phone call. Paul let _____
7. Sue is going to call me later. I told _____
8. Ann's mother taught _____

54.3 Complete these sentences with the verbs in the list. Sometimes *to* is necessary (*to go / to wait*, etc.); sometimes *to* is not necessary (*go/wait*, etc.).

> arrive   borrow   get   go   ~~leave~~   make   repeat   tell   think   wait

1. Please stay here. I don't want you <u>to leave</u> yet.
2. I didn't hear what she said, so I asked her _____ it.
3. "Should we begin?"   "No, let's _____ a few minutes."
4. Are they already here? I expected them _____ much later.
5. Kevin's parents didn't want him _____ married.
6. I want to stay here. You can't make me _____ with you.
7. "Is that your bicycle?"   "No, it's John's. He let me _____ it."
8. Rachel can't come to the party. She told me _____ you.
9. Would you like something to drink? Would you like me _____ some coffee?
10. "Kate doesn't like me."   "What makes you _____ that?"

I went to the store to . . .

A

Paula wanted some fruit, so she went to the store.

Why did she go to the store?
To get some fruit.

She went to the store **to get** some fruit.

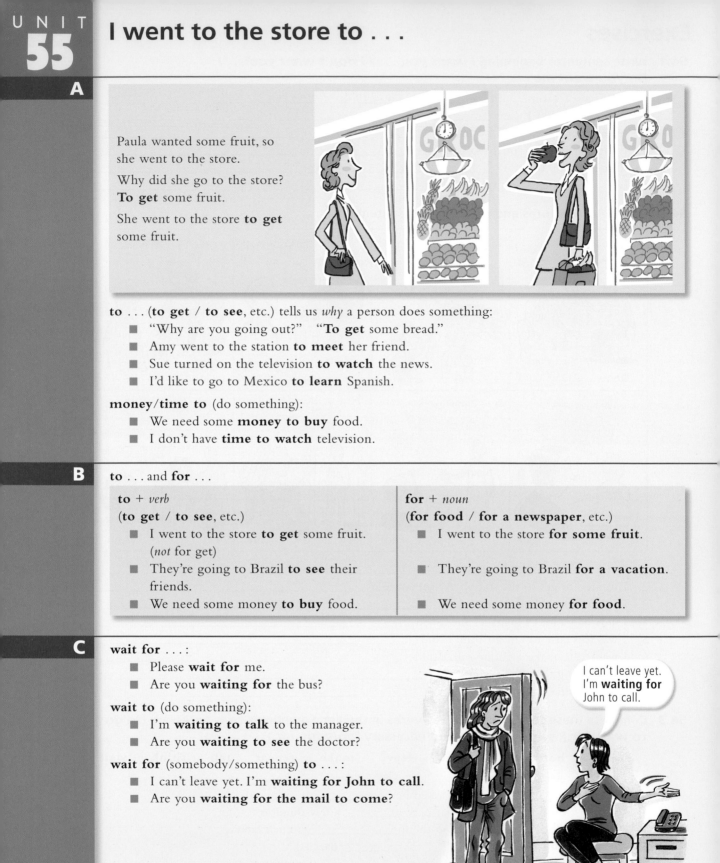

to . . . (**to get** / **to see**, etc.) tells us *why* a person does something:

- ■ "Why are you going out?" "**To get** some bread."
- ■ Amy went to the station **to meet** her friend.
- ■ Sue turned on the television **to watch** the news.
- ■ I'd like to go to Mexico **to learn** Spanish.

money/time to (do something):

- ■ We need some **money to buy** food.
- ■ I don't have **time to watch** television.

B

to . . . and **for . . .**

to + *verb* (**to get** / **to see**, etc.)	**for** + *noun* (**for food** / **for a newspaper**, etc.)
■ I went to the store **to get** some fruit. (*not* for get)	■ I went to the store **for some fruit**.
■ They're going to Brazil **to see** their friends.	■ They're going to Brazil **for a vacation**.
■ We need some money **to buy** food.	■ We need some money **for food**.

C

wait for . . . :

- ■ Please **wait for** me.
- ■ Are you **waiting for** the bus?

wait to (do something):

- ■ I'm **waiting to talk** to the manager.
- ■ Are you **waiting to see** the doctor?

wait for (somebody/something) **to . . . :**

- ■ I can't leave yet. I'm **waiting for John to call**.
- ■ Are you **waiting for the mail to come**?

I can't leave yet. I'm **waiting for** John to call.

go to . . . and **go for . . .** → Unit 56   **something to eat / nothing to do**, etc. → Unit 80
enough + to/for . . . → Unit 92   **too + to/for . . .** → Unit 93

Exercises

55.1 Write sentences beginning *I went to* . . . . Choose from the boxes.

| a coffee shop | the drugstore | + | buy some food | get some medicine |
| the post office | the supermarket | | get some stamps | meet a friend |

1. _I went to the post office to get some stamps._
2. I went _____
3. _____
4. _____

55.2 Complete the sentences. Choose from the box.

| to get some fresh air | to open this door | to read the newspaper |
| to see who it was | to wake him up | to watch the news |

1. I turned on the television _to watch the news_ .
2. Alice sat down in an armchair _____ .
3. Do I need a key _____ ?
4. I went for a walk by the river _____ .
5. I knocked on the door of David's room _____ .
6. The doorbell rang, so I looked out of the window _____ .

55.3 Use your own ideas to finish these sentences. Use *to* . . . .

1. I went to the store _to get some fruit_ .
2. I'm very busy. I don't have time _____ .
3. I called Ann _____ .
4. I'm going out _____ .
5. I borrowed some money _____ .

55.4 Write *to* or *for*.

1. I went to the store _to_ get some bread.
2. We went to a restaurant _____ have dinner.
3. Robert wants to go to college _____ study economics.
4. I'm going to Boston _____ an interview next week.
5. I'm going to Toronto _____ visit some friends of mine.
6. Do you have time _____ a cup of coffee?
7. I got up late this morning. I didn't have time _____ comb my hair.
8. Everybody needs money _____ live.
9. We didn't have any money _____ a taxi, so we walked home.
10. The office is very small. There's only enough room _____ a desk and chair.
11. *A:* Excuse me, are you waiting _____ use the phone?
     B: No, I'm waiting _____ somebody.

55.5 Complete these sentences. Choose from:

John / call   it / to arrive   you / tell me   the movie / begin

1. I can't go out yet. I'm waiting _for John to call_ .
2. I sat down in the movie theater and waited _____ .
3. We called an ambulance and waited _____ .
4. "Do you know what to do?" "No, I'm waiting _____ ."

go to . . .   go on . . .   go for . . .   go + -ing

A

go to . . . (**go to work** / **go to San Francisco** / **go to a concert**, etc.)

■ What time do you usually **go to work**?
■ I'm **going to China** next week.
■ Jean didn't want to **go to the concert**.
■ What time did you **go to bed** last night?
■ I **went to the dentist** yesterday.

go to →

go to sleep = start to sleep:

■ I was very tired and **went to sleep** quickly.

go home (without **to**)

■ I'm **going home** now. (*not* going to home)

B

go on . . .

go on	vacation a trip a tour an excursion a cruise strike

■ We're **going on vacation** next week.
■ Children often **go on school trips**.
■ When we were in Egypt, we **went on a tour** of the Pyramids.
■ Workers at the airport have **gone on strike**.
(= they are refusing to work)

C

go for . . .

go (somewhere) **for**	a walk a run a swim lunch dinner, etc.

■ "Where's Joan?"   "She **went for a walk**."
■ Do you **go for a run** every morning?
■ The water looks nice. I'm **going for a swim**.
■ Should we **go** out **for dinner**? I know a good restaurant.

D

go + -ing

We use **go + -ing** for many sports (**swimming/skiing**, etc.) and also **shopping**.

I **go** he is **going** we **went** they have **gone** she wants to **go**	**shopping** **swimming** **fishing** **sailing** **skiing** **jogging** **running**, etc.

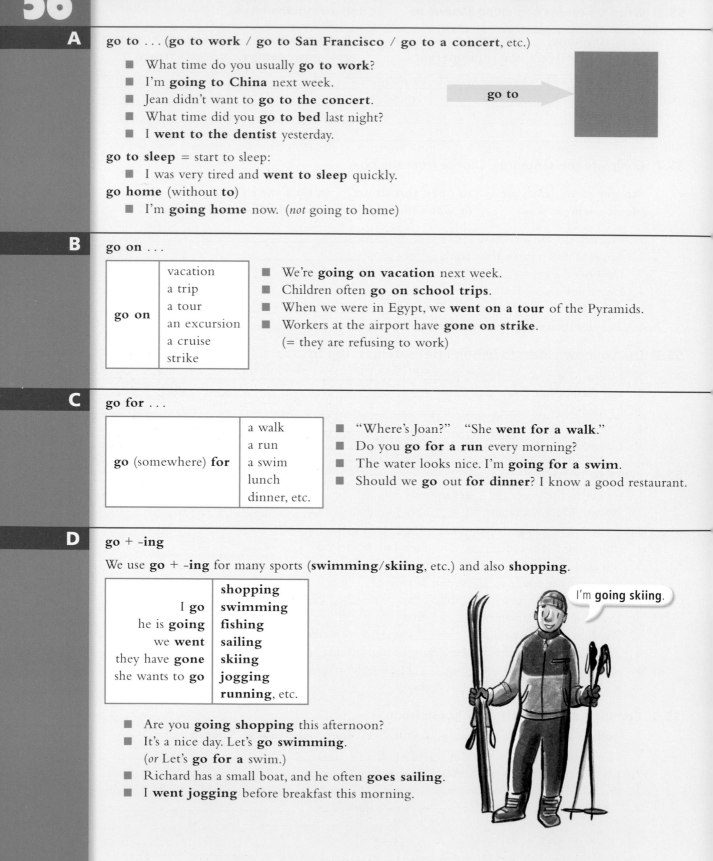

I'm **going skiing**.

■ Are you **going shopping** this afternoon?
■ It's a nice day. Let's **go swimming**.
(*or* Let's **go for a** swim.)
■ Richard has a small boat, and he often **goes sailing**.
■ I **went jogging** before breakfast this morning.

Exercises

56.1 Write *to/on/for* where necessary.

1. I'm going __*to*__ China next week.
2. Richard often goes ____−____ sailing. *(no preposition)*
3. Sue went _____ Mexico last year.
4. Would you like to go _____ the movies tonight?
5. Jack goes _____ jogging every morning.
6. I'm going out _____ a walk. Do you want to come?
7. I'm tired because I went _____ bed very late last night.
8. Jim is going _____ a trip _____ Turkey next week.
9. The weather was warm, and the river was clean, so we went _____ a swim.
10. The taxi drivers went _____ strike when I was in New York.
11. I need some stamps, so I'm going _____ the post office.
12. It's late. I have to go _____ home now.
13. Would you like to go _____ a tour of the city?
14. Do you want to go out _____ dinner this evening?
15. My parents are going _____ a cruise this summer.

56.2 Use the pictures to complete the sentences. Use *go/goes/going/went + -ing*.

| 1. *often* | 2. *last Saturday* | 3. *every day* | 4. *next winter* | 5. *later* | 6. *yesterday* |
| Richard | Diane | Gary | Nicole | Peter | Sarah |

1. Richard has a boat. He often __*goes sailing*__ .
2. Last Saturday Diane _____ .
3. Gary _____ every day.
4. Nicole is going to Colorado next winter. She is _____ .
5. Peter is going out later. He has to _____ .
6. Sarah _____ after work yesterday.

56.3 Complete the sentences. Use the words in the box. Use *to/on/for* if necessary.

| ~~a swim~~ | vacation | Hawaii | shopping | bed |
| a walk | home | riding | skiing | college |

1. The water looks nice. Let's go __*for a swim*__ .
2. After finishing high school, Tina went _____ , where she studied psychology.
3. I'm going _____ now. I have to buy a few things.
4. I was very tired last night. I went _____ early.
5. I wasn't enjoying the party, so I went _____ early.
6. We live near the mountains. In winter we go _____ almost every weekend.
7. Richard has a horse. He goes _____ a lot.
8. It's a beautiful day! Would you like to go _____ in the park?
9. *A:* Are you going _____ soon?
   B: Yes, next month. We're going _____ . We've never been there before.

get

get a letter / **get a job**, etc. (**get** + *noun*) = receive/buy/find:

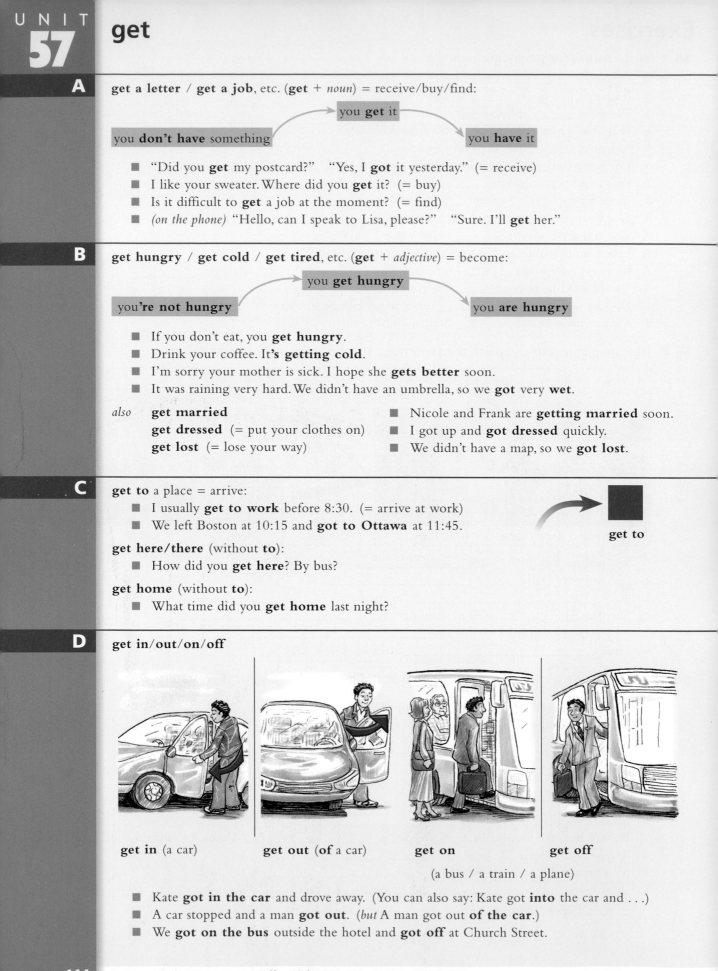

you **get** it

you **don't have** something → you **have** it

- "Did you **get** my postcard?"   "Yes, I **got** it yesterday." (= receive)
- I like your sweater. Where did you **get** it? (= buy)
- Is it difficult to **get** a job at the moment? (= find)
- *(on the phone)* "Hello, can I speak to Lisa, please?"   "Sure. I'll **get** her."

B

get hungry / **get cold** / **get tired**, etc. (**get** + *adjective*) = become:

you **get hungry**

you**'re not hungry** → you **are hungry**

- If you don't eat, you **get hungry**.
- Drink your coffee. It**'s getting cold**.
- I'm sorry your mother is sick. I hope she **gets better** soon.
- It was raining very hard. We didn't have an umbrella, so we **got** very **wet**.

also   **get married**
          get dressed (= put your clothes on)
          get lost (= lose your way)

- Nicole and Frank are **getting married** soon.
- I got up and **got dressed** quickly.
- We didn't have a map, so we **got lost**.

C

get to a place = arrive:

- I usually **get to work** before 8:30. (= arrive at work)
- We left Boston at 10:15 and **got to Ottawa** at 11:45.

get here/there (without **to**):

- How did you **get here**? By bus?

get home (without **to**):

- What time did you **get home** last night?

get to

D

get in/out/on/off

get in (a car)   **get out** (**of** a car)   **get on**   **get off**

(a bus / a train / a plane)

- Kate **got in the car** and drove away. (You can also say: Kate got **into** the car and . . .)
- A car stopped and a man **got out**. (*but* A man got out **of the car**.)
- We **got on the bus** outside the hotel and **got off** at Church Street.

get to → Unit 109   in/out/on/off → Units 111, 115   get up → Unit 115

Exercises

57.1 Complete these sentences. Use *get/gets* and choose from the box.

another one	a doctor	a lot of rain	~~my postcard~~	the job
a good salary	a new computer	a ticket	some milk	your jacket

1. Did you __*get my postcard*__ ? I sent it a week ago.
2. Where did you _____ ? It's very nice.
3. Quick! This man is sick. We have to _____ .
4. I want to return this phone. It doesn't work. Can I _____ , please?
5. Tom has an interview tomorrow. I hope he _____ .
6. When you go out, can you _____ ?
7. "Are you going to the concert?"   "Yes, if I can _____ ."
8. Margaret has a well-paid job. She _____ .
9. The weather is horrible here in winter. We _____ .
10. I'm going to _____ . The one I have is too slow.

57.2 Complete these sentences. Use *getting* + these words:

~~cold~~   dark   late   married   ready

1. Drink your coffee. It's __*getting cold*__ .
2. Turn on the light. It's _____ .
3. "I'm _____ next week."   "Really? Congratulations!"
4. "Where's Karen?"   "She's _____ to go out."
5. It's _____ . It's time to go home.

57.3 Complete the sentences. Use *get/gets/got* + these words:

angry   better   ~~hungry~~   lost   married   old   wet

1. If you don't eat, you __*get hungry*__ .
2. Don't go out in the rain. You'll _____ .
3. My brother _____ last year. His wife's name is Sarah.
4. Dan is always very calm. He never _____ .
5. We tried to find the hotel, but we _____ .
6. Everybody wants to stay young, but we all _____ .
7. Yesterday the weather wasn't so good at first, but it _____ during the day.

57.4 Write sentences with *I left* . . . and *got to* . . . .

1. home / 7:30 → work / 8:15
   __*I left home at 7:30 and got to work at 8:15.*__
2. Toronto / 10:15 → New York / 12:00
   I left Toronto at 10:15 and _____
3. the party / 11:15 → home / midnight
   _____
4. *Write a sentence about yourself.*
   I left _____

57.5 Write *got in / got out of / got on / got off*.

1. Kate __*got in*__ the car and drove away.
2. I _____ the bus and walked to my house from the bus stop.
3. Lisa _____ the car, locked the doors, and went into a store.
4. I made a stupid mistake. I _____ the wrong train.

115

do and make

A

Do is a general word for actions:

- What are you **doing** tonight? (*not* What are you making?)
- "Shall I open the window?"   "No, it's OK. I'll **do** it."
- Linda's job is very boring. She **does** the same thing every day.
- I **did** a lot of things yesterday.

What do you do? = What's your job?:

- "What do you **do**?"   "I work in a bank."

B

Make = produce/create. For example:

She's **making** coffee.   He has **made** a cake.   They **make** toys.   It was **made** in China.

Compare **do** and **make**:

- I **did** a lot yesterday. I **cleaned** my room, I **wrote** some letters, and I **made** a cake.
- *A:* What do you **do** in your free time? Read? Play sports?
  B: I **make** clothes. I **make** dresses and jackets. I also **make** toys for my children.

C

Expressions with **do**

do	homework housework (somebody) a favor an exercise (your) best the laundry the dishes

- Have the children **done their homework**?
- I hate **doing housework**, especially cleaning.
- Barbara, could you **do me a favor**?
- I have to **do four exercises** for homework tonight.
- I **did my best**, but I didn't win the race.
- Tim usually **does the laundry** on Saturdays.
- I cooked, so you should **do the dishes**.

D

Expressions with **make**

make	a mistake an appointment a phone call a list (a) noise a bed

- I'm sorry, I **made a mistake**.
- I need to **make an appointment** to see the doctor.
- Excuse me, I have to **make a phone call**.
- Have you **made a shopping list**?
- It's late. Don't **make any noise**.
- Sometimes I forget to **make my bed** in the morning.

We say **make a movie** *but* **take a picture**:

- When was **this movie made**?   *but*   When was **this picture taken**?

do/does/did (negatives and questions) → Units 44–45   make somebody do something → Unit 54

Exercises

58.1 Write *make/making/made* or *do/doing/did/done*.

1. "Shall I open the window?" "No, that's OK. I'll __*do*__ it."
2. What did you _____ last weekend? Did you leave town?
3. Do you know how to _____ bread?
4. Paper is _____ from wood.
5. Richard didn't help me. He sat in an armchair and _____ nothing.
6. "What do you _____ ?" "I'm a doctor."
7. I asked you to clean the bathroom. Have you _____ it?
8. "What do they _____ in that factory?" "Shoes."
9. I'm _____ some coffee. Would you like some?
10. Why are you angry with me? I didn't _____ anything wrong.
11. "What are you _____ tomorrow afternoon?" "I'm working."

58.2 What are these people doing?

1. ___*He's making a cake.*___
2. They _____
3. He _____
4. _____
5. _____
6. _____
7. _____
8. _____
9. _____
10. _____

58.3 Write *make* or *do* in the correct form.

1. I hate __*doing*__ housework, especially cleaning.
2. Why do you always _____ the same mistake?
3. "Can you _____ me a favor?" "It depends what it is."
4. "Have you _____ your homework?" "Not yet."
5. I need to see the dentist, but I haven't _____ an appointment.
6. Joe _____ his best, but he didn't pass his driver's test.
7. I painted the door, but I didn't _____ it very well.
8. How many phone calls did you _____ yesterday?
9. When you've finished Exercise 1, you can _____ Exercise 2.
10. There's something wrong with the car. The engine is _____ a strange noise.
11. It was a bad mistake. It was the worst mistake I've ever _____ .
12. Let's _____ a list of all the things we have to _____ today.

UNIT 59

have

A

have and **have got**

I have (something) or **I've got** (something) = it is mine:

- I **have** a new car.   *or*   **I've got** a new car.
- Sue **has** long hair.   *or*   Sue **has got** long hair.
- **Do** they **have** any children?   *or*   **Have** they **got** any children?
- Tim **doesn't have** a job.   *or*   Tim **hasn't got** a job.
- How much time **do** you **have**?   *or*   How much time **have** you **got**?

also

| I **have** | a headache / a toothache / a pain (in my leg, etc.) |
| I **'ve got** | a cold / a cough / a sore throat / a fever / the flu, etc. |

- I **have** a headache.   *or*   **I've got** a headache.
- **Do** you **have** a cold?   *or*   **Have** you **got** a cold?

The past is **I had** (without **got**) / **I didn't have** / **Did you have**?, etc.:

- When I first met Sue, she **had** short hair.
- He **didn't have** any money because he **didn't have** a job.
- **Did** you **have** enough time to do everything you wanted?

B

have breakfast / **have a good time**, etc.

In these expressions **have** = eat or drink. You can't use "have got."

have	breakfast / lunch / dinner
	a meal / a sandwich / (a) pizza, etc.
	a cup of coffee / a glass of milk, etc.
	something to eat/drink

- "Where's Liz?"   "She**'s having** lunch."
- I **don't** usually **have** breakfast.
- I **had** three cups of coffee this morning.
- "**Have** a cookie."   "Oh, thank you."

We also use **have** (*not* have got) in these expressions:

have	a party / a meeting
	a nice time / a good trip / fun, etc.
	a (nice) day / a (nice) weekend /
	a (great) vacation
	a (good) flight / a safe trip
	a dream / an accident
	an argument / a discussion
	a baby

- We**'re having** a party next week. Please come.
- Enjoy your vacation. **Have** a good trip!
- **I'm having** a bad day. Everything is going wrong. I hope I **have** a better day tomorrow.
- We **have** a 12-hour flight to Lima tomorrow.
- Mark **had** an accident on his first day in Rome.
- Boss, can we **have** a discussion about my pay?
- Sandra **has** just **had** a baby. It's a boy.

C

Compare:

have got *or* **have**

- **I've got** / I **have** three cups of coffee for this office.

have (*not* **have got**)

- I **have** coffee with my breakfast every morning.
  (*not* **I've got** coffee every morning)
- A: Where's Paul?
  B: He's on break. He**'s having** a cup of coffee.
  (= he's drinking it now)

I**'ve got** three cups of coffee for this office.

I'm on break. I**'m having** a cup of coffee.

I have / I've got → Unit 9   **I've (done)** (present perfect) → Units 16–17, 19–20   **I have to . . .** → Unit 34

Exercises

59.1 Write the correct form of *have* or *have got*.

1. ___I didn't have___ time to do the shopping yesterday.   (I / not / have)
2. " ___Does Lisa have___ OR ___Has Lisa got___ a car?"   (Lisa / have?)
   "No, she can't drive."
3. He can't open the door. _____ a key.   (he / not / have)
4. _____ a cold last week. He's better now.   (Gary / have)
5. What's wrong? _____ a headache?   (you / have?)
6. We wanted to go by taxi, but _____ enough money.   (we / not / have)
7. Liz is very busy. _____ much free time.   (she / not / have)
8. _____ any problems when you were on vacation?   (you / have?)

59.2 What are these people doing? Choose from the list:

an argument   **breakfast**   **a cup of tea**   **dinner**   **fun**   ~~a party~~

1. ___They're having a party.___
2. She _____
3. He _____
4. They _____
5. _____
6. _____

59.3 What do you say in these situations? Use *have*.

1. Barbara is going on vacation. What do you say to her before she goes?
   ___Have a nice vacation!___
2. You meet Claire at the airport. She has just gotten off her plane. Ask her about the flight.
   ___Did you have a good flight?___
3. Tim is going on a long trip. What do you say to him before he leaves?
   _____
4. It's Monday morning. You are at work. Ask Paula about her weekend.
   _____
5. Paul has just come back from vacation. Ask him about his vacation.
   _____
6. Rachel is going out tonight. What do you say to her before she goes?
   _____
7. Sue's little boy will be one year old next week. Is there going to be a birthday party? Ask her.
   _____

59.4 Complete the sentences. Use *have/had* and choose from the list.

an accident   **a glass of water**   **a baby**
a bad dream   ~~a party~~   **something to eat**

1. We ___had a party___ a few weeks ago. We invited 50 people.
2. "Should we _____ ?" "No, I'm not hungry."
3. I was thirsty, so I _____ .
4. I _____ last night. It woke me up.
5. Tina is a very good driver. She has never _____ .
6. Rachel is going to _____ . It will be her first child.

I/me   he/him   they/them, etc.

A

People

subject	I	we	you	he	she	they
object	**me**	**us**	**you**	**him**	**her**	**them**

subject			object	
I	**I** know Tom.	Tom knows **me**.	me
we	**We** know Tom.	Tom knows **us**.	us
you	**You** know Tom.	Tom knows **you**.	you
he	**He** knows Tom.	Tom knows **him**.	him
she	**She** knows Tom.	Tom knows **her**.	her
they	**They** know Tom.	Tom knows **them**.	them

B

Things

It's nice. I like **it**.

They're nice. I like **them**.

subject	it	they
object	it	them

- I don't want **this book**. You can have **it**.
- I don't want **these books**. You can have **them**.
- Diane never drinks **milk**. She doesn't like **it**.
- I never go to **parties**. I don't like **them**.

C

We use **me/her/them**, etc. (object) after a *preposition* (**for/to/with**, etc.):

- This letter isn't **for me**. It's **for you**.
- Who is that woman? Why are you looking **at her**?
- We're going to the movies. Do you want to come **with us**?
- Sue and Kevin are going to the movies. Do you want to go **with them**?
- "Where's the newspaper?"   "You're sitting **on it**."

give it/them to . . . :

- I want that book. Please give **it to me**.
- Robert needs these books. Can you give **them to him**, please?

my/his/their, etc. → Unit 61   **Give me that book / Give it to me** → Unit 97

Exercises

60.1 **Complete the sentences with *him/her/them*.**

1. I don't know those girls. Do you know __*them*__ ?
2. I don't know that man. Do you know _____ ?
3. I don't know those people. Do you know _____ ?
4. I don't know David's wife. Do you know _____ ?
5. I don't know Mr. Stevens. Do you know _____ ?
6. I don't know Sarah's parents. Do you know _____ ?
7. I don't know the woman in the black coat. Do you know _____ ?

60.2 **Complete the sentences. Use *I/me/you/she/her*, etc.**

1. **I** want to see **her**, but __*she*__ doesn't want to see __*me*__ .
2. **They** want to see **me**, but _____ don't want to see _____ .
3. **She** wants to see **him**, but _____ doesn't want to see _____ .
4. **We** want to see **them**, but _____ don't want to see _____ .
5. **He** wants to see **us**, but _____ don't want to see _____ .
6. **They** want to see **her**, but _____ doesn't want to see _____ .
7. **I** want to see **them**, but _____ don't want to see _____ .
8. **You** want to see **her**, but _____ doesn't want to see _____ .

60.3 **Write sentences beginning *I like* . . . , *I don't like* . . . , or *Do you like* . . . ?**

1. I don't eat tomatoes. __*I don't like them*__ .
2. George is a very nice man. I like _____ .
3. This jacket isn't very nice. I don't _____ .
4. This is my new car. Do _____ ?
5. Mrs. Clark is not very friendly. I _____ .
6. These are my new shoes. _____ ?

60.4 **Complete the sentences. Use *I/me/he/him*, etc.**

1. Who is that woman? Why are you looking at __*her*__ ?
2. "Do you know that man?" "Yes, I work with _____ ."
3. Where are the tickets? I can't find _____ .
4. I can't find my keys. Where are _____ ?
5. We're going out. You can come with _____ .
6. I have a new computer. Do you want to see _____ ?
7. Maria likes music. _____ plays the piano.
8. I don't like dogs. I'm afraid of _____ .
9. I'm talking to you. Please listen to _____ .
10. Where is Anna? I want to talk to _____ .
11. You can have these DVDs. I don't want _____ .
12. My brother has a new job, but _____ doesn't like _____ very much.

60.5 **Complete the sentences.**

1. I need that book. Can you __*give it to me*__ ?
2. He wants the key. Can you give _____ ?
3. She wants the keys. Can you _____ ?
4. I want that letter. Can you _____ ?
5. They want the money. Can you _____ ?
6. We want the photos. Can you _____ ?

my/his/their, etc.

A

| my umbrella | our umbrella | your umbrella | his umbrella | her umbrella | their umbrella |

I	→	**my**
we	→	**our**
you	→	**your**
he	→	**his**
she	→	**her**
they	→	**their**

I	like	**my**	house.
We	like	**our**	house.
You	like	**your**	house.
He	likes	**his**	house.
She	likes	**her**	house.
They	like	**their**	house.

it	→	**its**

Hawaii (= **it**) is famous for **its** beaches.

We use **my/your/his**, etc. + *noun*:

my hands	**his** new **car**	**her parents**
our clothes	**your** best **friend**	**their room**

B **his/her/their**

Donna

her car
(= Donna's car)

her husband
(= Donna's husband)

her children
(= Donna's children)

Andy

his bicycle

his sister

his parents

Mr. and
Mrs. Lee

their son

their daughter

their children

C **its** and **it's**

its   Hawaii is famous for **its** beaches.
it's (= it **is**)   I like Hawaii. **It's** a beautiful place. (= It **is** a beautiful place.)

Exercises

61.1 Complete the sentences in the same way.

1. I'm going to wash __my hands__ .
2. She's going to wash _____ hands.
3. We're going to wash _____ .
4. He's going to wash _____ .
5. They're going to wash _____ .
6. Are you going to wash _____ ?

61.2 Complete the sentences in the same way.

1. He __lives with his parents__ .
2. They live with _____ parents.
3. We _____ parents.
4. Jane lives _____ .
5. I _____ parents.
6. John _____ .
7. Do you live _____ ?
8. Most children _____ .

61.3 Look at the family tree, and complete the sentences with *his/her/their*.

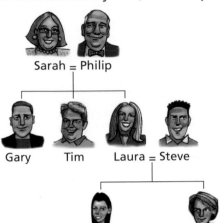

Sarah = Philip

Gary   Tim   Laura = Steve

Beth   Robert

1. I saw Sarah with __her__ husband, Philip.
2. I saw Laura and Steve with _____ children.
3. I saw Steve with _____ wife, Laura.
4. I saw Gary with _____ brother, Tim.
5. I saw Laura with _____ brother, Tim.
6. I saw Sarah and Philip with _____ son, Tim.
7. I saw Laura with _____ parents.
8. I saw Beth and Robert with _____ parents.

61.4 Write *my/our/your/his/her/their/its*.

1. Do you like __your__ job?
2. I know Mr. Watson, but I don't know _____ wife.
3. Alice and Tom live in San Francisco. _____ son lives in Mexico.
4. We're going to have a party. We're going to invite all _____ friends.
5. Anna is going out with _____ friends tonight.
6. I like tennis. It's _____ favorite sport.
7. "Is that _____ car?" "No, I don't have a car."
8. I want to call Maria. Do you know _____ phone number?
9. Do you think most people are happy with _____ jobs?
10. I'm going to wash _____ hair before I go out.
11. This is a beautiful tree. _____ leaves are a beautiful color.
12. John has a brother and a sister. _____ brother is 25, and _____ sister is 21.

61.5 Complete the sentences. Use *my/his/their*, etc. with these words:

coat   homework   house   husband   ~~job~~   key   name

1. Jim doesn't like __his job__ . It's not very interesting.
2. I can't get in. I don't have _____ .
3. Sally is married. _____ works in a bank.
4. Please take off _____ and sit down.
5. "What are the children doing?" "They're doing _____ ."
6. "Do you know that man?" "Yes, but I don't know _____ ."
7. We live on Main Street. _____ is on the corner of Main and First.

Whose is this? It's mine/yours/hers, etc.

A

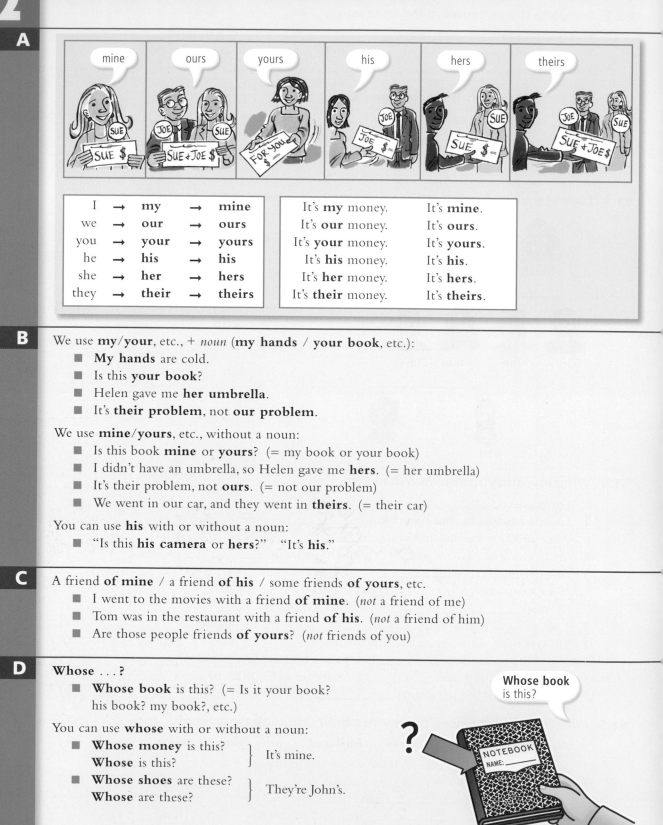

I	→	**my**	→	**mine**	It's **my** money.	It's **mine**.
we	→	**our**	→	**ours**	It's **our** money.	It's **ours**.
you	→	**your**	→	**yours**	It's **your** money.	It's **yours**.
he	→	**his**	→	**his**	It's **his** money.	It's **his**.
she	→	**her**	→	**hers**	It's **her** money.	It's **hers**.
they	→	**their**	→	**theirs**	It's **their** money.	It's **theirs**.

B

We use **my/your**, etc., + *noun* (**my hands / your book**, etc.):

- **My hands** are cold.
- Is this **your book**?
- Helen gave me **her umbrella**.
- It's **their problem**, not **our problem**.

We use **mine/yours**, etc., without a noun:

- Is this book **mine** or **yours**? (= my book or your book)
- I didn't have an umbrella, so Helen gave me **hers**. (= her umbrella)
- It's their problem, not **ours**. (= not our problem)
- We went in our car, and they went in **theirs**. (= their car)

You can use **his** with or without a noun:

- "Is this **his camera** or **hers**?" "It's **his**."

C

A friend **of mine** / a friend **of his** / some friends **of yours**, etc.

- I went to the movies with a friend **of mine**. (*not* a friend of me)
- Tom was in the restaurant with a friend **of his**. (*not* a friend of him)
- Are those people friends **of yours**? (*not* friends of you)

D

Whose . . . ?

- **Whose book** is this? (= Is it your book?
  his book? my book?, etc.)

You can use **whose** with or without a noun:

- **Whose money** is this?
  Whose is this? } It's mine.
- **Whose shoes** are these?
  Whose are these? } They're John's.

> Whose book
> is this?

my/his/their, etc. → Unit 61   I/me/my/mine → Unit 63   Kate's camera / my brother's car → Unit 65

Exercises

62.1 Complete the sentences with *mine/yours*, etc.

1. It's your money. It's __*yours*__ .
2. It's my bag. It's _____ .
3. It's our car. It's _____ .
4. They're her shoes. They're _____ .
5. It's their house. It's _____ .
6. They're your books. They're _____ .
7. They're my glasses. They're _____ .
8. It's his coat. It's _____ .

62.2 Choose the right word.

1. It's their/~~theirs~~ problem, not ~~our~~/ours. (*their* and *ours* are right)
2. This is a nice camera. Is it your/yours?
3. That's not my/mine umbrella. My/Mine is black.
4. Whose books are these? Your/Yours or my/mine?
5. Catherine is going out with her/hers friends tonight.
6. My/Mine room is bigger than her/hers.
7. They've got two children, but I don't know their/theirs names.
8. Can we use your washing machine? Our/Ours isn't working.

62.3 Complete these sentences. Use *friend(s) of mine/yours*, etc.

1. I went to the movies with a __*friend of mine*__ .
2. They went on vacation with some __*friends of theirs*__ .
3. She's going out with a _____ .
4. We had dinner with some _____ .
5. I played tennis with a _____ .
6. Tom is going to meet a _____ .
7. Do you know those people? Are they _____ ?

62.4 Look at the pictures. What are the people saying?

1. __Whose car is this?__   __It's theirs.__
2. _____ is this?   It's _____
3. _____ these?   They _____
4. _____   _____ ?
5. _____ ?   _____
6. _____ ?   _____

I/me/my/mine

I can see him, but he can't see **me**.

You give **me** your phone number, and I'll give you **mine**.

	I, etc. (→ Unit 60)	**me**, etc. (→ Unit 60)	**my**, etc. (→ Unit 61)	**mine**, etc. (→ Unit 62)
	I know Tom.	Tom knows **me**.	It's **my** car.	It's **mine**.
	We know Tom.	Tom knows **us**.	It's **our** car.	It's **ours**.
	You know Tom.	Tom knows **you**.	It's **your** car.	It's **yours**.
	He knows Tom.	Tom knows **him**.	It's **his** car.	It's **his**.
	She knows Tom.	Tom knows **her**.	It's **her** car.	It's **hers**.
	They know Tom.	Tom knows **them**.	It's **their** car.	It's **theirs**.

Study these examples:

- "Do **you** know that man?" "Yes, **I** know **him**, but **I** can't remember **his name**."
- **She** was very happy because **we** invited **her** to stay with **us** at **our house**.
- *A:* Where are the children? Have **you** seen them?
  B: Yes, **they** are playing with **their friends** in the park.
- That's **my pen**. Can you give it to **me**, please?
- "Is this **your hat**?" "No, it's **yours**."
- **He** didn't have an umbrella, so **she** gave **him hers**. (= she gave her umbrella to him)
- **I'm** going out with a friend of **mine** tonight. (*not* a friend of me)

myself/yourself, etc. → Unit 64 **Give me that book / Give it to me** → Unit 97

Exercises

63.1 Answer the questions in the same way.

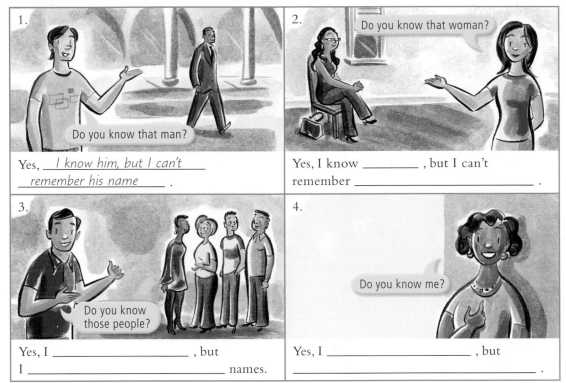

1.

Do you know that man?

Yes, _I know him, but I can't_
remember his name .

2.

Do you know that woman?

Yes, I know _____ , but I can't
remember _____ .

3.

Do you know
those people?

Yes, I _____ , but
I _____ names.

4.

Do you know me?

Yes, I _____ , but
_____ .

63.2 Complete the sentences in the same way.

1. We invited her _to stay with us at our house_ .
2. He invited us to stay with _____ at his house.
3. They invited me to stay with _____ house.
4. I invited them to stay _____ house.
5. She invited us to stay _____ house.
6. Did you invite him _____ house?

63.3 Complete the sentences in the same way.

1. I gave him _my_ address, and _he gave me his_ .
2. I gave her _my_ address, and she gave me _____ .
3. He gave me _his_ address, and I gave _____ .
4. We gave them _____ address, and they gave _____ .
5. She gave him _____ address, and he gave _____ .
6. You gave us _____ address, and we gave _____ .
7. They gave you _____ address, and you gave _____ .

63.4 Write **him/her/yours**, etc.

1. Where's Amanda? Have you seen _her_ ?
2. Where are my keys? Where did I put _____ ?
3. This letter is for Bill. Can you give it to _____ ?
4. We don't see _____ neighbors much. They're not at home very often.
5. "I can't find my pen. Can I use _____ ?" "Sure."
6. We're going to the movies. Why don't you come with _____ ?
7. Did your sister pass _____ driver's test?
8. Some people talk about _____ jobs all the time.
9. Last night I went out for dinner with a friend of _____ .

myself/yourself/themselves, etc.

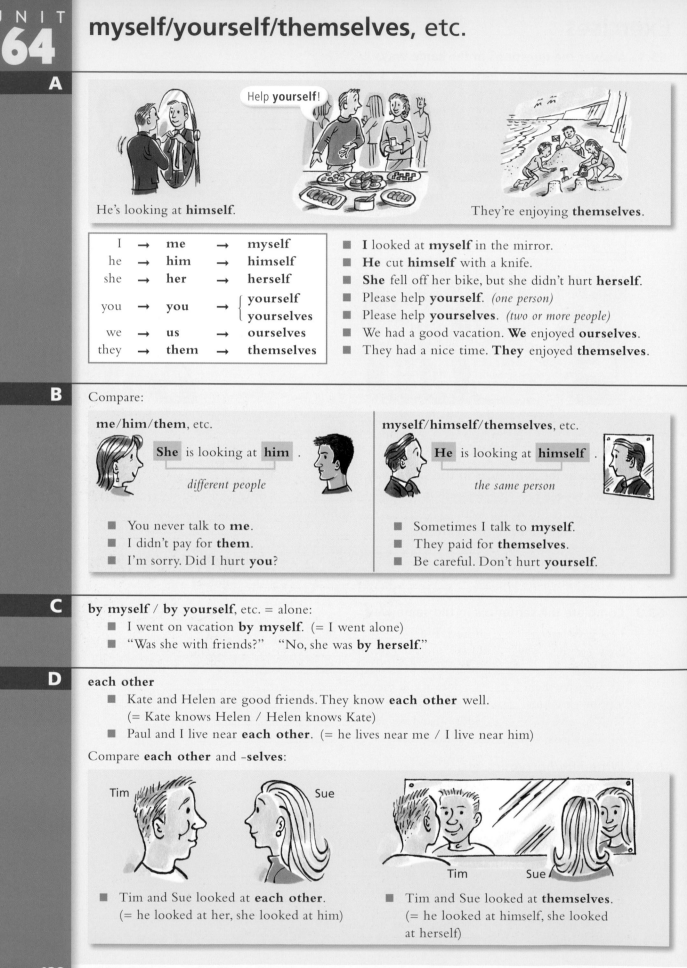

He's looking at **himself**.

Help **yourself**!

They're enjoying **themselves**.

I	→	me	→	myself
he	→	him	→	himself
she	→	her	→	herself
you	→	you	→	yourself / yourselves
we	→	us	→	ourselves
they	→	them	→	themselves

- I looked at **myself** in the mirror.
- **He** cut **himself** with a knife.
- **She** fell off her bike, but she didn't hurt **herself**.
- Please help **yourself**. *(one person)*
- Please help **yourselves**. *(two or more people)*
- We had a good vacation. **We** enjoyed **ourselves**.
- They had a nice time. **They** enjoyed **themselves**.

B

Compare:

me/him/them, etc.

She is looking at **him**.

different people

- You never talk to **me**.
- I didn't pay for **them**.
- I'm sorry. Did I hurt **you**?

myself/himself/themselves, etc.

He is looking at **himself**.

the same person

- Sometimes I talk to **myself**.
- They paid for **themselves**.
- Be careful. Don't hurt **yourself**.

C

by myself / **by yourself**, etc. = alone:

- I went on vacation **by myself**. (= I went alone)
- "Was she with friends?" "No, she was **by herself**."

D

each other

- Kate and Helen are good friends. They know **each other** well.
  (= Kate knows Helen / Helen knows Kate)
- Paul and I live near **each other**. (= he lives near me / I live near him)

Compare **each other** and **–selves**:

Tim Sue

Tim Sue

- Tim and Sue looked at **each other**.
  (= he looked at her, she looked at him)
- Tim and Sue looked at **themselves**.
  (= he looked at himself, she looked at herself)

Exercises

64.1 Complete the sentences with *myself/yourself*, etc.

1. He looked at __*himself*__ in the mirror.
2. I'm not angry with you. I'm angry with _____ .
3. Karen had a good time in Brazil. She enjoyed _____ .
4. My friends had a good time in Brazil. They enjoyed _____ .
5. I picked up a very hot plate and burned _____ .
6. He never thinks about other people. He only thinks about _____ .
7. I want to know more about you. Tell me about _____ . *(one person)*
8. Goodbye! Have a good trip and take care of _____ ! *(two people)*

64.2 Write sentences with *by myself* / *by yourself*, etc.

1. I went on vacation alone.   __*I went on vacation by myself.*__
2. When I saw him, he was alone.   When I saw him, he _____
3. Don't go out alone.   Don't _____
4. I went to the movies alone.   I _____
5. My sister lives alone.   My sister _____
6. Many people live alone.   Many people _____

64.3 Write sentences with *each other*.

1. __*They like each other.*__
2. They can't _____
3. They _____
4. _____
5. _____
6. _____

64.4 Complete the sentences. Use:
each other or **ourselves/yourselves/themselves** or **us/you/them**

1. Paul and I live near __*each other*__ .
2. Who are those people? Do you know __*them*__ ?
3. You can help Tom, and Tom can help you. So you and Tom can help _____ .
4. There's food in the kitchen. If you and Chris are hungry, you can help _____ .
5. We didn't go to Linda's party. She didn't invite _____ .
6. When we go on vacation, we always enjoy _____ .
7. Mary and Jane went to school together, but they never see _____ now.
8. Diane and I are very good friends. We've known _____ for a long time.
9. "Did you see Sam and Laura at the party?"   "Yes, but I didn't speak to _____ ."
10. Many people talk to _____ when they're alone.

-'s (**Kate's** camera / **my brother's** car, etc.)

A

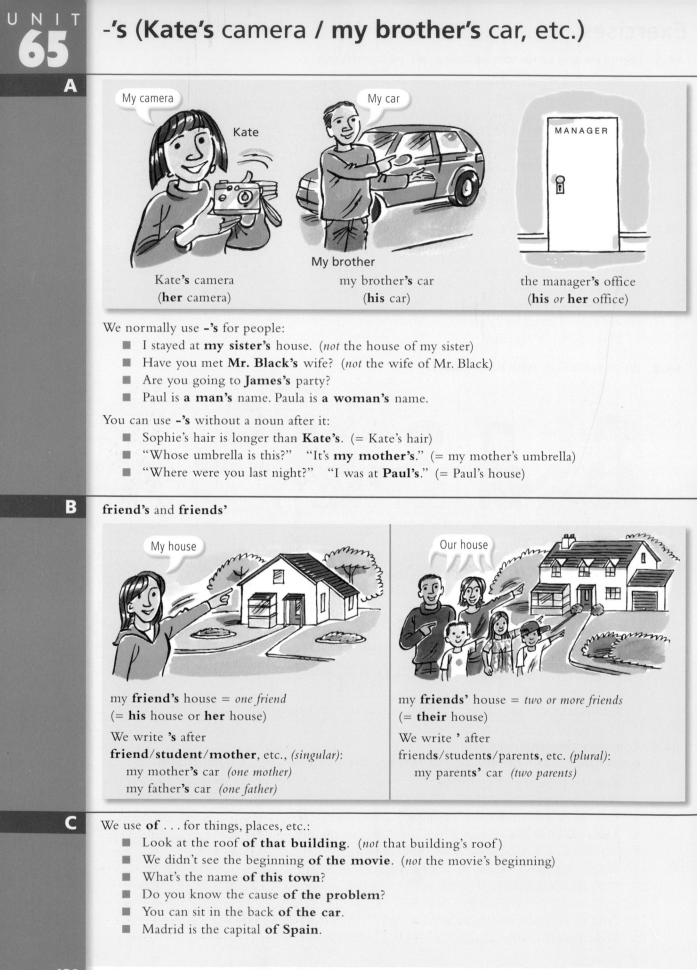

Kate's camera
(**her** camera)

my brother's car
(**his** car)

the manager's office
(**his** or **her** office)

We normally use **–'s** for people:

- I stayed at **my sister's** house. (*not* the house of my sister)
- Have you met **Mr. Black's** wife? (*not* the wife of Mr. Black)
- Are you going to **James's** party?
- Paul is **a man's** name. Paula is **a woman's** name.

You can use **–'s** without a noun after it:

- Sophie's hair is longer than **Kate's**. (= Kate's hair)
- "Whose umbrella is this?"   "It's **my mother's**." (= my mother's umbrella)
- "Where were you last night?"   "I was at **Paul's**." (= Paul's house)

B

friend's and **friends'**

my **friend's** house = *one friend*
(= **his** house or **her** house)

We write **'s** after
friend/student/mother, etc., *(singular)*:

   my mother's car *(one mother)*
   my father's car *(one father)*

my **friends'** house = *two or more friends*
(= **their** house)

We write **'** after
friend**s**/student**s**/parent**s**, etc. *(plural)*:

   my parent**s'** car *(two parents)*

C

We use **of** . . . for things, places, etc.:

- Look at the roof **of that building**. (*not* that building's roof)
- We didn't see the beginning **of the movie**. (*not* the movie's beginning)
- What's the name **of this town**?
- Do you know the cause **of the problem**?
- You can sit in the back **of the car**.
- Madrid is the capital **of Spain**.

mine/yours, etc. → Unit 62   whose . . . ? → Unit 62   -'s (he's / Kate's, etc.) → Appendix 4.5

Exercises

65.1 Look at the family tree. Complete the sentences about the people in the family.

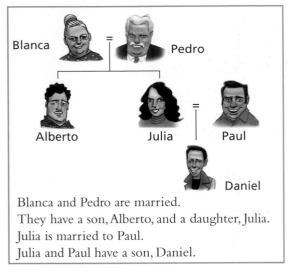

Blanca = Pedro

Alberto   Julia = Paul

Daniel

Blanca and Pedro are married.
They have a son, Alberto, and a daughter, Julia.
Julia is married to Paul.
Julia and Paul have a son, Daniel.

1. Pedro is ___Blanca's___ husband.
2. Julia is Daniel's ___mother___ .
3. Blanca is _____ wife.
4. Alberto is Julia's _____ .
5. Alberto is _____ uncle.
6. Julia is _____ wife.
7. Blanca is Daniel's _____ .
8. Julia is Alberto's _____ .
9. Paul is _____ husband.
10. Paul is Daniel's _____ .
11. Daniel is _____ nephew.

65.2 Look at the pictures and answer the questions. Use one word only.

Jane   Andy   Alice   Diane   Dave

1. Whose is this?
   Alice's

2. Whose is this?
   _____

3. And this?
   _____

4. And these?
   _____

5. And this?
   _____

6. And these?
   _____

65.3 Are these sentences OK? Change them where necessary.

1. I stayed at <u>the house of my sister</u>.   _my sister's house_
2. What is <u>the name of this village</u>?   _OK_
3. Do you like <u>the color of this coat</u>?   _____
4. Do you know <u>the phone number of Simon</u>?   _____
5. <u>The job of my brother</u> is very interesting.   _____
6. Write your name at <u>the top of the page</u>.   _____
7. For me, morning is <u>the best part of the day</u>.   _____
8. <u>The favorite color of Paula</u> is blue.   _____
9. When is <u>the birthday of your mother</u>?   _____
10. <u>The house of my parents</u> isn't very big.   _____
11. <u>The walls of this house</u> are very thin.   _____
12. The car stopped at <u>the end of the street</u>.   _____
13. Are you going to <u>the party of Sylvia</u> next week?   _____
14. <u>The manager of the hotel</u> is not here right now.   _____

a/an

He has **a** camera.

She's waiting for **a** taxi.

It's **a** beautiful day.

a ... = one thing or person:

- Rachel works in **a bank**. (*not* in bank)
- Can I ask **a question**? (*not* ask question)
- I don't have **a computer**.
- There's **a woman** at the bus stop.

an (*not* a) before **a/e/i/o/u**:

- Do you want **an a**pple or **a b**anana?
- I'm going to buy **a h**at and **an u**mbrella.
- There was **an i**nteresting program on TV last night.

also **an hour** (**h** is not pronounced: an hour)
but **a university** (pronounced *yuniversity*)
    a European country (pronounced *yuropean*)

another (= **an** + **other**) is one word:

- Can I have **another** cup of coffee?

We use **a/an** ... when we say what a thing or a person is. For example:

- The sun is **a star**.
- Football is **a game**.
- Dallas is **a city in Texas**.
- A mouse is **an animal**. It's **a small animal**.
- Joe is **a very nice person**.

We use **a/an** ... for jobs, etc.:

- *A:* What do you do?
  B: I'm **a dentist**. (*not* I'm dentist)
- "What does Mark do?"   "He's **an engineer**."
- Would you like to be **a teacher**?
- Beethoven was **a composer**.
- Picasso was **a famous painter**.
- Are you **a student**?

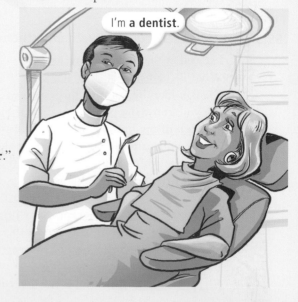

I'm **a dentist**.

a bottle / some water (countable/uncountable) → Units 68–69   **a/an** and **the** → Unit 70

Exercises

66.1 Write *a* or *an*.

1. __an__ old book
2. _____ window
3. _____ horse
4. _____ airport
5. _____ new airport
6. _____ organization
7. _____ university
8. _____ hour
9. _____ economic problem

66.2 What are these things? Choose from the box.

~~bird~~	flower	fruit	game	mountain
planet	river	tool	vegetable	musical instrument

1. A duck is __a bird__ .
2. A carrot is _____ .
3. Tennis is _____ .
4. A hammer is _____ .
5. Everest is _____ .
6. Saturn is _____ .
7. A banana is _____ .
8. The Amazon is _____ .
9. A rose is _____ .
10. A trumpet is _____ .

66.3 What are their jobs? Choose from the box and complete the sentences.

architect	~~dentist~~	electrician	nurse
photographer	sales clerk	taxi driver	

Can I help you?

1. __She's a dentist.__
2. He's _____
3. She _____
4. _____
5. _____
6. _____
7. _____
8. And you? I'm _____

66.4 Write sentences. Choose from the two boxes. Use *a/an* where necessary.

~~I want to ask you~~	Rebecca works in		old house	artist
Tom never wears	Jane wants to learn	+	party	~~question~~
I can't ride	Mike lives in		office	foreign language
My brother is	Tonight I'm going to		hat	bicycle

1. __I want to ask you a question.__
2. _____
3. _____
4. _____
5. _____
6. _____
7. _____
8. _____

train(s) bus(es) (singular and plural)

The plural of a noun is usually **-s**:

singular (= one)	→	*plural* (= two or more)
a flower	→	some **flowers**
a train	→	two **trains**
one week	→	a few **weeks**
a nice place	→	some nice **places**
this student	→	these **students**

a flower   some **flowers**

Spelling (see Appendix 5):

-s / -sh / -ch / -x → -es	bus → bu**ses**	dish → di**shes**
	church → chur**ches**	box → bo**xes**
also	potato → potato**es**	tomato → tomato**es**
-y → -ies	ba**by** → ba**bies**	dictiona**ry** → dictiona**ries**
	par**ty** → par**ties**	
but -**ay** / -**ey** / -**oy** → -**ys**	d**ay** → d**ays**	monk**ey** → monk**eys**	b**oy** → b**oys**
-**f** / -**fe** → -**ves**	shel**f** → shel**ves**	kni**fe** → kni**ves**	wi**fe** → wi**ves**

These things are plural in English:

scissors   glasses   pants   jeans   shorts   tights   pajamas

- Do you wear **glasses**?
- Where **are** the **scissors**? I need **them**.

You can also say **a pair of scissors** / **a pair of pants** / **a pair of pajamas**, etc.:
- I need **a** new **pair of jeans**. *or* I need **some** new **jeans**. (*not* a new jeans)

Some plurals do *not* end in **-s**:

this **man** → these **men**	one **foot** → two **feet**	that **sheep** → those **sheep**
a **woman** → some **women**	a **tooth** → all my **teeth**	a **fish** → a lot of **fish**
a **child** → many **children**	a **mouse** → some **mice**	

also a **person** → **two people** / **some people** / **a lot of people**, etc.:
- **She**'s a nice **person**.
but - **They** are nice **people**. (*not* nice persons)

People is plural (= they), so we say **people are** / **people have**, etc.:
- **A lot of people speak** English. (*not* speaks)
- I like **the people** here. **They are** very friendly.

Police is plural:
- **The police want** to talk to anybody who saw the accident. (*not* The police wants)

Exercises

67.1 Write the plural.

1. flower   _flowers_   5. umbrella _____   9. family _____
2. boat   _____   6. address _____   10. foot _____
3. woman _____   7. knife _____   11. holiday _____
4. city _____   8. sandwich _____   12. potato _____

67.2 Look at the pictures and complete the sentences.

1. There are a lot of ___sheep___ in the field.   4. Lucy has two _____ .
2. Gary is brushing his _____ .   5. There are a lot of _____ in the river.
3. There are three _____ at the bus stop.   6. The _____ are falling from the tree.

67.3 Are these sentences OK? Change the sentences where necessary.

1. I'm going to buy some flowers.   _OK_ _____
2. I need a new jeans.   _I need a new pair of jeans._ _____ OR
   I need some new jeans. _____
3. It's a lovely park with a lot of beautiful tree.   _____
4. There was a woman in the car with two mens.   _____
5. Sheep eat grass.   _____
6. David is married and has three childs.   _____
7. Most of my friend are student.   _____
8. He put on his pajama and went to bed.   _____
9. We went fishing, but we didn't catch many fish.   _____
10. Do you know many persons in this town?   _____
11. I like your pant. Where did you get it?   _____
12. Montreal is usually full of tourist.   _____
13. I don't like mice. I'm afraid of them.   _____
14. This scissor isn't very sharp.   _____

67.4 Which is right? Complete the sentences.

1. It's a nice place. Many people ___go___ there on vacation.   **go** _or_ **goes**?
2. Some people _____ always late.   **is** _or_ **are**?
3. The new city hall is not a very beautiful building. Most
   people _____ like it.   **don't** _or_ **doesn't**?
4. A lot of people _____ television every day.   **watch** _or_ **watches**?
5. Three people _____ injured in the accident.   **was** _or_ **were**?
6. How many people _____ in that house?   **live** _or_ **lives**?
7. _____ the police know the cause of the explosion?   **Do** _or_ **Does**?
8. The police _____ looking for the stolen car.   **is** _or_ **are**?
9. I need my glasses, but I can't find _____ .   **it** _or_ **them**?
10. I'm going to buy _____ new jeans today.   **a** _or_ **some**?

135

a bottle / some water
(countable/uncountable 1)

A

A noun can be *countable* or *uncountable*.

Countable nouns

For example: (a) **car**   (a) **man**   (a) **bottle**   (a) **house**   (a) **key**   (an) **idea**   (an) **accident**

You can use **one/two/three**, etc. + *countable nouns* (you can count them):

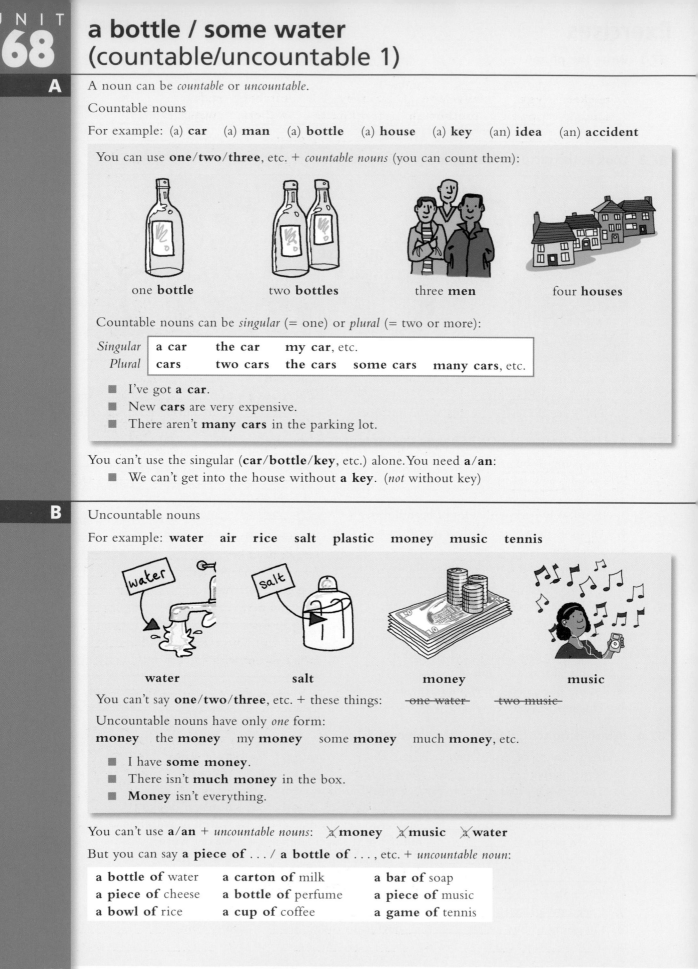

one **bottle**   two **bottles**   three **men**   four **houses**

Countable nouns can be *singular* (= one) or *plural* (= two or more):

Singular	**a car**	**the car**	**my car**, etc.	
Plural	**cars**	**two cars**	**the cars** **some cars** **many cars**, etc.	

- I've got **a car**.
- New **cars** are very expensive.
- There aren't **many cars** in the parking lot.

You can't use the singular (**car/bottle/key**, etc.) alone. You need **a/an**:

- We can't get into the house without **a key**. (*not* without key)

B

Uncountable nouns

For example: **water   air   rice   salt   plastic   money   music   tennis**

water   salt   money   music

You can't say **one/two/three**, etc. + these things: ~~one water~~   ~~two music~~

Uncountable nouns have only *one* form:

money   the **money**   my **money**   some **money**   much **money**, etc.

- I have **some money**.
- There isn't **much money** in the box.
- **Money** isn't everything.

You can't use **a/an** + *uncountable nouns*:   ✗**money**   ✗**music**   ✗**water**

But you can say **a piece of** . . . / **a bottle of** . . . , etc. + *uncountable noun*:

a bottle of water	**a carton of** milk	**a bar of** soap
a piece of cheese	**a bottle of** perfume	**a piece of** music
a bowl of rice	**a cup of** coffee	**a game of** tennis

a/an → Unit 66   countable/uncountable 2 → Unit 69

Exercises

68.1 What are these things? Some are countable and some are uncountable. Write *a/an* if necessary. The names of these things are:

bucket   egg   envelope   money   pitcher   ~~salt~~
sand   ~~spoon~~   toothbrush   toothpaste   wallet   water

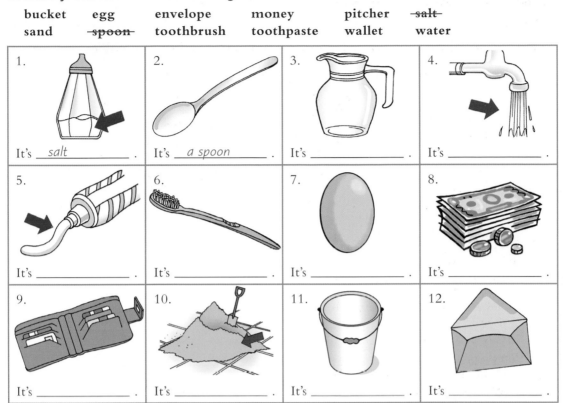

1. It's __salt__ .
2. It's __a spoon__ .
3. It's _____ .
4. It's _____ .
5. It's _____ .
6. It's _____ .
7. It's _____ .
8. It's _____ .
9. It's _____ .
10. It's _____ .
11. It's _____ .
12. It's _____ .

68.2 Some of these sentences are OK, but some need *a/an*. Write *a/an* where necessary.

1. I don't have watch. __a watch__
2. Do you like cheese? __OK__
3. I never wear hat. _____
4. Are you looking for job? _____
5. Kate doesn't eat meat. _____
6. Kate eats apple every day. _____
7. I'm going to party tonight. _____
8. Music is wonderful thing. _____
9. Jamaica is island. _____
10. I don't need key. _____
11. Everybody needs food. _____
12. I've got good idea. _____
13. Can you drive car? _____
14. Do you want cup of coffee? _____
15. I don't like coffee without milk. _____
16. Don't go out without coat. _____

68.3 What are these things? Write *a . . . of . . .* for each picture. Use the words in the boxes.

bar	bowl	~~carton~~		bread	honey	~~milk~~
cup	glass	jar	+	paper	soap	soup
loaf	piece	piece		tea	water	wood

1. __a carton of milk__
2. _____
3. _____
4. _____
5. _____
6. _____
7. _____
8. _____
9. _____

a cake / some cake / some cakes
(countable/uncountable 2)

A   a/an and some

> **a/an** + *singular countable nouns* (**car/apple/shoe**, etc.):
> - I need **a** new **car**.
> - Would you like **an** apple?
>
> **some** + *plural countable nouns* (**cars/apples/shoes**, etc.):
> - I need **some** new **shoes**.
> - Would you like **some apples**?
>
> **some** + *uncountable nouns* (**water/money/music**, etc.):
> - I need **some water**.
> - Would you like **some cheese**?
>   (*or* Would you like **a piece of** cheese?)

an apple

some apples

some cheese *or*
a piece of cheese

Compare **a** and **some**:
- Nicole bought **a hat**, **some shoes**, and **some perfume**.
- I read **a newspaper**, made **some phone calls**, and listened to **some music**.

B   Many nouns are sometimes countable and sometimes uncountable. For example:

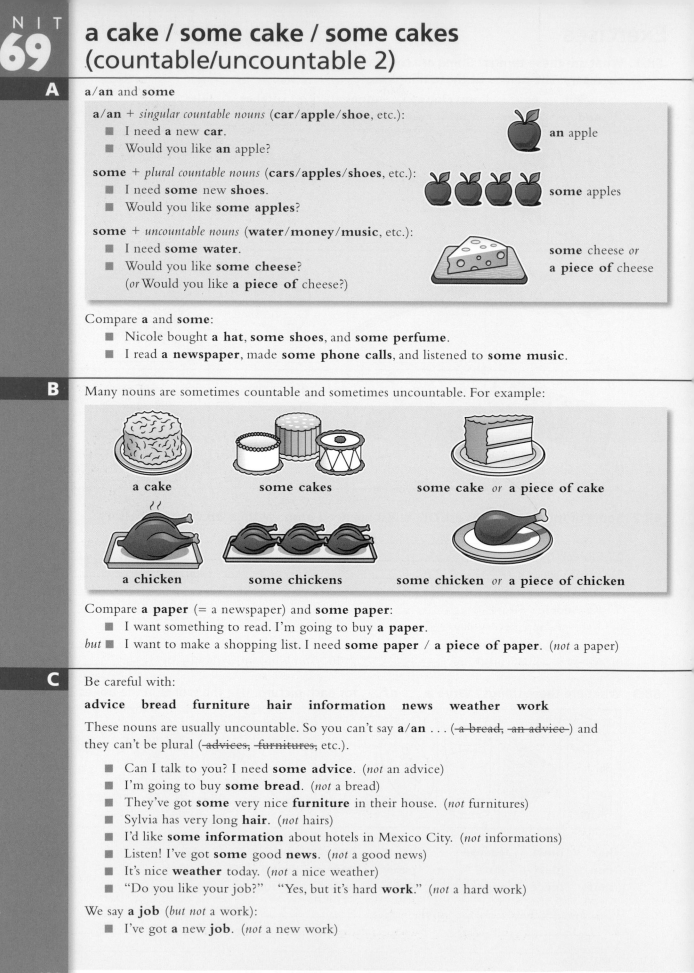

a cake   some cakes   some cake *or* a piece of cake

a chicken   some chickens   some chicken *or* a piece of chicken

Compare **a paper** (= a newspaper) and **some paper**:
- I want something to read. I'm going to buy **a paper**.

but - I want to make a shopping list. I need **some paper** / **a piece of paper**. (*not* a paper)

C   Be careful with:

advice   bread   furniture   hair   information   news   weather   work

These nouns are usually uncountable. So you can't say **a/an** . . . (~~a bread~~, ~~an advice~~) and they can't be plural (~~advices~~, ~~furnitures~~, etc.).

- Can I talk to you? I need **some advice**. (*not* an advice)
- I'm going to buy **some bread**. (*not* a bread)
- They've got **some** very nice **furniture** in their house. (*not* furnitures)
- Sylvia has very long **hair**. (*not* hairs)
- I'd like **some information** about hotels in Mexico City. (*not* informations)
- Listen! I've got **some** good **news**. (*not* a good news)
- It's nice **weather** today. (*not* a nice weather)
- "Do you like your job?"   "Yes, but it's hard **work**." (*not* a hard work)

We say **a job** (*but not* a work):
- I've got **a new job**. (*not* a new work)

Exercises

69.1 What did you buy? Use the pictures to write sentences (*I bought* . . .).

1. _____I bought some perfume, a hat, and some shoes._____
2. I bought _____
3. _____
4. _____

69.2 Write sentences with *Would you like a* . . . ? or *Would you like some* . . . ?

1. _____Would you like some cheese_____ ?   4. _____ ?
2. Would you like _____ ?   5. _____ ?
3. Would _____ ?   6. _____ ?

69.3 Write *a/an* or *some*.

1. I read __*a*__ book and listened to __*some*__ music.
2. I need _____ money. I want to buy _____ food.
3. We met _____ interesting people at the party.
4. I'm going to open _____ window to get _____ fresh air.
5. Rachel didn't eat much for lunch – only _____ apple and _____ bread.
6. We live in _____ big house. There's _____ nice yard with _____ beautiful trees.
7. I'm going to make a table. First I need _____ wood.
8. Listen to me carefully. I'm going to give you _____ advice.
9. I want to write a letter. I need _____ paper and _____ pen.

69.4 Which is right?

1. I'm going to buy some new ~~shoe~~ / shoes. (*shoes* is right)
2. Mark has brown eye / eyes.
3. Paula has short black hair / hairs.
4. The tour guide gave us some information / informations about the city.
5. We're going to buy some new chair / chairs.
6. We're going to buy some new furniture / furnitures.
7. It's hard to find a work / job these days.
8. We had wonderful weather / a wonderful weather when we were on vacation.

a/an and the

a/an

There are *three* windows here.
a window = window 1 or 2 or 3

- I have **a car**.
  (there are many cars and I have one)
- Can I ask **a question**?
  (there are many questions – can I ask one?)
- Is there **a hotel** near here? (there are many hotels – is there one near here?)
- Paris is **an interesting city**. (there are many interesting cities and Paris is one)
- Lisa is **a student**.
  (there are many students and Lisa is one)

the

Can you open **the** window?

There is only *one* window here –
the window.

- I'm going to wash **the car** tomorrow.
  (= my car)
- Can you repeat **the question**, please?
  (= the question that you asked)
- We enjoyed our vacation. **The hotel** was very nice. (= our hotel)
- Paris is **the capital of France**.
  (there is only one capital of France)
- Lisa is **the youngest student** in her class. (there is only one youngest student in her class)

Compare **a** and **the**:

- I bought **a jacket** and **a shirt** . **The jacket** was cheap, but **the shirt** was expensive.

  (= **the** jacket and **the** shirt **that I bought**)

We say **the** . . . when it is clear which thing or person we mean. For example:

the door / **the ceiling** / **the floor** / **the carpet** / **the light**, etc. *(of a room)*
the roof / **the backyard** / **the kitchen** / **the bathroom**, etc. *(of a house)*
the airport / **the police station** / **the bus station** / **the mayor's office**, etc. *(of a city)*

- "Where's Tom?" "In **the kitchen**."
  (= the kitchen of this house or apartment)
- Turn off **the light** and close **the door**.
  (= the light and the door of the room)
- Do you live far from **the airport**?
  (= the airport of your town)
- I'd like to speak to **the manager**, please.
  (= the manager of this store, etc.)

the ceiling

the light

the door

the floor

Exercises

70.1 Write *a/an* or *the*.

1. We enjoyed our trip. __*The*__ hotel was very nice.
2. "Can I ask __*a*__ question?" "Sure. What do you want to know?"
3. You look very tired. You need _____ vacation.
4. "Where's Tom?" "He's in _____ kitchen."
5. Eve is _____ interesting person. You should meet her.
6. *A:* Excuse me, can you tell me how to get to _____ post office?
   B: Yes, go straight and then take _____ next left.
7. *A:* Let's go and see _____ movie tonight.
   B: OK, that's _____ good idea.
8. It's _____ nice morning. Let's go for _____ walk.
9. Amanda is _____ student. When she finishes school, she wants to be _____ journalist.
   She lives with two friends in _____ apartment near _____ college where she is
   studying. _____ apartment is small, but she likes it.
10. Peter and Mary have two children, _____ boy and _____ girl. _____ boy is seven
    years old, and _____ girl is three. Peter works in _____ factory. Mary doesn't have
    _____ job outside the home right now.

70.2 Complete the sentences. Use *a* or *the* + these words:

airport   cup   dictionary   ~~door~~   floor   picture

1. Can you open *the door* , please?
2. How far is it to _____ _____ ?
3. Can I have _____ of coffee, please?
4. That's _____ nice _____ – I like it.
5. Can you pass me _____ _____ , please?
6. Why are you sitting on _____ ?

70.3 These sentences are not correct. Put in *a/an* or *the* where necessary.

1. Don't forget to turn off light when you go out.   *turn off the light*
2. Enjoy your trip, and don't forget to send me postcard.   _____
3. What is name of this town?   _____
4. Canada is very big country.   _____
5. What is largest city in Canada?   _____
6. I like this room, but I don't like color of carpet.   _____
7. "Are you OK?" "No, I've got headache."   _____
8. We live in old house near station.   _____
9. What is name of director of movie we saw last night?   _____

UNIT 71

the . . .

A

We use **the** when it is clear which thing or person we mean:

- What is **the name** of this street? (there is only one name)
- Who is **the best player** on your team? (there is only one best player)
- Can you tell me **the time**, please? (= the time *now*)
- My office is on **the first floor**. (= the first floor of the building)

Don't forget **the**:

- Do you live near **the airport**? (*not* near airport)
- Excuse me, where is **the nearest bank**? (*not* where is nearest . . .)

B

the same . . .

- We live on **the same street**. (*not* on same street)
- "Are these two books different?" "No, they're **the same**." (*not* they're same)

C

We say:

the sun / the moon / the world / the sky / the ocean / the country

- **The sky** is blue and **the sun** is shining.
- Do you live in a city or in **the country**?

the police / the fire department / the army (of a city, country, etc.)

- My brother is a soldier. He's in **the army**.
- What do you think of **the police**? Do they do a good job?

the top / the end / the middle / the left, etc.

- Write your name at **the top of** the page.
- My house is at **the end of** this block.
- The table is in **the middle of** the room.
- Do you drive on **the right** or on **the left** in your country?

the top

| the left | the middle | the right |

the bottom

(play) the piano / the guitar / the trumpet, etc. (musical instruments)

- Paula is learning to play **the piano**.

the radio

- I listen to **the radio** a lot.

the Internet

- Do you use **the Internet** much?

D

We do *not* use **the** with:

television/TV

- I watch **TV** a lot.
- What's on **television** tonight?

but Can you turn off **the television**? (= the TV set)

breakfast/lunch/dinner

- What did you have for **breakfast**? (*not* the breakfast)
- **Dinner** is ready!

next/last + week/month/year/summer/Monday, etc.

- I'm not working **next week**. (*not* the next week)
- Did you take a vacation **last summer**? (*not* the last summer)

a/an and the → Unit 70   the → Units 72–74   the oldest / the most expensive, etc. → Unit 91

Exercises

71.1 Put in **the** where necessary. Write **OK** if the sentence is already correct.

1. What is name of this street?   *the name*
2. What's on television tonight?   *OK*
3. Our apartment is on second floor.   _____
4. Would you like to go to moon?   _____
5. What is best hotel in this town?   _____
6. What time is lunch?   _____
7. How far is it to football stadium?   _____
8. We're taking a trip at end of May.   _____
9. What are you doing next weekend?   _____
10. I didn't like her first time I met her.   _____
11. I'm going out after dinner.   _____
12. Internet is a good place to get information.   _____
13. My sister got married last month.   _____
14. My dictionary is on top shelf on right.   _____
15. We live in country about 10 miles from nearest town.   _____

71.2 Complete the sentences. Use **the same** + these words:

    age   **color**   **problem**   ~~**street**~~   **time**

1. I live on North Street, and you live on North Street. We live on ___*the same street*___ .
2. I arrived at 8:30, and you arrived at 8:30. We arrived at _____ .
3. Jim is 25, and Sue is 25. Jim and Sue are _____ .
4. My shirt is dark blue, and so is my jacket. My shirt and jacket are _____ .
5. I have no money, and you have no money. We have _____ .

71.3 Look at the pictures and complete the sentences. Use **the** if necessary.

1. ___*The sun*___ is shining.
2. She's playing _____ .
3. They're having _____ .
4. He's watching _____ .
5. They're swimming in _____ .
6. Tim's name is at _____ of the list.

71.4 Complete these sentences. Choose from the list. Use **the** if necessary.

    capital   ~~**dinner**~~   **lunch**   **middle**   **name**   **police**   **sky**   **television**

1. We had ___*dinner*___ at a restaurant last night.
2. We stayed at a very nice hotel, but I don't remember _____ .
3. _____ is very clear tonight. You can see all the stars.
4. Sometimes there are some good programs on _____ late at night.
5. _____ stopped me because I was driving too fast.
6. Tokyo is _____ of Japan.
7. "What did you have for _____ ?" "A salad."
8. I woke up in _____ of the night.

go to work   go home   go to the movies

She's **at work**.   They're going **to school**.   He's **in bed**.

We say:

(go) **to work**, (be) **at work**, start **work**, finish **work**
- Bye! I'm **going to work** now. (*not* to the work)
- I **finish work** at 5:00 every day.

(go) **to school**, (be) **at school**, start **school**, finish **school**, etc.
- What did you learn **at school** today? (*not* at the school)
- Some children don't like **school**.

(go) **to college**, (be) **in college**
- Helen wants to **go to college** when she **finishes high school**.
- What did you study **in college**?

(go) **to class**, (be) **in class**
- I can't talk now. I have to **go to class**.
- I'll **be in class** until 5:00 today. I'll call you when I get out.

(go) **to prison/jail**, (be) **in prison/jail**
- Why is he **in prison**? What did he do?

(go) **to church**, (be) **in/at church**
- David usually goes **to church** on Sundays.

(go) **to bed**, (be) **in bed**
- I'm tired. I'm **going to bed**. (*not* to the bed)
- "Where's Jane?"   "She's **in bed**."

(go) **home**, (be) **(at) home**, etc.
- I'm tired. I'm **going home**. (*not* to home)
- Are you going out tonight, or are you **staying home**? (*or* **staying at home**)

B   We say:

(go to) **the movies / the theater / the bank / the post office / the hospital / the station / the airport**
- I never go to **the theater**, but I go to **the movies** a lot.
- "Are you going to **the bank**?"   "No, to **the post office**."
- The number 5 bus goes to **the airport**; the number 8 goes to **the train station**.

(go to) **the doctor**, **the dentist**
- You're not well. Why don't you go to **the doctor**?
- I have to go to **the dentist** tomorrow.

Exercises

72.1 **Where are these people? Complete the sentences. Sometimes you need *the*.**

1. He's in __bed__ .   3. She's in _____ .   5. They're at _____ .
2. They're at _____ .   4. She's at _____ .   6. He's in _____ .

72.2 **Complete the sentences. Choose from the list. Use *the* if necessary.**

~~bank~~   bed   ~~church~~   home   post office   school   station

1. I need to get some money. I have to go to __the bank__ .
2. David usually goes to __church__ on Sundays.
3. In the United States, children start _____ at the age of five.
4. There were a lot of people at _____ waiting for the train.
5. I called you last night, but you weren't at _____ .
6. I'm going to _____ now. Good night!
7. I'm going to _____ to get some stamps.

72.3 **Complete the sentences. Sometimes you need *the*.**

1. If you want to catch a plane, you __go to the airport__ .
2. If you want to see a movie, you go to _____ .
3. If you are tired and you want to sleep, you _____ .
4. If you rob a bank and the police catch you, you _____ .
5. If you have a problem with your teeth, you _____ .
6. If you want to study after you finish high school, you _____ .
7. If you are badly injured in an accident, you _____ .

72.4 **Are these sentences OK? Correct the sentences where necessary.**

1. We went to movies last night.   __to the movies__
2. I finish work at 5:00 every day.   __OK__
3. Lisa wasn't feeling well yesterday, so she went to doctor.   _____
4. I wasn't feeling well this morning, so I stayed in bed.   _____
5. Why is Angela always late for work?   _____
6. "Where are your children?" "They're at school."   _____
7. We have no money in bank.   _____
8. When I was younger, I went to church every Sunday.   _____
9. What time do you usually get home from work?   _____
10. Sorry I couldn't call you back earlier. I was in class.   _____
11. "Where should we meet?" "At station."   _____
12. Kate takes her children to school every day.   _____
13. Jim is sick. He's in hospital.   _____
14. Would you like to go to college?   _____
15. Would you like to go to theater tonight?   _____

I like **music**.   I hate **exams**.

Do not use **the** for general ideas:

- I like **music**, especially **classical music**.
  (*not* the music . . . the classical music)
- We don't eat **meat** very often. (*not* the meat)
- **Life** is not possible without **water**.
  (*not* The life . . . the water)
- I hate **exams**. (*not* the exams)
- Do you know where I can buy **foreign newspapers**?
- I'm not very good at writing **letters**.

Do not use **the** for games and sports:

- My favorite sports are **tennis** and **skiing**. (*not* the tennis . . . the skiing)

Do not use **the** for languages or school subjects (**history/geography/physics/biology**, etc.):

- Do you think **English** is difficult? (*not* the English)
- Tom's brother is studying **physics** and **chemistry**.

flowers or **the flowers**?

Compare:

- **Flowers** are beautiful.
  (= flowers in general)

- I don't like **cold weather**.
  (= cold weather in general)

- We don't eat **fish** very
  often. (= fish in general)

- Are you interested
  in **history**?
  (= history in general)

- I love your garden.
  The flowers are beautiful.
  (= the flowers in your
  garden)

- **The weather** isn't very
  good today.
  (= the weather today)

- We had a great meal last
  night. **The fish** was
  excellent.
  (= the fish we ate last
  night)

- Do you know much
  about **the history** of
  your country?

The flowers
are beautiful.

Exercises

73.1 What do you think about these things?

big cities	chocolate	computer games	dogs	exams
housework	jazz	museums	parties	tennis

Choose seven of these things and write sentences with:

I like . . .   I don't like . . .   I love . . .   I hate . . .   . . . is/are all right

1. _I hate exams._ OR _I like exams._ OR _Exams are all right. (etc)_
2. _____
3. _____
4. _____
5. _____
6. _____
7. _____
8. _____

73.2 Are you interested in these things? Write sentences with:

I'm (very) interested in . . .   I know a lot about . . .   I don't know much about . . .
I'm not interested in . . .   I know a little about . . .   I don't know anything about . . .

1. (history) _I'm very interested in history._
2. (politics) I _____
3. (sports) _____
4. (art) _____
5. (astronomy) _____
6. (economics) _____

73.3 Which is right?

1. My favorite sport is football / ~~the football.~~ (*football* is right)
2. I like this hotel. ~~Rooms~~ / The rooms are very nice. (*The rooms* is right)
3. Everybody needs friends / the friends.
4. Jane doesn't go to parties / the parties very often.
5. I went shopping at the mall this morning. Stores / The stores were very crowded.
6. "Where's milk / the milk?" "It's in the fridge."
7. I don't like milk / the milk. I never drink it.
8. "Do you play any sports?" "Yes, I play basketball / the basketball."
9. "What does your brother do?" "He sells computers / the computers."
10. We went for a swim in the river. Water / The water was very cold.
11. I don't like swimming in cold water / the cold water.
12. Excuse me, can you pass salt / the salt, please?
13. I like this town. I like people / the people here.
14. Vegetables / The vegetables are good for you.
15. Houses / The houses on this street are all the same.
16. I can't sing this song. I don't know words / the words.
17. I enjoy taking pictures / the pictures. It's my hobby.
18. Do you want to see pictures / the pictures that I took when I was on vacation?
19. English / The English is used a lot in international business / the international business.
20. Money / The money doesn't always bring happiness / the happiness.

the . . . (names of places)

A

Places (continents, countries, states, islands, towns, etc.)

In general we do *not* use **the** with names of places:

- **Quebec** is a province of **Canada**.
- **Bangkok** is the capital of **Thailand**.
- **Hawaii** is an island in the Pacific.
- **Peru** is in **South America**.

But we use **the** in names with **republic/states/kingdom**:

the Dominican **Republic**
the Czech **Republic**
the United **States** of America (**the** USA)
the United **Kingdom** (**the** UK)

B

the -s (plural names)

We use **the** with *plural* names of countries/islands/mountains:

the Netherlands   the Hawaiian Islands
the Philippines   the Andes

C

Seas, rivers, etc.

We use **the** with names of oceans/seas/rivers/canals:

the Atlantic (Ocean)   the Mediterranean (Sea)   the Amazon
the Nile (River)   the Panama Canal   the Black (Sea)

D

Places in towns (streets, buildings, etc.)

In general we do *not* use **the** with names of streets, squares, etc.:

- Kevin lives on **Central Avenue**.
- Where is **Main Street**, please?
- **Times Square** is in New York.

We do not use **the** with names of airports, stations, universities, and parks.

O'Hare International Airport   **Harvard University**
Pennsylvania Station   **Yosemite** (National Park)

But we use **the** with names of most hotels, museums, theaters, and monuments:

the Regent Hotel   the National Theater
the Metropolitan (Museum)   the Odeon (movie theater)
the Taj Mahal   the Lincoln Memorial

E

the . . . of . . .

We use **the** + names with **. . . of . . .** :

the Museum **of** Modern Art   the University **of** California
the Great Wall **of** China   the Statue **of** Liberty

We say **the north / the south / the east / the west** (of . . .):

- I've been to **the north of Italy**, but not to **the south**.

Exercises

74.1 Answer these geography questions. Choose from the box. Use *The* if necessary.

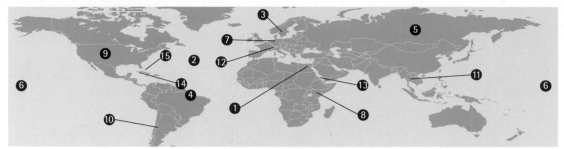

1. _Cairo_ _____ is the capital of Egypt.
2. _The Atlantic_ _____ is between Africa and America.
3. _____ is a country in northern Europe.
4. _____ is a river in South America.
5. _____ is the largest continent in the world.
6. _____ is the largest ocean.
7. _____ is a river in Europe.
8. _____ is a country in East Africa.
9. _____ is between Canada and Mexico.
10. _____ are mountains in South America.
11. _____ is the capital of Thailand.
12. _____ are mountains in central Europe.
13. _____ is between Saudi Arabia and Africa.
14. _____ is an island in the Caribbean.
15. _____ are a group of islands near Florida.

Alps
Amazon
Andes
Asia
~~**Atlantic**~~
Bahamas
Bangkok
~~**Cairo**~~
Jamaica
Kenya
Pacific
Red Sea
Rhine
Sweden
United States

74.2 Write *the* where necessary. If the sentence is already correct, write *OK*.

1. Kevin lives on Central Avenue. _OK_ _____
2. We went to see a play at National Theater. _at the National Theater_ _____
3. Have you ever been to China? _____
4. Have you ever been to Philippines? _____
5. Have you ever been to south of France? _____
6. Can you tell me where Washington Monument is? _____
7. Can you tell me where Hollywood Boulevard is? _____
8. Can you tell me where Museum of Art is? _____
9. Europe is bigger than Australia. _____
10. Belgium is smaller than Netherlands. _____
11. Which river is longer – Mississippi or Nile? _____
12. Did you go to National Gallery when you were in Washington? _____
13. We stayed at Park Hotel near Central Park. _____
14. How far is it from Times Square to Kennedy Airport? _____
15. Rocky Mountains are in North America. _____
16. Texas is famous for oil and cowboys. _____
17. I hope to go to United Kingdom next year. _____
18. Mary comes from west of Ireland. _____
19. Alan is a student at University of Michigan. _____
20. Panama Canal joins Atlantic Ocean and Pacific Ocean. _____

→ **Additional exercises 33–34** (pages 261–262)

this/that/these/those

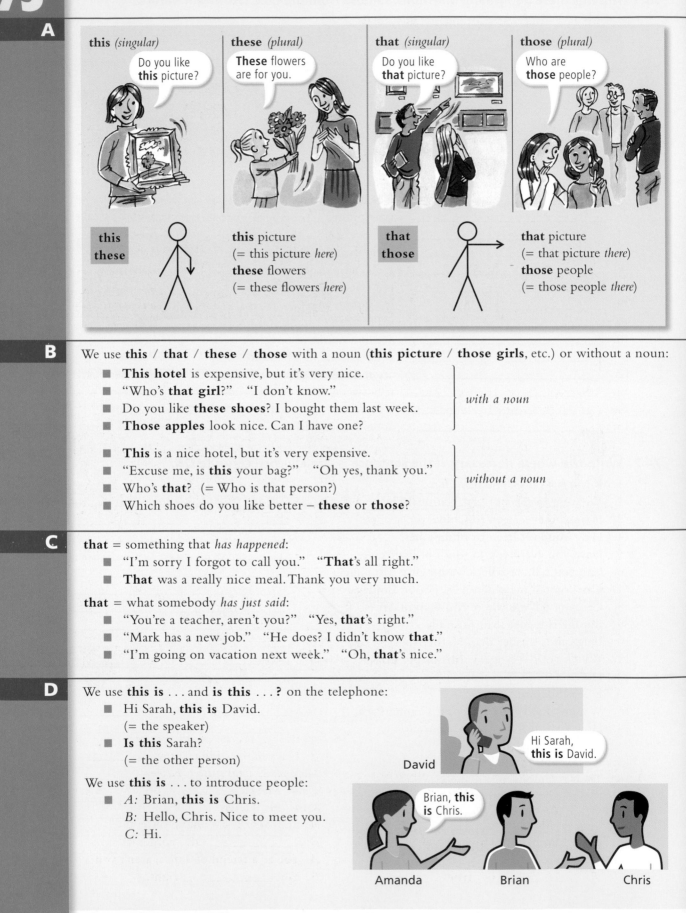

this (singular)

Do you like **this** picture?

these (plural)

These flowers are for you.

that (singular)

Do you like **that** picture?

those (plural)

Who are **those** people?

| this these |

this picture
(= this picture *here*)
these flowers
(= these flowers *here*)

| that those |

that picture
(= that picture *there*)
those people
(= those people *there*)

B

We use **this / that / these / those** with a noun (**this picture / those girls**, etc.) or without a noun:

- **This hotel** is expensive, but it's very nice.
- "Who's **that girl**?"   "I don't know."
- Do you like **these shoes**? I bought them last week.
- **Those apples** look nice. Can I have one?

} *with a noun*

- **This** is a nice hotel, but it's very expensive.
- "Excuse me, is **this** your bag?"   "Oh yes, thank you."
- Who's **that**? (= Who is that person?)
- Which shoes do you like better – **these** or **those**?

} *without a noun*

C

that = something that *has happened*:

- "I'm sorry I forgot to call you."   "**That**'s all right."
- **That** was a really nice meal. Thank you very much.

that = what somebody *has just said*:

- "You're a teacher, aren't you?"   "Yes, **that**'s right."
- "Mark has a new job."   "He does? I didn't know **that**."
- "I'm going on vacation next week."   "Oh, **that**'s nice."

D

We use **this is . . .** and **is this . . . ?** on the telephone:

- Hi Sarah, **this is** David.
  (= the speaker)
- **Is this** Sarah?
  (= the other person)

Hi Sarah, **this is** David.

David

We use **this is . . .** to introduce people:

- *A:* Brian, **this is** Chris.
  B: Hello, Chris. Nice to meet you.
  C: Hi.

Brian, **this is** Chris.

Amanda   Brian   Chris

Exercises

75.1 Complete the sentences. Use *this/that/these/those* + these words:

birds   dishes   house   postcards   seat   ~~shoes~~

1. Do you like *these shoes* ?
2. Who lives in _____ _____ ?
3. How much are _____ _____ ?
4. Look at _____ _____ .
5. Excuse me, is _____ _____ free?
6. _____ _____ are dirty.

75.2 Write questions: *Is this/that your . . . ?* or *Are these/those your . . . ?*

1. Is this your bag?
2.
3.
4.
5.
6.
7.
8.
9.
10.

75.3 Complete the sentences with *this is* or *that's* or *that*.

1. *A:* I'm sorry I'm late.
   B: ___That's___ all right.
2. *A:* I can't come to the party tomorrow.
   B: Oh, _____ too bad. Why not?
3. *(on the phone)*
   Sue: Hello, Jane. _____ Sue.
   Jane: Oh, hi Sue. How are you?
4. *A:* You're lazy.
   B: _____ not true!
5. *A:* Beth plays the piano very well.
   B: Does she? I didn't know _____ .
6. *Mark meets Paul's sister, Helen.*
   Paul: Mark, _____ my sister, Helen.
   Mark: Hi, Helen.
7. *A:* I'm sorry I was angry yesterday.
   B: _____ OK. Forget it!
8. *A:* You're a friend of Tim's, aren't you?
   B: Yes, _____ right.

one/ones

one (= a . . .)

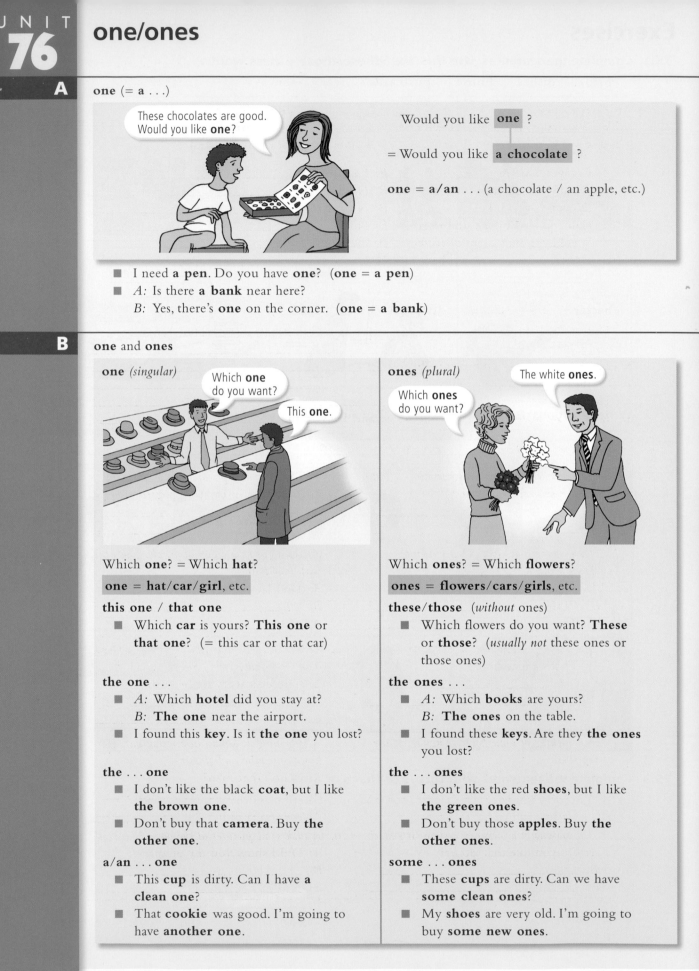

These chocolates are good. Would you like **one**?

Would you like **one** ?

= Would you like **a chocolate** ?

one = a/an . . . (a chocolate / an apple, etc.)

- I need **a pen**. Do you have **one**? (**one** = **a pen**)
- *A:* Is there **a bank** near here?
  B: Yes, there's **one** on the corner. (**one** = **a bank**)

one and **ones**

one *(singular)*

Which **one** do you want?

This **one**.

Which **one**? = Which **hat**?

one = **hat/car/girl**, etc.

this one / that one
- Which **car** is yours? **This one** or **that one**? (= this car or that car)

the one . . .
- *A:* Which **hotel** did you stay at?
  B: **The one** near the airport.
- I found this **key**. Is it **the one** you lost?

the . . . one
- I don't like the black **coat**, but I like **the brown one**.
- Don't buy that **camera**. Buy **the other one**.

a/an . . . one
- This **cup** is dirty. Can I have **a clean one**?
- That **cookie** was good. I'm going to have **another one**.

ones *(plural)*

Which **ones** do you want?

The white **ones**.

Which **ones**? = Which **flowers**?

ones = **flowers/cars/girls**, etc.

these/those *(without ones)*
- Which flowers do you want? **These** or **those**? (*usually not* these ones or those ones)

the ones . . .
- *A:* Which **books** are yours?
  B: **The ones** on the table.
- I found these **keys**. Are they **the ones** you lost?

the . . . ones
- I don't like the red **shoes**, but I like **the green ones**.
- Don't buy those **apples**. Buy **the other ones**.

some . . . ones
- These **cups** are dirty. Can we have **some clean ones**?
- My **shoes** are very old. I'm going to buy **some new ones**.

which . . . ? → Unit 48   another → Unit 66   this/that, etc. → Unit 75

Exercises

76.1 A asks B some questions. Use the information in the box to write B's answers. Use *one* (*not a/an* . . .) in the answers.

B doesn't need a car	B just had a cup of coffee
there's a drugstore on First Avenue	B is going to get a bike
~~B doesn't have a pen~~	B doesn't have an umbrella

1. *A:* Can you lend me a pen?   *B:* I'm sorry, __I don't have one__ .
2. *A:* Would you like to have a car?   *B:* No, I don't _____ .
3. *A:* Do you have a bike?   *B:* No, but _____ .
4. *A:* Can you lend me an umbrella?   *B:* I'm sorry, but _____ .
5. *A:* Would you like a cup of coffee?   *B:* No, thank you. _____ .
6. *A:* Is there a drugstore near here?   *B:* Yes, _____ .

76.2 Complete the sentences. Use *a/an* . . . *one*. Use the words in the list.

better   big   ~~clean~~   different   new   old

1. This cup is dirty. Can I have __a clean one__ ?
2. I'm going to sell my car and buy _____ .
3. That's not a very good picture. This is _____ .
4. I want today's newspaper. This is _____ .
5. This box is too small. I need _____ .
6. Why do we always go to the same restaurant? Let's go to _____ .

76.3 A is talking to B. Use the information to complete the conversations. Use *one/ones*.

1. *A stayed at a hotel. It was near the airport.* *A:* We stayed at a hotel. *B:* __Which one__ ? *A:* __The one near the airport.__	6. *A is looking at a picture. It's on the wall.* *A:* That's an interesting picture. *B:* _____ ? *A:* _____
2. *A sees some shoes in a store window.* *They're green.* *A:* I like those shoes. *B:* Which _____ ? *A:* The _____	7. *A sees a girl in a group of people. She's tall with long hair.* *A:* Do you know that girl? *B:* _____ ? *A:* _____
3. *A is looking at a house. It has a red door.* *A:* That's a nice house. *B:* _____ ? *A:* _____ with _____	8. *A is looking at some flowers in the garden.* *They're yellow.* *A:* Those flowers are beautiful. *B:* _____ ? *A:* _____
4. *A is looking at some CDs. They're on the top shelf.* *A:* Are those your CDs? *B:* _____ ? *A:* _____	9. *A is looking at a man in a restaurant. He has a mustache and glasses.* *A:* Who's that man? *B:* _____ ? *A:* _____ with _____
5. *A is looking at a jacket in a store. It's black.* *A:* Do you like that jacket? *B:* _____ ? *A:* _____	10. *A took some pictures at the party last week.* *A:* Did I show you my pictures? *B:* _____ ? *A:* _____

some and any

A

some	any

I have **some** money.

I **don't** have **any** money.

Use **some** in *positive* sentences:
- I'm going to buy **some** clothes.
- There's **some** ice in the fridge.
- We made **some** mistakes.

Use **any** in *negative* sentences:
- I'm **not** going to buy **any** clothes.
- There **isn't any** milk in the fridge.
- We **didn't** make **any** mistakes.

B

any and **some** in questions

In most questions (but not all) we use **any** (*not* **some**):
- Is there **any** ice in the fridge?
- Does he have **any** friends?
- Do you need **any** help?

We normally use **some** (*not* **any**) when we *offer* things (**Would you like . . . ?**):
- *A:* Would you like **some** coffee?
- *B:* Yes, please.

or when we *ask* for things (**Can I have . . . ?**, etc.):
- *A:* Can I have **some** soup, please?
- *B:* Yes. Help yourself.
- *A:* Can you lend me **some** money?
- *B:* Sure. How much do you need?

Do you have **any** money?

Would you like **some** coffee?

C

some and **any** without a noun

- I didn't take any pictures, but Jane took **some**. (= some pictures)
- You can have some coffee, but I don't want **any**. (= any coffee)
- I just made some coffee. Would you like **some**? (= some coffee)
- "Where's your luggage?" "I don't have **any**." (= any luggage)
- "Are there any cookies?" "Yes, there are **some** in the kitchen." (= some cookies)

D

something / somebody (*or* someone)	anything / anybody (*or* anyone)

something / somebody (*or* **someone**)
- She said **something**.
- I saw **somebody** (*or* **someone**).
- Would you like **something** to eat?
- **Somebody's** at the door.

anything / anybody (*or* **anyone**)
- She **didn't** say **anything**.
- I **didn't** see **anybody** (*or* **anyone**).
- Are you doing **anything** tonight?
- Where's Sue? Has **anybody** seen her?

a and **some** → Unit 69   **somebody/anything**, etc. → Unit 80

Exercises

77.1 Write *some* or *any*.

1. I bought __*some*__ cheese, but I didn't buy __*any*__ bread.
2. I'm going to the post office. I need _____ stamps.
3. There aren't _____ gas stations in this part of town.
4. Gary and Alice don't have _____ children.
5. Do you have _____ brothers or sisters?
6. There are _____ beautiful flowers in the garden.
7. Do you know _____ good hotels in Miami?
8. "Would you like _____ tea?"   "Yes, please."
9. When we were on vacation, we visited _____ very interesting places.
10. Don't buy _____ rice. We don't need _____ .
11. I went out to buy _____ oranges, but they didn't have _____ at the store.
12. I'm thirsty. Can I have _____ water, please?

77.2 Complete the sentences. Use *some* or *any* + the words in the box.

air	batteries	friends	fruit	help
languages	milk	pictures	questions	~~shampoo~~

1. I want to wash my hair. Is there __*any shampoo*__ ?
2. The police want to talk to you. They want to ask you _____ .
3. I don't have my camera, so I can't take _____ .
4. Do you speak _____ foreign _____ ?
5. Last night I went to a restaurant with _____ of mine.
6. Can I have _____ in my coffee, please?
7. This camera isn't working. There aren't _____ in it.
8. It's hot in this office. I'm going out for _____ fresh _____ .
9. *A:* Would you like _____ ?
   B: No, thank you. I've had enough to eat.
10. I can do this job alone. I don't need _____ .

77.3 Complete the sentences. Use *some* or *any*.

1. Jane didn't take any pictures, but __*I took some*__ . (I / take)
2. "Where's your luggage?"   " __*I don't have any*__ ." (I / not / have)
3. "Do you need any money?"   "No, thank you. _____ ." (I / have)
4. "Can you lend me some money?"   "I'm sorry, but _____ ." (I / not / have)
5. The tomatoes at the store didn't look very good, so _____ . (I / not / buy)
6. There were some nice oranges at the store, so _____ . (I / buy)
7. "How many phone calls did you make yesterday?"   " _____ ." (I / not / make)

77.4 Write *something/somebody* or *anything/anybody*.

1. A woman stopped me and said __*something*__ , but I didn't understand.
2. "What's wrong?"   "There's _____ in my eye."
3. Do you know _____ about politics?
4. I went to the store, but I didn't buy _____ .
5. _____ broke the window. I don't know who.
6. There isn't _____ in the bag. It's empty.
7. I'm looking for my keys. Has _____ seen them?
8. Would you like _____ to drink?
9. I didn't eat _____ because I wasn't hungry.
10. This is a secret. Please don't tell _____ .

not + any   no   none

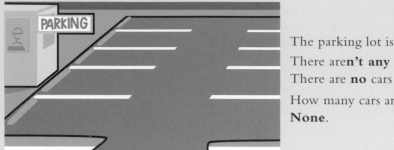

The parking lot is empty.

There are**n't any** cars
There are **no** cars ⎱ in the parking lot.

How many cars are there in the parking lot?
None.

not (-n't) + any

- There are**n't any** cars in the parking lot.
- Tracey and Jeff do**n't** have **any** children.
- You can have some coffee, but I do**n't** want **any**.

no + *noun* (**no cars** / **no garage**, etc.)

no . . . = **not any** *or* **not a**

- There are **no cars** in the parking lot. (= there are**n't any** cars)
- We have **no coffee**. (= we do**n't** have **any** coffee)
- It's a nice house, but there's **no garage**. (= there is**n't a** garage)

We use **no** . . . especially after **have/has** and **there is/are**.

negative verb + **any** = *positive verb* + **no**

- They **don't** have **any** children.   *or*   They **have no** children.
  (*not* They don't have no children)
- There **isn't any** sugar in your coffee.   *or*   There**'s no** sugar in your coffee.

No and **none**

Use **no** + *noun* (**no money** / **no children**, etc.):

- We have **no money**.
- Everything was OK. There were **no problems**.

Use **none** alone (*without* a noun):

- "How much money do you have?"   "**None.**" (= no money)
- "Were there any problems?"   "No, **none.**" (= no problems)

None and **no one**

none = 0 (zero)
no one = nobody

None is an answer for **How much**? / **How many**? (things or people):

- "**How much** money do you have?"   "**None.**" (= no money)
- "**How many** people did you meet?"   "**None.**" (= no people)

No one is an answer for **Who**?:

- "**Who** did you meet?"   "**No one.**"   *or*   "**Nobody.**"

Exercises

78.1 Write these sentences again with *no*.

1. We don't have any money.   *We have no money.*
2. There aren't any stores near here.   There are _____
3. Carla doesn't have any free time.   _____
4. There isn't a light in this room.   _____

Write these sentences again with *any*.

5. We have no money.   *We don't have any money.*
6. There's no milk in the fridge.   _____
7. There are no buses today.   _____
8. Tom has no brothers or sisters.   _____

78.2 Write *no* or *any*.

1. There's __*no*__ sugar in your coffee.
2. My brother is married, but he doesn't have _____ children.
3. Sue doesn't speak _____ foreign languages.
4. I'm afraid there's _____ coffee. Would you like some tea?
5. "Look at those birds!" "Birds? Where? I can't see _____ birds."
6. "Do you know where Jessica is?" "No, I have _____ idea."

Write *no*, *any*, or *none*.

7. There aren't _____ pictures on the wall.
8. The weather was cold, but there was _____ wind.
9. I wanted to buy some oranges, but they didn't have _____ at the store.
10. Everything was correct. There were _____ mistakes.
11. "How much luggage do you have?" " _____ ."
12. "How much luggage do you have?" "I don't have _____ ."

78.3 Complete the sentences. Use *any* or *no* + the words in the box.

air conditioning	answer	difference	friends	furniture
line	money	~~problems~~	questions	

1. Everything was OK. There were __*no problems*__ .
2. Jack and Emily would like to take a vacation, but they have _____ .
3. I'm not going to answer _____ .
4. He's always alone. He has _____ .
5. There is _____ between these two machines. They're exactly the same.
6. There wasn't _____ in the room. It was completely empty.
7. I tried to call you yesterday, but there was _____ .
8. The house is hot because there isn't _____ .
9. There was _____ outside the movie theater, so we didn't have to wait to get our tickets.

78.4 Write short answers (one or two words) to these questions. Use *none* where necessary.

1. How many letters did you write yesterday?   *Two.* OR *A lot.* OR *None.*
2. How many sisters do you have?   _____
3. How much coffee did you drink yesterday?   _____
4. How many pictures have you taken today?   _____
5. How many legs does a snake have?   _____

not + anybody/anyone/anything
nobody/no one/nothing

A

not + anybody / anyone
nobody / no one
(for *people*)

not + anything
nothing
(for *things*)

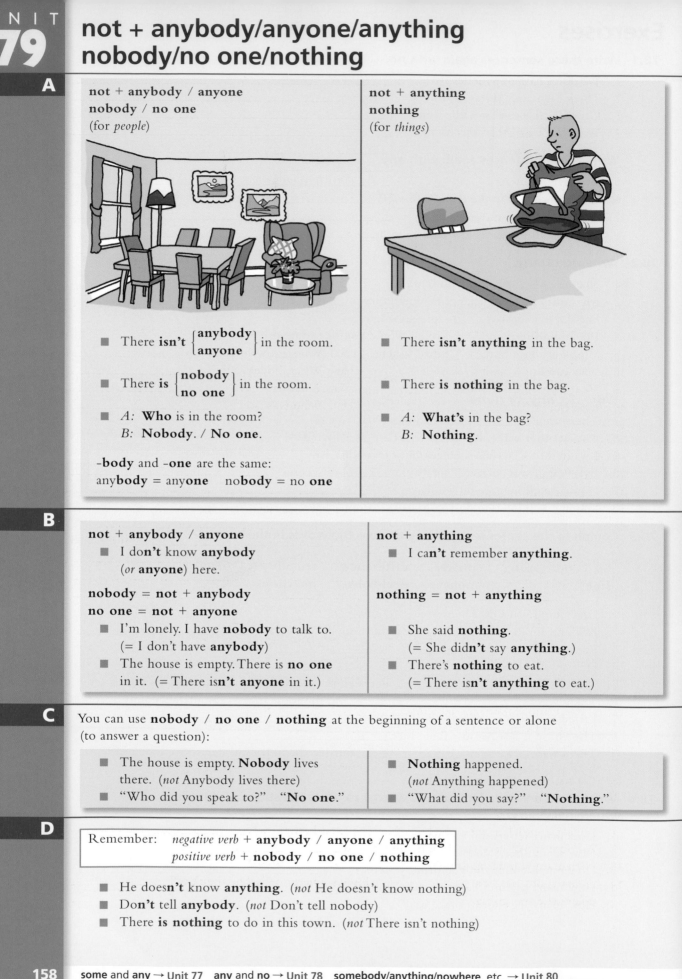

- There **isn't** {**anybody** / **anyone**} in the room.

- There **is** {**nobody** / **no one**} in the room.

- *A:* **Who** is in the room?
  B: **Nobody**. / **No one**.

-**body** and -**one** are the same:
any**body** = any**one**   no**body** = no **one**

- There **isn't anything** in the bag.

- There **is nothing** in the bag.

- *A:* **What's** in the bag?
  B: **Nothing**.

B

not + anybody / anyone
- I do**n't** know **anybody**
  (*or* **anyone**) here.

nobody = not + anybody
no one = not + anyone
- I'm lonely. I have **nobody** to talk to.
  (= I don't have **anybody**)
- The house is empty. There is **no one**
  in it. (= There is**n't anyone** in it.)

not + anything
- I ca**n't** remember **anything**.

nothing = not + anything
- She said **nothing**.
  (= She did**n't** say **anything**.)
- There's **nothing** to eat.
  (= There is**n't anything** to eat.)

C

You can use **nobody / no one / nothing** at the beginning of a sentence or alone
(to answer a question):

- The house is empty. **Nobody** lives
  there. (*not* Anybody lives there)
- "Who did you speak to?" "**No one**."

- **Nothing** happened.
  (*not* Anything happened)
- "What did you say?" "**Nothing**."

D

Remember: *negative verb* + **anybody / anyone / anything**
           positive verb + **nobody / no one / nothing**

- He does**n't** know **anything**. (*not* He doesn't know nothing)
- Do**n't** tell **anybody**. (*not* Don't tell nobody)
- There **is nothing** to do in this town. (*not* There isn't nothing)

some and **any** → Unit 77   **any** and **no** → Unit 78   **somebody/anything/nowhere**, etc. → Unit 80

Exercises

79.1 Write these sentences again with *nobody / no one* or *nothing*.

1. There isn't anything in the bag.   _There's nothing in the bag._
2. There isn't anybody in the office. There's _____
3. I don't have anything to do.   I _____
4. There isn't anything on TV.   _____
5. There wasn't anyone at home.   _____
6. We didn't find anything.   _____

79.2 Write these sentences again with *anybody/anyone* or *anything*.

1. There's nothing in the bag.   _There isn't anything in the bag._
2. There was nobody on the bus.   There wasn't _____
3. I have nothing to read.   _____
4. I have no one to help me.   _____
5. She heard nothing.   _____
6. We have nothing for dinner.   _____

79.3 Answer these questions with *nobody / no one* or *nothing*.

1a. What did you say? _Nothing._   5a. Who knows the answer? _____
2a. Who saw you? _Nobody._   6a. What did you buy? _____
3a. What do you want? _____ 7a. What happened? _____
4a. Who did you meet? _____ 8a. Who was late? _____

Now answer the same questions with full sentences.
Use *nobody / no one / nothing* or *anybody/anyone/anything*:

1b. _I didn't say anything._
2b. _Nobody saw me._
3b. I don't _____
4b. I _____
5b. _____ the answer.
6b. _____
7b. _____
8b. _____

79.4 Complete the sentences. Use:
    nobody / no one / nothing   or   *anybody/anyone/anything*

1. That house is empty. _Nobody_ lives there.
2. Jack has a bad memory. He can't remember _anything_ .
3. Be quiet! Don't say _____ .
4. I didn't know about the meeting. _____ told me.
5. "What did you have to eat?"   " _____ . I wasn't hungry."
6. I didn't eat _____ . I wasn't hungry.
7. Helen was sitting alone. She wasn't with _____ .
8. I'm sorry, I can't help you. There's _____ I can do.
9. I don't know _____ about car engines.
10. The museum is free. It doesn't cost _____ to go in.
11. I heard a knock at the door, but when I opened it, there was _____ there.
12. Antonio spoke very fast. I didn't understand _____ .
13. "What are you doing tonight?"   " _____ . Why?"
14. Helen is out of town. _____ knows where she is. She didn't tell _____
    where she was going.

somebody/anything/nowhere, etc.

A

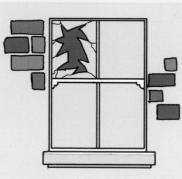

Chicago

Somebody (or **Someone**) has broken the window.

She has got **something** in her mouth.

Tom lives **somewhere** near Chicago.

somebody / **someone** = a person, but we don't know who	**something** = a thing, but we don't know what	**somewhere** = in/to a place, but we don't know where

B

People (**-body** *or* **-one**)

somebody *or* **someone**
anybody *or* **anyone**
nobody *or* **no one**

- There is **somebody** (or **someone**) at the door.
- Is there **anybody** (or **anyone**) at the door?
- There isn't **anybody** (or **anyone**) at the door.
- There is **nobody** (or **no one**) at the door.

-body and **-one** are the same: **somebody** = **someone**, **nobody** = **no one**, etc.

Things (**-thing**)

something
anything
nothing

- Lucy said **something**, but I didn't understand what she said.
- Are you doing **anything** this weekend?
- I was angry, but I did**n't** say **anything**.
- "What did you say?"   "**Nothing**."

Places (**-where**)

somewhere
anywhere
nowhere

- Ruth's parents live **somewhere** in Southern California.
- Did you go **anywhere** interesting on vacation?
- I'm staying here. I'm **not** going **anywhere**.
- I don't like this town. There is **nowhere** to go.

C

something / **anybody**, etc. + *adjective* (**big**/**cheap**/**interesting**, etc.)
- Did you meet **anybody interesting** at the party?
- We always go to the same place. Let's go **somewhere different**.
- "What's in that letter?"   "It's **nothing important**."

D

something / **anybody**, etc. + **to** . . .
- I'm hungry. I want **something to eat**. (= something that I can eat)
- Tony doesn't have **anybody to talk** to. (= anybody that he can talk to)
- There is **nowhere to go** in this town. (= nowhere where people can go)

some and **any** → Unit 77   **any** and **no** → Unit 78   **anybody/nothing**, etc. → Unit 79
everything/-body/-where → Unit 81

Exercises

80.1 Write *somebody* (or *someone*) / *something* / *somewhere*.

1. Lucy said __*something*__ . — What did she say?
2. I lost _____ . — What did you lose?
3. Sue and Tom went _____ . — Where did they go?
4. I'm going to call _____ . — Who are you going to call?

80.2 Write *nobody* (or *no one*) / *nothing* / *nowhere*.

1a. What did you say? — *Nothing.*
2a. Where are you going? — _____
3a. What do you want? — _____
4a. Who are you looking for? — _____

**Now answer the same questions with full sentences.
Use *not* + *anybody*/*anything*/*anywhere*.**

1b. __*I didn't say anything.*__   3b. _____
2b. I'm not _____   4b. _____

80.3 Write *somebody*/*anything*/*nowhere*, etc.

1. It's dark. I can't see __*anything*__ .
2. Tom lives __*somewhere*__ near San Francisco.
3. Do you know _____ about computers?
4. "Listen!" "What? I can't hear _____ ."
5. "What are you doing here?" "I'm waiting for _____ ."
6. We need to talk. There's _____ I want to tell you.
7. "Did _____ see the accident?" "No, _____ ."
8. We weren't hungry, so we didn't eat _____ .
9. "What's going to happen?" "I don't know. _____ knows."
10. "Do you know _____ in Tokyo?" "Yes, a few people."
11. "What's in that suitcase?" " _____ . It's empty."
12. I'm looking for my glasses. I can't find them _____ .
13. I don't like cold weather. I want to live _____ warm.
14. Is there _____ interesting on television tonight?
15. Have you ever met _____ famous?

80.4 Complete the sentences. Choose from the boxes.

something	anything	nothing		do	drink	eat	~~go~~
something	anywhere	~~nowhere~~		park	read	sit	stay
somewhere		nowhere					

1. We don't go out very much because there's __*nowhere to go*__ .
2. There isn't any food in the house. We don't have _____ .
3. I'm bored. I have _____ .
4. "Why are you standing?" "Because there isn't _____ ."
5. "Would you like _____ ?" "Yes, please – a glass of water."
6. If you're going downtown, take the bus. Don't drive because there's

   _____ .
7. I want _____ . I'm going to buy a magazine.
8. I need _____ in Seoul. Can you recommend a hotel?

every and **all**

Every

Every house on the street is the same.

every house on the street =
all the houses on the street

We use **every** + *singular noun* (**every house** / **every country**, etc.):

- Sarah has been to **every country** in Europe.
- **Every summer** we take a vacation at the beach.
- She looks different **every time** I see her.

Use a *singular verb* after **every** . . . :

- **Every house** on the street **is** the same. (*not* are the same)
- **Every country has** a national flag. (*not* have)

Compare **every** and **all**:

▪ **Every student** in the class passed the exam.	▪ **All the students** in the class passed the exam.
▪ **Every country has** a national flag.	▪ **All countries have** a national flag.

Every day and **all day**

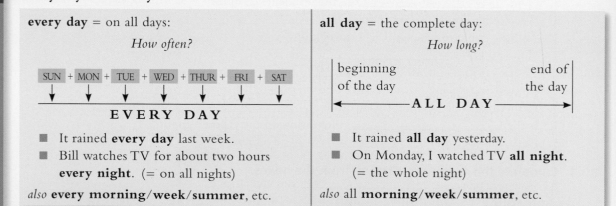

every day = on all days:

How often?

SUN + MON + TUE + WED + THUR + FRI + SAT

EVERY DAY

- It rained **every day** last week.
- Bill watches TV for about two hours **every night**. (= on all nights)

also **every morning/week/summer**, etc.

all day = the complete day:

How long?

beginning of the day   end of the day
◄———— **ALL DAY** ————►

- It rained **all day** yesterday.
- On Monday, I watched TV **all night**. (= the whole night)

also all **morning/week/summer**, etc.

Everybody (*or* everyone) / everything / everywhere

everybody or **everyone** (*people*) **everything** (*things*) **everywhere** (*places*)

- **Everybody** (*or* **Everyone**) needs friends.
  (= all people need friends)
- Do you have **everything** you need?
  (= all the things you need)
- I lost my watch. I've looked **everywhere** for it.
  (= I've looked in all places)

Use a *singular verb* after **everybody/everyone/everything**:

- **Everybody has** problems. (*not* Everybody have)

all → Unit 82

Exercises

81.1 **Complete the sentences. Use *every* + these words:**

> day   room   ~~student~~   time   word

1. _____Every student_____ in the class passed the exam.
2. My job is very boring. _____ is the same.
3. Kate is a very good chess player. When we play, she wins _____ .
4. _____ in the hotel has a TV.
5. "Did you understand what she said?" "Most of it, but not _____ ."

81.2 **Complete the sentences with *every day* or *all day*.**

1. Yesterday it rained __all day__ .
2. I buy a newspaper _____ , but sometimes I don't read it.
3. I'm not going out tomorrow. I'll be at home _____ .
4. I usually drink about four cups of coffee _____ .
5. Paula was sick yesterday, so she stayed in bed _____ .
6. I'm tired now because I've been working hard _____ .
7. Last year we went to the beach for a week, and it rained _____ .

81.3 **Write *every* or *all*.**

1. Bill watches TV for about two hours __every__ night.
2. Julia gets up at 6:30 _____ morning.
3. The weather was nice yesterday, so we sat outside _____ afternoon.
4. I'm leaving town on Monday. I'll be away _____ week.
5. "How often do you go skiing?" "_____ year. Usually in March."
6. *A:* Were you at home at 10 yesterday?
   B: Yes, I was at home _____ morning. I went out after lunch.
7. My sister loves new cars. She buys one _____ year.
8. I saw Sam at the party, but he didn't speak to me _____ night.
9. We take a vacation for two or three weeks _____ summer.

81.4 **Write *everybody*/*everything*/*everywhere*.**

1. _____Everybody_____ needs friends.
2. Chris knows _____ about computers.
3. I like the people here. _____ is very friendly.
4. This is a nice hotel. It's comfortable, and _____ is very clean.
5. Kevin never uses his car. He goes _____ on his motorcycle.
6. Let's have dinner. _____ is hungry.
7. Sue's house is full of books. There are books _____ .
8. You are right. _____ you say is true.

81.5 **Complete the sentences. Use one word only each time.**

1. Everybody __has__ problems.
2. Are you ready yet? Everybody _____ waiting for you.
3. The house is empty. Everyone _____ gone out.
4. Gary is very popular. Everybody _____ him.
5. This town is completely different now. Everything _____ changed.
6. I got home very late last night. I came in quietly because everyone _____ asleep.
7. Everybody _____ mistakes!
8. *A:* _____ everything clear? _____ everybody know what to do?
   B: Yes, we all understand.

all most some any no/none

A

Compare:

children/money/books, etc. (in general):	**the** children / **the** money / **these** books, etc:
■ **Children** like to play. (= children in general) ■ **Money** isn't everything. (= money in general) ■ I enjoy reading **books**. ■ Everybody needs **friends**.	■ Where are **the children**? (= our children) ■ I want to buy a car, but I don't have **the money**. (= the money for a car) ■ Have you read **these books**? ■ I often go out with **my friends**.

B

Most / **most of** . . . , some / **some of** . . . , etc.

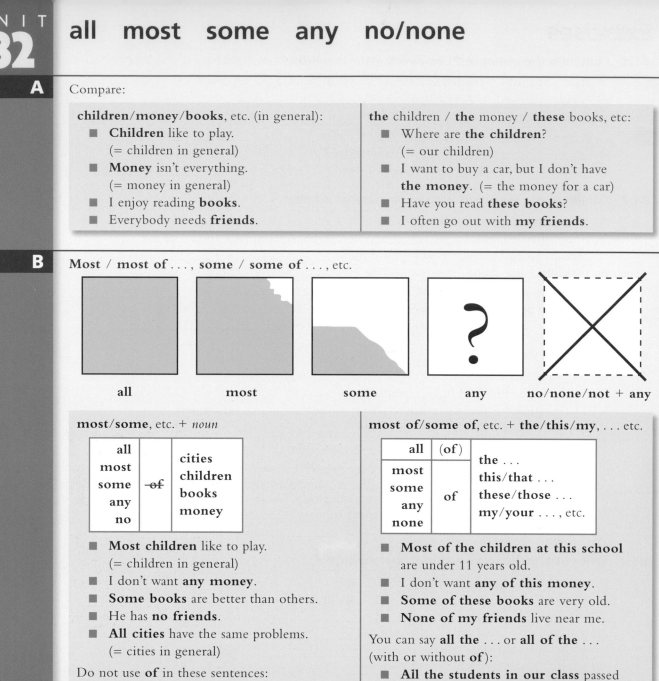

all   most   some   any   no/none/not + any

most/some, etc. + *noun*	**most of/some of**, etc. + **the/this/my**, . . . etc.

all most some any no	~~of~~	cities children books money

■ **Most children** like to play.
  (= children in general)
■ I don't want **any money**.
■ **Some books** are better than others.
■ He has **no friends**.
■ **All cities** have the same problems.
  (= cities in general)

Do not use **of** in these sentences:

■ **Most people** drive too fast.
  (*not* Most of people)
■ **Some birds** can't fly.
  (*not* Some of birds)

all	(of)	the . . .
most some any none	of	this/that . . . these/those . . . my/your . . . , etc.

■ **Most of the children at this school** are under 11 years old.
■ I don't want **any of this money**.
■ **Some of these books** are very old.
■ **None of my friends** live near me.

You can say **all the** . . . or **all of the** . . .
(with or without **of**):

■ **All the students in our class** passed the exam. (*or* **All of the students** . . .)
■ Silvia has lived in Miami **all her life**.
  (*or* . . . **all of her life**.)

C

All of it / **most of them** / **none of us**, etc.

all most some any none	of	it them us you

■ You can have **some of this cake**, but not **all of it**.
■ *A:* Do you know those people?
  B: **Most of them**, but not **all of them**.
■ **Some of us** are going out tonight. Why don't you come with us?
■ I've got a lot of books, but I haven't read **any of them**.
■ "How many of these books have you read?" "**None of them**."

the . . . (children / the children, etc.) → Unit 73   some and any → Unit 77   no/none/any → Unit 78
all and **every** → Unit 81

Exercises

82.1 Complete the sentences. Use the word in parentheses (*some*/*most*, etc.). Sometimes you need *of* (*some of* / *most of*, etc.).

1. <u>_Most_</u> children like to play. (most)
2. <u>_Some of_</u> this money is yours. (some)
3. _____ people never stop talking. (some)
4. _____ the stores downtown close at 6:00. (most)
5. You can change money in _____ banks. (most)
6. I don't like _____ the pictures in the living room. (any)
7. He's lost _____ his money. (all)
8. _____ my friends are married. (none)
9. Do you know _____ the people in this picture? (any)
10. _____ birds can fly. (most)
11. I enjoyed _____ the movie, but I didn't like the ending. (most)
12. _____ sports are very dangerous. (some)
13. We can't find anywhere to stay. _____ the hotels are full. (all)
14. Try _____ this cheese. It's delicious. (some)
15. The weather was bad when we were on vacation. It rained _____ the time. (most)

82.2 Look at the pictures and answer the questions. Use:

all / most / some / none   +   of them / of it

1. How many of the people are women?   <u>_Most of them._</u>
2. How many of the boxes are on the table? _____
3. How many of the men are wearing hats? _____
4. How many of the windows are open? _____
5. How many of the people are standing? _____
6. How much of the money is Ben's? _____

82.3 Are these sentences OK? Correct the sentences that are wrong.

1. (Most of children) like to play.   <u>_Most children_</u>
2. All the students failed the test.   <u>_OK_</u>
3. Some of people work too hard.   _____
4. Some of questions on the exam were very easy.   _____
5. I haven't seen any of those people before.   _____
6. All of insects have six legs.   _____
7. Have you read all these books?   _____
8. Most of students in our class are very nice.   _____
9. Most of my friends are going to the party.   _____
10. I'm very tired this morning – I was awake most of night.   _____

UNIT 83

both   either   neither

We use **both/either/neither** to talk about two things or people:

both   **either**   **neither** (*not* + **either**)

- Rebecca has two children. **Both** are married. (**both** = the two children)
- Would you like tea or coffee? You can have **either**. (**either** = tea or coffee)
- *A:* Do you want to go to the movies or the theater?
  B: **Neither**. I want to stay home. (**neither** = not the movies or the theater)

Compare **either** and **neither**:

- "Would you like **tea** or **coffee**?"
  - "**Either**. It doesn't matter." (= tea or coffee)
  - "I **don't** want **either**." (*not* I don't want neither)
  - "**Neither**." (= not tea or coffee)

Both / either / neither + *noun*

both + *plural*	**both**	**windows/books/children**, etc.
either / **neither** + *singular*	**either** / **neither**	**window/book/child**, etc.

- Last year I went to Miami and Seattle. I liked **both cities** very much.
- First I worked in an office and later in a store. **Neither job** was very interesting.
- There are two ways to get to the airport. You can go **either way**.

Both of . . . / either of . . . / neither of . . .

both	(**of**)	the . . .
either / **neither**	**of**	these/those . . . my/your/Paul's . . . , etc.

> I like **both of those** pictures.

- **Neither of my parents** is Canadian.
- I **haven't** read **either of these books**.

You can say **both of the/those/my** . . . or
both the/those/my . . . (with or without **of**):

- I like **both of** those pictures.   *or*   I like **both** those pictures.
- **Both of** Paul's sisters are married.   *or*   **Both** Paul's sisters are married.
- *but*   **Neither of** Paul's sisters is married. (*not* Neither Paul's sisters)

Both of them / neither of us

both / **either** / **neither**	**of**	**them** / **us** / **you**

- Paul has got two sisters. **Both of them** are married.
- Sue and I didn't eat anything. **Neither of us** was hungry.
- Who are those two people? I **don't** know **either of them**.

can't either / neither can I → Unit 43

Exercises

83.1 Write *both/either/neither*. Use *of* where necessary.

1. Last year I went to Miami and Seattle. I liked __both__ cities very much.
2. There were two pictures on the wall. I didn't like __either of__ them.
3. It was a good football game. _____ teams played well.
4. It wasn't a good football game. _____ team played well.
5. "Is your friend Canadian or American?"   "_____ . She's Australian."
6. We went away for two days, but the weather was bad. It rained _____ days.
7. *A:* I bought two newspapers. Which one do you want?
    B: _____ . It doesn't matter which one.
8. I invited Donna and Mike to the party, but _____ them came.
9. "Do you go to work by car or by bus?"   "_____ . I always walk."
10. "Which jacket do you prefer, this one or that one?"   "I don't like _____ them."
11. "Do you work, or are you a student?"   "_____ . I work, and I'm a student, too."
12. Paula and I didn't know the time because _____ us had a watch.
13. Helen has two sisters and a brother. _____ sisters are married.
14. Helen has two sisters and a brother. I know her brother, but I haven't met _____ her sisters.

83.2 Complete the sentences for the pictures. Use *Both . . .* and *Neither . . . .*

1. ___Both cups are___ _____ empty.
2. _____ are open.
3. _____ wearing a hat.
4. _____ beards.
5. _____ to the airport.
6. _____ right.

83.3 A man and a woman answered some questions. Their answers were the same. Write sentences with *Both/Neither of them . . . .*

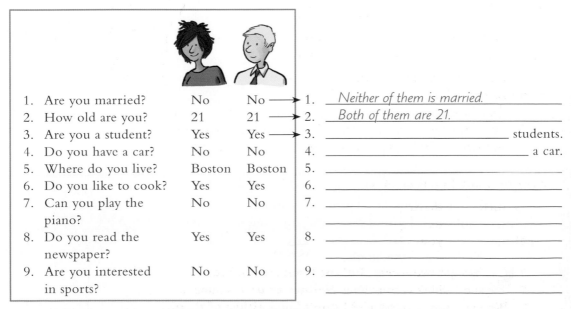

1. Are you married?	No	No	1. ___Neither of them is married.___
2. How old are you?	21	21	2. ___Both of them are 21.___
3. Are you a student?	Yes	Yes	3. _____ students.
4. Do you have a car?	No	No	4. _____ a car.
5. Where do you live?	Boston	Boston	5. _____
6. Do you like to cook?	Yes	Yes	6. _____
7. Can you play the piano?	No	No	7. _____
8. Do you read the newspaper?	Yes	Yes	8. _____
9. Are you interested in sports?	No	No	9. _____

a lot   much   many

A

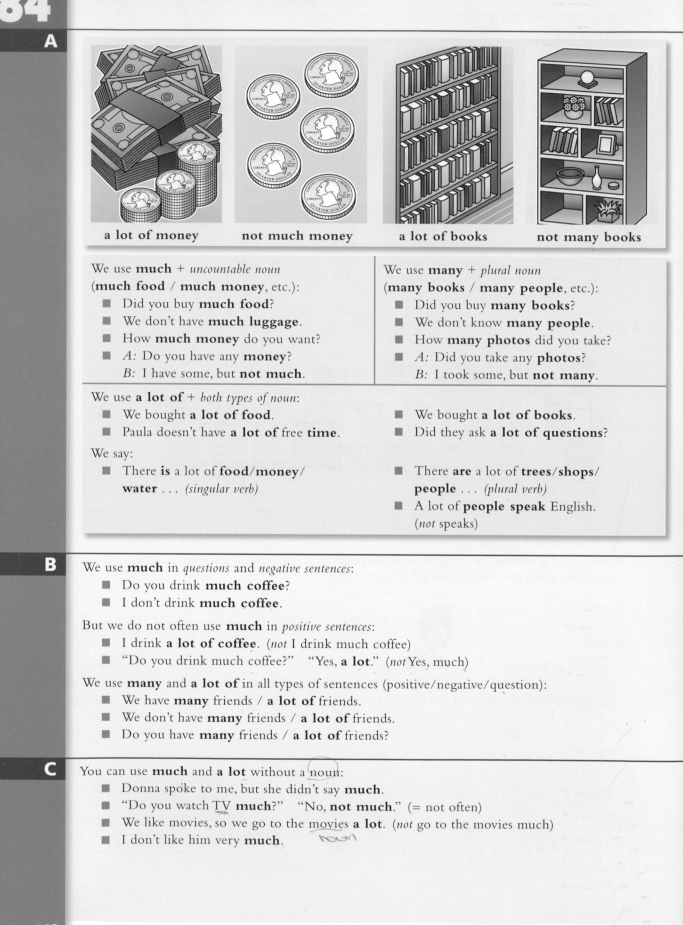

a lot of money   not much money   a lot of books   not many books

We use **much** + *uncountable noun*
(**much food** / **much money**, etc.):
- Did you buy **much food**?
- We don't have **much luggage**.
- How **much money** do you want?
- *A:* Do you have any **money**?
  B: I have some, but **not much**.

We use **many** + *plural noun*
(**many books** / **many people**, etc.):
- Did you buy **many books**?
- We don't know **many people**.
- How **many photos** did you take?
- *A:* Did you take any **photos**?
  B: I took some, but **not many**.

We use **a lot of** + *both types of noun*:
- We bought **a lot of food**.
- Paula doesn't have **a lot of** free **time**.

We say:
- There **is** a lot of **food/money/water** … *(singular verb)*

- We bought **a lot of books**.
- Did they ask **a lot of questions**?

- There **are** a lot of **trees/shops/people** … *(plural verb)*
- A lot of **people speak** English.
  (*not* speaks)

B

We use **much** in *questions* and *negative sentences*:
- Do you drink **much coffee**?
- I don't drink **much coffee**.

But we do not often use **much** in *positive sentences*:
- I drink **a lot of coffee**. (*not* I drink much coffee)
- "Do you drink much coffee?"   "Yes, **a lot**." (*not* Yes, much)

We use **many** and **a lot of** in all types of sentences (positive/negative/question):
- We have **many** friends / **a lot of** friends.
- We don't have **many** friends / **a lot of** friends.
- Do you have **many** friends / **a lot of** friends?

C

You can use **much** and **a lot** without a noun:
- Donna spoke to me, but she didn't say **much**.
- "Do you watch TV **much**?"   "No, **not much**." (= not often)
- We like movies, so we go to the movies **a lot**. (*not* go to the movies much)
- I don't like him very **much**.

countable/uncountable → Units 68–69

Exercises

84.1 Write *much* or *many*.

1. Did you buy __*much*__ food?
2. There aren't _____ hotels in this town.
3. We don't have _____ gas. We need to stop and get some.
4. Were there _____ people on the train?
5. Did _____ students fail the exam?
6. Paula doesn't have _____ money.
7. I wasn't hungry, so I didn't eat _____ .
8. I don't know where Gary lives these days. I haven't seen him for _____ years.

Write *How much* or *How many*.

9. _____ people are coming to the party?
10. _____ milk should I get at the store?
11. _____ bread did you buy?
12. _____ players are there on a football team?

84.2 Complete the sentences. Use *much* or *many* with these words:

~~books~~   countries   luggage   people   time   times

1. I don't read very much. I don't have __*many books*__ .
2. Hurry up! We don't have _____ .
3. Do you travel a lot? Have you been to _____ ?
4. Tina hasn't lived here very long, so she doesn't know _____ .
5. "Do you have _____ ?" "No, only this bag."
6. I know Tokyo very well. I've been there _____ .

84.3 Complete the sentences. Use *a lot of* + these words:

accidents   ~~books~~   fun   interesting things   traffic

1. I like reading. I have __*a lot of books*__ .
2. We enjoyed our visit to the museum. We saw _____ .
3. This road is very dangerous. There are _____ .
4. We enjoyed our vacation. We had _____ .
5. It took me a long time to drive here. There was _____ .

84.4 In some of these sentences *much* is not natural. Change the sentences or write *OK*.

1. Do you drink <u>much coffee</u>?   *OK*
2. I drink <u>much tea</u>.   *a lot of tea*
3. It was a cold winter. We had <u>much snow</u>.   _____
4. There wasn't <u>much snow</u> last winter.   _____
5. It costs <u>much money</u> to travel around the world. _____
6. This pen was cheap. It didn't cost <u>much</u>.   _____
7. Do you know <u>much</u> about computers?   _____
8. "Do you have any luggage?" "Yes, <u>much</u>."   _____

84.5 Write sentences about these people. Use *much* and *a lot*.

1. Jim loves movies. (go to the movies)   *He goes to the movies a lot.*
2. Nicole thinks TV is boring. (watch TV)   *She doesn't watch TV much.*
3. Tina is a good tennis player. (play tennis) She _____
4. Martin doesn't like to drive. (use his car) He _____
5. Paul spends most of the time at home. (go out) _____
6. Sue has been all over the world. (travel)   _____

(a) little   (a) few

A

(a) **little** + *uncountable noun*:

(a) **little** water
(a) **little** time
(a) **little** money
(a) **little** soup

a little water

(a) **few** + *plural noun*:

(a) **few** books
(a) **few** questions
(a) **few** people
(a) **few** days

a few books

B

a little = some but not much

- She didn't eat anything, but she drank **a little water**.
- I speak **a little Spanish**.
  (= some Spanish but not much)
- *A:* Can you speak Spanish?
  B: **A little**.

a few = some but not many

- Excuse me, I have to make **a few phone calls**.
- We're going away for **a few days**.
- I speak **a few words** of Spanish.
- *A:* Do you have any stamps?
  B: Yes, **a few**. Do you want one?

C

~~a~~ **little** (*without* **a**) = almost no *or* almost nothing

- There was **little food** in the fridge. It was almost empty.

You can say **very little**:
- Dan is very thin because he eats **very little**. (= almost nothing)

~~a~~ **few** (*without* **a**) = almost no

- There were **few people** in the theater. It was almost empty.

You can say **very few**:
- Your English is very good. You make **very few mistakes**.

D

little and **a little**

A little is a *positive* idea:
- They have **a little** money, so they're not poor. (= they have some money)

Little (or **very little**) is a *negative* idea:
- They have (**very**) **little** money. They are very poor. (= almost no money)

few and **a few**

A few is a *positive* idea:
- I have **a few** friends, so I'm not lonely. (= I have some friends)

Few (or **very few**) is a *negative* idea:
- I'm sad and I'm lonely. I have (**very**) **few** friends. (= almost no friends)

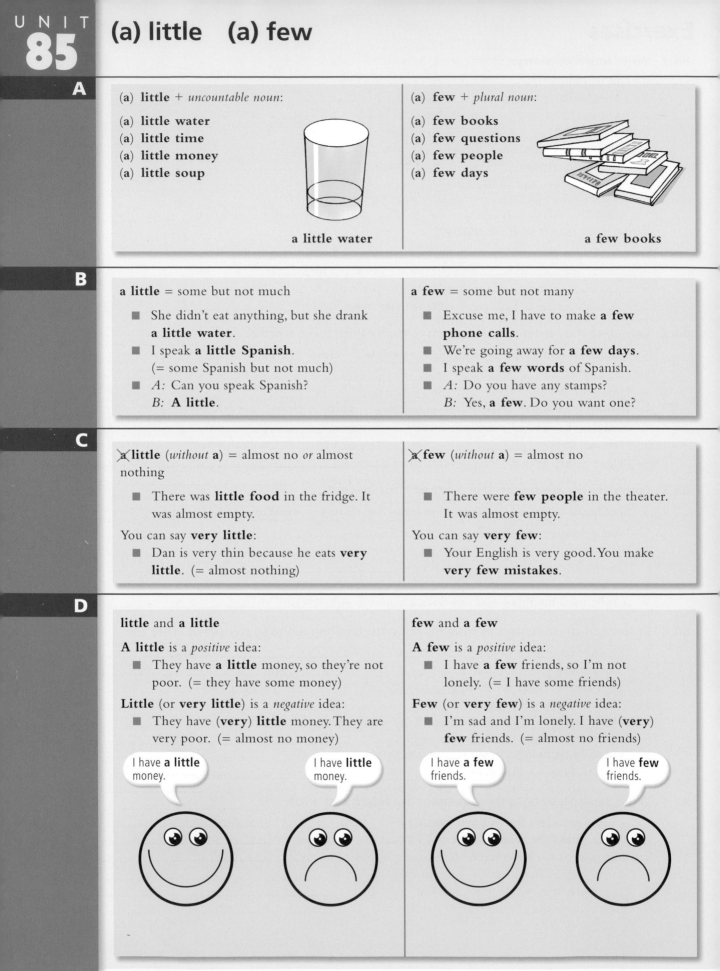

I have **a little** money.

I have **little** money.

I have **a few** friends.

I have **few** friends.

countable/uncountable → **Units 68–69**

Exercises

85.1 Answer the questions with *a little* or *a few*.

1. "Do you have any money?"   "Yes, __*a little*__ ."
2. "Do you have any envelopes?"   "Yes, _____ ."
3. "Do you want sugar in your coffee?"   "Yes, _____ , please."
4. "Did you take any pictures when you were on vacation?"   "Yes, _____ ."
5. "Does your friend speak English?"   "Yes, _____ ."
6. "Are there any good restaurants in this town?"   "Yes, _____ ."

85.2 Write *a little* or *a few* + these words:

chairs   days   fresh air   friends   milk   Russian   times   ~~years~~

1. Martin speaks Italian well. He lived in Italy for __*a few years*__ .
2. Can I have _____ in my coffee, please?
3. "When did Julia leave?"   "_____ ago."
4. "Do you speak any foreign languages?"   "I can speak _____ ."
5. "Are you going out alone?"   "No, I'm going with _____ ."
6. "Have you ever been to Mexico?"   "Yes, _____ ."
7. There wasn't much furniture in the room – just a table and _____ .
8. I'm going out for a walk. I need _____ .

85.3 Complete the sentences. Use *very little* or *very few* + these words:

coffee   hotels   ~~mistakes~~   people   rain   time   work

1. Your English is very good. You make __*very few mistakes*__ .
2. I drink _____ . I don't like it.
3. The weather here is very dry in summer. There is _____ .
4. It's difficult to find a place to stay in this town. There are _____ .
5. Hurry up. We've got _____ .
6. The town is very quiet at night. _____ go out.
7. Some people in the office are very lazy. They do _____ .

85.4 Write *little / a little* or *few / a few*.

1. There was __*little*__ food in the fridge. It was almost empty.
2. "When did Sarah go out?"   "_____ minutes ago."
3. I can't decide now. I need _____ time to think about it.
4. There was _____ traffic, so we arrived earlier than we expected.
5. The bus service isn't very good at night – there are _____ buses after 9:00.
6. "Would you like some soup?"   "Yes, _____ , please."
7. They sent us a map, so we had _____ trouble finding their house.

85.5 Right or wrong? Change the sentences where necessary. Write *OK* if the sentence is correct.

1. We're going away for few days next week.   __*for a few days*__
2. Everybody needs little luck.   _____
3. I can't talk to you now – I've got few things to do. _____
4. I eat very little meat – I don't like it very much. _____
5. Excuse me, can I ask you few questions?   _____
6. There were little people on the bus – it was almost empty. _____
7. Martin is a very private person. Few people know him well. _____

old/nice/interesting, etc. (adjectives)

A

*Adjective + noun (**nice day** / **blue eyes**, etc.)*

	adjective + noun	
It's a	**nice**	**day** today.
Laura has	**brown**	**eyes**.
There's a very	**old**	**church** in this town.
Do you like	**Italian**	**food**?
I don't speak any	**foreign**	**languages**.
There are some	**beautiful yellow**	**flowers** in the garden.

The adjective is *before* the noun:

- They live in a **modern house**. (*not* a house modern)
- Have you met any **famous people**? (*not* people famous)

The ending of an adjective is always the same:

   a **different** place   **different** places (*not* differents)

B

Be (**am/is/was**, etc.) *+ adjective*

- The weather **is nice** today.
- These flowers **are** very **beautiful**.
- **Are** you **cold**? Should I close the window?
- **I'm hungry**. Can I have something to eat?
- The movie **wasn't** very **good**. It was **boring**.
- Please **be quiet**. I'm reading.

I'm hungry.

C

Look/feel/smell/taste/sound *+ adjective*

You **look tired**.
Yes, I **feel tired**.
You **sound happy**.
It **smells good**.
It **tastes good**.

- "You **look tired**."   "Yes, I **feel tired**."
- Gary told me about his new job. It **sounds** very **interesting**.
- I'm not going to eat this fish. It doesn't **smell good**.

Compare:

He	is feels looks	tired.

They	are look sound	happy.

It	is smells tastes	good.

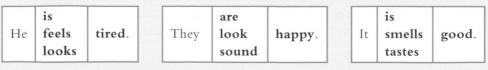

get + adjective (**get hungry/tired**, etc.) → Unit 57   **something/anybody** + adjective → Unit 80

Exercises

86.1 Put the words in the right order.

1. (new / live in / house / they / a)   *They live in a new house.*
2. (like / jacket / I / that / green)   I _____
3. (music / like / do / classical / you?)   Do _____
4. (had / wonderful / a / I / trip)   _____
5. (went to / restaurant / a / Japanese / we)   _____

86.2 The words below are adjectives (*dark*/*foreign*, etc.) or nouns (*air*/*job*, etc.). Use an adjective and a noun to complete each sentence.

air	dangerous	~~foreign~~	hot	knife	long	vacation
clouds	dark	fresh	job	~~languages~~	sharp	water

1. Do you speak any _foreign languages_ ?
2. Look at those _____ . It's going to rain.
3. Sue works very hard, and she's very tired. She needs a _____ .
4. You need _____ to make tea.
5. Can you open the window? We need some _____ .
6. I need a _____ to cut these onions.
7. Firefighting is a _____ .

86.3 Write sentences for the pictures. Choose from the boxes.

feel(s)	look(s)	~~sound(s)~~		~~happy~~	nice	surprised
look(s)	smell(s)	taste(s)	+	new	sick	terrible

1. You _sound happy_ .
2. It _____ .
3. I _____ .
4. You _____ .
5. They _____ .
6. It _____ .

86.4 A and B don't agree. Complete B's sentences. Use *feel*/*look*, etc.

A

B

	A	B	
1.	You look tired.	I do? I _don't feel tired_ .	(feel)
2.	This is a new coat.	It is? It doesn't _____ .	(look)
3.	I'm American.	You are? You _____ .	(sound)
4.	You look cold.	Really? I _____ .	(feel)
5.	These bags are heavy.	They are? They _____ .	(look)
6.	That soup looks good.	Maybe, but it _____ .	(taste)

quickly/badly/suddenly, etc. (adverbs)

A

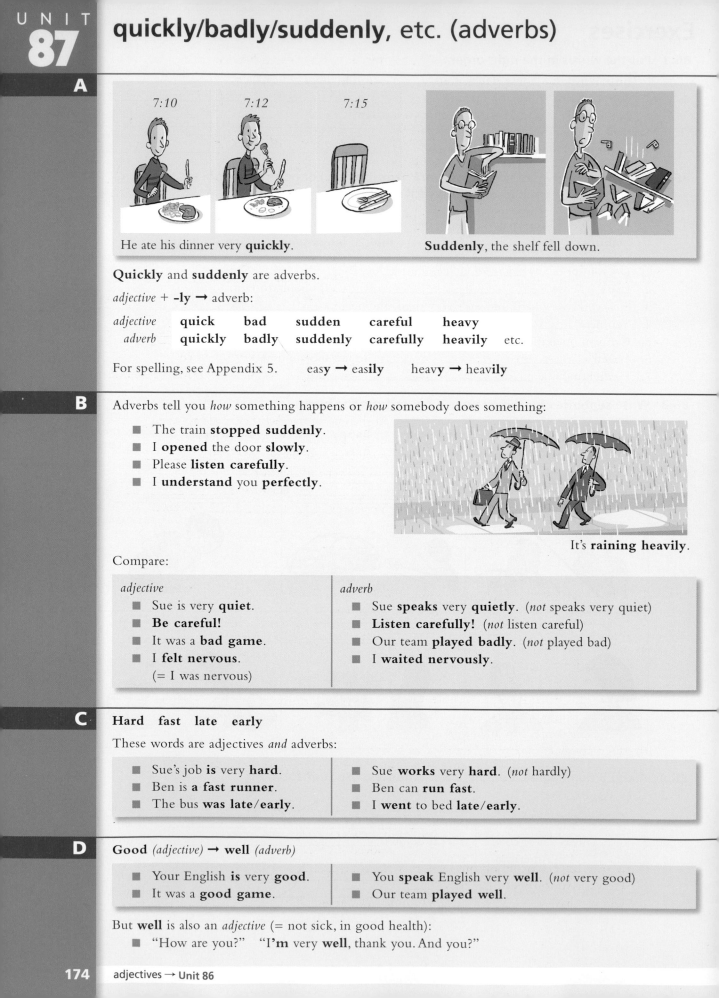

7:10   7:12   7:15

He ate his dinner very **quickly**.

Suddenly, the shelf fell down.

Quickly and **suddenly** are adverbs.

adjective + **–ly** → adverb:

adjective	**quick**	**bad**	**sudden**	**careful**	**heavy**	
adverb	**quickly**	**badly**	**suddenly**	**carefully**	**heavily**	etc.

For spelling, see Appendix 5.   easy → eas**ily**   heavy → heav**ily**

B

Adverbs tell you *how* something happens or *how* somebody does something:

- The train **stopped suddenly**.
- I **opened** the door **slowly**.
- Please **listen carefully**.
- I **understand** you **perfectly**.

It's **raining heavily**.

Compare:

adjective	*adverb*
■ Sue is very **quiet**.	■ Sue **speaks** very **quietly**. (*not* speaks very quiet)
■ **Be careful!**	■ **Listen carefully!** (*not* listen careful)
■ It was a **bad game**.	■ Our team **played badly**. (*not* played bad)
■ I **felt nervous**.	■ I **waited nervously**.
(= I was nervous)	

C

Hard   fast   late   early

These words are adjectives *and* adverbs:

- Sue's job **is** very **hard**.
- Ben is **a fast runner**.
- The bus **was late/early**.

- Sue **works** very **hard**. (*not* hardly)
- Ben can **run fast**.
- I **went** to bed **late/early**.

D

Good (*adjective*) → **well** (*adverb*)

- Your English **is** very **good**.
- It was a **good game**.

- You **speak** English very **well**. (*not* very good)
- Our team **played well**.

But **well** is also an *adjective* (= not sick, in good health):

- "How are you?"   "I**'m** very **well**, thank you. And you?"

Exercises

87.1 Look at the pictures and complete the sentences with these adverbs:

angrily   badly   dangerously   fast   ~~heavily~~   quietly

1. It's raining __*heavily*__ .
2. He sings very _____ .
3. They came in _____ .
4. She shouted at me _____ .
5. She can run very _____ .
6. He was driving _____ .

87.2 Complete the sentences. Choose from the boxes.

come	know	sleep	win		~~carefully~~	clearly	hard	well
explain	~~listen~~	think	work	**+**	carefully	easily	quickly	well

1. I'm going to tell you something very important, so please __*listen carefully*__ .
2. They _____ . At the end of the day they're always tired.
3. I'm tired this morning. I didn't _____ last night.
4. You play chess much better than me. When we play, you always _____ .
5. _____ before you answer the question.
6. I've met Alice a few times, but I don't _____ her very _____ .
7. Our teacher doesn't _____ things very _____ . We never understand him.
8. Helen! I need your help. _____ !

87.3 Which is right?

1. Don't eat so ~~quick~~ / quickly. It's not good for you. (*quickly* is right)
2. Why are you <u>angry / angrily</u>? I didn't do anything.
3. Can you speak <u>slow / slowly</u>, please?
4. Come on, Dave! Why are you always so <u>slow / slowly</u>?
5. Bill is a very <u>careful / carefully</u> driver.
6. Jane is studying <u>hard / hardly</u> for her exams.
7. "Where's Diane?"   "She was here, but she left <u>sudden / suddenly</u>."
8. Please be <u>quiet / quietly</u>. I'm studying.
9. Some companies pay their workers very <u>bad / badly</u>.
10. Those oranges look <u>nice / nicely</u>. Can I have one?
11. I don't remember much about the accident. Everything happened <u>quick / quickly</u>.

87.4 Write *good* or *well*.

1. Your English is very __*good*__ . You speak it very __*well*__ .
2. Jackie did very _____ on the quiz today.
3. The party was very _____ . I enjoyed it a lot.
4. Martin has a difficult job, but he does it _____ .
5. How are your parents? Are they _____ ?
6. Did you have a _____ vacation? Was the weather _____ ?

old/older   expensive / more expensive

A

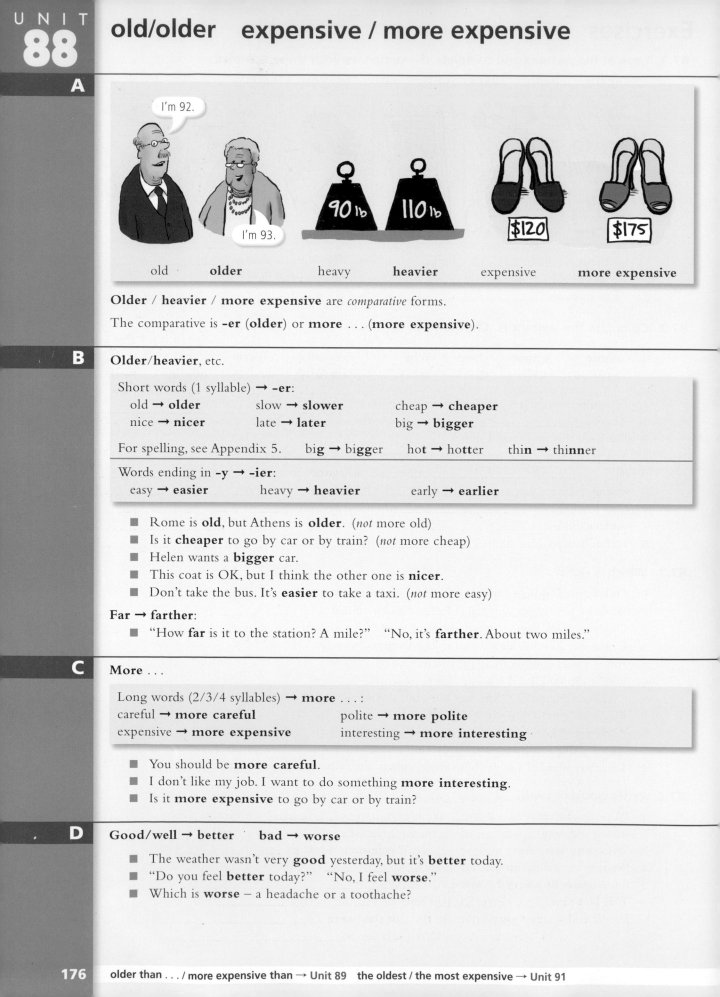

I'm 92.

I'm 93.

90 lb   110 lb

$120 $175

old   ·   **older**   heavy   **heavier**   expensive   **more expensive**

Older / **heavier** / **more expensive** are *comparative* forms.

The comparative is **-er** (**older**) or **more** . . . (**more expensive**).

B   **Older**/**heavier**, etc.

Short words (1 syllable) → **-er**:
old → **older**   slow → **slower**   cheap → **cheaper**
nice → **nicer**   late → **later**   big → **bigger**

For spelling, see Appendix 5.   bi**g** → bi**gg**er   hot → ho**tt**er   thi**n** → thi**nn**er

Words ending in **-y** → **-ier**:
easy → **easier**   heavy → **heavier**   early → **earlier**

■ Rome is **old**, but Athens is **older**. (*not* more old)
■ Is it **cheaper** to go by car or by train? (*not* more cheap)
■ Helen wants a **bigger** car.
■ This coat is OK, but I think the other one is **nicer**.
■ Don't take the bus. It's **easier** to take a taxi. (*not* more easy)

Far → farther:
■ "How **far** is it to the station? A mile?"   "No, it's **farther**. About two miles."

C   **More** . . .

Long words (2/3/4 syllables) → **more** . . . :
careful → **more careful**   polite → **more polite**
expensive → **more expensive**   interesting → **more interesting**

■ You should be **more careful**.
■ I don't like my job. I want to do something **more interesting**.
■ Is it **more expensive** to go by car or by train?

D   **Good/well → better   bad → worse**

■ The weather wasn't very **good** yesterday, but it's **better** today.
■ "Do you feel **better** today?"   "No, I feel **worse**."
■ Which is **worse** – a headache or a toothache?

Exercises

88.1 Look at the pictures and write the comparative (*older / more interesting*, etc.).

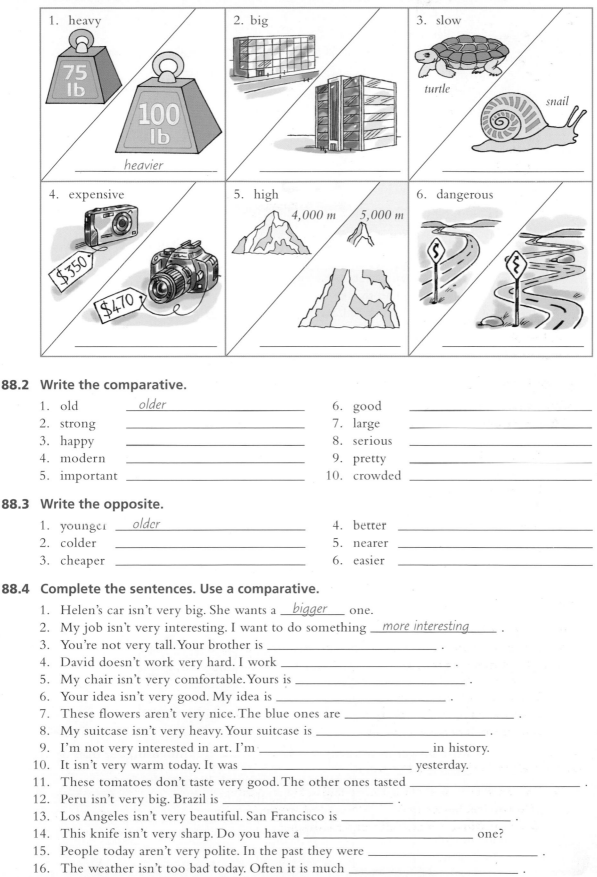

1. heavy   75 lb   100 lb   _heavier_
2. big
3. slow   *turtle*   *snail*
4. expensive $350 $470
5. high   4,000 m   5,000 m
6. dangerous

88.2 Write the comparative.

1. old   _older_
2. strong   _____
3. happy   _____
4. modern   _____
5. important   _____
6. good   _____
7. large   _____
8. serious   _____
9. pretty   _____
10. crowded   _____

88.3 Write the opposite.

1. younger   _older_
2. colder   _____
3. cheaper   _____
4. better   _____
5. nearer   _____
6. easier   _____

88.4 Complete the sentences. Use a comparative.

1. Helen's car isn't very big. She wants a __*bigger*__ one.
2. My job isn't very interesting. I want to do something __*more interesting*__ .
3. You're not very tall. Your brother is _____ .
4. David doesn't work very hard. I work _____ .
5. My chair isn't very comfortable. Yours is _____ .
6. Your idea isn't very good. My idea is _____ .
7. These flowers aren't very nice. The blue ones are _____ .
8. My suitcase isn't very heavy. Your suitcase is _____ .
9. I'm not very interested in art. I'm _____ in history.
10. It isn't very warm today. It was _____ yesterday.
11. These tomatoes don't taste very good. The other ones tasted _____ .
12. Peru isn't very big. Brazil is _____ .
13. Los Angeles isn't very beautiful. San Francisco is _____ .
14. This knife isn't very sharp. Do you have a _____ one?
15. People today aren't very polite. In the past they were _____ .
16. The weather isn't too bad today. Often it is much _____ .

older than . . . more expensive than . . .

A

I'm **taller than** you.

Hotel Prices
[per room per night]

Capitol Hotel	$350
Grand Hotel	$130
Western Hotel	$175

She's **taller than** him.

The Capitol Hotel is **more expensive than** the Grand Hotel.

We use **than** after comparatives (**older than** . . . / **more expensive than** . . . , etc.):

- Athens is **older than** Rome.
- Are oranges **more expensive than** bananas?
- It's easier to take a taxi **than** to take the bus.
- "How are you today?"   "Not bad. **Better than** yesterday."
- The restaurant is **more crowded than** usual.

B

We usually say: than **me** / than **him** / than **her** / than **us** / than **them**.

You can say:

- I can run faster **than him**.   *or*   I can run faster **than he can**.
- You are a better singer **than me**.   *or*   You are a better singer **than I am**.
- I got up earlier **than her**.   *or*   I got up earlier **than she did**.

C

More / less than . . .

- *A:* How much did your shoes cost? Fifty dollars?
  B: No, **more than** that. (= **more than** $50)
- The movie was very short – **less than** an hour.
- They've got **more money than** they need.
- You go out **more than** me.

```
60 ─
        MORE THAN 50
           ▲
50 ─       │
           ▼
40 ─    LESS THAN 50
```

D

A little older / much older, etc.

Box A is **a little bigger** than Box B.

Box C is **much bigger** than Box D.

a little **much**	bigger older better more difficult more expensive	than . . .

- Canada is **much bigger** than France.
- Sue is a **little older** than Gary – she's 25 and he's 24.
- The hotel was **much more expensive** than I expected.
- You go out **much more** than me.

Exercises

89.1 Write sentences about Liz and Ben. Use *than*.

Liz   Ben

1. I'm 26.	1. I'm 24.
2. I'm not a very good swimmer.	2. I'm a very good swimmer.
3. I'm 5 feet 10 inches tall.	3. I'm 5 feet 8 inches tall.
4. I start work at 8:00.	4. I start work at 8:30.
5. I don't work very hard.	5. I work very hard.
6. I don't have much money.	6. I have a lot of money.
7. I'm a very good driver.	7. I'm not a very good driver.
8. I'm not very patient.	8. I'm very patient.
9. I'm not a very good dancer.	9. I'm a good dancer.
10. I'm very intelligent.	10. I'm not very intelligent.
11. I speak Spanish very well.	11. I don't speak Spanish very well.
12. I don't go to the movies very much.	12. I go to the movies a lot.

1. Liz _is older than Ben_____ .
2. Ben _is a better swimmer than Liz_____ .
3. Liz is _____ .
4. Liz starts _____ Ben.
5. Ben _____ .
6. Ben has _____ .

7. Liz is a _____ .
8. Ben _____ .
9. Ben _____ .
10. Liz _____ .
11. Liz _____ .
12. Ben _____ .

89.2 Complete the sentences. Use *than*.

1. He isn't very tall. You're _taller than him_____ OR _taller than he is_____ .
2. She isn't very old. You're _____ .
3. I don't work very hard. You work _____ .
4. He doesn't watch TV very much. You _____ .
5. I'm not a very good cook. You _____ .
6. We don't know many people. You _____ .
7. They don't have much money. You _____ .
8. I can't run very fast. You can _____ .
9. She hasn't been here very long. You _____ .
10. They didn't get up very early. You _____ .
11. He wasn't very surprised. You _____ .

89.3 Complete the sentences with *a little* or *much* + comparative (*older/better*, etc.).

1. Emma is 18 months old. Gary is 16 months old.
   Emma _is a little older than Gary_____ .
2. Jack's mother is 52. His father is 69.
   Jack's mother _____ .
3. My camera cost $100. Yours cost $96.
   My camera _____ .
4. Yesterday I felt terrible. Today I feel OK.
   I feel _____ .
5. Today the temperature is 12 degrees Celsius. Yesterday it was 10 degrees Celsius.
   It's _____ .
6. Sarah is an excellent volleyball player. I'm not very good.
   Sarah _____ .

not as . . . as

Not as . . . as

I'm 93.   I'm 96.

She's old, but she's **not as old as** he is.   Box A is**n't as big as** Box B.

- Rome is **not as old as** Athens. (= Athens is older)
- The Grand Hotel is**n't as expensive as** the Western. (= the Western is **more expensive**)
- I do**n't** play soccer **as often as** you. (= you play **more often**)
- The weather is better than it was yesterday. It is**n't as cold**. (= as cold **as it was yesterday**)

Not as much as . . . / not as many as . . .

- I don't have **as much money as** you. (= you have **more money**)
- I don't know **as many people as** you. (= you know **more people**)
- I don't go out **as much as** you. (= you go out **more**)

Compare **not as . . . as** and **than**:

- Rome is **not as old as** Athens.
  Athens is **older than** Rome. (*not* older as Rome)
- Tennis is**n't as popular as** soccer.
  Soccer is **more popular than** tennis.
- I do**n't** go out **as much as** you.
  You go out **more than** me.

We usually say: as **me** / as **him** / as **her**, etc.
You can say:

- She's not as old **as him**.   *or*   She's not as old **as he is**.
- You don't work as hard **as me**.   *or*   You don't work as hard **as I do**.

We say **the same as** . . . :

- The weather today is **the same as** yesterday.
- My hair is **the same color as** yours.
- I arrived at **the same time as** Tim.

Exercises

90.1 Look at the pictures and write sentences about A, B, and C.

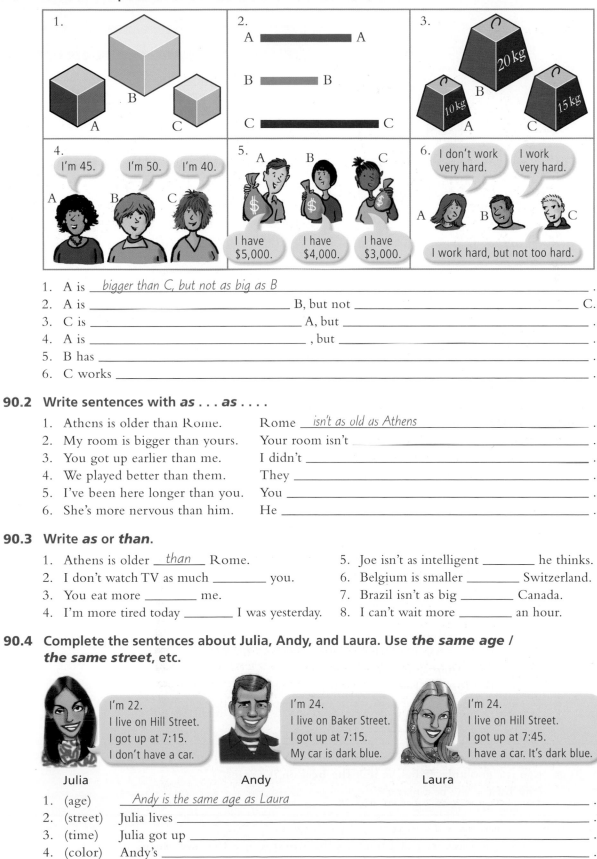

1. A is _bigger than C, but not as big as B_ .
2. A is _____ B, but not _____ C.
3. C is _____ A, but _____ .
4. A is _____ , but _____ .
5. B has _____ .
6. C works _____ .

90.2 Write sentences with as . . . as . . . .

1. Athens is older than Rome.   Rome _isn't as old as Athens_ .
2. My room is bigger than yours.   Your room isn't _____ .
3. You got up earlier than me.   I didn't _____ .
4. We played better than them.   They _____ .
5. I've been here longer than you.   You _____ .
6. She's more nervous than him.   He _____ .

90.3 Write as or than.

1. Athens is older _than_ Rome.
2. I don't watch TV as much _____ you.
3. You eat more _____ me.
4. I'm more tired today _____ I was yesterday.
5. Joe isn't as intelligent _____ he thinks.
6. Belgium is smaller _____ Switzerland.
7. Brazil isn't as big _____ Canada.
8. I can't wait more _____ an hour.

90.4 Complete the sentences about Julia, Andy, and Laura. Use the same age / the same street, etc.

Julia: I'm 22. I live on Hill Street. I got up at 7:15. I don't have a car.

Andy: I'm 24. I live on Baker Street. I got up at 7:15. My car is dark blue.

Laura: I'm 24. I live on Hill Street. I got up at 7:45. I have a car. It's dark blue.

1. (age)   _Andy is the same age as Laura_ .
2. (street) Julia lives _____ .
3. (time)   Julia got up _____ .
4. (color) Andy's _____ .

the oldest   the most expensive

A

MOTEL PRICES IN

JAMESTOWN
[Per room per night]

Best West Motel	$135	Oak Tree Motel	$85
Sleep Inn	$105	Cozy Cabins	$60
Rainbow Motel	$95	Lake View Inn	$50

Box A is **bigger than** Box B.

Box A is **bigger than** all the other boxes.

Box A is **the biggest** box.

The Best West Motel is **more expensive than** the Sleep Inn.

The Best West Motel is **more expensive than** all the other motels in town.

The Best West Motel is **the most expensive** motel in town.

Bigger / older / more expensive, etc. are *comparative* forms (→ Unit 88).

Biggest / oldest / most expensive, etc. are *superlative* forms.

B

The superlative form is **-est** (**oldest**) or **most . . .** (**most expensive**).

Short words (**old/cheap/nice**, etc.) → **the -est**:
    old → **the oldest**   cheap → **the cheapest**   nice → **the nicest**
but   good → **the best**   bad → **the worst**

For spelling see Appendix 5.   **big** → the big**g**est   hot → the hottest

Words ending in **-y** (**easy/heavy**, etc.) → **the -iest**:
    easy → **the easiest**   heavy → **the heaviest**   pretty → **the prettiest**

Long words (**careful/expensive/interesting**, etc.) → **the most . . .**:
    careful → **the most careful**   interesting → **the most interesting**

C

We say **the** oldest . . . / **the** most expensive . . . , etc. (with **the**):
- The church is very old. It's **the oldest** building in the town.
  (= it is **older than** all the other buildings)
- What is **the longest** river in the world?
- Money is important, but it isn't **the most important** thing in life.
- Excuse me, where is **the nearest** bank?

D

You can use **the oldest / the best / the most expensive**, etc. without a noun:
- Ken is a good player, but he isn't **the best** on the team.
  (**the best** = the best player)

E

You can use *superlative* + **I've ever . . . / you've ever . . .** , etc.:
- The movie was very bad. I think it's **the worst** movie **I've ever seen**.
- What is **the most unusual** thing **you've ever done**?

Exercises

91.1 Write sentences with comparatives (*older*, etc.) and superlatives (*the oldest*, etc.).

1.

big/small
(A/D)   *A is bigger than D.*
(A)   *A is the biggest.*
(B)   *B is the smallest.*

2.

A —————— A
B ———— B
C ———————— C
D ——————————— D

long/short
(C/A)   C is _____ A.
(D)   D is _____
(B)   B is _____

3.

I'm 23.   I'm 19.   I'm 24.   I'm 21.

A   B   C   D

young/old
(D/C)   D _____
(C)   _____
(B)   _____

4.

$25 $45 $50 $30
A   B   C   D

expensive/cheap
(D/A)   _____
(C)   _____
(A)   _____

5.

RESTAURANT A excellent
RESTAURANT B not bad
RESTAURANT C good but not wonderful
RESTAURANT D awful

good/bad
(A/C)   _____
(A)   _____
(D)   _____

91.2 Complete the sentences. Use a superlative (*the oldest*, etc.).

1. This building is very old. It's _the oldest building_ in town.
2. It was a very happy day. It was _____ of my life.
3. It's a very good movie. It's _____ I've ever seen.
4. She's a very popular singer. She's _____ in the country.
5. It was a very bad mistake. It was _____ I've ever made.
6. It's a very pretty city. It's _____ I've ever seen.
7. It was a very cold day. It was _____ of the year.
8. He's a very boring person. He's _____ I've ever met.

91.3 Write sentences with a superlative (*the longest*, etc.). Choose from the boxes.

Sydney Alaska	high	city	river	Africa	South America
Everest the Nile	large	country	state	Australia	the world
Brazil Jupiter	long	mountain	planet	the United States	the solar system

1. _Sydney is the largest city in Australia._
2. Everest _____
3. _____
4. _____
5. _____
6. _____

183

enough

A

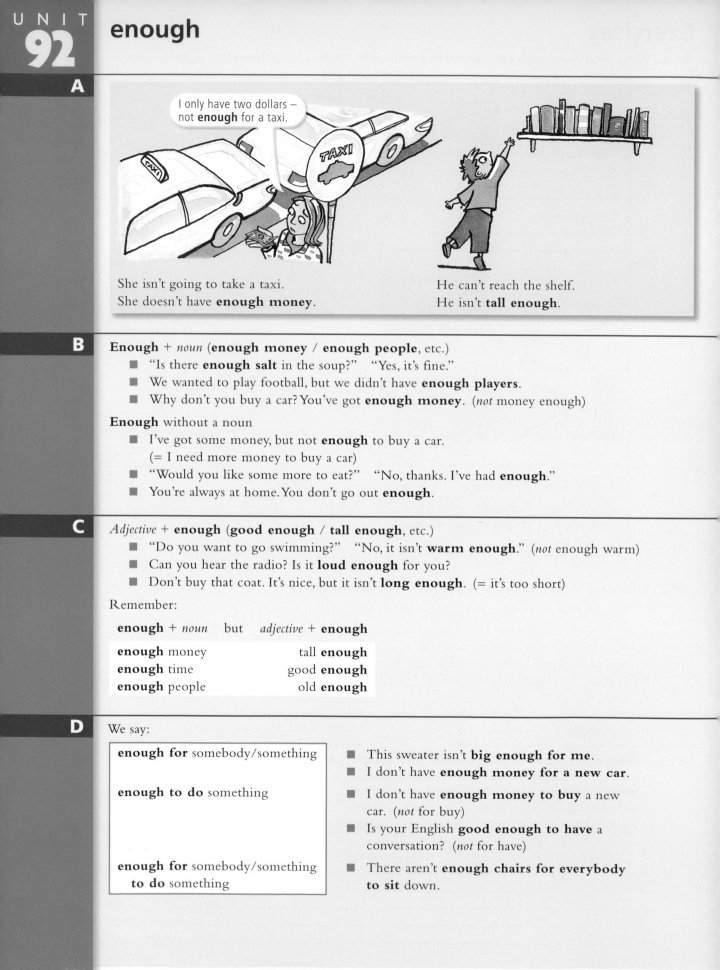

I only have two dollars – not **enough** for a taxi.

She isn't going to take a taxi.
She doesn't have **enough money**.

He can't reach the shelf.
He isn't **tall enough**.

B

Enough + *noun* (**enough money** / **enough people**, etc.)

- ■ "Is there **enough salt** in the soup?" "Yes, it's fine."
- ■ We wanted to play football, but we didn't have **enough players**.
- ■ Why don't you buy a car? You've got **enough money**. (*not* money enough)

Enough without a noun

- ■ I've got some money, but not **enough** to buy a car.
  (= I need more money to buy a car)
- ■ "Would you like some more to eat?" "No, thanks. I've had **enough**."
- ■ You're always at home. You don't go out **enough**.

C

Adjective + **enough** (**good enough** / **tall enough**, etc.)

- ■ "Do you want to go swimming?" "No, it isn't **warm enough**." (*not* enough warm)
- ■ Can you hear the radio? Is it **loud enough** for you?
- ■ Don't buy that coat. It's nice, but it isn't **long enough**. (= it's too short)

Remember:

enough + *noun* but *adjective* + **enough**

enough money	tall **enough**
enough time	good **enough**
enough people	old **enough**

D

We say:

enough for somebody/something	■ This sweater isn't **big enough for me**.
	■ I don't have **enough money for a new car**.
enough to do something	■ I don't have **enough money to buy** a new car. (*not* for buy)
	■ Is your English **good enough to have** a conversation? (*not* for have)
enough for somebody/something **to do** something	■ There aren't **enough chairs for everybody to sit** down.

Exercises

92.1 Look at the pictures and complete the sentences. Use *enough* + these words:

chairs   ~~money~~   paint   wind

1. She doesn't have _enough money_ .
2. There aren't _____ .
3. She doesn't have _____ .
4. There isn't _____ .

92.2 Look at the pictures and complete the sentences. Use these adjectives + *enough*:

big   long   strong   ~~tall~~

1. He _isn't tall enough_ .
2. The car _____ .
3. His legs aren't _____ .
4. He _____ .

92.3 Complete the sentences. Use *enough* with these words:

big   eat   ~~loud~~   old   practice   ~~salt~~   space   time   tired

1. "Is there _enough salt_ in the soup?"   "Yes, it's fine."
2. Can you hear the radio? Is it _loud enough_ for you?
3. He can quit school if he wants – he's _____ .
4. When I visited New York last year, I didn't have _____ to see all
    the things I wanted to see.
5. This house isn't _____ for a large family.
6. Tina is very thin. She doesn't _____ .
7. My office is very small. There isn't _____ .
8. It's late, but I don't want to go to bed now. I'm not _____ .
9. Lisa isn't a very good tennis player because she doesn't _____ .

92.4 Complete the sentences. Use *enough* with these words:

1. We don't have _enough money to buy_ a new car.   (money / buy)
2. This knife isn't _____ tomatoes. (sharp / cut)
3. The water wasn't _____ swimming. (warm / go)
4. Do we have _____ sandwiches? (bread / make)
5. We played well, but not _____ the game. (well / win)
6. I don't have _____ the newspaper. (time / read)

too

A

The shoes are **too big** for him.

There is **too much** sugar in it.

Yuck!

B

Too + *adjective / adverb* (**too big** / **too hard**, etc.)

- Can you turn the radio down?
  It's **too loud**. (= louder than I want)
- I can't work. I'm **too tired**.
- I think you work **too hard**.

It's **too loud**.

C

Too much / **too many** = more than you want, more than is good:

- I don't like the weather here. There is **too much rain**. (= more rain than is good)
- Let's go to another restaurant. There are **too many people** here.
- Emily studies all the time. I think she studies **too much**.
- Traffic is a problem in this town. There are **too many cars**.

D

Compare **too** and **not enough**:

too big

- The hat is **too big** for him.
- The radio is **too loud**. Can you turn it down, please?
- There's **too much sugar** in my coffee.
  (= more sugar than I want)
- I don't feel very well. I ate **too much**.

not big enough

- The hat is**n't big enough** for him. (= it's **too small**)
- The radio is**n't loud enough**. Can you turn it up, please?
- There's **not enough sugar** in my coffee.
  (= I need more sugar)
- You're very thin. You do**n't** eat **enough**.

E

We say:

too ... for somebody/something
too ... to do something
too ... for somebody **to do** something

- These shoes are **too big for me**.
- It's a small house – **too small for a large family**.

- I'm **too tired to go** out. (*not* for go out)
- It's **too cold to sit** outside.

- She speaks **too fast for me to understand**.

to ... and for ... → Unit 55   much/many → Unit 84   enough → Unit 92

Exercises

93.1 Look at the pictures and complete the sentences. Use *too* + these words:

big   crowded   fast   heavy   ~~loud~~   low

1. The music is ___too loud___ .
2. The box is _____ .
3. The net is _____ .
4. She's driving _____ .
5. The ball is _____ .
6. The museum is _____ .

93.2 Write *too / too much / too many* or *enough*.

1. You're always at home. You don't go out ___enough___ .
2. I don't like the weather here. There's ___too much___ rain.
3. I can't wait for them. I don't have _____ time.
4. There was nowhere to sit on the beach. There were _____ people.
5. You're always tired. I think you work _____ hard.
6. "Did you have _____ to eat?"   "Yes, thank you."
7. You drink _____ coffee. It's not good for you.
8. You don't eat _____ vegetables. You should eat more of them.
9. I don't like the weather here. It's _____ cold.
10. Our team didn't play well. We made _____ mistakes.
11. "Would you like some ice in your tea?"   "Yes, but not _____ ."

93.3 Complete the sentences. Use *too* or *enough* with these words:

1. I couldn't work. I ___was too tired___ . (tired)
2. Can you turn the radio up, please? It ___isn't loud enough___ . (loud)
3. I don't want to walk home. It's _____ . (far)
4. Don't buy anything in that store. It _____ . (expensive)
5. You can't put all your things in this bag. It _____ . (big)
6. I couldn't do the exercise. It _____ . (difficult)
7. Your work needs to be better. It _____ . (good)
8. I can't talk to you now. I _____ . (busy)
9. I thought the movie was boring. It _____ . (long)

93.4 Complete the sentences. Use *too* (+ adjective) + *to* . . . .

1. (I'm not going out / cold)   It's ___too cold to go out___ .
2. (I'm not going to bed / early)   It's _____ .
3. (they're not getting married / young)   They're _____ .
4. (nobody goes out at night / dangerous)
   It's _____ .
5. (don't call Sue now / late)
   It's _____ .
6. (I didn't say anything / surprised)
   I was _____ .

He **speaks English** very well. (word order 1)

Verb + object

Sue **reads** **a newspaper** every day.
subject *verb* *object*

The *verb* (**reads**) and the *object* (**a newspaper**) are usually together. We say:

- Sue **reads a newspaper** every day.
  (*not* Sue reads every day a newspaper)

Sue (subject) *a newspaper (object)*

	verb + object
He **speaks**	**English** very well. (*not* He speaks very well English)
I **like**	**Italian food** very much. (*not* I like very much . . .)
Did you **watch**	**television** all night? (*not* Did you watch all night . . .)
Paul often **wears**	**a black hat**. (*not* Paul wears often . . .)
We **invited**	**a lot of people** to the party.
I **opened**	**the door** slowly.
Why do you always **make**	**the same mistake**?
I'm going to **borrow**	**some money** from the bank.

Where and when

We went **to a party** **last night** .
where? *when?*

Place *(where?)* is usually before time *(when?)*. We say:

- We went **to a party last night**. (*not* We went last night to a party)

	place (where?)	+	time (when? how long? how often?)	
Lisa walks	**to work**		**every day**.	(*not* . . . every day to work)
Will you be	**at home**		**tonight**?	(*not* . . . tonight at home)
I usually go	**to bed**		**early**.	(*not* . . . early to bed)
We arrived	**at the airport**		**at 7:00**.	
They've lived	**in the same house**		**for 20 years**.	
Joe's father has been	**in the hospital**		**since June**.	

Exercises

94.1 Right or wrong? Correct the sentences that are wrong.

1. Did you watch (all night television)? _Did you watch television all night?_
2. Sue reads a newspaper every day. _OK_
3. I like very much this picture. _____
4. Tom started last week his new job. _____
5. I want to speak English fluently. _____
6. Jane bought for her friend a present. _____
7. I drink every day three cups of coffee. _____
8. Don't eat your dinner too quickly! _____
9. I borrowed from my brother 50 dollars. _____

94.2 Put the words in order.

1. (the door / opened / I / slowly) _I opened the door slowly._
2. (a new computer / I / last week / bought) I _____
3. (finished / Paul / quickly / his work) _____
4. (Emily / very well / French / doesn't speak) _____
5. (a lot of shopping / did / I / yesterday) _____
6. (New York / do you know / well?) _____
7. (we / enjoyed / very much / the party) _____
8. (the problem / carefully / I / explained) _____
9. (we / at the airport / some friends / met) _____
10. (did you buy / in Canada / that jacket?) _____
11. (every day / do / the same thing / we) _____
12. (football / don't like / very much / I) _____

94.3 Put the words in order.

1. (to work / every day / walks / Lisa) _Lisa walks to work every day._
2. (at the hotel / I / early / arrived) I _____
3. (goes / every year / to Puerto Rico / Julia) Julia _____
4. (we / since 2002 / here / have lived) We _____
5. (in Florida / Sue / in 1984 / was born)
   Sue _____
6. (didn't go / yesterday / Paul / to work)
   Paul _____
7. (to a wedding / last weekend / went / Helen)
   Helen _____
8. (I / in bed / this morning / my breakfast / had)
   I _____
9. (in September / Barbara / to college / is going)
   Barbara _____
10. (I / a beautiful bird / this morning / in the garden / saw)
    I _____
11. (many times / have been / my parents / to Tokyo)
    My _____
12. (my umbrella / I / last night / left / in the restaurant)
    I _____
13. (to the movies / tomorrow night / are you going?)
    Are _____
14. (the children / I / took / this morning / to school)
    I _____

always/usually/often, etc.
(word order 2)

These words (**always**/**never**, etc.) are with the verb in the middle of a sentence:

always	often	ever	rarely	also	already	all
usually	sometimes	never	seldom	just	still	both

- My brother **never speaks** to me.
- She**'s always** late.
- Do you **often go** to restaurants?
- I **sometimes eat** too much. (*or* **Sometimes** I eat too much.)
- "Don't forget to call Laura." "I**'ve already called** her."
- I've got three sisters. They**'re all** married.

Always/**never**, etc. are *before* the verb:

	verb
always	go
often	play
never	have
etc.	etc.

- I **always drink** coffee in the morning.
  (*not* I drink always coffee)
- Helen **often goes** to Chicago on business.
  (*not* Helen goes often)
- You **sometimes look** unhappy.
- They **usually have** dinner at 7:00.
- We **rarely** (*or* **seldom**) **watch** television.
- Richard is a good swimmer. He **also plays** tennis and volleyball.
  (*not* He plays also tennis)
- I've got three sisters. They **all live** in the same city.

But **always**/**never**, etc. are *after* **am/is/are/was/were**:

am	
is	always
are	often
was	never
were	etc.

- I **am always tired**. (*not* I always am tired)
- They **are never** at home during the day.
- It **is usually** very cold here in the winter.
- When I was a child, I **was often** late for school.
- "Where's Laura?" "She**'s still** in bed."
- I've got two brothers. They**'re both** doctors.

Always/**never**, etc. are *between* two verbs (**have . . . been** / **can . . . find**, etc.):

verb 1		*verb 2*
will		go
can	always	find
do	often	remember
etc.	never	etc.
have	etc.	gone
has		been
		etc.

- I **will always remember** you.
- It **doesn't often rain** here.
- Do you **usually drive** to work?
- I **can never find** my keys.
- **Have** you **ever been** to Egypt?
- **Did** the phone **just ring**?
- The children **have all finished** their homework.

---

always/never + simple present → Unit 5   **just/already** + present perfect → Unit 20   **all** → Units 81–82
both → Unit 83   **still** → Unit 96

Exercises

95.1 Read Paul's answers to the questions. Write sentences about Paul with *often*/*never*, etc.

Paul

1.	Do you ever play tennis?	Yes, often.
2.	Do you get up early?	Yes, always.
3.	Are you ever late for work?	No, never.
4.	Do you ever get angry?	Sometimes.
5.	Do you ever go swimming?	Rarely.
6.	Are you at home in the evenings?	Yes, usually.

Paul often plays tennis.

He _____

He _____

_____

_____

_____

95.2 Write these sentences with *never*/*always*/*usually*, etc.

1. My brother speaks to me. (never)   *My brother never speaks to me.*
2. Susan is polite. (always)   Susan _____
3. I finish work at 5:00. (usually)   I _____
4. Sarah has started a new job. (just)   Sarah _____
5. I go to bed before midnight. (rarely)   _____
6. The bus isn't late. (usually)   _____
7. I don't eat fish. (often)   _____
8. I will forget what you said. (never)   _____
9. Have you lost your passport? (ever)   _____
10. Do you work in the same place? (still)   _____
11. They stay at the same hotel. (always)   _____
12. Jane doesn't work on Saturdays. (usually)   _____
13. Is Tina here? (already)   _____
14. What do you have for breakfast? (usually)   _____
15. I can remember his name. (never)   _____

95.3 Write sentences with *also*.

1. Do you play football? (basketball)   *Yes, and I also play basketball.*
2. Do you speak Italian? (French)   Yes, and I _____
3. Are you tired? (hungry)   Yes, and _____
4. Have you been to Mexico? (Guatemala)   Yes, _____
5. Did you buy any clothes? (some books)   _____

95.4 Write sentences with *both* and *all*.

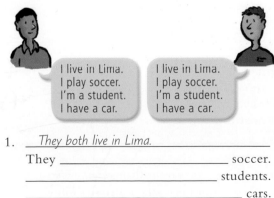

1. _They both live in Lima._

    They _____ soccer.

    _____ students.

    _____ cars.

2. They _____ married.

    They _____ Venezuela.

    _____

still   yet   already

A Still

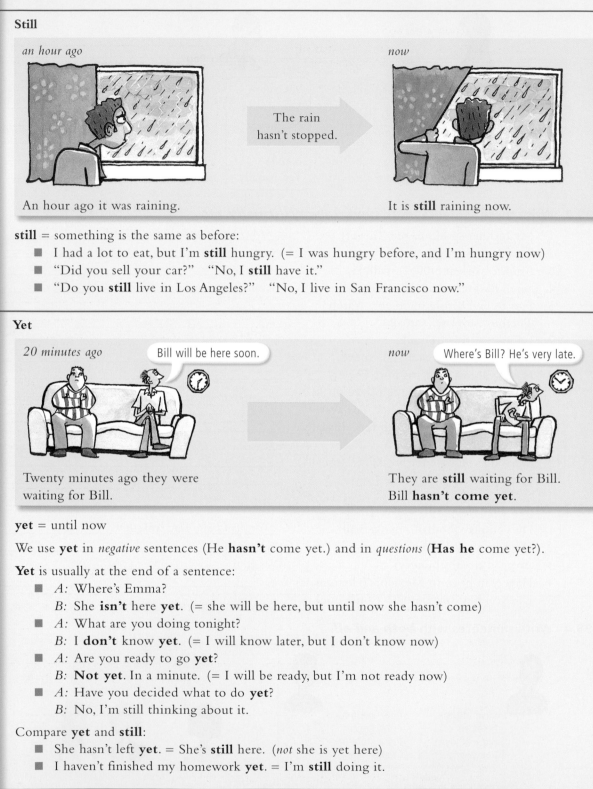

an hour ago   *now*

The rain hasn't stopped.

An hour ago it was raining.   It is **still** raining now.

still = something is the same as before:

■ I had a lot to eat, but I'm **still** hungry. (= I was hungry before, and I'm hungry now)

■ "Did you sell your car?"   "No, I **still** have it."

■ "Do you **still** live in Los Angeles?"   "No, I live in San Francisco now."

B Yet

20 minutes ago   Bill will be here soon.   *now*   Where's Bill? He's very late.

Twenty minutes ago they were   They are **still** waiting for Bill.
waiting for Bill.   Bill **hasn't come yet**.

yet = until now

We use **yet** in *negative* sentences (He **hasn't** come yet.) and in *questions* (**Has he** come yet?).

Yet is usually at the end of a sentence:

■ *A:* Where's Emma?
  B: She **isn't** here **yet**. (= she will be here, but until now she hasn't come)

■ *A:* What are you doing tonight?
  B: I **don't** know **yet**. (= I will know later, but I don't know now)

■ *A:* Are you ready to go **yet**?
  B: **Not yet**. In a minute. (= I will be ready, but I'm not ready now)

■ *A:* Have you decided what to do **yet**?
  B: No, I'm still thinking about it.

Compare **yet** and **still**:

■ She hasn't left **yet**. = She's **still** here. (*not* she is yet here)

■ I haven't finished my homework **yet**. = I'm **still** doing it.

C Already = earlier than expected:

■ "What time is Joe coming?"   "He's **already** here." (= earlier than we expected)

■ "I'm going to tell you what happened."   "That's not necessary. I **already** know."

■ Sarah isn't coming to the movies with us. She has **already** seen the film.

already/yet + present perfect/simple past → Unit 20   word order (**still/already**) → Unit 95

Exercises

96.1 You meet Tina. The last time you saw her was two years ago. You ask her some questions with *still*.

Tina – two years ago

1. I play the piano.
4. I'm studying Japanese.
2. I have an old car.
5. I go to the movies a lot.
3. I'm a student.
6. I want to be a teacher.

1. _Do you still play the piano?_
2. Do you _____
3. Are _____
4. _____
5. _____
6. _____

96.2 Write three sentences for each situation. Look at the example carefully.

| | before | now |

1.
(before) _They were waiting for the bus._
(still) _They are still waiting._
(yet) _The bus hasn't come yet._

2. I'm looking for a job.
(before) He was _____
(still) He _____
(yet) _____ yet.

3.
(before) She _____ asleep.
(still) _____
(yet) _____

4.
dinner   dinner
(before) They _____
(still) _____
(yet) _____

96.3 Write questions with *yet*.

1. You and Sue are going out together. You are waiting for her to get ready. Maybe she is ready now. You ask her: _Are you ready yet?_
2. You are waiting for Helen to arrive. She wasn't here 10 minutes ago. Maybe she is here now. You ask somebody: _____ Helen _____
3. Anna had a blood test and is waiting for the results. Maybe she has gotten her results. You ask her: _____ you _____
4. A few days ago you spoke to Tom. He wasn't sure where to go for his vacation. Maybe he has decided. You ask him: _____

96.4 Complete the sentences. Use *already*.

1.	What time is Joe coming?	_He's already_ here.
2.	Do you and Joe want to see the movie?	No, we _'ve already seen_ it.
3.	I have to see Julia before she leaves.	It's too late. She _____ .
4.	Do you need a pen?	No, thanks. I _____ one.
5.	Should I pay the bill?	No, that's OK. I _____ .
6.	Should I tell Paul about the meeting?	No, he _____ . I told him.

Give me that book!   Give it to me!

A

give   lend   pass   send   show

After these verbs (**give** / **lend**, etc.), there are two possible structures:

give something to somebody
- I gave **the keys to Sarah**.

give somebody something
- I gave **Sarah the keys**.

Sarah

B

Give something to somebody

		something	to somebody
That's my book.	**Give**	it	**to** me.
These are Sue's keys. Can you	**give**	them	**to** her?
Can you	**give**	these flowers	**to** your mother?
I	**lent**	my car	**to** a friend of mine.
Did you	**send**	a postcard	**to** Kate?
We've seen these pictures. You	**showed**	them	**to** us yesterday.

C

Give somebody something

		somebody	something
	Give	me	that book. It's mine.
Tom	**gave**	his mother	some flowers.
I	**lent**	Joe	some money.
How much money did you	**lend**	him?	
I	**sent**	you	an e-mail. Did you get it?
Nicole	**showed**	us	her vacation photos.
Can you	**pass**	me	the salt, please?

You can also say "**buy** / **get** somebody something":
- I **bought** my mother some flowers. (= I bought some flowers **for** my mother.)
- Can you **get** me a newspaper when you go out? (= get a newspaper **for** me)

D

You can say:
- I **gave** the keys **to Sarah**.
- *and* I **gave Sarah** the keys.
   (*but not* I gave to Sarah the keys)

- That's my book. Can you **give** it **to me**?
- *and* Can you **give me** that book?
   (*but not* Can you give to me that book?)

We prefer the first structure (**give** something **to** somebody) with **it** or **them**:
- I gave **it to her**. (*not* I gave her it)
- Here are the keys. Give **them to your father**. (*not* Give your father them)

it/him/them, etc. → Unit 60

Exercises

97.1 Mark had some things that he didn't want. He gave them to different people.

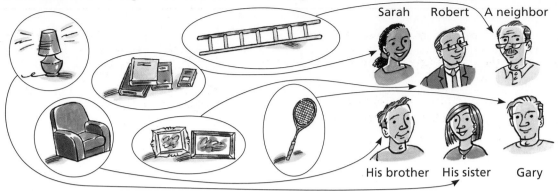

Write sentences beginning **He gave** . . . .

1. What did Mark do with the armchair? _He gave it to his brother._
2. What did he do with the tennis racket? He gave _____
3. What happened to the books? He _____
4. What about the lamp? _____
5. What did he do with the pictures? _____
6. And the ladder? _____

97.2 You gave presents to your friends. You decided to give them the things in the pictures.
Write a sentence for each person.

1. _I gave Paul a book_   4. _____
2. I gave _____   5. _____
3. I _____   6. _____

97.3 Write questions beginning **Can you give me** . . . **?** / **Can you pass me** . . . **?**, etc.

1. (you want the salt) (pass) _Can you pass me the salt?_
2. (you need an umbrella) (lend) Can you _____
3. (you want my address) (give) Can _____ your _____
4. (you need 20 dollars) (lend) _____
5. (you want some information) (send) _____
6. (you want to see the letter) (show) _____
7. (you want some stamps) (get) _____

97.4 Which is right?

1. ~~I gave to Sarah the keys.~~ / I gave Sarah the keys. (*I gave Sarah the keys* is right)
2. I'll <u>lend to you some money</u> if you want. / I'll <u>lend you some money</u> if you want.
3. Did you <u>send the letter me</u>? / Did you <u>send the letter to me</u>?
4. I want to <u>buy for you a present</u>. / I want to <u>buy you a present</u>.
5. Can you <u>pass to me the sugar</u>, please? / Can you <u>pass me the sugar</u>, please?
6. This is Lisa's bag. Can you <u>give it to her</u>? / Can you <u>give her it</u>?
7. I <u>showed to the police officer my driver's license</u>. /
   I <u>showed the police officer my driver's license</u>.

and but or so because

A

| and | but | or | so | because |

We use these words *(conjunctions)* to join two sentences. They make one longer sentence from two shorter sentences:

sentence A   The car stopped. —— The driver got out.   *sentence B*

The car stopped, **and** the driver got out.

B   And/but/or

sentence A		*sentence B*
We stayed at home	**and**	(we)* watched television.
My sister is married	**and**	(she)* lives in Houston.
He doesn't like her,	**and**	she doesn't like him.
I bought a newspaper,	**but**	I didn't read it.
It's a nice house,	**but**	it doesn't have a garage.
Do you want to go out,	**or**	are you too tired?

*It is not necessary to repeat "we" and "she."

In lists, we use commas (,). We use **and** before the last thing:

■ I got home, had something to eat, sat down in an armchair, **and** fell asleep.

■ Karen is at work, Sue has gone shopping, **and** Chris is playing football.

C   So (the result of something)

sentence A		*sentence B*
It was very hot,	**so**	I opened the window.
Joe plays a lot of sports,	**so**	he's very fit.
They don't like to travel,	**so**	they haven't been to many places.

D   Because (the reason for something)

sentence A		*sentence B*
I opened the window	**because**	it was very hot.
Joe can't come to the party	**because**	he's leaving town.
Lisa is hungry	**because**	she didn't have breakfast.

Because is also possible at the beginning. We use a comma.

■ **Because it was very hot**, I opened the window.

E

In these examples there is more than one conjunction:

■ It was late **and** I was tired, **so** I went to bed.

■ I love New York, **but** I wouldn't like to live there **because** it's too big.

Exercises

98.1 Write sentences. Choose from the boxes and use *and*/*but*/*or*.

I̶ ̶s̶t̶a̶y̶e̶d̶ ̶a̶t̶ ̶h̶o̶m̶e̶.̶
I̶ ̶b̶o̶u̶g̶h̶t̶ ̶a̶ ̶n̶e̶w̶s̶p̶a̶p̶e̶r̶.̶
I went to the window.
I wanted to call you.
I jumped into the river.
I usually drive to work.
Do you want me to come with you?

I didn't have your number.
Should I wait here?
I̶ ̶d̶i̶d̶n̶'̶t̶ ̶r̶e̶a̶d̶ ̶i̶t̶.̶
I took the bus this morning.
I̶ ̶w̶a̶t̶c̶h̶e̶d̶ ̶t̶e̶l̶e̶v̶i̶s̶i̶o̶n̶.̶
I swam to the other side.
I looked out.

1. _I stayed at home and watched television._
2. _I bought a newspaper, but I didn't read it._
3. I _____
4. _____
5. _____
6. _____
7. _____

98.2 Look at the pictures and complete the sentences. Use *and*/*but*/*so*/*because*.

1. It was very hot, _so he opened the window._
2. They couldn't play tennis _____
3. They went to the museum, _____
4. Bill wasn't hungry, _____
5. Helen was late _____
6. Sue said _____

98.3 Write sentences about what you did yesterday. Use *and*/*but*, etc.

1. (and)   _Last night I stayed at home and studied._
2. (because)   _I went to bed very early because I was tired._
3. (but)   _____
4. (and)   _____
5. (so)   _____
6. (because)   _____

When . . .

'A

When I went out, it was raining.

This sentence has two parts:

| when I went out | + | it was raining |

You can say:

- **When I went out**, it was raining. *or*
  It was raining when I went out.

We write a comma (,) if **When** . . . is at the beginning:

- { **When** you're tired, don't drive.
  { Don't drive **when** you're tired.

- { Helen was 25 **when** she got married.
  { **When** Helen got married, she was 25.

We do the same in sentences with **before/while/after**:

- { Always look both ways **before** you cross the street.
  { **Before** you cross the street, always look both ways.

- { **While** I was waiting for the bus, it began to rain.
  { It began to rain **while** I was waiting for the bus.

- { He never played football again **after** he broke his leg.
  { **After** he broke his leg, he never played football again.

B

When I am . . . / When I go . . . , etc.

Next week Sarah is going to New York.
She has a friend, Lisa, who lives in New York,
but Lisa is also going away – to Mexico.
So they won't see each other in New York.

Lisa **will be** in Mexico **when** Sarah **is** in
New York.

The time is *future* (**next week**), but we say:
- . . . **when** Sarah **is** in New York.
  (*not* when Sarah will be)

I'll be in Mexico
when you're here.

Sarah   Lisa

We use the *present* (**I am / I go**, etc.) with a *future meaning* after **when**:

- **When** I **get** home tonight, I'm going to take a shower. (*not* When I will get home)
- I can't talk to you now. I'll talk to you later **when** I **have** more time.

We do the same after **before/while/after/until**:

- Please close the window **before** you **go** out. (*not* before you will go)
- Rachel is going to stay in our apartment **while** we **are** away. (*not* while we will be)
- I'll wait here **until** you **come** back. (*not* until you will come back)

Exercises

99.1 Write sentences beginning with *When*. Choose from the boxes.

When +
| I went out |
| I'm tired |
| I called her |
| I go on vacation |
| the program ended |
| I got to the hotel |

+
| I turned off the TV |
| I always go to the same place |
| there were no rooms |
| it was raining |
| there was no answer |
| I like to watch TV |

1. *When I went out, it was raining.*
2. _____
3. _____
4. _____
5. _____
6. _____

99.2 Complete the sentences using the following:

somebody broke into the house	before they came here	when they heard the news
before they crossed the street	while they were away	they didn't believe me
they went to live in France		

1. They looked both ways *before they crossed the street.*
2. They were very surprised _____
3. After they got married, _____
4. Their house was damaged in a storm _____
5. Where did they live _____ ?
6. While we were asleep, _____
7. When I told them what happened, _____

99.3 Which is right?

1. ~~I stay~~ / I'll stay here until you come / ~~you'll come~~ back. (*I'll stay* and *you come* are right)
2. I'm going to bed when I finish / I'll finish my work.
3. We must do something before it's / it will be too late.
4. Helen is moving away soon. I'm / I'll be very sad when she leaves / she'll leave.
5. Don't go out yet. Wait until the rain stops / will stop.
6. We come / We'll come and visit you when we're / we'll be in Toronto again.
7. When I come / I'll come to see you tomorrow, I bring / I'll bring your DVDs.
8. I'm going to Quebec next week. I hope to see some friends of mine while I'm / I'll be there.
9. "I need your address." "OK, I give / I'll give it to you before I go / I'll go."
10. I'm not ready yet. I tell / I'll tell you when I'm / I'll be ready.

99.4 Use your own ideas to complete these sentences.

1. Can you close the window before *you go out* _____ ?
2. What are you going to do when _____ ?
3. When I have enough money, _____ .
4. I'll wait for you while _____ .
5. When I start my new job, _____ .
6. Will you be here when _____ ?

A

Should we take the bus or a taxi?

If we take the bus, it will be cheaper.

We'll get there more quickly **if we take a taxi**.

If can be at the beginning of a sentence or in the middle:

If at the beginning

If we take the bus,	it will be cheaper.
If you don't hurry,	you'll miss the train.
If you're hungry,	have something to eat.
If the phone rings,	can you answer it, please?

if in the middle

It will be cheaper	**if** we take the bus.
You'll miss the train	**if** you don't hurry.
I'm going to the concert	**if** I can get a ticket.
Is it OK	**if** I use your phone?

In conversation, we often use the **if**-part of the sentence alone:

- "Are you going to the concert?"   "Yes, **if I can get a ticket**."

B

If you see Ann tomorrow . . . , etc.

After **if**, we use the present (*not* will). We say **if** you **see** . . . (*not* if you will see):

- **If** you **see** Ann tomorrow, can you ask her to call me?
- **If** I**'m** late tonight, don't wait for me. (*not* if I will be)
- What should we do **if** it **rains**? (*not* if it will rain)
- **If** I **don't feel** well tomorrow, I'll stay home.

C

If and **when**

If I go out = it is possible that I will go out, but I'm not sure:

- *A:* Are you going out later?
  B: Maybe. **If I go out**, I'll close the windows.

When I go out = I'm going out (for sure):

- *A:* Are you going out later?
  B: Yes, I am. **When I go out**, I'll close the windows.

Compare **when** and **if**:

- **When** I get home tonight, I'm going to take a shower.
- **If** I'm late tonight, don't wait for me. (*not* When I'm late)
- We're going to play basketball **if** it doesn't rain. (*not* when it doesn't rain)

Exercises

100.1 Write sentences beginning with *If*. Choose from the boxes.

If +

~~you don't hurry~~
you pass the driving test
you fail the driving test
you don't want this magazine
you want those pictures
you're busy now
you're hungry
you need money

+

we can have lunch now
you can have them
I can lend you some
you'll get your license
~~you'll be late~~
I'll throw it away
we can talk later
you can take it again

1. *If you don't hurry, you'll be late.* _____
2. If you pass _____
3. If _____
4. _____
5. _____
6. _____
7. _____
8. _____

100.2 Which is right?

1. If I'm / ~~I'll be~~ late tonight, don't wait for me. (*I'm* is right)
2. Will you call me if <u>I give</u> / I'll give you my phone number?
3. If there <u>is</u> / will be a fire, the alarm will ring.
4. If I don't see you tomorrow morning, <u>I call</u> / I'll call you in the afternoon.
5. <u>I'm</u> / I'll be surprised if Martin and Jane <u>get</u> / will get married.
6. <u>Do you go</u> / Will you go to the party if <u>they invite</u> / they'll invite you?

100.3 Use your own ideas to complete these sentences.

1. I'm going to the concert if ___*I can get a ticket.*___
2. If you don't hurry, ___*you'll miss the train.*___
3. I don't want to disturb you if _____
4. If you go to bed early tonight, _____
5. Turn the television off if _____
6. Tina won't pass her driving test if _____
7. If I have time tomorrow, _____
8. We can go to the beach tomorrow if _____
9. I'll be surprised if _____

100.4 Write *if* or *when*.

1. ___*If*___ I'm late tonight, don't wait for me.
2. I'm going shopping now. _____ I come back, we can have lunch.
3. I'm thinking of going to see Tim. _____ I go, will you come with me?
4. _____ you don't want to go out tonight, we can stay at home.
5. Is it OK _____ I close the window?
6. John is still in high school. _____ he finishes, he wants to go to college.
7. Do you want to go on a picnic tomorrow _____ the weather is good?
8. We're going to Mexico City next week. We're going to look for a hotel _____ we get there. I don't know what we'll do _____ we don't find a room.

If I had . . .   If we went . . . , etc.

A

Dan likes fast cars, but he doesn't have one.
He doesn't have enough money.

If he had the money, he **would buy** a fast car.

Usually **had** is *past*, but in this sentence **had** is
not past. **If he had** the money = if he had the
money *now* (but he doesn't have it).

If	I you it they, etc.	**had/knew/lived/went** (etc.) . . . , **didn't have / didn't know** (etc.) . . . , **were** . . . , **could** . . . ,	I you it they, etc.	**would(n't)** **could(n't)**	buy . . . be . . . have . . . go . . . , etc.

You can say:

- **If he had** the money, he would buy a car.
- *or*   He would buy a car **if he had** the money.

I'd / she'd / they'd, etc. = I **would** / she **would** / they **would**, etc.:

- I don't know the answer. **If I knew** the answer, **I'd tell** you.
- It's raining, so we're not going out. We**'d get** wet **if** we **went** out.
- Jane lives in a city. She likes cities. She **wouldn't be** happy **if** she **lived** in the country.
- **If you didn't have** a job, what **would** you **do**? (but you *have* a job)
- I'm sorry I can't help you. **I'd help** you **if I could**. (but I *can't*)
- **If we had** a car, we **could travel** more. (but we *don't* have a car, so we *can't* travel much)

B

If (I) **was/were** . . .

I wouldn't go out **if I were** you.

You can say **if** I/he/she/it **was** *or* **if** I/he/she/it **were**:

- It's not a very nice place. I wouldn't go there **if I
  were you**. (*or* . . . **if I was** you)
- It would be nice **if the weather was** better.
  (*or* . . . **if the weather were** better)
- What would Tom do **if he were** here?
  (*or* . . . **if he was** here)

C

Compare:

if I have / if it is, etc.	**if I had / if it was**, etc.
- I want to go and see Helen. **If I have** time, I **will go** today. (= maybe I'll have time, so maybe I'll go)	- I want to go and see Helen. **If I had** time, I **would go** today. (= I don't have time today, so I will not go)
- I like that jacket. **I'll buy** it **if** it **isn't** too expensive. (= maybe it will not be too expensive)	- I like that jacket, but it's very expensive. **I'd buy** it **if** it **wasn't** so expensive. (= it is expensive, so I'm not going to buy it)
- **I'll help** you **if I can**. (= maybe I can help)	- **I'd help** you **if I could**, but I can't.

if we go / if I have / if I can, etc. → Unit 100

Exercises

101.1 Complete the sentences.

1. I don't know the answer. If I __knew__ the answer, I'd tell you.
2. I have a car. I couldn't travel very much if I __didn't have__ a car.
3. I don't want to go out. If I _____ to go out, I'd go.
4. We don't have a key. If we _____ a key, we could get into the house.
5. I'm not hungry. I would have something to eat if I _____ hungry.
6. Sue enjoys her work. She wouldn't do it if she _____ it.
7. He can't speak any foreign languages. If he _____ speak a foreign language, maybe he would get a better job.
8. You don't try hard enough. If you _____ harder, you would have more success.
9. I have a lot to do today. If I _____ so much to do, we could go out.

101.2 Put the verb in the correct form.

1. If __he had__ the money, he would buy a fast car. (he / have)
2. Jane likes living in a city. __She wouldn't be__ happy if she lived in the country. (she / not / be)
3. If I wanted to learn Italian, _____ to Italy. (I / go)
4. I haven't told Helen what happened. She'd be angry if _____ . (she / know)
5. If _____ a map, I could show you where I live. (we / have)
6. What would you do if _____ a lot of money? (you / win)
7. It's not a very good hotel. _____ there if I were you. (I / not / stay)
8. If _____ closer to Miami, we would go there more often. (we / live)
9. I'm sorry you have to go now. _____ nice if you had more time. (it / be)
10. I'm not going to take the job. I'd take it if _____ better. (the salary / be)
11. I don't know anything about cars. If my car broke down, _____ what to do. (I / not / know)
12. If you could change one thing in the world, what _____ ? (you / change)

101.3 Complete the sentences. Use the following (with the verb in the correct form):

we (have) a bigger house	it (be) a little cheaper	I (watch) it
we (buy) a bigger house	every day (be) the same	I (be) bored
we (have) some pictures on the wall	the air (be) cleaner	

1. I'd buy that jacket if __it was a little cheaper__ .
2. If there was a good movie on TV tonight, _____ .
3. This room would be nicer if _____ .
4. If there wasn't so much traffic, _____ .
5. Life would be boring if _____ .
6. If I had nothing to do, _____ .
7. We could invite all our friends to stay if _____ .
8. If we had more money, _____ .

101.4 Complete the sentences. Use your own ideas.

1. I'd be happier if __I had less work__ .
2. If I could go anywhere in the world, _____ .
3. I wouldn't be very happy if _____ .
4. I'd buy _____ if _____ .
5. If I saw an accident in the street, _____ .
6. The world would be a better place if _____ .

A

I can speak six languages.

Jack

> I met a woman. **She** can speak six languages.
> └─────── 2 sentences ───────┘

she → who

> ┌─────── 1 sentence ───────┐
> I met **a woman who** can speak six languages.

> Jack was wearing a hat. **It** was too big for him.
> └─────── 2 sentences ───────┘

it → that or which

> ┌─────── 1 sentence ───────┐
> Jack was wearing **a hat that** was too big for him.
> *or*
> Jack was wearing **a hat which** was too big for him.

B   **Who** is for people (*not* things):

A thief is **a person**	**who** steals things.	
Do you know **anybody**	**who** can play the piano?	
The man	**who** called	didn't give his name.
The people	**who** work in the office	are very friendly.

C   **That** is for things or people:

An airplane is **a machine**	**that** flies.	
Emma lives in **a house**	**that** is 100 years old.	
The people	**that** work in the office	are very friendly.

You can use **that** for people, but **who** is more common.

D   **Which** is for things (*not* people):

An airplane is **a machine**	**which** flies. (*not* a machine who . . .)
Emma lives in **a house**	**which** is 100 years old.

Do not use **which** for people:
-   Do you remember **the woman who** played the piano at the party?
    (*not* the woman which . . .)

Exercises

102.1 Choose from the boxes and write sentences: *A . . . is a person who* . . . . Use a dictionary if necessary.

a thief	a dentist	doesn't tell the truth	is sick in the hospital
a butcher	a fool	takes care of your teeth	steals things
a musician	a genius	is very intelligent	does stupid things
a patient	a liar	plays a musical instrument	sells meat

1. _A thief is a person who steals things._
2. A butcher is a person _____
3. A musician _____
4. _____
5. _____
6. _____
7. _____
8. _____

102.2 Make one sentence from two.

1. (A man called. He didn't give his name.)
   The man who called didn't give his name.
2. (A woman opened the door. She was wearing a yellow dress.)
   The woman _____ a yellow dress.
3. (Some students took the test. Most of them passed.)
   Most of the students _____
4. (A police officer stopped our car. He wasn't very friendly.)
   The _____

102.3 Write *who* or *which*.

1. I met a woman __who__ can speak six languages.
2. What's the name of the man _____ just started working in your office?
3. What's the name of the river _____ flows through the town?
4. Where is the picture _____ was hanging on the wall?
5. Do you know anybody _____ wants to buy a car?
6. You always ask questions _____ are difficult to answer.
7. I have a friend _____ is very good at fixing cars.
8. I think everybody _____ went to the party really enjoyed it.
9. Why does he always wear clothes _____ are too small for him?

102.4 Right or wrong? Correct the mistakes.

1. A thief is a person which steals things.   _a person who steals_
2. An airplane is a machine that flies.   _OK_
3. A coffee maker is a machine who makes coffee. _____
4. Have you seen the money that was on the table? _____
5. I don't like people which never stop talking. _____
6. I know somebody that can help you.   _____
7. I know somebody who works in that store.   _____
8. Correct the sentences who are wrong.   _____
9. My neighbor bought a car who cost $60,000.   _____

the people **we met**
the hotel **you stayed at** (relative clauses 2)

A

| The man is carrying a bag.
 It's very heavy. | } *2 sentences* |

The bag (that) **he is carrying** is very heavy.
└──────────── *1 sentence* ────────────┘

| Kate won some money.
 What is she going to do with it? | } *2 sentences* |

What is Kate going to do with **the money** (that) **she won**?
└──────────── *1 sentence* ────────────┘

Kate

You can say:

- The bag **that** he is carrying . . . *or* The bag he is carrying . . . (with or without **that**)
- . . . the money **that** Kate won? *or* . . . the money Kate won?

You do not need **that/who/which** when it is the *object*:

subject	*verb*	*object*	
The man	was carrying	a bag	→ **the bag** (that) **the man was carrying**
Kate	won	some money	→ **the money** (that) **Kate won**
You	wanted	some books	→ **the books** (that) **you wanted**
We	met	some people	→ **the people** (who) **we met**

- Did you find **the books you wanted**? (*or* . . . the books **that** you wanted?)
- **The people we met** were very friendly. (*or* The people **who** we met . . .)
- **Everything I said** was true. (*or* Everything **that** I said . . .)

We say:

- The movie **we saw** was very good. (*not* The movie we saw it was . . .)

B

Sometimes there is a *preposition* (**to/in/at**, etc.) after the verb:

Eve **is talking to** a man.	→	Do you know **the man Eve is talking to**?
We **stayed at** a hotel.	→	**The hotel we stayed at** was near the station.
I **told** you **about** some books.	→	These are **the books I told you about**.

We say:

. . . the books **I told you about**. (*not* the books I told you about them)

You can say (a place) **where** . . . :

- **The hotel where** we stayed was near the station. (= The hotel we stayed at . . .)

C

You must use **who/that/which** when it is the *subject* (→ Unit 102):

- I met a woman **who can speak** six languages. (**who** is the subject)
- Jack was wearing a hat **that was** too big for him. (**that** is the subject)

a person who . . . , a thing that/which . . . (relative clauses 1) → Unit 102

Exercises

103.1 Make one sentence from two.

1. (Helen took some pictures. Have you seen them?)
   Have you seen the pictures Helen took?
2. (You gave me a pen. I've lost it.)
   I've lost the _____
3. (Sue is wearing a jacket. I like it.)
   I like the _____
4. (I gave you some flowers. Where are they?)
   Where are the _____ ?
5. (He told us a story. I didn't believe it.)
   I _____
6. (You bought some oranges. How much were they?)
   How _____ ?

103.2 Make one sentence from two.

1. (I was carrying a bag. It was very heavy.)
   The bag I was carrying was very heavy.
2. (You cooked a meal. It was excellent.)
   The _____
3. (I'm wearing shoes. They aren't very comfortable.)
   The shoes _____
4. (We invited some people to dinner. They didn't come.)
   The _____

103.3 You ask your friend some questions. Complete the sentences.

1. Your friend stayed at a hotel. You ask:
   What's the name of _the hotel you stayed at?_
2. Your friend was talking to some people. You ask:
   Who are the people _____ ?
3. Your friend was looking for some keys. You ask:
   Did you find the _____ ?
4. Your friend is going to a party. You ask:
   Where is the _____ ?
5. Your friend was talking about a movie. You ask:
   What's the name of _____ ?
6. Your friend is listening to some music. You ask:
   What's that _____ ?
7. Your friend was waiting for an e-mail. You ask:
   Did you get _____ ?

103.4 Complete the questions. Use *where*.

1. John stayed at a hotel. You ask him:
   Did you like _the hotel where you stayed_ ?
2. Sue had dinner in a restaurant. You ask her:
   What's the name of the restaurant _____ ?
3. Sarah lives in a town. You ask her:
   How big is the _____ ?
4. Richard works in a factory. You ask him:
   Where exactly is _____ ?

at 8:00   on Monday   in April

A   At

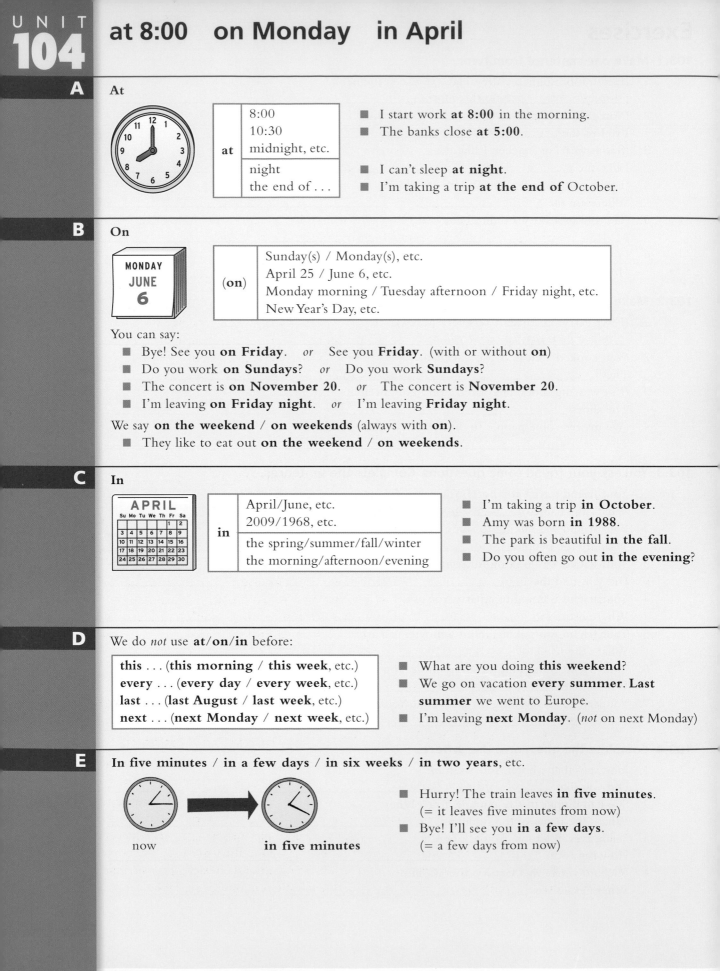

at	8:00 10:30 midnight, etc.
	night the end of . . .

- I start work **at 8:00** in the morning.
- The banks close **at 5:00**.

- I can't sleep **at night**.
- I'm taking a trip **at the end of** October.

B   On

(on)	Sunday(s) / Monday(s), etc. April 25 / June 6, etc. Monday morning / Tuesday afternoon / Friday night, etc. New Year's Day, etc.

You can say:
- Bye! See you **on Friday**.   *or*   See you **Friday**. (with or without **on**)
- Do you work **on Sundays**?   *or*   Do you work **Sundays**?
- The concert is **on November 20**.   *or*   The concert is **November 20**.
- I'm leaving **on Friday night**.   *or*   I'm leaving **Friday night**.

We say **on the weekend / on weekends** (always with **on**).
- They like to eat out **on the weekend / on weekends**.

C   In

in	April/June, etc. 2009/1968, etc.
	the spring/summer/fall/winter the morning/afternoon/evening

- I'm taking a trip **in October**.
- Amy was born **in 1988**.
- The park is beautiful **in the fall**.
- Do you often go out **in the evening**?

D

We do *not* use **at/on/in** before:

this . . . (**this morning / this week**, etc.)
every . . . (**every day / every week**, etc.)
last . . . (**last August / last week**, etc.)
next . . . (**next Monday / next week**, etc.)

- What are you doing **this weekend**?
- We go on vacation **every summer**. **Last summer** we went to Europe.
- I'm leaving **next Monday**. (*not* on next Monday)

E

In five minutes / in a few days / in six weeks / in two years, etc.

now   in five minutes

- Hurry! The train leaves **in five minutes**.
  (= it leaves five minutes from now)
- Bye! I'll see you **in a few days**.
  (= a few days from now)

Exercises

104.1 Write *at* or *in*.

1. Amy was born __in__ 1988.
2. I got up _____ 8:00 this morning.
3. I like to get up early _____ the morning.
4. I like to look at the stars _____ night.
5. My brother got married _____ May.
6. We often go to the beach _____ the summer.
7. Let's meet _____ 7:30 tomorrow night.
8. The company started _____ 1989.
9. I'll send you the money _____ the end of the month.
10. The café is open _____ the evening. It closes _____ midnight.

104.2 Write *at/on/in*.

1. __on__ June 6
2. __in__ the evening
3. _____ half past two
4. _____ Wednesday
5. _____ 1997
6. _____ September
7. _____ September 24
8. _____ Thursday
9. _____ 11:45
10. _____ New Year's Eve
11. _____ noon
12. _____ the morning
13. _____ Friday morning
14. _____ Saturday night
15. _____ night
16. _____ the end of the day
17. _____ the weekend
18. _____ the winter

104.3 Which sentence is correct – A, B, or both of them?

	A	B	
1.	I'm taking a trip in October.	I'm taking a trip on October.	__A__
2.	Do you work Sundays?	Do you work on Sundays?	__both__
3.	I always feel tired at the evening.	I always feel tired in the evening.	_____
4.	I'm leaving next Saturday.	I'm leaving on next Saturday.	_____
5.	Tim started his new job on May 18.	Tim started his new job May 18.	_____
6.	Laura finished high school in 2002.	Laura finished high school 2002.	_____
7.	We meet on every Tuesday.	We meet every Tuesday.	_____
8.	We don't often go out in night.	We don't often go out at night.	_____
9.	I can't meet you Thursday.	I can't meet you on Thursday.	_____
10.	Lisa saw Sam Monday night.	Lisa saw Sam on Monday night.	_____
11.	I'm leaving in the end of this month.	I'm leaving at the end of this month.	_____
12.	Tim goes to the gym on Fridays.	Tim goes to the gym Fridays.	_____

104.4 Write sentences with *in* . . . .

1. It's 8:25 now. The train leaves at 8:30.   _The train leaves in five minutes._
2. It's Monday today. I'll call you on Thursday.   I'll _____ days.
3. Today is June 14. My exam is on June 28.   My _____
4. It's 3:00 now. Tom will be here at 3:30.   Tom _____

104.5 Write *at/on/in* if necessary. Sometimes the sentence is already complete, and no word is necessary.

1. They like to eat out __on__ weekends.
2. I'm going __–__ next Friday. *(already complete)*
3. I always feel tired _____ the evening.
4. Will you be at home _____ this evening?
5. We went to France _____ last summer.
6. Laura was born _____ 1994.
7. What are you doing _____ the weekend?
8. I call Robert _____ every Sunday.
9. Should we play tennis _____ next Sunday?
10. I couldn't go to the party _____ last weekend.
11. I'm going out. I'll be back _____ an hour.
12. I don't often go out _____ night.

from . . . to   until   since   for

A **From . . . to . . .**

- We lived in Japan **from** 1996 **to** 2005.
- I work **from** Monday **to** Friday.

You can also say **from** . . . **until** . . . :

- We lived in Japan **from** 1996 **until** 2005.

from Monday to Friday

Monday — *Friday*

B **Until . . .**

| until | Friday
December
3:00
I come back |

- They're leaving town tomorrow.
  They'll be away **until Friday**.
- I went to bed early, but I wasn't tired.
  I read a book **until 3:00 a.m.**
- Wait here **until I come back**.

until Friday

Friday

You can also say **till** (= **until**):

- Wait here **till** I come back.

Compare:

- "**How long** will you be away?" "**Until** Monday."
- "**When** are you coming back?" "**On** Monday."

C **Since** + a time in the past (to now)

We use **since** after the *present perfect* (**have been** / **have done**, etc.):

| since | Monday
2002
2:30
I arrived |

- Joe is in the hospital. He has been
  in the hospital **since Monday**.
  (= from Monday to now)
- Sue and Dave have been
  married **since 2002**.
  (= from 2002 to now)
- It has been raining **since I arrived**.

since Monday

Monday — *now*

Compare:

- We lived in Japan **from** 1996 **to** 2005.
  We lived in Japan **until** 2005.
- Now we live in Denver. We came to Denver **in** 2005.
  We have lived in Denver **since** 2005. (= from 2005 until now)

We use **for** (*not* **since**) + a period of time (**three days** / **10 years**, etc.):

- Joe has been in the hospital **for three days**. (*not* since three days)

D **For** + a period of time

| for | three days
10 years
five minutes
a long time |

- Gary stayed with us **for
  three days**.
- I'm going away **for
  a few weeks**.
- I'm going away **for the weekend**.
- They've been married **for 10 years**.

for three days

Sunday   *Monday*   *Tuesday*

present perfect + **for/since** → Units 17–18   present perfect (**I have lived**) and simple past (**I lived**) → Unit 21

Exercises

105.1 Read the information and complete the sentences. Use *from . . . to* / *until* / *since*.

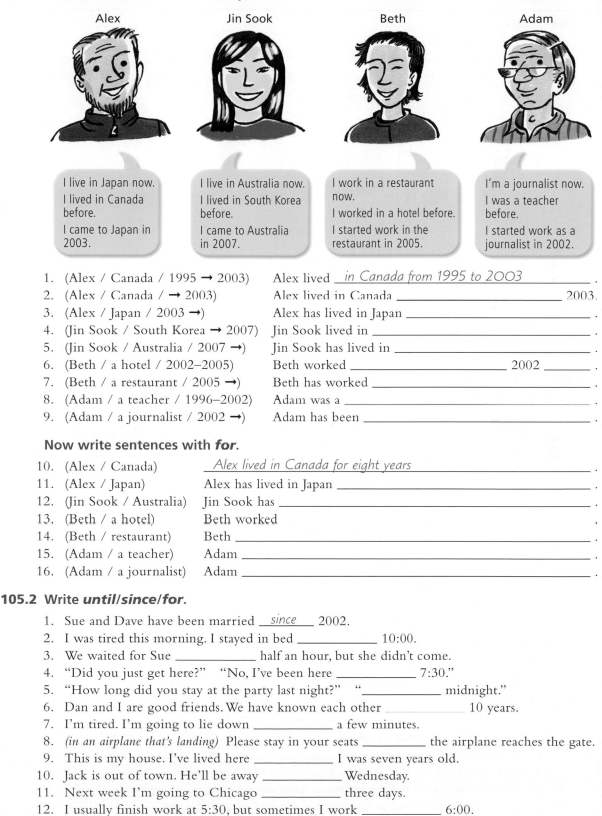

Alex Jin Sook Beth Adam

> **Alex:** I live in Japan now. I lived in Canada before. I came to Japan in 2003.

> **Jin Sook:** I live in Australia now. I lived in South Korea before. I came to Australia in 2007.

> **Beth:** I work in a restaurant now. I worked in a hotel before. I started work in the restaurant in 2005.

> **Adam:** I'm a journalist now. I was a teacher before. I started work as a journalist in 2002.

1. (Alex / Canada / 1995 → 2003) Alex lived _in Canada from 1995 to 2003_ .
2. (Alex / Canada / → 2003) Alex lived in Canada _____ 2003.
3. (Alex / Japan / 2003 →) Alex has lived in Japan _____ .
4. (Jin Sook / South Korea → 2007) Jin Sook lived in _____ .
5. (Jin Sook / Australia / 2007 →) Jin Sook has lived in _____ .
6. (Beth / a hotel / 2002–2005) Beth worked _____ 2002 _____ .
7. (Beth / a restaurant / 2005 →) Beth has worked _____ .
8. (Adam / a teacher / 1996–2002) Adam was a _____ .
9. (Adam / a journalist / 2002 →) Adam has been _____ .

Now write sentences with *for*.

10. (Alex / Canada) _Alex lived in Canada for eight years_ .
11. (Alex / Japan) Alex has lived in Japan _____ .
12. (Jin Sook / Australia) Jin Sook has _____ .
13. (Beth / a hotel) Beth worked _____ .
14. (Beth / restaurant) Beth _____ .
15. (Adam / a teacher) Adam _____ .
16. (Adam / a journalist) Adam _____ .

105.2 Write *until*/*since*/*for*.

1. Sue and Dave have been married _since_ 2002.
2. I was tired this morning. I stayed in bed _____ 10:00.
3. We waited for Sue _____ half an hour, but she didn't come.
4. "Did you just get here?" "No, I've been here _____ 7:30."
5. "How long did you stay at the party last night?" "_____ midnight."
6. Dan and I are good friends. We have known each other _____ 10 years.
7. I'm tired. I'm going to lie down _____ a few minutes.
8. *(in an airplane that's landing)* Please stay in your seats _____ the airplane reaches the gate.
9. This is my house. I've lived here _____ I was seven years old.
10. Jack is out of town. He'll be away _____ Wednesday.
11. Next week I'm going to Chicago _____ three days.
12. I usually finish work at 5:30, but sometimes I work _____ 6:00.
13. "How long have you known Anna?" "_____ we were in high school."
14. Where have you been? I've been waiting for you _____ 20 minutes.

before   after   during   while

A

Before, during, and after

before the movie   **during** the movie   **after** the movie

- Everybody feels nervous **before a test**.
- I fell asleep **during the movie**.
- We were tired **after our visit** to the museum.

B

Before, while, and after

before we played   **while** we were playing   **after** we played

- Don't forget to close the window **before you go out**.
- I often fall asleep **while I'm reading**.
- They watched TV **after they did the dishes**.

C

During, while, and for

We use **during** + *noun* (during **the movie**). We use **while** + *verb* (while **I'm reading**):
- We didn't speak **during the meal**.
but   We didn't speak **while we were eating**. (*not* during we were eating)

Use **for** (*not* during) + *a period of time* (**three days / two hours / a year**, etc.):
- We played basketball **for two hours**. (*not* during two hours)
- I lived in Florida **for a year**. (*not* during a year)

D

You can use **before/after** + **-ing** (**before going / after eating**, etc.):
- I always have breakfast **before going** to work. (= before I go to work)
- **After doing** the dishes, they watched TV. (= after they did)

Remember: We say **before going** (*not* before to go), **after doing** (*not* after to do), etc.:
- **Before eating** the apple, I washed it carefully. (*not* before to eat)
- I started work **after reading** the newspaper. (*not* after to read)

past continuous (I was -ing) → Units 13–14   before/after/while/when → Unit 99
for → Unit 105   prepositions + -ing → Unit 113

Exercises

106.1 Complete the sentences. Choose from the boxes.

after	during		lunch	the end	they went to Mexico
before	while	+	the concert	~~the test~~	you're waiting
			the course	the night	

1. Everybody was nervous _before the test_ .
2. I usually work four hours in the morning and another three hours _____ .
3. The movie was really boring. We left _____ .
4. Anna went to night school to learn German. She learned a lot _____ .
5. My aunt and uncle lived in Chicago _____ .
6. *A:* Somebody broke a window _____ . Did you hear anything?
   B: No, I was asleep all the time.
7. Would you like to sit down _____ ?
8. "Are you going home _____ ?" "Yes, I have to get up early tomorrow."

106.2 Write *during*/*while*/*for*.

1. We didn't speak __while__ we were eating.
2. We didn't speak __during__ the meal.
3. Gary called _____ you were out.
4. I stayed in Rome _____ five days.
5. Sally didn't read any newspapers _____ she was on vacation.
6. The students looked very bored _____ the class.
7. I fell out of bed _____ I was asleep.
8. Last night I watched TV _____ three hours.
9. I don't usually watch TV _____ the day.
10. Do you ever watch TV _____ you are having dinner?

106.3 Complete the sentences. Use *-ing* (*doing*, *having*, etc.).

1. After __doing__ the dishes, they watched TV.
2. I felt sick after _____ too much chocolate.
3. I'm going to ask you a question. Think carefully before _____ it.
4. I felt awful when I got up this morning. I felt better after _____ a shower.
5. After _____ my work, I left the office and went home.
6. Before _____ to a foreign country, you should try and learn a little of
   the language.

106.4 Write sentences with *before* + *-ing* and *after* + *-ing*.

1. They did the dishes. Then they watched TV.
   After _doing the dishes, they watched TV._
2. John finished high school. Then he worked in a bookstore for two years.
   John worked _____
3. I read for a few minutes. Then I went to sleep.
   Before _____
4. We walked for three hours. We were very tired.
   After _____
5. Let's have a cup of coffee. Then we'll go out.
   Let's _____

in at on (places 1)

A   In

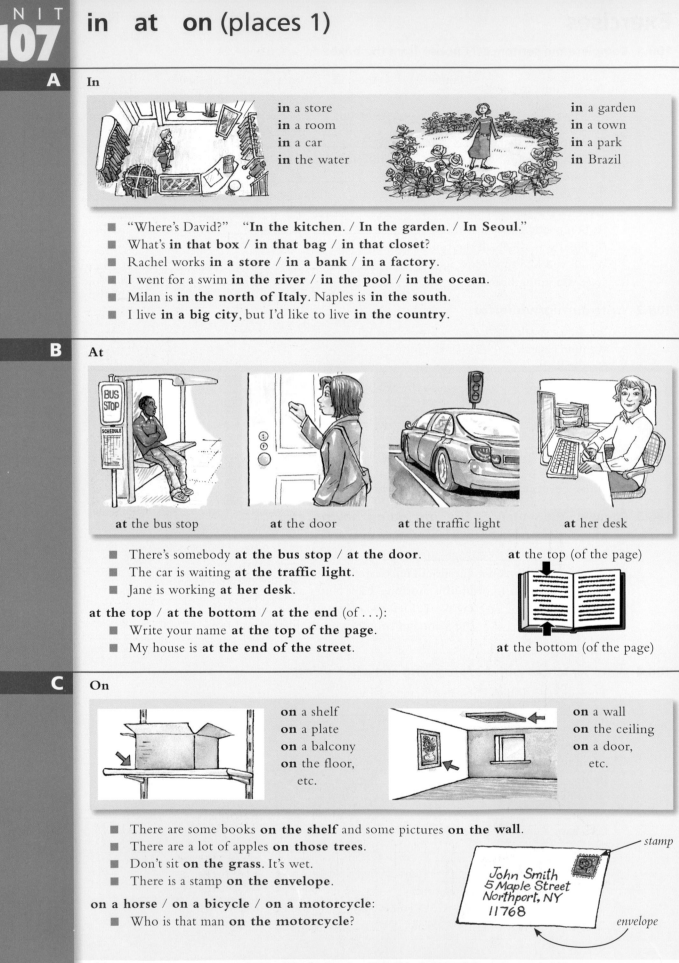

in a store
in a room
in a car
in the water

in a garden
in a town
in a park
in Brazil

- ■ "Where's David?" "In the kitchen. / In the garden. / In Seoul."
- ■ What's in that box / in that bag / in that closet?
- ■ Rachel works in a store / in a bank / in a factory.
- ■ I went for a swim in the river / in the pool / in the ocean.
- ■ Milan is in the north of Italy. Naples is in the south.
- ■ I live in a big city, but I'd like to live in the country.

B   At

at the bus stop   at the door   at the traffic light   at her desk

- ■ There's somebody at the bus stop / at the door.
- ■ The car is waiting at the traffic light.
- ■ Jane is working at her desk.

at the top / at the bottom / at the end (of . . .):
- ■ Write your name at the top of the page.
- ■ My house is at the end of the street.

at the top (of the page)

at the bottom (of the page)

C   On

on a shelf
on a plate
on a balcony
on the floor,
    etc.

on a wall
on the ceiling
on a door,
    etc.

- ■ There are some books on the shelf and some pictures on the wall.
- ■ There are a lot of apples on those trees.
- ■ Don't sit on the grass. It's wet.
- ■ There is a stamp on the envelope.

on a horse / on a bicycle / on a motorcycle:
- ■ Who is that man on the motorcycle?

stamp

John Smith
5 Maple Street
Northport, NY
11768

envelope

the top / the bottom, etc. → Unit 71   at/on/in (time) → Unit 104   in/at/on (places 2) → Unit 108

Exercises

107.1 Look at the pictures and answer the questions. Use *in/at/on*.

1. (the kitchen)
2. (the box)
3. (the box)
4. (the wall)
5. (the bus stop)
6. (the field)
7. (the balcony)
8. (the pool)
9. (the window)
10. (the ceiling)
11. (the table)
12. (the table)

1. Where is he? _In the kitchen._
2. Where are the shoes? _____
3. Where is the pen? _____
4. Where is the clock? _____
5. Where is the bus? _____
6. Where are the horses? _____
7. Where are they standing? _____
8. Where is she swimming? _____
9. Where is he standing? _____
10. Where is the spider? _____
11. Where is he sitting? _____
12. Where is she sitting? _____

107.2 Write *in/at/on*.

1. Don't sit _on_ the grass. It's wet.
2. What do you have _____ your bag?
3. Look! There's a man _____ the roof. What's he doing?
4. There are a lot of fish _____ this river.
5. Our house is number 45 – the number is _____ the door.
6. "Is the post office near here?"   "Yes, turn left _____ the traffic light."
7. I have a small vegetable garden _____ the backyard.
8. My sister lives _____ Prague.
9. There's a small park _____ the top of the hill.
10. I think I heard the doorbell. There's somebody _____ the door.
11. Munich is a large city _____ the south of Germany.
12. There's a gas station _____ the end of the block.
13. It's difficult to carry a lot of things _____ a bicycle.
14. I looked at the list of names. My name was _____ the bottom.
15. There is a mirror _____ the wall _____ the living room.

in at on (places 2)

A In

in bed	■ "Where's Kate?" "She's **in bed**."
in the hospital	■ David's father is sick. He's **in the hospital**.
in the sky	■ I like to look at the stars **in the sky** at night.
in the world	■ What's the largest city **in the world**?
in a newspaper / **in** a book	■ I read about the accident **in the newspaper**.
in a photograph / **in** a picture	■ You look sad **in this photograph**.
in a car / **in** a taxi	■ Did you come here **in your car**?
in the middle (of . . .)	■ There's a big tree **in the middle** of the yard.

B At

at work / **at** school	■ "Where's Kate?" "She's **at work**."
at the station / **at** the airport	■ Do you want me to meet you **at the station**?
at the post office / **at** the supermarket	■ I saw your brother **at the post office** today.
at Jane's (house) / **at** my sister's (house) / **at** the doctor's / **at** the hairdresser's, etc.	■ *A:* Where were you yesterday? *B:* **At my sister's**.
	■ I saw Tom **at the doctor's**.
at a concert / **at** a party / **at** a football game, etc.	■ There weren't many people **at the party**.

You can say **be/stay home** or **be/stay at home** (with or without **at**).
  ■ Is Tom **at home**? *or* Is Tom **home**?

Often it is possible to use **at** or **in** for buildings (hotels, restaurants, etc.):
  ■ We stayed **at** a nice hotel. *or* We stayed **in** a nice hotel.

C

You can say **at school** or **in school**, but there is a difference.

She's **at** school = she's there now
  ■ "Where's your sister? Is she home?" "No, she's **at school**."

She's **in** school = she's a student (in high school / college / medical school, etc.)
  ■ "Does your sister have a job?" "No, she's still **in school**."

D On

on a bus   **on** the second floor   **on** the way from A to B

on a bus / **on** a train / **on** a plane / **on** a ship	■ Did you come here **on the bus**?
on the first floor (*or* ground floor), **on** the second floor, etc.	■ The office is **on the second floor**. (*not* in the second floor)
on the way (to . . .) / **on** the way home	■ I met Ann **on the way** to work / **on the way** home.
on a street	■ My brother lives **on** a nice street.

Exercises

108.1 Look at the pictures and answer the questions. Use *in/at/on*.

1. (the hospital)
2. (the airport)
3. (bed)
4. (a ship)
5. (the sky)
6. (a party)
7. (the doctor's)
8. (the second floor)
9. (work)
10. (a plane)
11. (a taxi)
12. (a wedding)

RESTAURANT 2nd FLOOR

1. Where is she? _In the hospital._
2. Where are they? _____
3. Where is he? _____
4. Where are they? _____
5. Where are the stars? _____
6. Where are they? _____
7. Where is Steve? _____
8. Where is the restaurant? _____
9. Where is she? _____
10. Where are they? _____
11. Where are they? _____
12. Where are they? _____

108.2 Write *in/at/on*.

1. "Where's your sister? Is she home?"   "No, she's __at__ school."
2. There was a big table _____ the middle of the room.
3. What is the longest river _____ the world?
4. Were there many people _____ the concert last night?
5. Will you be _____ home tomorrow afternoon?
6. Who is the man _____ this picture? Do you know him?
7. "Is your son going to get married soon?"   "No, he's still _____ college."
8. Gary is coming by bus. I'm going to meet him _____ the station.
9. Charlie is _____ the hospital. He had an operation yesterday.
10. How many pages are there _____ this book?
11. "Are you hungry after your trip?"   "Yes, there was nothing to eat _____ the plane."
12. I'm sorry I'm late. My car broke down _____ the way here.
13. "Is Tom here?"   "No, he's _____ his brother's."
14. Don't believe everything you read _____ the newspaper!
15. I walked to work, but I came home _____ the bus.
16. *A: (on the phone)* Can I speak to Anne, please?
    B: No, sorry. She'll be _____ the university until 5:00 today.

to in at (places 3)

A

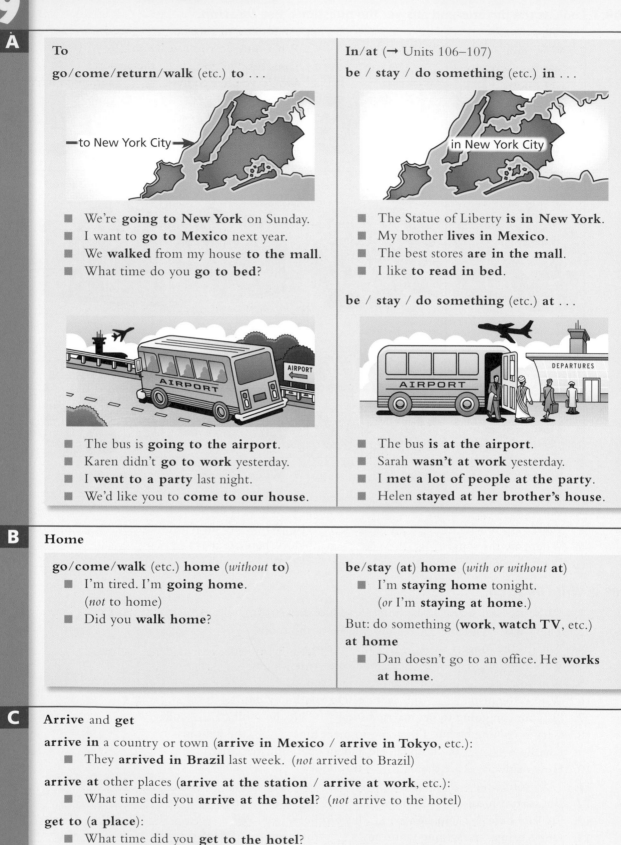

To

go/come/return/walk (etc.) **to** . . .

—to New York City→

- We're **going to New York** on Sunday.
- I want to **go to Mexico** next year.
- We **walked** from my house **to the mall**.
- What time do you **go to bed**?

- The bus is **going to the airport**.
- Karen didn't **go to work** yesterday.
- I **went to a party** last night.
- We'd like you to **come to our house**.

In/at (→ Units 106–107)

be / stay / do something (etc.) **in** . . .

in New York City

- The Statue of Liberty **is in New York**.
- My brother **lives in Mexico**.
- The best stores **are in the mall**.
- I like **to read in bed**.

be / stay / do something (etc.) **at** . . .

DEPARTURES

- The bus **is at the airport**.
- Sarah **wasn't at work** yesterday.
- I **met a lot of people at the party**.
- Helen **stayed at her brother's house**.

B

Home

go/come/walk (etc.) **home** (*without* **to**)
- I'm tired. I'm **going home**.
  (*not* to home)
- Did you **walk home**?

be/stay (**at**) **home** (*with or without* **at**)
- I'm **staying home** tonight.
  (*or* I'm **staying at home**.)

But: do something (**work**, **watch TV**, etc.)
at home
- Dan doesn't go to an office. He **works at home**.

C

Arrive and get

arrive in a country or town (**arrive in Mexico** / **arrive in Tokyo**, etc.):
- They **arrived in Brazil** last week. (*not* arrived to Brazil)

arrive at other places (**arrive at the station** / **arrive at work**, etc.):
- What time did you **arrive at the hotel**? (*not* arrive to the hotel)

get to (a place):
- What time did you **get to the hotel**?
- What time did you **get to Tokyo**?

get home / **arrive home** (no preposition):
- I was tired when I **got home**. *or* I was tired when I **arrived home**.

been to → Unit 16   get (to . . .) → Unit 57   in/at → Units 107–108

Exercises

109.1 Write *to* or *in*.

1. I like reading _*in*_ bed.
2. We're going _____ Italy next month.
3. Sue is on vacation _____ Mexico right now.
4. I have to go _____ the bank today.
5. I was tired, so I stayed _____ bed.
6. What time do you usually go _____ bed?
7. Does this bus go _____ the airport?
8. Would you like to live _____ another country?

109.2 Write *to* or *at* if necessary. Sometimes no preposition is necessary.

1. Paula didn't go _*to*_ work yesterday.
2. I'm tired. I'm going __–__ home. *(already complete)*
3. Tina is sick. She went _____ the doctor.
4. Would you like to come _____ a party on Saturday?
5. "Is Liz _____ home?" "No, she went _____ work."
6. There were 20,000 people _____ the football game.
7. Why did you go _____ home early last night?
8. A boy jumped into the river and swam _____ the other side.
9. There were a lot of people waiting _____ the bus stop.
10. We had dinner _____ a restaurant, and then we went back _____ the hotel.

109.3 Write *to*, *at*, or *in* if necessary. Sometimes no preposition is necessary.

1. Joe is coming tomorrow. I'm meeting him _*at*_ the airport.
2. We're going _____ a concert tomorrow night.
3. I went _____ Chile last year.
4. How long did you stay _____ Chile?
5. Next year we hope to go _____ Japan to visit some friends.
6. Do you want to go _____ the movies tonight?
7. Did you park your car _____ the station?
8. After the accident, three people were taken _____ the hospital.
9. How often do you go _____ the dentist?
10. "Is Sarah here?" "No, she's _____ Helen's."
11. My house is _____ the end of the block on the left.
12. I went _____ Maria's house, but she wasn't _____ home.
13. There were no taxis, so we had to walk _____ home.
14. "Who did you meet _____ the party?" "I didn't go _____ the party."

109.4 Write *to*, *at*, or *in* if necessary. Sometimes the sentence is already complete, and no word is necessary.

1. What time do you usually get _____ work?
2. What time do you usually get _____ home?
3. What time did you arrive _____ the party?
4. When did you arrive _____ Dallas?
5. What time does the plane get _____ Paris?
6. We arrived _____ home very late.

109.5 Complete these sentences about yourself. Use *to/in/at*.

1. At 3:00 this morning I was _*in bed*_____ .
2. Yesterday I went _____ .
3. At 11:00 yesterday morning I was _____ .
4. One day I'd like to go _____ .
5. I don't like going _____ .
6. At 9:00 last night I was _____ .

next to, between, under, etc.

A

Next to / between / in front of / in back of

Alice is **next to** Bob.   *or*   Alice is **beside** Bob.
Bob is **between** Alice and Carla.
Don is **in front of** Bob.
Eric is **in back of** Bob.

also
Alice is **on the left**.
Carla is **on the right**.
Bob is **in the middle** (of the group).

B

Across from / in front of

Anne is sitting **in front of** Bruce.
Anne is sitting **across from** Chris.
Chris is sitting **across from** Anne.

C

By (= next to)

by the window

- Who is that man standing **by the window**?
- Our house is **by the ocean**. (= next to the ocean)
- If you feel cold, why don't you sit **by the fire**?

D

Under

under the table   **under** a tree

- The cat is **under the table**.
- The girl is standing **under a tree**.
- I'm wearing a jacket **under my coat**.

E

Above and below

A   A is **above the line**.
    (= higher than the line)

B   B is **below the line**.
    (= lower than the line)

The pictures are **above the shelves**.

The shelves are **below the pictures**.

Exercises

110.1 Where are the people in the picture? Complete the sentences.

Alan   Barbara   Kevin

Donna   Emily   Fred

1. Kevin is standing _in back of_ Fred.
2. Fred is sitting _____ Emily.
3. Emily is sitting _____ Barbara.
4. Emily is sitting _____ Donna and Fred.
5. Donna is sitting _____ Emily.
6. Fred is sitting _____ Kevin.
7. Alan is standing _____ Donna.
8. Alan is standing _____ left.
9. Barbara is standing _____ middle.

110.2 Look at the pictures and complete the sentences.

5. Movie Palace NOW SHOWING...2 mins
   Opening TODAY

7. NOVEMBER

11. Anna   Paul

12. LEFT

1. The cat is _under_ the table.
2. There is a big tree _____ the house.
3. The plane is flying _____ the clouds.
4. She is standing _____ the piano.
5. The movie theater is _____ the right.
6. She's sitting _____ the phone.
7. The calendar is _____ the clock.
8. The cabinet is _____ the sink.
9. There are some shoes _____ the bed.
10. The plant is _____ the piano.
11. Paul is sitting _____ Anna.
12. In Japan people drive _____ the left.

110.3 Write sentences about the picture.

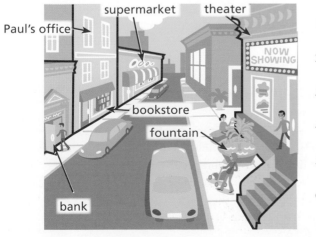

supermarket   theater

Paul's office

NOW SHOWING

bookstore

fountain

bank

1. (next to) _The bank is next to the_
   bookstore.
2. (in front of) The _____ in front of
   _____
3. (across from) _____
   _____
4. (next to) _____
   _____
5. (above) _____
   _____
6. (between) _____
   _____

up, over, through, etc.

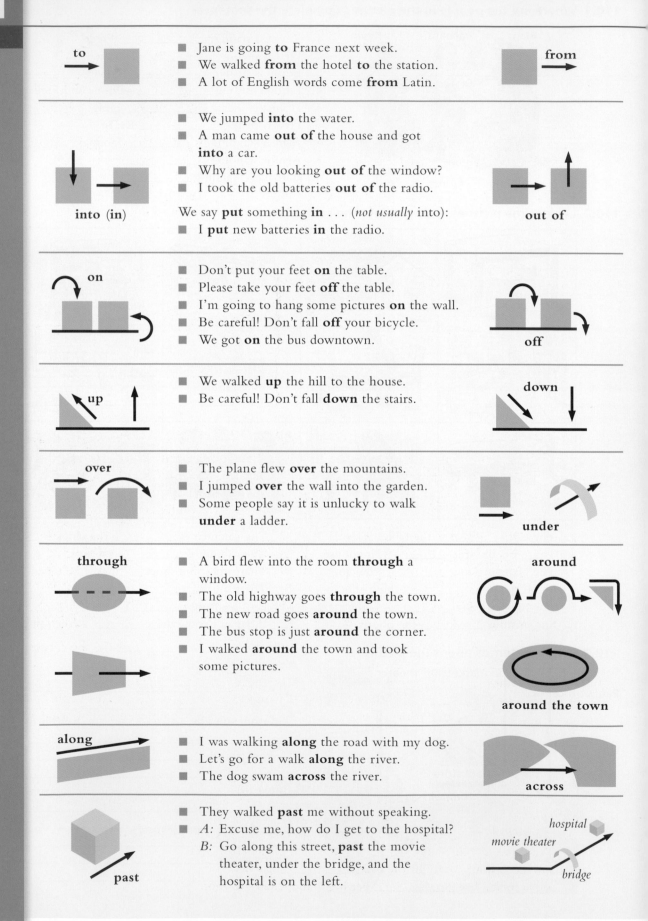

to
- Jane is going **to** France next week.
- We walked **from** the hotel **to** the station.
- A lot of English words come **from** Latin.

from

into (in)
- We jumped **into** the water.
- A man came **out of** the house and got **into** a car.
- Why are you looking **out of** the window?
- I took the old batteries **out of** the radio.

We say **put** something in . . . (*not usually* into):
- I **put** new batteries **in** the radio.

out of

on
- Don't put your feet **on** the table.
- Please take your feet **off** the table.
- I'm going to hang some pictures **on** the wall.
- Be careful! Don't fall **off** your bicycle.
- We got **on** the bus downtown.

off

up
- We walked **up** the hill to the house.
- Be careful! Don't fall **down** the stairs.

down

over
- The plane flew **over** the mountains.
- I jumped **over** the wall into the garden.
- Some people say it is unlucky to walk **under** a ladder.

under

through
- A bird flew into the room **through** a window.
- The old highway goes **through** the town.
- The new road goes **around** the town.
- The bus stop is just **around** the corner.
- I walked **around** the town and took some pictures.

around

around the town

along
- I was walking **along** the road with my dog.
- Let's go for a walk **along** the river.
- The dog swam **across** the river.

across

past
- They walked **past** me without speaking.
- *A:* Excuse me, how do I get to the hospital?
  B: Go along this street, **past** the movie theater, under the bridge, and the hospital is on the left.

hospital
movie theater
bridge

get in/on, etc. → Unit 57   **in/on** → Units 107–108   **to** → Unit 109   **fall off / run away**, etc. → Unit 115

Exercises

111.1 Somebody asks you how to get to a place.
You say which way to go. Look at the pictures
and write sentences beginning **Go** . . . .

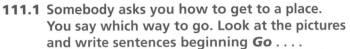

1. *Go past
the church.*
2. Go _____ the bridge.
3. _____ the hill.
4. _____ the steps.
5. _____ this street.
6. _____
7. _____
8. _____
9. _____
10. _____

111.2 Look at the pictures and complete the sentences.

1. The dog swam __*across*__ the river.
2. A book fell _____ the shelf.
3. A plane flew _____ the town.
4. A woman got _____ the car.
5. A girl ran _____ the street.
6. Suddenly a car came _____ the corner.
7. They drove _____ the town.
8. They got _____ the train.
9. The moon travels _____ the earth.
10. They got _____ the house _____ a window.

111.3 Complete the sentences. Use **over/from/to**, etc.

1. I looked _____ the window and watched the people in the street.
2. My house is near here. It's just _____ the corner.
3. "Where's my phone?" "You put it _____ your bag."
4. How far is it _____ here _____ the airport?
5. We walked _____ the museum for an hour and saw a lot of interesting things.
6. You can put your coat _____ the back of the chair.
7. In tennis, you have to hit the ball _____ the net.
8. Silvia took a key _____ her bag and opened the door.

223

on   at   by   with   about

A

On

on vacation
on television
on the radio
on the phone
on fire
on time (= not late)

- Jane isn't at work this week. She's **on vacation**.
- We watched the news **on television**.
- We listened to the news **on the radio**.
- I spoke to Rachel **on the phone** last night.
- The house is **on fire**! Call the fire department.
- "Was the train late?"   "No, it was **on time**."

B

At

at (the age of) 21 / at 50 kilometers an hour / at 100 degrees, etc.:

- Lisa got married **at 21**. (*or* . . . **at the age of 21**.)
- A car uses more gas **at 70 miles an hour** than **at 55**.
- Water boils at **100 degrees Celsius**.

C

By

by car / by bus / by plane / by bike, etc.:

- Do you like traveling **by train**?
- Jane usually goes to work **by bike**.

but **on foot**:

- You can't get there **by car**. You have to go **on foot**. (= you have to walk)

a book **by** . . . / a painting **by** . . . / a piece of music **by** . . . , etc.:

- Have you read any books **by Charles Dickens**?
- **Who** is that painting **by**? Picasso?

by after the passive (→ Unit 22):

- I was bitten **by a dog**.

by bus

on foot

the title → **HARD TIMES**
by
the writer → **CHARLES DICKENS**

D

With/Without

- Did you stay at a hotel or **with friends**?
- Wait for me. Please don't go **without me**.
- Do you like your coffee **with** or **without milk**?
- I cut the paper **with a pair of scissors**.

a man **with** a beard / a woman **with** glasses, etc.:

- Do you know that man **with the beard**?
- I'd like to have a house **with a big yard**.

a man **with a** beard

a woman **with** glasses

E

About

talk/speak/think/hear/know about . . . :

- Some people **talk about their work** all the time.
- I don't **know** much **about cars**.

a book / a question / a program / information, etc. **about** . . . :

- There was **a program about** volcanoes on TV last night. Did you see it?

by → Units 22, 64, 110   **at/on** → Units 104, 107–108   preposition + -ing → Unit 113

Exercises

112.1 Complete the sentences. Use *on* + these words:

the phone   ~~the radio~~   television   time   vacation

1. We heard the news ___on the radio___ .
2. Please don't be late. Try to get here _____ .
3. I won't be here next week. I'm going _____ .
4. "Did you see Linda?" "No, but I talked to her _____ ."
5. "What's _____ tonight?" "Nothing that I want to watch."

112.2 Look at the pictures. Complete the sentences with *at/by/with*, etc.

1. I cut the paper ___with___ a pair of scissors.
2. Last year they took a trip around the world _____ boat.
3. Who is the woman _____ short hair?
4. They are talking _____ the weather.
5. The car is _____ fire.
6. She's listening to some music _____ Mozart.
7. The plane is flying _____ 600 miles an hour.
8. They're _____ vacation.
9. Do you know the man _____ sunglasses?
10. He's reading a book _____ grammar _____ Vera P. Bull.

112.3 Complete the sentences. Use *at/by/with*, etc.

1. In tennis, you hit the ball _____ a racket.
2. It's cold today. Don't go out _____ a coat.
3. *Hamlet*, *Othello*, and *Macbeth* are plays _____ William Shakespeare.
4. Do you know anything _____ computers?
5. My grandmother died _____ the age of 98.
6. How long does it take to go from New York to Los Angeles _____ plane?
7. I didn't go to the football game, but I watched it _____ television.
8. My house is the one _____ the red door on the right.
9. These trains are very fast. They can travel _____ very high speeds.
10. You can't get there _____ car. There's no road.
11. Can you give me some information _____ hotels in this town?
12. I was arrested _____ two police officers and taken to the police station.
13. The buses here are very good. They're almost always _____ time.
14. What would you like to drink _____ your meal?
15. We traveled from Los Angeles to Seattle _____ train.
16. The museum has some paintings _____ Frida Kahlo.

afraid of . . . , good at . . . , etc.
of/at/for, etc. (prepositions) + -ing

A   Afraid of . . . / **good at** . . . , etc. *(adjective + preposition)*

Help!

He's afraid of me.

I'm not very good at math.

I'm fed up with my job.

IN

afraid of . . .	■ Are you **afraid of** dogs?
angry/mad at somebody	■ Why are you **mad at** me? What did I do?
angry/mad about something	■ Are you **angry about** last night? (= something that happened last night)
different from . . .	■ Lisa is very **different from** her sister.
fed up with . . .	■ I'm **fed up with** my job. I want to do something different. (= I've had enough of my job)
full of . . .	■ The room was **full of people**.
good at . . .	■ Are you **good at** math?
bad at . . .	■ Tina is very **bad at** tennis.
interested in . . .	■ I'm not **interested in** sports.
married to . . .	■ Sue is **married to** a dentist. (= her husband is a dentist)
nice/kind of somebody to . . .	■ It was **kind of** you to help us. Thank you very much.
be **nice/kind to** somebody	■ David is very friendly. He's always very **nice to** me.
sorry about a situation	■ I'm afraid I can't help you. I'm **sorry about** that.
sorry for/about doing something	■ I'm **sorry for/about** not calling you yesterday. (*or* I'm sorry I didn't call you)
be/feel **sorry for** somebody	■ I feel **sorry for** them. They are in a very difficult situation.

B   Of/at/for, etc. + **-ing**

After a preposition (**of/at/for**, etc.), a verb ends in **-ing**:

I'm not very good **at**	**telling**	stories.
Are you fed up **with**	**doing**	the same thing every day?
I'm sorry **for**	not **calling**	you yesterday.
Thank you **for**	**helping**	me.
Mark is thinking **of**	**buying**	a new car.
Tom left **without**	**saying**	goodbye. (= he didn't say goodbye)
After	**doing**	the housework, they went shopping.

before/after -ing → Unit 106   think about/of → Unit 114

Exercises

113.1 Look at the pictures and complete the sentences with *of*/*with*/*in*, etc.

1. He's afraid __*of*__ dogs.
2. She's interested _____ science.
3. She's married _____ a soccer player.
4. She's very good _____ languages.
5. He's fed up _____ the weather.
6. *A:* Can I help you?
   B: Thanks, that's very kind _____ you.

113.2 Complete the sentences with *in*/*of*/*about*, etc.

1. I'm not interested __*in*__ sports.
2. I'm not very good _____ sports.
3. I like Sarah. She's always very nice _____ me.
4. I'm sorry _____ your broken window. It was an accident.
5. He's very brave. He isn't afraid _____ anything.
6. It was very nice _____ Jane to let us stay in her apartment.
7. Life today is very different _____ life 50 years ago.
8. Are you interested _____ politics?
9. I feel sorry _____ her, but I can't help her.
10. Chris was angry _____ what happened.
11. These boxes are very heavy. They are full _____ books.
12. What's wrong? Are you mad _____ me?

113.3 Complete the sentences.

1. I'm not very __*good at telling*__ stories. (good / tell)
2. I wanted to go to the movies, but Paula wasn't _____ . (interested / go)
3. Sue isn't very _____ up in the morning. (good / get)
4. Let's go! I'm _____ . (fed up / wait)
5. I'm _____ you up in the middle of the night. (sorry / wake)
6. Sorry I'm late! _____ . (thank you / wait)

113.4 Complete the sentences. Use *without -ing*.

1. (Tom left / he didn't say goodbye) __*Tom left without saying goodbye.*__
2. (Sue walked past me / she didn't speak)
   Sue walked _____
3. (don't do anything / ask me first)
   Don't _____
4. (I went out / I didn't lock the door)
   I _____

113.5 Write sentences about yourself.

1. (interested) __*I'm interested in sports.*__
2. (afraid) I'm _____
3. (not very good) I'm not _____
4. (not interested) _____
5. (fed up) _____

listen to . . . , look at . . . , etc.
(verb + preposition)

A

ask (somebody) **for** . . .	■ A man stopped me and **asked** me **for** money.
belong to . . .	■ Does this book **belong to** you? (= Is this your book?)
happen to . . .	■ I can't find my pen. What's **happened to** it?
listen to . . .	■ **Listen to** this music. It's great.
look at . . .	■ He's **looking at** his watch. ■ **Look at** these flowers! They're beautiful. ■ Why are you **looking at** me like that?
look for . . .	■ She's lost her key. She's **looking for** it. ■ I'm **looking for** Sarah. Have you seen her?
speak/talk to somebody **about** something	■ Did you **talk to** Paul **about** the problem? ■ (on the phone) Can I **speak to** Chris, please?
take care of . . .	■ When Pat is at work, a friend of hers **takes care** of her children. ■ Don't lose this book. **Take care of** it.
thank somebody **for** . . .	■ **Thank** you very much **for** your help.
think about . . . or **think of** . . .	■ He never **thinks about** (or **of**) other people. ■ Mark is **thinking of** (or **about**) buying a new computer.
wait for . . .	■ **Wait for** me. I'm almost ready.
write (to) . . .	■ I tried calling the company, but they didn't answer, so I **wrote to** them. (or I **wrote** them)

B

Call, **e-mail**, and **text**

call somebody, **e-mail somebody**, **text somebody** (no preposition)

■ I have to **call** my parents tonight. (*not* call to . . .)
■ *A:* Could you use your cell phone when you were in Europe?
   B: No. My friends and family **e-mailed** me instead of calling.
■ Let Sam know where to meet us. **E-mail** or **text** him before he leaves work.

C

Depend

We say **depend on** . . . :

■ *A:* Do you like eating in restaurants?
   B: Sometimes. It **depends on** the restaurant. (*not* it depends of)

You can say **it depends what/where/how**, etc., with or without **on**:

■ *A:* Do you want to come out with us?
   B: It **depends where** you're going.   *or*   It **depends on where** you're going.

wait → Unit 55   **preposition + -ing** → Unit 113

Exercises

114.1 Look at the pictures and complete the sentences with *to/for/at*, etc.

1. She's looking __at__ her watch.
2. He's listening _____ the radio.
3. They're waiting _____ a taxi.
4. Paul is talking _____ Jane.
5. They're looking _____ a picture.
6. Sue is looking _____ Tom.

114.2 Complete the sentences with a preposition (*to/for/about*, etc.) if necessary.

1. Thank you very much __for__ your help.
2. This isn't my umbrella. It belongs _____ a friend of mine.
3. Who's going to take care _____ your dog while you're out of town?
4. *(on the phone)* Can I speak _____ Steven Davis, please?
5. *(on the phone)* Thank you _____ calling. Goodbye.
6. Excuse me, I'm looking _____ Hill Street. Can you tell me where it is?
7. We're thinking _____ going to Australia next year.
8. We asked the waiter _____ tea, but he brought us coffee.
9. "Do you like to read books?" "It depends _____ the book."
10. John was talking, but nobody was listening _____ what he was saying.
11. I want to take your picture. Please look _____ the camera and smile.
12. We waited _____ Karen until 2:00, but she didn't come.
13. What happened _____ Ella last night? Why didn't she come to the party?
14. Don't forget to call _____ your mother tonight.
15. He's alone all day. He never talks _____ anybody.
16. "How much does it cost to stay at this hotel?" "It depends _____ the room."
17. It will be faster if you e-mail _____ me, but you can also write _____ me at this address.
18. Catherine is thinking _____ changing jobs.
19. I looked _____ the newspaper, but I didn't read it carefully.
20. When you're sick, you need somebody to take care _____ you.
21. Barry is looking _____ a job. He wants to work in a hotel.
22. I don't want everyone to hear my conversation with Jane. I'll text _____ her.

114.3 Answer these questions with *It depends* . . . .

1. Do you want to go out with us?
2. Do you like to eat in restaurants?
3. Do you enjoy watching TV?
4. Can you do something for me?
5. Are you leaving town this weekend?
6. Can you lend me some money?

It depends where you're going.
It depends on the restaurant.
It depends _____
It _____
_____
_____

go in, fall off, run away, etc.
(phrasal verbs 1)

A *phrasal verb* is a verb (**go/look/be**, etc.) + **in/out/up/down**, etc.

---

in

get in

- Kate opened the door of the car and **got in**. (= **into** the car)
- I waited outside the store. I didn't **go in**.

out

look out

- I went to the window and **looked out**.
- A car stopped, and a woman **got out**. (= **out of** the car)

---

on

get on

- The bus came, and I **got on**.

off

fall off

- Be careful! Don't **fall off**.

---

up

stand up

- She **stood up** and left the room.
- I usually **get up** early. (= get out of bed)
- We **looked up** at the stars in the sky.

down

fall down

- The picture **fell down**.
- Would you like to **sit down**?
- **Lie down** on the floor.

---

away *or* **off**

run away

- The thief **ran away**. (*or* . . . **ran off**)
- Emma got into the car and **drove away**. (*or* . . . **drove off**)

be/go away (= in/to another place)
- Tim has **gone away** for a few days.

back

go *come back*

- Go away and don't **come back**!
- We went out for dinner and then **went back** to our hotel.

be back
- Tim is away. He'll **be back** on Monday.

---

over

move over *pull over*

- There was an empty seat, so he **moved over**.
- I was tired of driving and **pulled over**.

around

John!

turn around

- Somebody shouted my name, so I **turned around**.
- We went for a long walk. After an hour we **turned around** and went back.

---

get → Unit 57   **put on / take off**, etc. (phrasal verbs 2) → Unit 116   more phrasal verbs → Appendix 6

Exercises

115.1 Look at the pictures and complete the sentences. Use these verbs + *in/out/up*, etc.

got   got   ~~looked~~   looked   rode   sat   turned   went

1. I went to the window and ___looked out___ .
2. The door was open, so we _____ .
3. He heard a plane, so he _____ .
4. She got on her bike and _____ .
5. I said hello, and he _____ .
6. The bus stopped, and she _____ .
7. There was a free seat, so she _____ .
8. A car stopped, and two men _____ .

115.2 Complete the sentences. Use *out/away/back*, etc.

1. "What happened to the picture on the wall?" "It fell ___down___ ."
2. Please don't walk _____ . I have something to tell you.
3. Lisa heard a noise in back of her, so she turned _____ to see what it was.
4. I'm going _____ now to do some shopping. I'll be _____ at 5:00.
5. I'm really tired. I'm going to lie _____ on the sofa.
6. I can't see the movie screen. Would you please move _____ ?
7. Mark is from Utah. He lives in Boston now, but he wants to go _____ to Utah.
8. We don't have a key to the house, so we can't get _____ .
9. I was very tired this morning. I couldn't get _____ .
10. *A:* "When are you going _____ ?"
    B: "On the fifth. And I'm coming _____ on the twenty-fourth."

115.3 Before you do this exercise, study the verbs in Appendix 6 (page 242). Complete the sentences. Choose a verb from the box + *on/off/up*, etc. If necessary, put the verb into the correct form.

break	get	go	slow	take	work	
fall	give	hold	speak	~~wake~~		+ along/on/off/up/down/over/out

1. I went to sleep at 10:00 and ___woke up___ at 8:00 the next morning.
2. "It's time to go." "_____ a minute. I'm not ready yet."
3. The train _____ and finally stopped.
4. I like flying, but I'm always nervous when the plane _____ .
5. Tony doesn't see his sister much. They don't _____ very well.
6. It's difficult to hear you. Can you _____ a little?
7. This car isn't very good. It has _____ many times.
8. When babies try to walk, they sometimes _____ .
9. Ben isn't in good shape because he doesn't _____ at the gym anymore.
10. I tried to find a job, but I _____ . It was impossible.
11. The fire alarm _____ , and everyone had to leave the building.

put on your shoes   put your shoes on
(phrasal verbs 2)

A

Sometimes a phrasal verb (**put on** / **take off**, etc.) has an *object*. For example:

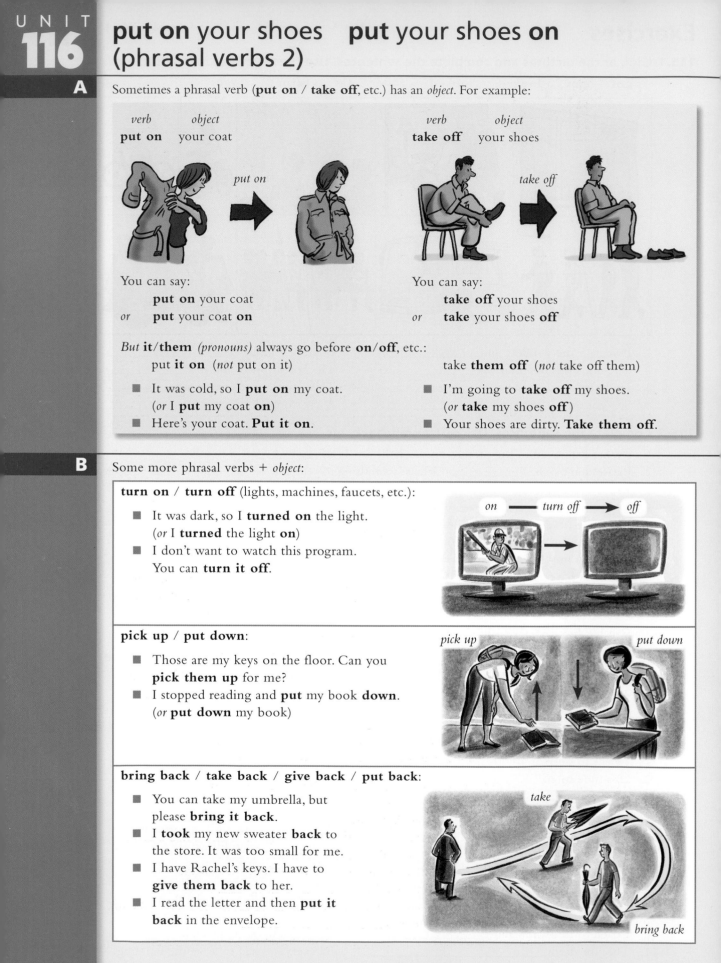

verb	*object*		*verb*	*object*
put on	your coat		**take off**	your shoes

put on → *take off*

You can say:

> **put on** your coat
or > **put** your coat **on**

You can say:

> **take off** your shoes
or > **take** your shoes **off**

But **it**/**them** *(pronouns)* always go before **on**/**off**, etc.:

> put **it on** (*not* put on it)

> take **them off** (*not* take off them)

- It was cold, so I **put on** my coat.
  (*or* I **put** my coat **on**)
- Here's your coat. **Put it on**.

- I'm going to **take off** my shoes.
  (*or* **take** my shoes **off**)
- Your shoes are dirty. **Take them off**.

B

Some more phrasal verbs + *object*:

turn on / turn off (lights, machines, faucets, etc.):

- It was dark, so I **turned on** the light.
  (*or* I **turned** the light **on**)
- I don't want to watch this program.
  You can **turn it off**.

on —— *turn off* → *off*

pick up / put down:

- Those are my keys on the floor. Can you
  pick them up for me?
- I stopped reading and **put** my book **down**.
  (*or* **put down** my book)

pick up   *put down*

bring back / take back / give back / put back:

- You can take my umbrella, but
  please **bring it back**.
- I **took** my new sweater **back** to
  the store. It was too small for me.
- I have Rachel's keys. I have to
  give them back to her.
- I read the letter and then **put it
  back** in the envelope.

take

bring back

go in / **fall off**, etc. (phrasal verbs 1) → **Unit 115**   more phrasal verbs + object → **Appendix 7**

Exercises

116.1 Look at the pictures. What did these people do?

1. He _____turned on the light_____ .
2. She _____ .
3. He _____ .
4. She _____ .
5. He _____ .
6. She _____ .

116.2 You can write these sentences in three different ways. Complete the table.

1.	I turned on the radio.	_I turned the radio on._	_I turned it on._
2.	He put on his jacket.	He _____	He _____
3.	She _____	She took her glasses off.	_____
4.	I picked up the phone.	_____	_____
5.	They gave back the key.	_____	_____
6.	_____	We turned the lights off.	_____

116.3 Complete the sentences. Use these verbs with *it* or *them*.

bring back   pick up   take back   turn off   ~~turn on~~

1. I wanted to watch something on television, so I _____turned it on_____ .
2. My new lamp doesn't work. I'm going to _____ to the store.
3. There were some gloves on the floor, so I _____ and put them on the table.
4. When I finished working on the computer, I _____ .
5. Thank you for lending me these books. I won't forget to _____ .

116.4 Before you do this exercise, study the verbs in Appendix 7 (page 243). Complete the sentences using one of the following verbs. Sometimes you will also need to use *it/them/me*.

fill out   knock over   put out   ~~tear down~~   try on
give up   look up   show around   throw away   ~~turn down~~

1. They ___tore___ a lot of houses ___down___ when they built the new road.
2. That music is very loud. Can you ___turn it down___ ?
3. I _____ a glass and broke it.
4. "What does this word mean?"   "Here's a dictionary. You can _____ ."
5. I want to keep these magazines. Please don't _____ .
6. I _____ a pair of shoes at the store, but I didn't buy them.
7. I visited a school last week. One of the teachers _____ .
8. "Do you play the piano?"   "No, I started to learn, but I _____ after a month."
9. Somebody gave me a form and told me to _____ .
10. Smoking isn't allowed here. Please _____ your cigarette _____ .

APPENDIX 1
Active and passive

1.1 Present and past

	Active	Passive
Simple present	■ We **make** butter from milk. ■ Somebody **cleans** these rooms every day. ■ People never **invite** me to parties. ■ How **do** they **make** butter?	■ Butter **is made** from milk. ■ These rooms **are cleaned** every day. ■ I **am** never **invited** to parties. ■ How **is** butter **made**?
Simple past	■ Somebody **stole** my car last week. ■ Somebody **stole** my keys yesterday. ■ They **didn't invite** me to the party. ■ When **did** they **build** these houses?	■ My car **was stolen** last week. ■ My keys **were stolen** yesterday. ■ I **wasn't invited** to the party. ■ When **were** these houses **built**?
Present continuous	■ They **are building** a new airport at this time. (= it isn't finished) ■ They **are building** some new houses near the river.	■ A new airport **is being built** at this time. ■ Some new houses **are being built** near the river.
Past continuous	■ When I was here a few years ago, they **were building** a new airport. (= it wasn't finished at that time)	■ When I was here a few years ago, a new air port **was being built**.
Present perfect	■ Look! They **have painted** the door. ■ These shirts are clean. Somebody **has washed** them. ■ Somebody **has stolen** my car.	■ Look! The door **has been painted**. ■ These shirts are clean. They **have been washed**. ■ My car **has been stolen**.
Past perfect	■ Tina said that somebody **had stolen** her car.	■ Tina said that her car **had been stolen**.

1.2 *Will / can / must / have to*, etc.

Active

- Somebody **will clean** the office tomorrow.
- Somebody **must clean** the office at night.
- I think they**'ll invite** you to the party.
- They **can't repair** my watch.
- You **should wash** this sweater by hand.

- They **are going to build** a new airport.
- Somebody **has to wash** these clothes.
- They **had to take** the injured man to the hospital.

Passive

- The office **will be cleaned** tomorrow.
- The office **must be cleaned** at night.
- I think you**'ll be invited** to the party.
- My watch **can't be repaired**.
- This sweater **should be washed** by hand.

- A new airport **is going to be built**.
- These clothes **have to be washed**.
- The injured man **had to be taken** to the hospital.

Infinitive	Simple past	Past participle
be	was/were	been
beat	beat	beaten
become	became	become
begin	began	begun
bite	bit	bitten
blow	blew	blown
break	broke	broken
bring	brought	brought
build	built	built
buy	bought	bought
catch	caught	caught
choose	chose	chosen
come	came	come
cost	cost	cost
cut	cut	cut
do	did	done
draw	drew	drawn
drink	drank	drunk
drive	drove	driven
eat	ate	eaten
fall	fell	fallen
feel	felt	felt
fight	fought	fought
find	found	found
fly	flew	flown
forget	forgot	forgotten
get	got	gotten
give	gave	given
go	went	gone
grow	grew	grown
hang	hung	hung
have	had	had
hear	heard	heard
hide	hid	hidden
hit	hit	hit
hold	held	held
hurt	hurt	hurt
keep	kept	kept
know	knew	known
leave	left	left
lend	lent	lent
let	let	let

Infinitive	Simple past	Past participle
lie	lay	lain
light	lit	lit
lose	lost	lost
make	made	made
mean	meant (ment)*	meant (ment)*
meet	met	met
pay	paid	paid
put	put	put
quit	quit	quit
read (reed)*	read (red)*	read (red)*
ride	rode	ridden
ring	rang	rung
rise	rose	risen
run	ran	run
say	said (sed)*	said (sed)*
see	saw	seen
sell	sold	sold
send	sent	sent
shine	shone	shone
shoot	shot	shot
show	showed	shown
shut	shut	shut
sing	sang	sung
sit	sat	sat
sleep	slept	slept
speak	spoke	spoken
spend	spent	spent
stand	stood	stood
steal	stole	stolen
swim	swam	swum
take	took	taken
teach	taught	taught
tear	tore	torn
tell	told	told
think	thought	thought
throw	threw	thrown
understand	understood	understood
wake	woke	woken
wear	wore	worn
win	won	won
write	wrote	written

* pronunciation

Irregular verbs in groups

The simple past and past participle are the same:

The simple past and past participle are different:

1.
cost	→ cost	let	→ let
cut	→ cut	put	→ put
hit	→ hit	quit	→ quit
hurt	→ hurt	shut	→ shut

1.
break	→ broke	→ broken
choose	→ chose	→ chosen
speak	→ spoke	→ spoken
steal	→ stole	→ stolen
wake	→ woke	→ woken

2.
lend	→ lent	lose	→ lost
send	→ sent	shoot	→ shot
spend	→ spent	light	→ lit
build	→ built	sit	→ sat

keep	→ kept
sleep	→ slept

feel	→ felt
leave	→ left
meet	→ met
mean	→ meant (ment)*

2.
drive	→ drove	→ driven
ride	→ rode	→ ridden
rise	→ rose	→ risen
write	→ wrote	→ written

beat	→ beat	→ beaten
bite	→ bit	→ bitten
hide	→ hid	→ hidden

3.
bring	→ brought
buy	→ bought
fight	→ fought
think	→ thought

catch	→ caught
teach	→ taught

3.
eat	→ ate	→ eaten
fall	→ fell	→ fallen
forget	→ forgot	→ forgotten
get	→ got	→ gotten
give	→ gave	→ given
see	→ saw	→ seen
take	→ took	→ taken

4.
sell	→ sold
tell	→ told

find	→ found
have	→ had
hear	→ heard (herd)*
hold	→ held
read	→ read (red)*
say	→ said (sed)*

pay	→ paid
make	→ made

stand	→ stood
understand	→ understood

4.
blow	→ blew	→ blown
grow	→ grew	→ grown
know	→ knew	→ known
throw	→ threw	→ thrown
fly	→ flew	→ flown
draw	→ drew	→ drawn
show	→ showed	→ shown

5.
begin	→ began	→ begun
drink	→ drank	→ drunk
swim	→ swam	→ swum
ring	→ rang	→ rung
sing	→ sang	→ sung
run	→ ran	→ run

6.
come	→ came	→ come
become	→ became	→ become

* pronunciation

APPENDIX 4
Short forms (he's / I'd / don't, etc.)

4.1 In spoken English we usually pronounce *I am* as one word. The short form (*I'm*) is a way of writing this:

I am	→	I'm
it is	→	it's
they have	→	they've, etc.

- **I'm** feeling tired this morning.
- "Do you like this jacket?"   "Yes, **it's** nice."
- "Where are your friends?"   "**They've** gone home."

When we write short forms, we use ' *(an apostrophe)*:

I ~~a~~m → I'm   he ~~i~~s → he's   you ~~ha~~ve → you've   she ~~wi~~ll → she'll

4.2 We use these forms with *I/he/she*, etc.:

am → 'm	I'm						
is → 's		he's	she's	it's			
are → 're					we're	you're	they're
have → 've	I've				we've	you've	they've
has → 's		he's	she's	it's			
had → 'd	I'd	he'd	she'd		we'd	you'd	they'd
will → 'll	I'll	he'll	she'll		we'll	you'll	they'll
would → 'd	I'd	he'd	she'd		we'd	you'd	they'd

- **I've** got some new shoes.
- **We'll** probably go out tonight.
- **It's** 10:00. **You're** late again.

's = is *or* **has**:
- She**'s** going out tonight. (she**'s** going = she **is** going)
- She**'s** gone out. (she**'s** gone = she **has** gone)

'd = would *or* **had**:
- *A:* What would you like to eat?
  B: **I'd** like a salad, please. (**I'd** like = I **would** like)
- I told the police that **I'd** lost my passport. (**I'd** lost = I **had** lost)

Do not use **'m/'s/'d**, etc. at the end of a sentence (see Unit 41):
- "Are you tired?"   "Yes, I **am**." (*not* Yes, I'm.)
- She isn't tired, but he **is**. (*not* he's)

4.3 We use short forms with *I/you/he/she*, etc., but you can use short forms (especially *'s*) with other words, too:
- **Who's** your favorite singer? (= who **is**)
- **What's** the time? (= what **is**)
- **There's** a big tree in the yard. (= there **is**)
- **My sister's** working in London. (= my sister **is** working)
- **Paul's** gone out. (= Paul **has** gone out)
- **What color's** your car? (= What color **is** your car?)

APPENDIX 4
Short forms (**he's** / **I'd** / **don't**, etc.)

4.4 Negative short forms (see Unit 44):

isn't	(= is not)	**don't**	(= do not)	**can't**	(= cannot)
aren't	(= are not)	**doesn't**	(= does not)	**couldn't**	(= could not)
wasn't	(= was not)	**didn't**	(= did not)	**won't**	(= will not)
weren't	(= were not)			**wouldn't**	(= would not)
hasn't	(= has not)			**shouldn't**	(= should not)
haven't	(= have not)			**mustn't**	(= must not)
hadn't	(= had not)				

- We went to her house, but she **wasn't** at home.
- "Where's David?"   "I **don't** know. I **haven't** seen him."
- You work all the time. You **shouldn't** work so hard.
- I **won't** be here tomorrow. (= I will not)

4.5 **'s** (*apostrophe + s*)

's can mean different things:

(1) **'s** = **is** *or* **has** (see section 4.2 of this appendix)

(2) **let's** = let **us** (see Unit 37)
- It's a beautiful day. **Let's** go outside. (= **Let us** go outside.)

(3) Kate**'s** camera = her camera
my brother**'s** car = his car
the manager**'s** office = his/her office, etc.
(see Unit 65)

Compare:
- **Kate's** camera was very expensive. (**Kate's** camera = **her** camera)
- **Kate's** a very good photographer. (**Kate's** = Kate **is**)
- **Kate's** got a new camera. (Kate**'s** got = Kate **has** got)

APPENDIX 5
Spelling

5.1 Words + -s and -es (birds/watches, etc.)

noun + **s** (plural) (see Unit 67)

bird ➔ bird**s**   mistake ➔ mistake**s**   hotel ➔ hotel**s**

verb + **s** (he/she/it **-s**) (see Unit 5)

think ➔ think**s**   live ➔ live**s**   remember ➔ remember**s**

but

+ **es** after **-s** / **-sh** / **-ch** / **-x**

bu**s** ➔ bus**es**   pa**ss** ➔ pass**es**   addre**ss** ➔ address**es**
di**sh** ➔ dish**es**   wa**sh** ➔ wash**es**   fini**sh** ➔ finish**es**
wat**ch** ➔ watch**es**   tea**ch** ➔ teach**es**   sandwi**ch** ➔ sandwich**es**
bo**x** ➔ box**es**

also

potato ➔ potato**es**   tomato ➔ tomato**es**
do ➔ do**es**   go ➔ go**es**

-f / **-fe** ➔ **-ves**

shel**f** ➔ shel**ves**   kni**fe** ➔ kni**ves**   *but*   roo**f** ➔ roo**fs**

5.2 Words ending in -y (baby ➔ babies / study ➔ studied, etc.)

-y ➔ **-ies**

stud**y** ➔ stud**ies** (*not* studys)   famil**y** ➔ famil**ies** (*not* familys)
stor**y** ➔ stor**ies**   cit**y** ➔ cit**ies**   bab**y** ➔ bab**ies**
tr**y** ➔ tr**ies**   marr**y** ➔ marr**ies**   fl**y** ➔ fl**ies**

-y ➔ **-ied** (see Unit 11)

stud**y** ➔ stud**ied** (*not* studyed)
tr**y** ➔ tr**ied**   marr**y** ➔ marr**ied**   cop**y** ➔ cop**ied**

-y ➔ **-ier** / **-iest** (see Units 88, 91)

eas**y** ➔ eas**ier**/eas**iest** (*not* easyer/easyest)
happ**y** ➔ happ**ier**/happ**iest**   luck**y** ➔ luck**ier**/luck**iest**
heav**y** ➔ heav**ier**/heav**iest**   funn**y** ➔ funn**ier**/funn**iest**

-y ➔ **-ily** (see Unit 87)

eas**y** ➔ eas**ily** (*not* easyly)
happ**y** ➔ happ**ily**   heav**y** ➔ heav**ily**   luck**y** ➔ luck**ily**

y does not change to **i** if the ending is **-ay** / **-ey** / **-oy** / **-uy**:

holid**ay** ➔ holid**ays** (*not* holidaies)
enj**oy** ➔ enj**oys**/enj**oyed**   st**ay** ➔ st**ays**/st**ayed**   b**uy** ➔ b**uys**   k**ey** ➔ k**eys**

but

say ➔ **said**   **pay** ➔ **paid**   (*irregular verbs*)

APPENDIX 5
Spelling

5.3 *-ing*

Verbs that end in **-e** (mak**e**/writ**e**/driv**e**, etc.) → ~~e~~**ing**	
mak**e** → mak**ing** write → writ**ing** come → com**ing** dance → danc**ing**	

Verbs that end in **-ie** → **-ying**:	
lie → **lying** **die** → **dying** **tie** → **tying**	

5.4 stop → stopped, big → bigger, etc.

Vowels and consonants:

Vowel letters: a e i o u
Consonant letters: b c d f g k l m n p r s t w y

Sometimes a word ends in a *vowel* + a *consonant*. For example: st**op**, b**ig**, g**et**.
Before **-ing/-ed/-er/-est**, the consonant (**p**/**g**/**t**, etc.) becomes **pp**/**gg**/**tt**, etc.
For example:

	V+C			
stop	ST **O P**	p → **pp**	sto**pp**ing	sto**pp**ed
run	R **U N**	n → **nn**	ru**nn**ing	
get	G **E T**	t → **tt**	ge**tt**ing	
swim	SW **I M**	m → **mm**	swi**mm**ing	
big	B **I G**	g → **gg**	bi**gg**er	bi**gg**est
hot	H **O T**	t → **tt**	ho**tt**er	ho**tt**est
thin	TH **I N**	n → **nn**	thi**nn**er	thi**nn**est

V = *vowel*
C = *consonant*

This does *not* happen:
(1) if the word ends in *two* consonant letters (C + C):

	C+C		
help	HE **L P**	he**lp**ing	he**lp**ed
work	WO **R K**	wor**k**ing	wor**k**ed
fast	FA **S T**	fa**st**er	fa**st**est

(2) if the word ends in two vowel letters + a consonant letter (V + V + C):

	V+V+C		
need	N **E E D**	nee**d**ing	nee**d**ed
wait	W **A I T**	wai**t**ing	wai**t**ed
cheap	CH **E A P**	chea**p**er	chea**p**est

(3) in longer words (two syllables or more) if the last part of the word is *not* stressed:

	stress	
happen	**HAP**-pen	→ happe**n**ing/happe**n**ed (*not* happe**nn**ed)
visit	**VIS**-it	→ visi**t**ing/visi**t**ed
remember	re-**MEM**-ber	→ remembe**r**ing/remembe**r**ed

but

prefer	pre-**FER**	*(stress at the end)* →	prefe**rr**ing/prefe**rr**ed
begin	be-**GIN**	*(stress at the end)* →	begi**nn**ing

(4)   if the word ends in **-y** or **-w**. (At the end of words, **y** and **w** are not consonants.)
enjo**y** → enjo**y**ing/enjo**y**ed   sno**w** → sno**w**ing/sno**w**ed   fe**w** → fe**w**er/fe**w**est

Phrasal verbs (take off / give up, etc.)

This is a list of some important phrasal verbs (see Unit 115).

out	**look out / watch out** = *be careful*
	■ **Look out!** There's a car coming.
	work out = *exercise* (to become stronger or more fit)
	■ Sarah **works out** at the gym two or three times a week.

work out

on	**come on** = *be quick / hurry*
	■ **Come on!** Everybody is waiting for you.
	go on = *continue*
	■ I'm sorry I interrupted. **Go on.**
	(= continue what you were saying)
	■ How long will this hot weather **go on**?
	keep on = *continue (talking, etc.)*
	■ I asked them to be quiet, but they **kept on** talking.
	hold on = *wait*
	■ Can you **hold on** a minute? (= can you wait?)

Hold on a minute.

off	**take off** = *leave the ground (for planes)*
	■ The plane **took off** 20 minutes late but arrived on time.
	go off = *explode (a bomb, etc.) or ring (an alarm, an alarm clock, etc.)*
	■ A bomb **went off** and caused a lot of damage.
	■ A car alarm **goes off** if somebody tries to break into the car.

take off

go off

up	**clean up** = *make neat or clean*
	■ After the party, it took two hours to **clean up**.
	give up = *stop trying*
	■ I know it's difficult, but don't **give up**. (= don't stop trying)
	grow up = *become an adult*
	■ What does your son want to do when he **grows up**?
	hurry up = *do something more quickly*
	■ **Hurry up!** We don't have much time.
	speak up = *speak more loudly*
	■ I can't hear you. Can you **speak up**, please?
	wake up = *stop sleeping*
	■ I often **wake up** in the middle of the night.

grow up

wake up

down	**slow down** = *go more slowly*
	■ You're driving too fast. **Slow down!**
	break down = *stop working (for cars, machines, etc.)*
	■ Sue was very late because her car **broke down**.

break down

along	**get along** = *be together without problems*
	■ Sam doesn't visit his parents often. He doesn't **get along** with his father.

over	**fall over** = *lose your balance*
	■ I **fell over** because my shoes were too big for me.

fall over

Phrasal verbs + object (**put out** a fire / **try on** clothes, etc.)

This is a list of some important phrasal verbs + object (see Unit 116).

out

fill out a form = *complete a form*
- Can you **fill out this form**, please?

put out a fire, a cigarette, etc.
- The fire department arrived and **put the fire out**.

cross out a mistake, a word, etc.
- If you make a mistake, **cross it out**.

fill out

put out   *cross out*

on

try on clothes = *put on clothes to see if they fit you*
- *(in a store)* Where can I **try these pants on**?

up

give up something = *stop doing/having something*
- Sue **gave up her job** when her baby was born. (= she stopped working)
- Tom's doctor told him he had to **give up smoking**.

look up a word in a dictionary, etc.
- I didn't know the meaning of the word, so I **looked it up** in a dictionary.

turn up the TV, radio, music, heat, etc. = *make it louder or warmer*
- Can you **turn the radio up**? I can't hear it.

wake up somebody who is sleeping
- I have to get up early tomorrow. Can you **wake me up** at 6:30?

down

tear down a building = *demolish it*
- They are going to **tear down** the school and build a new one.

tear down

turn down the TV, radio, music, heat, etc. = *make it quieter or less warm*
- The music is too loud. Can you **turn it down**?

over

knock over a cup, a glass, a person, etc.
- Be careful. Don't **knock your cup over**.

knock over

away

throw away garbage, things you don't want
- These apples are bad. Should I **throw them away**?
- Don't **throw away that picture**. I want it.

throw away

put something **away** = *put it in the place where you usually keep it*
- After they finished playing, the children **put their toys away**.

Garbage

back

pay somebody **back** = *give back money that you borrowed*
- Thank you for lending me the money. I'll **pay you back** next week.

around

show somebody **around** = *take somebody on a tour of a place*
- We visited a factory last week. The manager **showed us around**.

Additional Exercises

List of exercises:

---

am/is/are   Units 1–2

1 Write sentences for the pictures. Use the words in the boxes + *is/isn't/are/aren't*.

~~The windows~~	**on the table**	1.	_The windows are open._
~~Lisa~~	**hungry**	2.	_Lisa isn't happy._
Kate	**asleep**	3.	Kate _____
The children	~~open~~	4.	_____
Gary	**full**	5.	_____
The books	**near the station**	6.	_____
The hotel	**a doctor**	7.	_____
The bus	~~happy~~	8.	_____

---

244 ADDITIONAL EXERCISES

2 Complete the sentences.

1. "Are you hungry?"   "No, but __I'm__ thirsty."
2. "__How are__ your parents?"   "They're fine."
3. "Is Anna at home?"   "No, _____ at work."
4. "_____ my keys?"   "On your desk."
5. Where is Paul from? _____ American or Canadian?
6. _____ very hot today. The temperature is 38 degrees Celsius.
7. "Are you a teacher?"   "No, _____ a student."
8. "_____ your umbrella?"   "Green."
9. Where's your car? _____ in the parking lot?
10. "_____ tired?"   "No, I'm fine."
11. "These shoes are nice. How _____ ?"   "Seventy-five dollars."

Present continuous (*I'm working* / *are you working?*, etc.)   Units 3–4

3 Use the words in parentheses to write sentences.

1. *A:* Where are your parents?
   B: __They're watching TV._____ (they / watch / TV)
2. *A:* Paula is going out.
   B: __Where's she going?_____ (where / she / go?)
3. *A:* Where's David?
   B: _____ (he / take / a shower)
4. *A:* _____ (the children / play?)
   B: No, they're asleep.
5. *A:* _____ (it / rain?)
   B: No, not any more.
6. *A:* Where are Sue and Steve?
   B: _____ (they / come / now)
7. *A:* _____ (why / you / stand / here?)
   B: _____ (I / wait / for somebody)

Simple present (*I work* / *she doesn't work* / *do you work?*, etc.)   Units 5–7

4 Complete the sentences. Use the simple present.

1. __Sue always gets__ to work early.   (Sue / always / get)
2. __We don't watch__ TV very often.   (we / not / watch)
3. How often __do you wash__ your hair?   (you / wash)
4. I want to go to the movies, but _____ to go. (Sam / not / want)
5. _____ to go out tonight?   (you / want)
6. _____ near here?   (Helen / live)
7. _____ a lot of people.   (Sarah / know)
8. I enjoy traveling, but _____ very much.   (I / not / travel)
9. What time _____ in the morning?   (you / usually / get up)
10. My parents are usually at home at night.
    _____ very often.   (they / not / go out)
11. _____ work at 5:00.   (Tom / always / leave)
12. *A:* What _____ ?   (Julia / do)
    B: _____ in a hotel.   (she / work)

Simple present, *am/is/are* and *have (got)*

5 **Read the questions and Claire's answers. Then write sentences about Claire.**

Claire

1.	Are you married?	No.
2.	Do you live in Houston?	Yes.
3.	Are you a student?	Yes.
4.	Do you have a car?	No.
5.	Do you go out a lot?	Yes.
6.	Do you have a lot of friends?	Yes.
7.	Do you like Houston?	No.
8.	Do you like to dance?	Yes.
9.	Are you interested in sports?	No.

1. _She isn't married._
2. _She lives in Houston._
3. _____
4. _____
5. _____
6. _____
7. _____
8. _____
9. _____

6 **Complete the questions.**

1. _What's your name_____ ?
    _____ married?
    Where _____ ?
    _____ any children?
    How _____ ?

    Brian.
    Yes, I am.
    On State Street.
    Yes, a daughter.
    She's three.

2. _____ ?
    _____ ?
    _____ your job?
    _____ a car?
    _____ to work by car?

    I'm 29.
    I work in a supermarket.
    No, I hate it.
    Yes, I do.
    No, I usually go by bus.

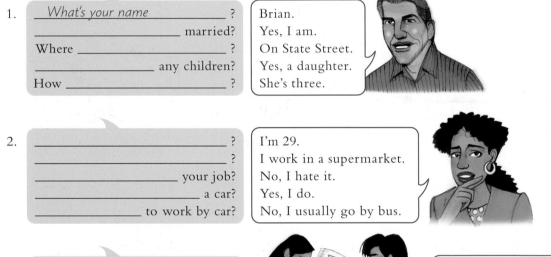

3. _Who is this man_____ ?
    _____ ?
    _____ ?
    _____ in New York?

    That's my brother.
    Michael.
    He's a travel agent.
    No, in Los Angeles.

7 **Write sentences from these words. All the sentences are present.**

1. (Sarah often / tennis)   _Sarah often plays tennis._
2. (my parents / a new car)   _My parents have a new car._   OR
                                    My parents have got a new car.
3. (my shoes / dirty)   _My shoes are dirty._
4. (Sonia / 32 years old)   Sonia _____
5. (I / two sisters)   _____
6. (we often / TV at night)   _____
7. (Jane never / a hat)   _____
8. (my car / a flat tire)   _____
9. (these flowers / beautiful)   _____
10. (Mary / German very well)   _____

Present continuous (*I'm working*) and simple present (*I work*)

8 **Complete the sentences.**

1. Please be quiet.
   I'm working (I/work).

2. *Do you go* (you/go) to the movies a lot?

3. What _____ _____ (you/cook)?

4. Jack _____ (play) the piano very well.

5. _____ (I/leave) now. Goodbye!

6. _____ (it/rain). Can I take this umbrella?

7. _____ (I/not/watch) TV very much.

8. Excuse me, _____ _____ (we/look) for the museum.

9. What's this word? How _____ (you/pronounce) it?

---

9 **Which is right?**

1. "Are you speaking / Do you speak English?" "Yes, a little." (*Do you speak* is right)
2. Sometimes <u>we're going / we go</u> away on weekends.
3. It's a nice day today. The sun <u>is shining / shines</u>.
4. *(You meet Kate in the street.)* Hello, Kate. Where <u>are you going / do you go</u>?
5. How often <u>are you taking / do you take</u> a vacation?
6. Emily is a writer. <u>She's writing / She writes</u> children's books.
7. <u>I'm never reading / I never read</u> newspapers.
8. "Where are Michael and Jane?" "<u>They're watching / They watch</u> TV in the living room."
9. Helen is in her office. <u>She's talking / She talks</u> to somebody.
10. What time <u>are you usually having / do you usually have</u> dinner?
11. John isn't at home right now. <u>He's visiting / He visits</u> some friends.
12. "Would you like some coffee?" "No, thanks. <u>I'm not drinking / I don't drink</u> coffee."

10 **Complete the sentences. Use one word only.**

1. I got up early and __took__ a shower.
2. Tom was tired last night, so he _____ to bed early.
3. I _____ this pen on the floor. Is it yours?
4. Kate got married when she _____ 23.
5. Helen is learning to drive. She _____ her first lesson yesterday.
6. "I've got a new job."   "Yes, I know. David _____ me."
7. "Where did you buy that book?"   "It was a present. Jane _____ it to me."
8. We _____ hungry, so we had something to eat.
9. "Did you enjoy the movie?"   "Yes, I _____ it was very good."
10. "Did Andy come to your party?"   "No, we _____ him, but he didn't come."

11 **Look at the questions and Kevin's answers. Write sentences about Kevin when he was a child.**

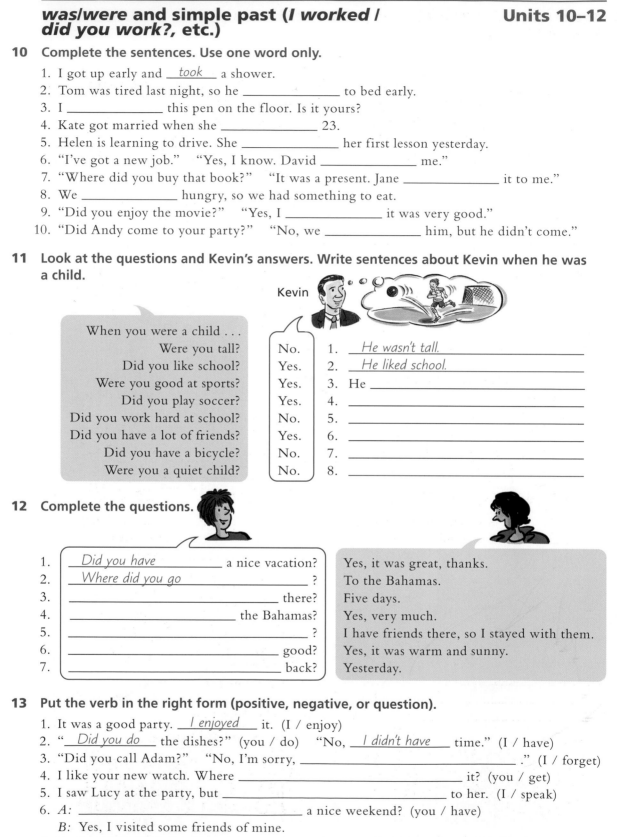

Kevin

When you were a child . . .

Were you tall?	No.	1.	*He wasn't tall.*
Did you like school?	Yes.	2.	*He liked school.*
Were you good at sports?	Yes.	3.	He _____
Did you play soccer?	Yes.	4.	_____
Did you work hard at school?	No.	5.	_____
Did you have a lot of friends?	Yes.	6.	_____
Did you have a bicycle?	No.	7.	_____
Were you a quiet child?	No.	8.	_____

12 **Complete the questions.**

1. *Did you have* _____ a nice vacation?   Yes, it was great, thanks.
2. *Where did you go* _____ ?   To the Bahamas.
3. _____ there?   Five days.
4. _____ the Bahamas?   Yes, very much.
5. _____ ?   I have friends there, so I stayed with them.
6. _____ good?   Yes, it was warm and sunny.
7. _____ back?   Yesterday.

13 **Put the verb in the right form (positive, negative, or question).**

1. It was a good party. __I enjoyed__ it. (I / enjoy)
2. "__Did you do__ the dishes?" (you / do)   "No, __I didn't have__ time." (I / have)
3. "Did you call Adam?"   "No, I'm sorry, _____." (I / forget)
4. I like your new watch. Where _____ it? (you / get)
5. I saw Lucy at the party, but _____ to her. (I / speak)
6. *A:* _____ a nice weekend? (you / have)
   B: Yes, I visited some friends of mine.
7. Paul wasn't well yesterday, so _____ to work. (he / go)
8. "Is Mary here?"   "Yes, _____ five minutes ago." (she / arrive)
9. Where _____ before he moved here? (Robert / live)
10. The restaurant wasn't expensive. _____ very much. (the meal / cost)

14 Complete the sentences. Use the simple past or past continuous.

1. It _was raining_ (rain) when we _went_ (go) out.

2. Good morning.
Jane   Paul
When I arrived at the office, Jane and Paul _____ (work) at their desks.

3. I _____ (open) the window because it was hot.

4. Sue
The phone _____ (ring) when Sue _____ (cook) dinner.

5. I _____ (hear) a noise outside, so I _____ (look) out of the window.

6. Tom
Tom _____ (look) out of the window when the accident _____ (happen).

7. Richard
Richard had a book in his hand, but he _____ (not/read) it. He _____ (watch) TV.

8. Erin
Erin bought a magazine, but she _____ (not/read) it. She didn't have time.

9. I _____ (finish) lunch, _____ (pay) the bill, and _____ (leave) the restaurant.

10. Hi, Kate!
Kate
I _____ (see) Kate this morning. I _____ (walk) along the street and she _____ (wait) for the bus.

15 Complete the sentences. Use one of these forms:

> simple present (**I work/drive**, etc.)   present continuous (**I am working/driving**, etc.)
> simple past (**I worked/drove**, etc.)   past continuous (**I was working/driving**, etc.)

1. You can turn off the TV. I *'m not watching* (not / watch) it.
2. Last night Jenny ___*fell*___ (fall) asleep while she ___*was reading*___ (read).
3. Listen! Somebody _____ (play) the piano.
4. "Do you have my key?"   "No, I _____ (give) it back to you."
5. David is very lazy. He _____ (not / like) to work hard.
6. Where _____ (your parents / go) on vacation last year?
7. I _____ (see) Diane yesterday. She _____ (drive) her new car.
8. *A:* _____ (you / watch) TV very much?
   B: No, I don't have a TV.
9. *A:* What _____ (you / do) at 6:00 last Sunday morning?
   B: I was in bed asleep.
10. Andy isn't at home very much. He _____ (go) out a lot.
11. I _____ (try) to find a job right now. It's very hard.
12. I'm tired this morning. I _____ (not / sleep) very well last night.

Present perfect (*I have done* / *she has been,* etc.)   Units 16–21

16 Look at the pictures and complete the sentences. Use the present perfect.

250 **ADDITIONAL EXERCISES**

5. _____ to Chile?

Yes, I went there a few years ago.

6. How long _____ here?

Since 2005.

7. Do you know Alan?

Alan

Yes, we _____ each other for years.

8. The weather is terrible today. It _____ all day.

17 Complete the sentences (1, 2, or 3 words).

1. Mark and Liz are married. They _have been_ married for five years.
2. David has been watching TV _since_ 5:00.
3. Martin is at work. He _____ at work since 8:30.
4. "Did you just arrive in Miami?" "No, I've been here _____ five days."
5. I've known Helen _____ we were in high school.
6. "My brother lives in Los Angeles." "Really? How long _____ there?"
7. George has had the same job _____ 20 years.
8. Some friends of ours are staying with us. They _____ here since Monday.

18 Complete the sentences. Write about yourself.

1. I've never _ridden a horse._
2. I've _been to Montreal_ many times.
3. I've just _____
4. I've _____
   (once / twice / a few times / many times)
5. I haven't _____ yet.
6. I've never _____
7. I've _____ since _____
8. I've _____ for _____

Present perfect (*I have done*, etc.) and simple past (*I did*, etc.)

Units 19–21

19 Present perfect or simple past? Complete the sentences (positive or negative).

1. *A:* Do you like London?
   B: I don't know. I __*haven't been*__ there.

2. *A:* Have you seen Kate?
   B: Yes, I __*saw*__ her five minutes ago.

3. *A:* That's a nice sweater. Is it new?
   B: Yes, I _____ it last week.

4. *A:* Are you tired this morning?
   B: Yes, I _____ to bed late last night.

5. *A:* Is the new French movie good?
   B: Yes, really good. I _____ it three times.

6. *A:* Do you like your new job?
   B: I _____ . My first day is next Monday.

7. *A:* The weather isn't very nice today, is it?
   B: No, but it _____ nice yesterday.

8. *A:* Was Helen at the party on Saturday?
   B: I don't think so. I _____ her there.

9. *A:* Is your son still in school?
   B: No, he _____ college two years ago.

10. *A:* Is Silvia married?
    B: Yes, she _____ married for five years.

11. *A:* Have you heard of George Washington?
    B: Of course. He _____ the first president of the United States.

12. *A:* How long does it take to make a pizza?
    B: I don't know. I _____ a pizza.

20 Write sentences with the present perfect or simple past.

1. *A:* Have you been to Thailand?
   B: Yes, __*I went there last year.*__ (I / go / there / last year)

2. *A:* Do you like London?
   B: I don't know. __*I've never been there.*__ (I / never / there)

3. *A:* Where is Paul these days?
   B: He's living in Chicago. He _____ (live / there / since last May)

4. *A:* Has Catherine gone home?
   B: Yes, _____ (she / leave / at 4:00)

5. *A:* New York is my favorite city.
   B: It is? _____ ? (how many times / you / there?)

6. *A:* You look tired.
   B: Yes, _____ (I / tired / all day)

7. *A:* I can't find my address book. Have you seen it?
   B: _____ (it / on the table / last night)

8. *A:* Do you know the Japanese restaurant on First Street?
   B: Yes, _____ (I / eat / there a few times)

9. *A:* Paula and Sue are here.
   B: Are they? _____ ? (what time / they / get / here?)

21 **Present perfect or simple past? Complete the sentences.**

1. *A:* ___Have you been___ to France?
   B: Yes, many times.
   A: When _____ the last time?
   B: Two years ago.

2. *A:* Is this your car?
   B: Yes, it is.
   A: How long _____ it?
   B: It's new. I _____ it yesterday.

3. *A:* Where do you live?
   B: On Maple Street.
   A: How long _____ there?
   B: Five years. Before that _____ on Mill Road.
   A: How long _____ on Mill Road?
   B: About three years.

4. *A:* What do you do?
   B: I work in a store.
   A: How long _____ there?
   B: Nearly two years.
   A: What _____ before that?
   B: I _____ a taxi driver.

22 **Write sentences about yourself.**

1. (yesterday morning) ___I was late for work yesterday morning.___
2. (last night) _____
3. (yesterday afternoon) _____
4. (. . . days ago) _____
5. (last week) _____
6. (last year) _____

Present, past, and present perfect

23 Which is right?

1. " _Is Sue working? (C)_ " "No, she's on vacation."

   A Does Sue work?　　**B** Is working Sue?　　**C** Is Sue working?　　**D** Does work Sue?

2. "Where _____ ?" "In Dallas."

   A lives your uncle　　**B** does your uncle live　　**C** your uncle lives　　**D** does live your uncle

3. I speak Italian, but _____ French.

   A I no speak　　**B** I'm not speaking　　**C** I doesn't speak　　**D** I don't speak

4. "Where's Tom?" "_____ a shower at the moment."

   A He's taking　　**B** He take　　**C** He takes　　**D** He has taken

5. Why _____ angry with me yesterday?

   A were you　　**B** was you　　**C** you were　　**D** have you been

6. My favorite movie is *Cleo's Dream*. _____ it four times.

   A I'm seeing　　**B** I see　　**C** I was seeing　　**D** I've seen

7. I _____ out last night. I was too tired.

   A don't go　　**B** didn't went　　**C** didn't go　　**D** haven't gone

8. Liz is from Chicago. She _____ there all her life.

   A is living　　**B** has lived　　**C** lives　　**D** lived

9. My friend _____ for me when I arrived.

   A waited　　**B** has waited　　**C** was waiting　　**D** has been waiting

10. "How long _____ English?" "Six months."

    A do you learn　　**B** are you learning　　**C** you are learning　　**D** have you been learning

11. Joel is Canadian, but he lives in Peru. He has been there _____ .

    A for three years　　**B** since three years　　**C** three years ago　　**D** during three years

12. "What time _____ ?" "About an hour ago."

    A has Lisa called　　**B** Lisa has called　　**C** did Lisa call　　**D** is Lisa calling

13. What _____ when you saw her?

    A did Sue wear　　**B** was Sue wearing　　**C** has Sue worn　　**D** was wearing Sue

14. "Can you drive?" "No, _____ a car, but I want to learn."

    A I never drive　　**B** I'm never driving　　**C** I've never driven　　**D** I was never driving

15. I saw Helen at the station when I was going to work this morning, but she _____ me.

    A didn't see　　**B** don't see　　**C** hasn't seen　　**D** didn't saw

24 **Complete the sentences.**

1. These houses __were built__ (build) 20 years ago. Before that there was a movie theater here, but the building _____ (damage) in a fire and had to _____ (tear down).

2. This bridge _____ (build) in 1955. Now it _____ (use) by hundreds of people every day. The bridge _____ (paint) now.

3. This street _____ (call) Kennedy Street. It used to _____ (call) Hill Street, but the name _____ (change) a few years ago.

4. This is a bicycle factory. Bicycles _____ (make) here since 1961. It's the largest bicycle factory in the country. Thousands of bicycles _____ (produce) here every year.

25 **Complete the sentences.**

1. We __were invited__ (invite) to the party, but we didn't go.
2. The museum is very popular. Every year it _____ (visit) by thousands of people.
3. Many buildings _____ (damage) in the storm last week.
4. A new road is going to _____ (build) next year.
5. "Where's your jacket?"   "It _____ (clean). It will be ready tomorrow."
6. She's famous now, but in a few years her name will _____ (forget).
7. "Are you happy with your washing machine?"   "Not really. It _____ _____ (repair) three times since we bought it."
8. Milk should _____ (keep) in a fridge.
9. _____ (you / ever / bite) by a snake?
10. My bag _____ (steal) from my car yesterday afternoon.

26 **Write a new sentence with the same meaning.**

1. Somebody has stolen my keys.   _My keys have been stolen._
2. Somebody stole my car last week.   My car _____ .
3. Somebody wants you on the phone.   You _____ .
4. Somebody has eaten all the bananas. All the _____ .
5. Somebody will repair the machine.   The _____ .
6. Somebody is watching us.   We _____ .
7. Somebody has to do the housework.   The _____ .

27 Active or passive? Complete the sentences.

1. They _are building_ (build) a new airport now.
2. These shirts are clean now. They _have been washed_ OR _were washed_ (wash).
3. "How did you fall?" "Somebody _____ (push) me."
4. "How did you fall?" "I _____ (push)."
5. I can't find my bag. Somebody _____ (take) it!
6. My watch is broken. It _____ (repair) at the moment.
7. Who _____ (invent) the camera?
8. When _____ (the camera / invent)?
9. These shirts are clean now. They _____ (wash).
10. These shirts are clean now. I _____ (wash) them.
11. The letter was for me, so why _____ (they / send) it to you?
12. The information will _____ (send) to you as soon as possible.

Future   Units 26–29

28 Which is the best alternative?

1. _We're having (B)_ a party next Sunday. I hope you can come.
   A We have   **B** We're having   **C** We'll have

2. Do you know about Karen? _____ her job. She told me last week.
   A She quits   **B** She's going to quit   **C** She'll quit

3. There's a program on TV that I want to watch. _____ in five minutes.
   A It starts   **B** It's starting   **C** It will start

4. The weather is nice now, but I think _____ later.
   A it rains   **B** it's raining   **C** it will rain

5. "What _____ next weekend?" "Nothing. I have no plans."
   A do you do   **B** are you doing   **C** will you do

6. "When you see Tina, can you ask her to call me?" "OK, _____ her."
   A I ask   **B** I'm going to ask   **C** I'll ask

7. "What would you like to drink, tea or coffee?" "_____ tea, please."
   A I have   **B** I'm going to have   **C** I'll have

8. Don't take that newspaper away. _____ it.
   A I read   **B** I'm going to read   **C** I'll read

9. Rachel is sick, so _____ to the party tomorrow night.
   A she doesn't come   **B** she isn't coming   **C** she won't come

10. I want to meet Sarah at the station. What time _____ ?
    A does her train arrive   **B** is her train going to arrive   **C** is her train arriving

11. "Will you be at home tomorrow night?" "No, _____ ."
    A I go out   **B** I'm going out   **C** I'll go out

12. "_____ you tomorrow?" "Yes, fine."
    A Do I call   **B** Am I going to call   **C** Shall I call

Past, present, and future

29 Complete the sentences.

1. *A:* ___Did you go___ (you / go) out last night?
   B: No, _____ (I / stay) home.
   A: What _____ (you / do)?
   B: _____ (I / watch) TV.
   A: _____ (you / go) out tomorrow night?
   B: Yes, _____ (I / go) to the movies.
   A: What movie _____ (you / see)?
   B: _____ (I / not / know). _____ (I / not / decide) yet.

2. *A:* Are you visiting here?
   B: Yes, we are.
   A: How long _____ (you / be) here?
   B: _____ (we / arrive) yesterday.
   A: And how long _____ (you / stay)?
   B: Until the end of next week.
   A: And _____ (you / like) it here?
   B: Yes, _____ (we / have) a wonderful time.

3. *A:* Oh, _____ (I / just / remember) – _____
   (Karen / call) while you were out.
   B: _____ (she / always / call) when I'm not here.
   _____ (she / leave) a message?
   A: No, but _____ (she / want) you to call her back as soon as possible.
   B: OK, _____ (I / call) her now.
   _____ (you / know) her number?
   A: It's in my address book. _____ (I / get) it for you.

4. *A:* _____ (I / go) out with Chris and Steve tonight.
   _____ (you / want) to come with us?
   B: Yes, where _____ (you / go)?
   A: To the Italian restaurant on North Avenue. _____ (you / ever / eat) there?
   B: Yes, _____ (I / be) there two or three times. In fact I
   _____ (go) there last night, but I'd love to go again!

5. *A:* _____ (I / lose) my glasses again.
   _____ (you / see) them?
   B: _____ (you / wear) them
   when _____ (I / come) in.
   A: Well, _____ (I / not / wear)
   them now, so where are they?
   B: _____ (you / look) in the kitchen?
   A: No, _____ (I / go) and look now.

Past, present, and future   Units 3–23, 26–29, 53, 55, 99, 106

30 Rachel is talking about her best friend, Carolyn. Put the verbs in the correct form.

Carolyn is my best friend. I remember very well the first time
(1) _____ (we / meet). It was our first day at high
school, and (2) _____ (we / sit) next to each other in
the first class. (3) _____ (we / not / know) any other
students in our class, and so (4) _____ (we / become)
friends. We found that (5) _____ (we / like) the
same things, especially music and sports, and so
(6) _____ (we / spend) a lot of time together.

(7) _____ (we / finish) school five years ago, but
(8) _____ (we / meet) as often as we can. For the last
six months Carolyn (9) _____ (be) in Mexico – right
now (10) _____ (she / work) in a school as a teaching
assistant. (11) _____ (she / come) back to the States
next month, and when (12) _____ (she / come) back,
(13) _____ (we / have) lots of things to talk about.
(14) _____ (it / be) really nice to see her again.

Rachel

31 Nick and his friend Jon are from London. They are traveling around the world. Read the
e-mails between Nick and his parents, and put the verbs in the correct form.

Dear Mom and Dad,

We're in Los Angeles, the first stop on our round-the-world
trip! (1) _*We arrived*_ (we / arrive) here yesterday, and now
(2) _____ (we / stay) at a hotel near the
airport. The flight was twelve hours, but
(3) _____ (we / enjoy) it.
(4) _____ (we / watch) some movies and
(5) _____ (sleep) for a few hours, which is
unusual for me – usually (6) _____
(I / not / sleep) well on planes.

Today is a rest day for us and (7) _____
(we / not / do) anything special, but tomorrow
(8) _____ (we / go) to Hollywood
(9) _____ (see) the movie studios.
(10) _____ (we / not / decide) yet what
to do after Los Angeles. Jon (11) _____
(want) to drive up the coast to San Francisco, but I'd prefer
(12) _____ (go) south to San Diego.

I hope all is well with you – (13) _____
(I / send) you another e-mail next week.

Love,

Nick

INTERNET CAFÉ

Nick

San Francisco

USA

Los Angeles

Pacific
Ocean

San Diego

MEXICO

258 ADDITIONAL EXERCISES

Dear Nick,

Thanks for your e-mail. It's good to hear that (14) _____
(you / have) a good time. We're fine – Ellie and Jo (15) _____
(study) hard for their exams next month. Dad has been busy at work, and last week
(16) _____ (he / have) a lot of important meetings. He's a little
tired – I think (17) _____ (he / need) a good rest.

Keep in touch!
Love,
Mom

A month later . . .

Hi Mom and Dad,

(18) _____ (we / be) in California for a month now.
(19) _____ (we / get) back to Los Angeles yesterday after
(20) _____ (see) many wonderful places. I think the place
(21) _____ (I / like) most was Yosemite National Park – it's
beautiful there and (22) _____ (we / go) biking a lot. The day
before (23) _____ (we / leave), Jon
(24) _____ (have) an accident on his bike. Luckily
(25) _____ (he / not / injure), but the bike
(26) _____ (damage).

(27) _____ (we / change) our travel plans since my last
message: now (28) _____ (we / leave) for Hawaii on Monday
(not Tuesday). (29) _____ (we / stay) there for a week before
(30) _____ (fly) to New Zealand.
(31) _____ (that / be) different, I'm sure!

All the best to Ellie and Jo for their exams.
Love,
Nick

Hi Nick,

Have a good time in Hawaii! Ellie and Jo (32) _____ (finish)
their exams yesterday – (33) _____ (I / let) you know when
(34) _____ (we / get) the results.

We're all OK. Dad and I (35) _____ (look) forward to our
vacation next month. (36) _____ (we / go) to Italy for two
weeks – (37) _____ (we / send) you an e-mail from there.

Take care!
Love,
Mom

32　**Which is correct?**

1. Don't forget ___to turn (B)___ off the light before you go out.
   A turn　**B** to turn　**C** turning

2. It's late. I should _____ now.
   A go　**B** to go　**C** going

3. I'm sorry, but I don't have time _____ to you now.
   A for talking　**B** to talk　**C** talking

4. Gary is always in the kitchen. He enjoys _____ .
   A cook　**B** to cook　**C** cooking

5. We've decided _____ away for a few days.
   A go　**B** to go　**C** going

6. You're making too much noise. Can you please stop _____ ?
   A shout　**B** to shout　**C** shouting

7. Would you like _____ to dinner on Sunday?
   A come　**B** to come　**C** coming

8. That bag is too heavy for you. Let me _____ you.
   A help　**B** to help　**C** helping

9. There's a swimming pool near my house. I go _____ every day.
   A to swim　**B** to swimming　**C** swimming

10. Did you use a dictionary _____ the letter?
    A to translate　**B** for translating　**C** for translate

11. I'd love _____ a car like yours.
    A have　**B** to have　**C** having

12. Could you _____ me with this bag, please?
    A help　**B** to help　**C** helping

13. I don't mind _____ here, but I'd prefer to sit by the window.
    A sit　**B** to sit　**C** sitting

14. Do you want _____ you?
    A that I help　**B** me to help　**C** me helping

15. I usually read the newspaper before _____ work.
    A start　**B** to start　**C** starting

16. I wasn't feeling very well, but the medicine made me _____ better.
    A feel　**B** to feel　**C** feeling

17. Shall I call the restaurant _____ a table?
    A for reserve　**B** for reserving　**C** to reserve

18. Tom looked at me without _____ anything.
    A say　**B** saying　**C** to say

33 **Complete the sentences.**

1. Can you pass __the sugar__, please?

2. Do you have _____?
   No, I can't drive.

3. Do we have any milk?
   Yes, there's some in _____.

4. What do you do?
   I'm _____.

5. I don't feel very well. I don't want to go to _____.

6. What did you do last night?
   I went to _____.

7. Shall we walk home?
   No, let's take _____.

8. Can you play _____?
   Yes, but not very well.

9. I'm interested in _____.

10. What's the difference between those cars?
    Nothing, they're _____.

34 Write *a/an* or *the* if necessary. If *a/an/the* are not necessary, leave an empty space (–).

1. Who is __the__ best player on your team?
2. I don't watch __–__ TV very often.
3. "Is there __a__ bank near here?"   "Yes, at __the__ end of this block."
4. I can't ride _____ horse.
5. _____ sky is very clear tonight.
6. Do you live here, or are you _____ tourist?
7. What did you have for _____ lunch?
8. Who was _____ first president of _____ United States?
9. "What time is it?"   "I don't know. I don't have _____ watch."
10. I'm sorry, but I've forgotten your name. I can never remember _____ names.
11. What time is _____ next train to Boston?
12. Kate never sends _____ e-mails. She prefers to call people.
13. "Where's Sue?"   "She's in _____ backyard."
14. Excuse me, I'm looking for _____ Majestic Hotel. Is it near here?
15. Gary was sick _____ last week, so he didn't go to _____ work.
16. Everest is _____ highest mountain in _____ world.
17. I usually listen to _____ radio while I'm having _____ breakfast.
18. I like _____ sports. My favorite sport is _____ basketball.
19. Julia is _____ doctor. Her husband is _____ art teacher.
20. My apartment is on _____ second floor. Turn left at _____ top of _____ stairs, and it's on _____ right.
21. After _____ dinner, we watched _____ TV.
22. I've been to _____ northern Mexico but not to _____ south.

Prepositions   Units 104–109, 112

35 Write a preposition (*in/for/by,* etc.).

1. Helen is studying math __in__ college.
2. What is the longest river _____ Europe?
3. Is there anything _____ TV tonight?
4. We arrived _____ the hotel after midnight.
5. "Where's Mike?"   "He's _____ vacation."
6. Tom hasn't gotten up yet. He's still _____ bed.
7. Lisa is away. She's been away _____ Monday.
8. The next meeting is _____ April 15.
9. We traveled across Canada _____ train.
10. There's too much sugar _____ my coffee.
11. Kevin lived in Las Vegas _____ six months. He didn't like it very much.
12. Were there a lot of people _____ the party?
13. I don't know any of the people _____ this photo.
14. The train was very slow. It stopped _____ every station.
15. I like this room. I like the pictures _____ the walls.
16. "Did you paint that picture?"   "No, it was given to me _____ a friend of mine."
17. I'm going away _____ a few days. I'll be back _____ Thursday.
18. Silvia has gone _____ Italy. She's _____ Milan right now.
19. Emma quit school _____ sixteen and got a job _____ a bookstore.

Study Guide

This guide will help you decide which units you need to study.

Each sentence can be completed using one or more of the alternatives (A, B, C, etc.). You have to decide which alternative (A, B, C, etc.) is right. SOMETIMES MORE THAN ONE ALTERNATIVE IS CORRECT.

If you don't know or if you are not sure which alternatives are correct, study the unit(s) in the list on the right. You will find the correct sentence in the unit.

There is an Answer Key to this Study Guide on page 306.

IF YOU ARE NOT SURE WHICH ANSWER IS RIGHT, STUDY UNIT(S)

Present

1.1 _____ . Can you close the window, please?   **1**
   A I cold   **B** I'm cold   **C** I have cold   **D** It has cold

1.2 Tom _____ in politics.   **1**
   A isn't interested   **B** not interested   **C** doesn't interested
   D doesn't interest

1.3 "_____ ?"   "No, she's out."   **2**
   A Is at home your mother   **B** Does your mother at home
   C Is your mother at home   **D** Are your mother at home

1.4 These postcards are nice. _____   **2**
   A How much are they?   **B** How many are they?
   C How much they are?   **D** How much is they?

1.5 Look, there's Sarah. _____ a brown coat.   **3, 24**
   A She wearing   **B** She has wearing   **C** She is wearing
   D She's wearing

1.6 You can turn off the television. _____ it.   **3, 24**
   A I'm not watch   **B** I'm not watching   **C** I not watching
   D I don't watching

1.7 "_____ today?"   "Yes, he is."   **4, 24**
   A Is working Paul   **B** Is work Paul   **C** Is Paul work
   D Is Paul working

1.8 Look, there's Emily! _____   **4, 24**
   A Where she is going?   **B** Where she go?   **C** Where's she going?
   D Where she going?

1.9 The earth _____ around the sun.   **5, 24**
   A going   **B** go   **C** goes   **D** does go   **E** is go

1.10 We _____ late on weekends.   **5, 24, 95**
   A often sleep   **B** sleep often   **C** often sleeping   **D** are often sleep

1.11 We _____ television very often.   **6, 24**
   A not watch   **B** doesn't watch   **C** don't watch   **D** don't watching
   E watch not

1.12 "_____ on Sundays?" "No, not usually."   **7, 24**

    A Do you work   **B** Are you work   **C** Does you work

    D Do you working   **E** Work you

1.13 I don't understand this sentence. What _____ ?   **7, 24**

    A mean this word   **B** means this word   **C** does mean this word

    D does this word mean   **E** this word means

1.14 Please be quiet. _____   **8, 24**

    A I working.   **B** I work.   **C** I'm working.   **D** I'm work.

1.15 Tom _____ a shower every morning.   **8**

    A takes   **B** taking   **C** is taking   **D** take

1.16 What _____ on weekends?   **7, 8, 24**

    A do you usually   **B** are you usually doing   **C** are you usually do

    D do you usually do   **E** you do usually

1.17 Sarah isn't feeling well. _____ a headache.   **9, 59**

    A She have   **B** She have got   **C** She has   **D** She's got

1.18 Mr. and Mrs. Harris _____ any children.   **9, 59**

    A don't have   **B** doesn't have   **C** no have   **D** haven't got

    E hasn't got

Past

2.1 The weather _____ last week.   **10**

    A is nice   **B** was nice   **C** were nice   **D** nice   **E** had nice

2.2 Why _____ late this morning?   **10**

    A you was   **B** did you   **C** was you   **D** you were   **E** were you

2.3 Terry _____ in a bank from 2001 to 2008.   **11**

    A work   **B** working   **C** works   **D** worked   **E** was work

2.4 Caroline _____ to the movies three times last week.   **11**

    A go   **B** went   **C** goes   **D** got   **E** was

2.5 I _____ television yesterday.   **12, 24**

    A didn't watch   **B** didn't watched   **C** wasn't watched

    D don't watch   **E** didn't watching

2.6 "How _____ ?" "I don't know. I didn't see it."   **12**

    A happened the accident   **B** did happen the accident

    C does the accident happen   **D** did the accident happen

    E the accident happened

2.7 What _____ at 11:30 yesterday?   **13**

    A were you doing   **B** was you doing   **C** you were doing

    D were you do   **E** you was doing

2.8 Jack was reading a book when the phone _____ .

A ringing   **B** ring   **C** rang   **D** was ringing   **E** was ring

14

2.9 I saw Lucy and Steve this morning. They _____ at the bus stop.

A waiting   **B** waited   **C** were waiting   **D** was waiting
E were waited

14

2.10 Dave _____ in a factory. Now he works in a supermarket.

A working   **B** works   **C** work   **D** use to work
E used to work

15

Present perfect

3.1 "Where's Rebecca?" "_____ to bed."

A She is gone   **B** She has gone   **C** She goes   **D** She have gone
E She's gone

19

3.2 "Are Diane and Paul here?" "No, they _____ ."

A don't arrive yet   **B** have already arrived   **C** haven't already arrived
D haven't arrived yet

20

3.3 My sister _____ by plane.

A has never travel   **B** has never traveled   **C** is never traveled
D has never been traveled   **E** have never traveled

16, 24

3.4 _____ that woman before, but I can't remember where.

A I see   **B** I seen   **C** I've saw   **D** I've seen   **E** I've seeing

16, 24

3.5 "How long _____ married?" "Since 1998."

A you are   **B** you have been   **C** has you been   **D** are you
E have you been

17

3.6 "Do you know Lisa?" "Yes, _____ her for a long time."

A I knew   **B** I've known   **C** I know   **D** I am knowing

17

3.7 Richard has been in Canada _____ .

A for six months   **B** since six months   **C** six months ago
D in six months

18, 105

3.8 "When did Tom leave?" "_____ ."

A For ten minutes   **B** Since ten minutes   **C** Ten minutes ago
D In ten minutes

18

3.9 We _____ a vacation last year.

A don't take   **B** haven't taken   **C** hasn't taken   **D** didn't take
E didn't took

21

3.10 Where _____ on Sunday afternoon? I couldn't find you.

A you were   **B** you have been   **C** was you   **D** have you been
E were you

21

Passive

4.1 This house _____ 100 years ago.

    A is built   **B** is building   **C** was building   **D** was built   **E** built

    22, 24

4.2 We _____ to the party last week.

    A didn't invite   **B** didn't invited   **C** weren't invited
    D wasn't invited   **E** haven't been invited

    22, 24

4.3 "Where _____ born?" "In Cairo."

    A you are   **B** you were   **C** was you   **D** are you   **E** were you

    22

4.4 My car is at the garage. It _____ .

    A is being repaired   **B** is repairing   **C** have been repaired
    D repaired   **E** repairs

    23

4.5 I can't find my keys. I think _____ .

    A they've been stolen   **B** they are stolen   **C** they've stolen
    D they're being stolen

    23

Verb forms

5.1 It _____ , so we didn't need an umbrella.

    A wasn't rained   **B** wasn't rain   **C** didn't raining   **D** wasn't raining

    24

5.2 Somebody _____ this window.

    A has broke   **B** has broken   **C** has breaked   **D** has break

    25

Future

6.1 Andrew _____ tennis tomorrow.

    A is playing   **B** play   **C** plays   **D** is play

    26

6.2 _____ out tonight?

    A Are you going   **B** Are you go   **C** Do you go   **D** Go you
    E Do you going

    26

6.3 "What time is the concert tonight?" "It _____ at 7:30."

    A is start   **B** is starting   **C** starts   **D** start   **E** starting

    26

6.4 What _____ to the wedding next week?

    A are you wearing   **B** are you going to wear   **C** do you wear
    D you are going to wear

    27

6.5 I think Kelly _____ her driver's test.

    A passes   **B** will pass   **C** will be pass   **D** will passing

    28

6.6 _____ to the movies on Saturday. Do you want to come with us?

    A We go   **B** We'll go   **C** We're going   **D** We will going

    26, 28

6.7 "_____ you tomorrow, OK?" "OK, bye."

    A I call   **B** I calling   **C** I'm calling   **D** I'll call

    29

6.8 There's a good program on TV tonight. _____ it.

    A I watch   **B** I'll watch   **C** I'm going to watch   **D** I'll watching

    27, 29

6.9 It's a nice day. _____ for a walk?

    A Do we go   **B** Shall we go   **C** Should we go   **D** We go
    E Go we

    29

Modals, imperative, etc.

7.1 _____ to the movies tonight, but I'm not sure.

A I'll go   **B** I'm going   **C** I may go   **D** I might go

30

7.2 "_____ here?"   "Sure."

A Can I sit   **B** Do I sit   **C** May I sit   **D** Can I to sit

30, 31

7.3 I'm having a party next week, but Paul and Rachel _____ .

A can't come   **B** can't to come   **C** can't coming   **D** couldn't come

31

7.4 Before Maria came to the United States, she _____ understand much English.

A can   **B** can't   **C** not   **D** couldn't   **E** doesn't

31

7.5 We _____ walk home last night. There were no buses.

A have to   **B** had to   **C** must   **D** must to   **E** must have

32, 34

7.6 You worked 10 hours today. You _____ tired.

A must   **B** can   **C** must be   **D** can be   **E** must to be

32

7.7 It's a good movie. You _____ go and see it.

A should to   **B** ought to   **C** ought   **D** should   **E** have

33

7.8 What time _____ go to the dentist tomorrow?

A you must   **B** you have to   **C** have you to   **D** do you have to

34

7.9 We _____ wait very long for the bus – it came in a few minutes.

A don't have to   **B** hadn't to   **C** didn't have to   **D** didn't had to
E mustn't

34

7.10 "_____ some coffee?"   "No, thank you."

A Are you liking   **B** You like   **C** Would you like   **D** Do you like

35

7.11 I don't really want to go out. _____ home.

A I rather stay   **B** I'd rather stay   **C** I'd rather to stay
D I'd prefer to stay

36

7.12 Please _____ . Stay here with me.

A don't go   **B** you no go   **C** go not   **D** you don't go

37

7.13 It's a nice day. _____ out.

A Let's to go   **B** Let's go   **C** Let's going   **D** We go

37

There and *it*

8.1 Excuse me, _____ a hotel near here?

A has there   **B** is there   **C** there is   **D** is it

38

8.2 _____ a lot of accidents on this road. It's very dangerous.

A Have   **B** It has   **C** There have   **D** They are   **E** There are

38

8.3 I was hungry when I got home, but _____ anything to eat.

A there wasn't   **B** there weren't   **C** it wasn't   **D** there hasn't been

39

8.4 _____ two miles from our house to downtown.

A It's   **B** It has   **C** There is   **D** There are

40

8.5 _____ true that you're moving to Dallas?

A Is there   **B** Is it   **C** Is   **D** Are you

40

IF YOU ARE NOT SURE WHICH ANSWER IS RIGHT, STUDY UNIT(S)

Auxiliary verbs

9.1 I haven't seen the movie, but my sister _____ .   **41**
A does **B** is **C** has seen **D** has **E** hasn't

9.2 I don't like hot weather, but Sue _____ .   **41**
A does **B** doesn't **C** do **D** does like **E** likes

9.3 "Nicole got married last week." "_____ ? Really?"   **42**
A Got she **B** She got **C** She did **D** She has

9.4 You haven't met my mother, _____ ?   **42**
A haven't you **B** have you **C** did you **D** you have
E you haven't

9.5 Bill doesn't watch TV. He doesn't read newspapers, _____ .   **43**
A too **B** either **C** neither **D** never

9.6 "I'd like to go to Australia." "_____ ."   **43**
A So do I **B** So am I **C** So would I **D** Neither do I
E So I would

9.7 Sue _____ much on weekends.   **44**
A don't **B** doesn't **C** don't do **D** doesn't do

Questions

10.1 "When _____ ?" "I'm not sure. More than 100 years ago."   **45**
A did the telephone invent **B** has the telephone invented
C was invented the telephone **D** was the telephone invented
E the telephone was invented

10.2 "I broke my finger last week." "How _____ that?"   **45**
A did you **B** you did **C** you did do **D** did you do

10.3 Why _____ me last night? I was waiting for you to call.   **45**
A didn't you call **B** you not call **C** you don't call **D** you didn't call

10.4 "Who _____ in this house?" "I don't know."   **46**
A lives **B** does live **C** does lives **D** living

10.5 What _____ when you told him the story?   **46**
A said Paul **B** did Paul say **C** Paul said **D** did Paul said

10.6 "Tom's father is in the hospital." "_____ "   **47**
A In which hospital he is? **B** In which hospital he is in?
C Which hospital he is in? **D** Which hospital is he in?

10.7 Did you have a good vacation? _____   **47**
A How was the weather like? **B** What was the weather like?
C What the weather was like? **D** Was the weather like?

10.8 _____ taller – Joe or Gary?   **48**
A Who is **B** What is **C** Which is **D** Who has

10.9 There are four umbrellas here. _____ is yours?   **48, 76**
A What **B** Who **C** Which **D** How **E** Which one

10.10 How long _____ to cross the Atlantic by ship?

    A is it **B** does it need **C** does it take **D** does it want

    49

10.11 I don't remember what _____ at the party.

    A Jenny was wearing **B** was wearing Jenny **C** was Jenny wearing

    50

10.12 "Do you know _____ ?" "Yes, I think so."

    A if Jack is at home **B** is Jack at home **C** whether Jack is at home

    D that Jack is at home

    50

Reported speech

11.1 I saw Steve a week ago. He said that _____ me, but he didn't.

    A he call **B** he calls **C** he'll call **D** he's going to call

    E he would call

    51

11.2 "Why did Tim go to bed so early?" "He _____ ."

    A said he was tired **B** said that he was tired **C** said me he was tired

    D told me he was tired **E** told that he was tired

    51

-ing and to . . .

12.1 You shouldn't _____ so hard.

    A working **B** work **C** to work **D** worked

    52

12.2 It's late. I _____ now.

    A must to go **B** have go **C** have to going **D** have to go

    52

12.3 Tina has decided _____ her car.

    A sell **B** to sell **C** selling **D** to selling

    53

12.4 I don't mind _____ early.

    A get up **B** to get up **C** getting up **D** to getting up

    53

12.5 Do you like _____ early?

    A get up **B** to get up **C** getting up **D** to getting up

    53

12.6 Do you want _____ you some money?

    A me lend **B** me lending **C** me to lend **D** that I lend

    54

12.7 He's very funny. He makes _____ .

    A me laugh **B** me laughing **C** me to laugh **D** that I laugh

    54

12.8 Paula went to the store _____ some fruit.

    A for get **B** for to get **C** for getting **D** to get **E** get

    55

Go, get, do, make, and have

13.1 The water looks nice. I'm going _____ .

    A for a swim **B** on a swim **C** to swimming **D** swimming

    56

13.2 I'm sorry your mother is sick. I hope she _____ better soon.

    A has **B** makes **C** gets **D** goes

    57

13.3 Kate _____ the car and drove away.

    A went into **B** went in **C** got in **D** got into

    57

13.4 "Shall I open the window?" "No, it's OK. I'll _____ it."

    A do **B** make **C** get **D** open

    58

13.5 I'm sorry, I _____ a mistake.   **58**
    A did **B** made **C** got **D** had

13.6 _____ enough time to do everything you wanted?   **59**
    A Have you **B** Had you **C** Do you have **D** Did you have

Pronouns and possessives

14.1 I don't want this book. You can have _____ .   **60, 63**
    A it **B** them **C** her **D** him

14.2 Sue and Kevin are going to the movies. Do you want to go with _____ ?   **60, 63**
    A her **B** they **C** them **D** him

14.3 I know Donna, but I don't know _____ husband.   **61, 63**
    A their **B** his **C** she **D** her

14.4 Hawaii is famous for _____ beaches.   **61**
    A his **B** its **C** it's **D** their

14.5 I didn't have an umbrella, so Helen gave me _____ .   **62, 63**
    A her **B** hers **C** her umbrella **D** she's

14.6 I went to the movies with a friend of _____ .   **62, 63**
    A mine **B** my **C** me **D** I **E** myself

14.7 We had a good vacation. We enjoyed _____ .   **64**
    A us **B** our **C** ours **D** ourself **E** ourselves

14.8 Kate and Helen are good friends. They know _____ well.   **64**
    A each other **B** them **C** themselves **D** theirselves

14.9 Have you met _____ ?   **65**
    A the wife of Mr. Black **B** Mr. Black wife **C** the wife Mr. Black
    D Mr. Black's wife **E** the Mr. Black's wife

14.10 Have you seen _____ ?   **65**
    A the car of my parents **B** my parent's car **C** my parents' car
    D my parents car

A and *the*

15.1 I'm going to buy _____ .   **66, 68**
    A hat and umbrella **B** a hat and a umbrella
    C a hat and an umbrella **D** an hat and an umbrella

15.2 "What do you do?" "_____ ."   **66**
    A I dentist **B** I'm a dentist **C** I'm dentist **D** I do dentist

15.3 I'm going shopping. I need _____ .   **67**
    A some new jeans **B** a new jeans **C** a new pair of jeans
    D a new pair jeans

15.4 I like the people here. _____ very friendly.   **67**
    A She is **B** They are **C** They is **D** It is **E** He is

15.5 We can't get into the house without _____ .   **68**
    A some key **B** a key **C** key

15.6 I'd like _____ about hotels in Mexico City.

A some information **B** some informations **C** an information

69

15.7 We enjoyed our vacation. _____ was very nice.

A Hotel **B** A hotel **C** An hotel **D** The hotel

70, 71

15.8 The table is in _____ .

A middle of room **B** middle of the room
C the middle of the room **D** the middle of room

71

15.9 What did you have for _____ ?

A the breakfast **B** breakfast **C** a breakfast

71

15.10 I finish _____ at 5:00 every day.

A the work **B** work **C** a work

72

15.11 I'm tired. I'm going _____ .

A in bed **B** in the bed **C** to a bed **D** to the bed **E** to bed

72

15.12 We don't eat _____ very often.

A the meat **B** some meat **C** a meat **D** meat

73

15.13 _____ is in New York.

A The Times Square **B** Times Square

74

15.14 My friends are staying at _____ .

A the Regent Hotel **B** Regent Hotel

74

Determiners and pronouns

16.1 "I'm going on vacation next week." "Oh, _____ nice."

A it's **B** this is **C** that's

75

16.2 "Is there a bank near here?" "Yes, there's _____ on the corner."

A some **B** it **C** one **D** a one

76

16.3 This cup is dirty. Can I have _____ ?

A clean one **B** a clean one **C** clean **D** a clean

76

16.4 I'm going shopping. I'm going to buy _____ clothes.

A any **B** some

77

16.5 "Where's your luggage?" "I don't have _____ ."

A one **B** some **C** any

77

16.6 Tracey and Jeff _____ .

A have no children **B** don't have no children
C don't have any children **D** have any children

78, 79

16.7 "How much money do you have?" "_____ ."

A No **B** No one **C** Any **D** None

78

16.8 There is _____ in the room. It's empty.

A anybody **B** nobody **C** anyone **D** no one

79, 80

16.9 "What did you say?" "_____ ."

A Nothing **B** Nobody **C** Anything **D** Anybody

79, 80

16.10 I'm hungry. I want _____ .

     A something for eat   **B** something to eat   **C** something for eating

80

16.11 It rained _____ last week.

     A all day   **B** all days   **C** every days   **D** every day

81

16.12 _____ friends.

     A Everybody need   **B** Everybody needs   **C** Everyone need
     D Everyone needs

81

16.13 _____ children like to play.

     A Most   **B** The most   **C** Most of   **D** The most of

82

16.14 I like _____ those pictures.

     A both   **B** both of   **C** either   **D** either of

83

16.15 I haven't read _____ these books.

     A neither   **B** neither of   **C** either   **D** either of

83

16.16 Do you have _____ friends?

     A a lot of   **B** much   **C** many   **D** much of   **E** many of

84

16.17 We like movies, so we go to the movies _____ .

     A a lot of   **B** much   **C** many   **D** a lot

84

16.18 There were _____ people in the theater. It was almost empty.

     A a little   **B** few   **C** little   **D** a few of

85

16.19 They have _____ money, so they're not poor.

     A a little   **B** a few   **C** few   **D** little   **E** little of

85

Adjectives and adverbs

17.1 I don't speak any _____ .

     A foreign languages   **B** languages foreign   **C** languages foreigns

86

17.2 He ate his dinner very _____ .

     A quick   **B** quicker   **C** quickly

87

17.3 You speak English very _____ .

     A good   **B** fluent   **C** well   **D** slow

87

17.4 Helen wants _____ .

     A a more big car   **B** a car more big   **C** a car bigger   **D** a bigger car

88

17.5 "Do you feel better today?" "No, I feel _____ ."

     A good   **B** worse   **C** more bad   **D** more worse

88

17.6 Athens is older _____ Rome.

     A as   **B** than   **C** that   **D** of

89

17.7 I can run faster _____ .

     A than him   **B** that he can   **C** than he can   **D** as he can   **E** as he

89

17.8 Tennis isn't _____ soccer.

     A popular as   **B** popular than   **C** as popular than
     D so popular that   **E** as popular as

90

17.9   The weather today is the same _____ yesterday.   **90**

   A as   **B** that   **C** than   **D** like

17.10   The Best West Motel is _____ in town.   **91**

   A the more expensive motel   **B** the most expensive motel
   C the motel most expensive   **D** the motel the more expensive
   E the motel more expensive

17.11   The movie was very bad. I think it's the _____ movie I've   **91**
   ever seen.

   A worse   **B** baddest   **C** most bad   **D** worst   **E** more worse

17.12   Why don't you buy a car? You've got _____ .   **92**

   A enough money   **B** money enough   **C** enough of money

17.13   Is your English _____ a conversation?   **92**

   A enough good to have   **B** good enough for have   **C** enough good for
   D good enough to have

17.14   I'm _____ out.   **93**

   A too tired for go   **B** too much tired for going   **C** too tired to go
   D too much tired to go

Word order

18.1   Sue is interested in the news. She _____ .   **94**

   A reads every day a newspaper   **B** reads a newspaper every day
   C every day reads a newspaper

18.2   _____ coffee in the morning.   **95**

   A I drink always   **B** Always I drink   **C** I always drink

18.3   _____ during the day.   **95**

   A They are at home never   **B** They are never at home
   C They never are at home   **D** Never they are at home

18.4   "Where's Emma?"   "She _____ ."   **96**

   A isn't here yet   **B** isn't here already   **C** isn't here still

18.5   I locked the door, and I gave _____ .   **97**

   A Sarah the keys   **B** to Sarah the keys   **C** the keys Sarah
   D the keys to Sarah

Conjunctions and clauses

19.1   I can't talk to you now. I'll talk to you later when _____   **99**
   more time.

   A I'll have   **B** I had   **C** I have   **D** I'm going to have

19.2   _____ late tonight, don't wait for me.   **100**

   A If I'm   **B** If I'll be   **C** When I'm   **D** When I'll be

19.3   I don't know the answer. If I _____ the answer, I'd tell you.   **101**

   A know   **B** would know   **C** have known   **D** knew

19.4   I like that jacket. _____ it if it wasn't so expensive.   **101**

   A I buy   **B** I'll buy   **C** I bought   **D** I'd bought   **E** I'd buy

19.5　Emma lives in a house _____ is 100 years old.

　　　A who　**B** that　**C** which　**D** it　**E** what

102

19.6　The people _____ work in the office are very friendly.

　　　A who　**B** that　**C** they　**D** which　**E** what

102

19.7　Did you find the books _____ ?

　　　A who you wanted　　**B** that you wanted　　**C** what you wanted

　　　D you wanted　　**E** you wanted it

103

19.8　I met _____ can speak six languages.

　　　A a woman who　　**B** a woman which　　**C** a woman　　**D** a woman she

103

Prepositions

20.1　Bye! See you _____ .

　　　A Friday　**B** at Friday　**C** in Friday　**D** on Friday

104

20.2　Hurry! The train leaves _____ five minutes.

　　　A at　**B** on　**C** from　**D** after　**E** in

104

20.3　"How long will you be away?"　"_____ Monday."

　　　A On　**B** To　**C** Until　**D** Till　**E** Since

105

20.4　We played basketball yesterday. We played _____ two hours.

　　　A in　**B** for　**C** since　**D** during

106

20.5　I always have breakfast before _____ to work.

　　　A I go　**B** go　**C** to go　**D** going

106

20.6　Write your name _____ the top of the page.

　　　A at　**B** on　**C** in　**D** to

107

20.7　There are a lot of apples _____ those trees.

　　　A at　**B** on　**C** in　**D** to

107

20.8　What's the largest city _____ the world?

　　　A at　**B** on　**C** in　**D** of

108

20.9　The office is _____ the second floor.

　　　A at　**B** on　**C** in　**D** to

108

20.10　I met a lot of people _____ the party.

　　　A on　**B** to　**C** in　**D** at

109

20.11　I want to go _____ Mexico next year.

　　　A at　**B** on　**C** in　**D** to

109

20.12　What time did you arrive _____ the hotel?

　　　A at　**B** on　**C** in　**D** to

109

20.13　"Where is Don in this picture?"　"Don is _____ Bob."

　　　A at front of　　**B** in the front of　　**C** in front of　　**D** in front from

110

20.14　I jumped _____ the wall into the garden.

　　　A on　**B** through　**C** across　**D** over　**E** above

111

20.15　Jane isn't at work this week. She's _____ vacation.

　　　A on　**B** in　**C** for　**D** to　**E** at

112

20.16 Do you like traveling _____ ? **112**
   A with train   **B** with the train   **C** in train   **D** on train
   E by train

20.17 I'm not very good _____ telling stories. **113**
   A on   **B** with   **C** at   **D** in   **E** for

20.18 Tom left without _____ goodbye. **113**
   A say   **B** saying   **C** to say   **D** that he said

20.19 I have to call _____ tonight. **114**
   A with my parents   **B** to my parents   **C** at my parents   **D** my parents

20.20 "Do you like eating in restaurants?"   "Sometimes. It depends **114**
   _____ the restaurant."
   A in   **B** at   **C** of   **D** on   **E** over

Phrasal verbs

21.1 A car stopped and a woman got _____ . **115**
   A off   **B** down   **C** out   **D** out of

21.2 It was cold, so I _____ . **116**
   A put on my coat   **B** put my coat on   **C** put the coat on me
   D put me the coat on

21.3 I have Rachel's keys. I have to _____ to her. **116**
   A give back   **B** give them back   **C** give back them   **D** give it back

Answer Key to Exercises

UNIT 1

1.1
2. they're
3. it isn't / it's not
4. that's
5. I'm not
6. you aren't / you're not

1.2
2. 'm/am
3. is
4. are
5. 's/is
6. are
7. is . . . are
8. 'm/am . . . is

1.3
2. I'm / I am
3. He's / He is
4. they're / they are
5. It's / It is
6. You're / You are
7. She's / She is
8. Here's / Here is

1.4
Example answers:
1. My name is Robert.
2. I'm from Brazil.
3. I'm 25.
4. I'm a cook.
5. My favorite colors are black and white.
6. I'm interested in plants.

1.5
2. 're/are cold.
3. 's/is hot.
4. He's / He is afraid.
5. They're / They are hungry.
6. She's / She is angry.

1.6
2. 's/is windy today.
   or isn't / 's not windy today.
3. hands are cold. *or* hands aren't / are not cold.
4. Brazil is a very big country.
5. Diamonds aren't / are not cheap.
6. Toronto isn't / is not in the United States.
8. I'm / I am hungry. *or* I'm not / I am not hungry.
9. I'm / I am a good swimmer. *or* I'm not / I am not a good swimmer.

10. I'm / I am interested in politics. *or* I'm not / I am not interested in politics.

UNIT 2

2.1
2. f
3. h
4. c
5. a
6. e
7. b
8. i
9. d

2.2
3. Is your job interesting?
4. Are the stores open today?
5. Where are you from?
6. Are you interested in sports?
7. Is the post office near here?
8. Are your children at school?
9. Why are you late?

2.3
2. Where's / Where is
3. How old are
4. How much are
5. What's / What is
6. Who's / Who is
7. What color are

2.4
2. Are you Australian?
3. How old are you?
4. Are you a teacher?
5. Are you married?
6. Is your wife a lawyer?
7. Where's / Where is she from?
8. What's / What is her name?
9. How old is she?

2.5
2. Yes, I am. *or* No, I'm not.
3. Yes, it is. *or* No, it isn't. / No, it's not.
4. Yes, they are. *or* No, they aren't. / No, they're not.
5. Yes, it is. *or* No, it isn't. / No, it's not.
6. Yes, I am. *or* No, I'm not.

UNIT 3

3.1
2. 's/is waiting
3. 're/are playing
4. He's / He is lying

5. They're / They are having
6. She's / She is sitting

3.2
2. 's/is cooking
3. 're/are standing
4. 's/is swimming
5. 're/are staying
6. 's/is taking
7. 're/are building
8. 'm/am leaving

3.3
3. 's/is sitting on the floor.
4. She isn't / She's not reading a book.
5. She isn't / She's not playing the piano.
6. She's / She is laughing.
7. She's / She is wearing a hat.
8. She isn't / She's not writing a letter.

3.4
3. I'm sitting on a chair. *or* I'm not sitting on a chair.
4. I'm eating. *or* I'm not eating.
5. It's raining. *or* It isn't raining. / It's not raining.
6. I'm studying English.
7. I'm listening to music. *or* I'm not listening to music.
8. The sun is shining. *or* The sun isn't shining.
9. I'm wearing shoes. *or* I'm not wearing shoes.
10. I'm not reading a newspaper.

UNIT 4

4.1
2. Are you leaving now?
3. Is it raining?
4. Are you enjoying the movie?
5. Is that clock working?
6. Are you waiting for a bus?

4.2
2. is . . . going?
3. are you eating?
4. are you crying?
5. are they looking at?
6. is he laughing?

4.3

3. Are you listening to me?
4. Where are your friends going?
5. Are your parents watching television?
6. What is Jessica cooking?
7. Why are you looking at me?
8. Is the bus coming?

4.4

2. Yes, I am.   *or*   No, I'm not.
3. Yes, I am.   *or*   No, I'm not.
4. Yes, it is.   *or*   No, it isn't. / No, it's not.
5. Yes, I am.   *or*   No, I'm not.
6. Yes, I am.   *or*   No, I'm not.

UNIT 5

5.1

2. thinks   5. has
3. flies   6. finishes
4. dances

5.2

2. live   5. They go
3. She eats   6. He sleeps
4. He plays

5.3

2. open   7. costs
3. closes   8. cost
4. teaches   9. boils
5. meet   10. like . . . likes
6. washes

5.4

2. I never go to the movies.
3. Martina always works hard.
4. Children usually like chocolate.
5. Julia always enjoys parties.
6. I often forget people's names.
7. Tim never watches television.
8. We usually have dinner at 6:30.
9. Jenny always wears nice clothes.

5.5

Example answers:

2. I sometimes read in bed.
3. I often get up before 7:00.
4. I never go to work by bus.
5. I always drink coffee in the morning.

UNIT 6

6.1

2. doesn't play the piano very well.
3. don't know my phone number.
4. We don't work very hard.
5. Mike doesn't have a car.
6. You don't do the same thing every day.

6.2

1. doesn't like classical music. like (*or* I don't like)
2. don't like boxing. likes boxing. like (*or* I don't like) boxing.
3. Bill and Rose like horror movies. Carol doesn't like horror movies. I like (*or* I don't like) horror movies.

6.3

Example answers:

2. I never go to the theater.
3. I don't ride a bicycle very often.
4. I never eat in restaurants.
5. I travel by train a lot.

6.4

2. doesn't use
3. don't go
4. doesn't wear
5. don't know
6. doesn't cost
7. don't see

6.5

3. don't know
4. doesn't talk
5. drinks
6. don't believe
7. like
8. doesn't eat

UNIT 7

7.1

2. Do . . . play tennis?
3. Does . . . live near here?
4. Do Tom's friends play tennis? / Do they play tennis?
5. Does your brother speak English? / Does he speak English?
6. Do you do yoga every morning?

7. Does Paul often travel on business? / Does he often travel on business?
8. Do you want to be famous?
9. Does Anna work hard? / Does she work hard?

7.2

3. How often do you watch TV?
4. What do you want for dinner?
5. Do you like football?
6. Does your brother like football?
7. What do you do in your free time?
8. Where does your sister work?
9. Do you ever go to the movies?
10. What does this word mean?
11. Does it often snow here?
12. What time do you usually go to bed?
13. How much does it cost to call Mexico?
14. What do you usually have for breakfast?

7.3

2. Do you enjoy / Do you like
3. do you start
4. Do you work
5. do you get
6. does he do
7. does he teach
8. Does he enjoy / Does he like

7.4

2. Yes, I do.   *or*   No, I don't.
3. Yes, I do.   *or*   No, I don't.
4. Yes, it does.   *or*   No, it doesn't.
5. Yes, I do.   *or*   No, I don't.

UNIT 8

8.1

2. No, she isn't.
   Yes, she does.
   She's playing the piano.
3. Yes, he does.
   Yes, he is.
   He's washing a window.
4. No, they aren't.
   Yes, they do.
   They teach.

8.2

2. don't   6. do
3. are   7. does
4. does   8. doesn't
5. 's/is . . . don't

8.3

4. 's/is singing
5. She wants
6. do you read
7. you're / you are sitting
8. I don't / I do not understand
9. I'm / I am going . . . Are you coming
10. does your father finish
11. I'm not / I am not listening
12. He's / He is cooking
13. doesn't usually drive . . . usually walks
14. doesn't like . . . She prefers

UNIT 9

9.1

2. he's got
3. they've got
4. she hasn't got
5. it's got
6. I haven't got

9.2

2. 's got a computer. *or* has a computer.
3. He hasn't got a dog. *or* He doesn't have a dog.
4. He hasn't got a cell phone. *or* He doesn't have a cell phone.
5. He's got a watch. *or* He has a watch.
6. He's got two brothers and a sister. *or* He has two brothers and a sister.
7. I've got a computer. / I have a computer. *or* I haven't got a computer. / I don't have a computer.
8. I've got a dog. / I have a dog. *or* I haven't got a dog. / I don't have a dog.
9. I've got a bike. / I have a bike. *or* I haven't got a bike. / I don't have a bike.
10. *(Example answer)* I've got a brother and a sister.

9.3

3. He has a new job.
4. They don't have much money.
5. Do you have an umbrella?
6. We have a lot of work to do.
7. I don't have your phone number.
8. Does your father have a car?
9. How much money do we have?

9.4

3. has
4. don't
5. got
6. have
7. doesn't

9.5

3. have four wheels.
4. has a lot of friends.
5. don't have a key.
6. has six legs.
7. don't have much time.

UNIT 10

10.1

2. were at the movies.
3. was at the station.
4. Mr. and Mrs. Hall were in/at a restaurant.
5. Ben was at the beach.
6. *(Example answer)* I was at work.

10.2

2. is . . . was
3. 'm/am
4. was
5. were
6. 're/are
7. Was
8. was
9. are . . . were

10.3

2. wasn't . . . was
3. was . . . were
4. Were . . . was . . . wasn't. *or* wasn't. . . was.
5. were
6. weren't . . . were

10.4

2. Was your exam difficult?
3. Where were Sue and Chris last week?
4. How much was your new camera?
5. Why were you angry yesterday?
6. Was the weather nice last week?

UNIT 11

11.1

2. opened
3. started . . . ended
4. wanted
5. happened

6. rained
7. enjoyed . . . stayed
8. died

11.2

2. saw   8. thought
3. played   9. copied
4. paid   10. knew
5. visited   11. put
6. bought   12. spoke
7. went

11.3

2. got   9. checked
3. had   10. had
4. left   11. waited
5. drove   12. departed
6. got   13. arrived
7. parked   14. took
8. walked

11.4

2. lost her keys
3. met her friends
4. bought two newspapers.
5. went to the movies.
6. ate an orange.
7. took a shower.
8. came (to see us)

11.5

Example answers:

2. I got up late yesterday.
3. I met some friends at lunchtime.
4. I went to the supermarket.
5. I called a lot of people.
6. I lost my keys.

UNIT 12

12.1

2. didn't work   4. didn't have
3. didn't go   5. didn't do

12.2

2. Did you enjoy the party?
3. Did you have a nice vacation?
4. Did you finish work early?
5. Did you sleep well last night?

12.3

2. got up before 7:00. *or* didn't get up before 7:00.
3. I took a shower. *or* I didn't take a shower.
4. I bought a magazine. *or* I didn't buy a magazine.

5. I ate meat.   *or*
   I didn't eat meat.
6. I went to bed before 10:30.
   or   I didn't go to bed before
   10:30.

12.4
2. did you get to work
3. Did you win
4. did you go
5. did it cost
6. Did you go to bed late
7. Did you have a nice time
8. did it happen / did that happen

12.5
2. bought   6. didn't have
3. Did it rain   7. did you do
4. didn't stay   8. didn't know
5. opened

UNIT 13

13.1
2. were at the supermarket.
   were buying food.
3. was in his car. He was driving.
4. Tracey was at the station. She
   was waiting for a train.
5. Mr. and Mrs. Hall were in the
   park. They were walking.
6. *(Example answer)* I was at a
   café. I was having coffee with
   some friends.

13.2
2. was playing tennis.
3. she was reading a/the
   newspaper.
4. she was cooking (lunch).
5. she was having/eating breakfast.
6. she was cleaning the kitchen.

13.3
2. What were you doing
3. Was it raining
4. Why was Sue driving
5. Was Tim wearing

13.4
2. He was carrying a bag.
3. He wasn't going to the dentist.
4. He was eating an ice cream
   cone.
5. He wasn't carrying an
   umbrella.
6. He wasn't going home.
7. He was wearing a hat.
8. He wasn't riding a bicycle.

UNIT 14

14.1
1. happened . . . was painting
   . . . fell
2. arrived . . . got . . . were
   waiting
3. was walking . . . met . . .
   was going . . . was carrying
   . . . stopped

14.2
2. was studying
3. did the mail arrive . . .
   came . . . was having
4. didn't go
5. were you driving . . .
   stopped . . . wasn't driving
6. Did your team win . . .
   didn't play
7. did you break . . . were
   playing . . . hit . . . broke
8. Did you see . . . was wearing
9. were you doing
10. lost . . . did you get . . .
    climbed

UNIT 15

15.1
2. used to play
3. She used to be
4. They used to live
5. He used to wear glasses.
6. used to be a hotel.

15.2
2. used to play
3.–6.
   She used to go out three or
   four nights a week. / She used
   to go out a lot.
   She used to play a musical
   instrument. / She used to play
   the guitar.
   She used to read a lot. / She
   used to like to read.
   She used to take two or three
   trips a year. / She used to
   travel a lot.

15.3
3. used to have
4. used to be
5. go/commute
6. used to eat
7. watches
8. used to live
9. get
10. did . . . use to play

UNIT 16

16.1
3. you ever been to South Korea?
4. Have you ever lost your
   passport?
5. Have you ever flown in a
   helicopter?
6. Have you ever won a race?
7. Have you ever been to Peru?
8. Have you ever driven a bus?
9. Have you ever broken your
   leg?

16.2
Helen:
2. 's/has been to South Korea
   once.
3. She's / She has never won a
   race.
4. She's / She has flown in a
   helicopter a few times.
You (example answers):
5. 've/have never been to New
   York.
6. I've / I have played tennis
   many times.
7. I've / I have never driven a
   truck.
8. I've / I have been late for
   work a few times.

16.3
2–6.
   's/has done a lot of interesting
   things.
   She's / She has traveled all
   over the world.   *or*
   She's / She has been all over
   the world.
   She's / She has been married
   three times.
   She's / She has written 10
   books.
   She's / She has met a lot of
   interesting people.

16.4
3. Have you ever written
4. She's / She has never met
5. they've / they have read
6. I've / I have never been . . .
   my brother has been
7. She's / She has seen . . . I've /
   I have never seen
8. I've / I have traveled

UNIT 17

17.1
3. 've/have been
4. 's/has been
5. 've/have lived *or* 've/have been living
6. 's/has worked *or* 's/has been working
7. 's/has had
8. 've/have been studying

17.2
2. have they been there / in Brazil?
3. have . . . known her/Amy?
4. How long has she been studying Italian?
5. How long has he lived / been living in Seattle?
6. How long have you been a teacher?
7. How long has it been raining?

17.3
2. has lived in South Korea all her life.
3. have been on vacation since Sunday.
4. has been shining all day.
5. has been waiting for 10 minutes.
6. has had a beard since he was 20.

17.4
2. I know
3. I've known
4. have you been waiting
5. works
6. She has been reading
7. have you lived
8. I've had
9. is . . . He has been

UNIT 18

18.1
3. for
4. since
5. since
6. for
7. for
8. for . . . since

18.2
Example answers:
2. A year ago.
3. A few weeks ago.
4. Two hours ago.
5. Six months ago.

18.3
3. for 20 years.
4. 20 years ago.
5. an hour ago.
6. a few days ago.
7. for six months.
8. for a long time

18.4
2. been here since Tuesday.
3. raining for an hour.
4. known Sue since 2002.
5. been married for six months.
6. been studying medicine (at the university) for three years.
7. played / been playing the piano since he was seven years old.

18.5
Example answers:
2. I've been to New York three times.
3. I've been studying English for six months.
4. I've known Chris for a long time.
5. I've had a headache since I got up this morning.

UNIT 19

19.1
2. 's/has closed the door
3. 've/have gone to bed
4. 's/has stopped raining
5. 's/has taken a shower
6. picture has fallen down

19.2
2. I've / I have written them a letter.
3. She's / She has broken her arm.
4. They've / They have moved to Seattle.
5. I've / I have made a big mistake.
6. I've / I have lost my wallet. Have you seen it anywhere?
7. Have you heard? Mark has gotten married.
9. Brian took my bike again without asking.
10. Did you tell your friends the good news?
11. We didn't / did not pay the electric bill.

UNIT 20

20.1
2. 's/has just gotten up.
3. 've/have just bought a car.
4. has just started.

20.2
2. 've/have already seen
3. 've/have already called him/ Tom.
4. 's/has already left /gone to work.
5. 've/have already read it.
6. 's/has already started (it).

20.3
2. Have you told your father about the accident yet?
3. I've / I have just eaten a big dinner, so I'm not hungry.
4. Jenny can watch TV because she's / she has already done her homework.
5. You can't go to bed – you haven't brushed your teeth yet.
6. You can't talk to Pete because he's / he has just gone home.
7. Nicole has just gotten out of the hospital, so she can't go to work.
9. The mail carrier didn't come yet.
10. I just spoke to your sister.
11. Did Mario buy a new computer yet?
12. Ted and Alice didn't tell anyone they're getting married yet.
13. We already did our packing for our trip.
14. I just swam a mile.

20.4
2. Have . . . met your new neighbors yet?
3. Have you paid your phone bill yet?
4. Has Tom/he sold his car yet?

UNIT 21

21.1
2. started (it)
3. arrived
4. she went out
5. I wore it

21.2
3. I finished
4. *OK*

5. did you finish
6. *OK*
7. died
8. were you / did you go

21.3
3. played
4. did you go
5. Have you ever met
6. wasn't / was not
7. 's/has visited
8. turned
9. lived
10. haven't / have not been

21.4
1. Did you have
   was
2. 's/has won
   Have you seen
   saw
3. 's/has had . . . was . . .
   worked . . . didn't enjoy
4. 've/have seen . . . 've/have
   never spoken . . . Have you
   ever spoken
   met

UNIT 22

22.1
3. is made from sand.
4. Stamps are sold in a post office.
5. This word isn't / is not used
   very often.
6. Are we allowed to park here?
7. How is this word pronounced?
9. was painted last month.
10. My phone was stolen a few
    days ago.
11. Three people were injured in
    the accident.
12. When was this bridge built?
13. I wasn't / was not woken up by
    the noise.
14. How were these windows
    broken?
15. Were you invited to Jon's
    party last week?

22.2
2. Soccer is played in most . . .
3. Why was the letter sent to . . . ?
4. . . . where cars are repaired.
5. Where were you born?
6. How many languages are
   spoken . . . ?
7. . . . but nothing was stolen.
8. When was the bicycle
   invented?

22.3
3. is made
4. were damaged
5. was given
6. are shown
7. were invited
8. was made
9. was stolen . . . was found

22.4
2. was born in São Paulo.
3. parents were born in Rio de
   Janeiro.
4. was born in . . .
5. My mother was born in . . .

UNIT 23

23.1
2. is being built.
3. are being cleaned/washed.
4. is being cut.

23.2
3. has been broken.
4. is being repaired.
5. The car has been damaged.
6. The houses are being
   torn down.
7. The trees have been cut down.
8. They have been invited to
   a party.

23.3
3. has been repaired / was
   repaired
4. was repaired
5. are made
6. were they built
7. Is the computer being used
   (*or* Is anybody using the
   computer)
8. are they called
9. were stolen
10. was damaged . . . hasn't / has
    not been repaired

UNIT 24

24.1
3. are   7. do
4. Does   8. Is
5. Do   9. does
6. Is   10. Are

24.2
2. don't
3. 'm/am not
4. isn't
5. don't

6. doesn't
7. 'm/am not
8. 're not / aren't

24.3
2. Did   7. were
3. were   8. Has
4. was   9. did
5. Has   10. have
6. did

24.4
2. was   6. 've/have
3. Have   7. is
4. are   8. was
5. were   9. has

24.5
3. eaten   8. understand
4. enjoying   9. listening
5. damaged   10. pronounced
6. use   11. open
7. gone

UNIT 25

25.1
3. said   10. happened
4. brought   11. heard
5. paid   12. put
6. enjoyed   13. caught
7. bought   14. watched
8. sat   15. understood
9. left

25.2
2. began   begun
3. ate   eaten
4. drank   drunk
5. drove   driven
6. spoke   spoken
7. wrote   written
8. came   come
9. knew   known
10. took   taken
11. went   gone
12. gave   given
13. threw   thrown
14. got   gotten

25.3
3. slept   10. built
4. saw   11. learned
5. rained   12. ridden
6. lost . . . seen 13. known
7. stolen   14. fell . . . hurt
8. went   15. ran . . . run
9. finished

25.4

2. told
3. won
4. met
5. woken up
6. swam
7. thought
8. spoken
9. cost
10. driven
11. sold
12. flew

UNIT 26

26.1

2. is going
3. is meeting Dave.
4. Karen is having
5. Tom and Sue are going to a party.

26.2

2. Are you working next week?
3. What are you doing tomorrow night?
4. What time are your friends coming?
5. When is Liz going on vacation?

26.3

Example answers:

3. I'm going away this weekend.
4. I'm playing basketball tomorrow.
5. I'm meeting a friend tonight.
6. I'm going to the movies on Thursday night.

26.4

3. Karen is getting
4. are going . . . are they going
5. ends
6. I'm not going
7. I'm going . . . We're meeting
8. are you getting . . . leaves
9. does the movie begin
10. are you doing . . . I'm working

UNIT 27

27.1

2. 'm going to take a bath.
3. 'm going to buy a car.
4. 're going to play soccer.

27.2

3. 'm/am going to walk
4. 's/is going to stay
5. 'm/am going to eat
6. 're/are going to give
7. 's/is going to lie down
8. Are . . . going to watch
9. is . . . going to do

27.3

2. is going to fall (down).
3. is going to turn (left).
4. 's/is going to kick the ball.

27.4

Example answers:

1. I'm going to call Maria tonight.
2. I'm going to get up early tomorrow.
3. I'm going to buy some shoes tomorrow.

UNIT 28

28.1

2. she'll be
3. she was
4. she'll be
5. she's
6. she was
7. she'll be

28.2

Example answers:

2. I'll be at home.
3. I'll probably be in bed.
4. I'll be at work.
5. I don't know where I'll be.

28.3

2. 'll/will
3. won't
4. won't
5. 'll/will
6. 'll/will
7. won't

28.4

3. think we'll win the game.
4. I don't think I'll be here tomorrow.
5. I think Sue will like her present.
6. I don't think they'll get married.
7. I don't think you'll like the movie.

28.5

2. are you doing
3. They're leaving
4. will lend
5. I'm going
6. will call
7. He's working
8. won't take
9. are coming

UNIT 29

29.1

2. I'll send
3. I'll eat
4. I'll sit
5. I'll do
6. I'll stay
7. I'll show

29.2

2. think I'll have
3. I don't think I'll play
4. I think I'll buy
5. I don't think I'll buy

29.3

2. I'll do
3. I watch
4. I'll go
5. is going to buy
6. I'll give
7. Are you doing . . . I'm going
8. I'm working
9. I'll buy

29.4

2. g
3. b
4. e
5. i
6. a
7. h
8. c
9. f

UNIT 30

30.1

2. might see you tomorrow.
3. Sarah might forget to call.
4. It might snow today.
5. I might be late tonight.
6. Mark might not be here next week.
7. I might not have time to go out.

30.2

2. might take a trip.
3. I might see her on Monday.
4. I might have fish.
5. I might take a taxi.
6. I might buy/get a new car.

30.3

3. might get up early.
4. He isn't / He's not working tomorrow.
5. He might be at home tomorrow morning.
6. He might watch television.
7. He's going out in the afternoon.
8. He might go shopping.

30.4

Example answers:

1. I might read a newspaper.
2. I might go out with some friends at night.
3. I might have an egg for breakfast.

UNIT 31

31.1
2. Can you ski?
3. Can you play chess?
4. Can you run 10 kilometers?
5. Can you drive (a car)?
6. Can you ride (a horse)?

Example answers:
7. I can/can't swim.
8. I can/can't ski.
9. I can/can't play chess.
10. I can/can't run 10 kilometers.
11. I can/can't drive (a car).
12. I can/can't ride (a horse).

31.2
2. can see
3. can't hear
4. can't find
5. can speak

31.3
2. couldn't eat
3. can't decide
4. couldn't find
5. can't go
6. couldn't go

31.4
2. Can/Could you pass the salt (please)?
3. Can/Could you turn down the radio (please)?
4. Can/Could I have your phone number (please)?
5. Can/Could I look at your newspaper (please)? *or* Can/Could I have a look at your newspaper (please)?
6. Can/Could I use your pen (please)?

UNIT 32

32.1
2. must be hungry
3. must be good
4. must be very happy
5. must be for you
6. must be in the kitchen

32.2
2. must like
3. must have
4. must drink
5. must work

32.3
3. must not
4. must
5. must not
6. must not
7. must

32.4
2. must know
3. must wear
4. must get
5. must take
6. must be

32.5
3. must
4. had to
5. mustn't
6. must
7. mustn't
8. had to

UNIT 33

33.1
2. You should go
3. You should eat
4. you should visit
5. you should wear
6. You should read

33.2
2. shouldn't eat so much.
3. She shouldn't work so
4. He shouldn't drive so fast.

33.3
2. I should learn (to drive)?
3. Do you think I should get another job?
4. Do you think I should invite Gary (to the party)?

33.4
3. I think you should sell it.
4. I think she should take a trip.
5. I don't think they should get married.
6. I don't think you should go to work.
7. I think he should go to the doctor.
8. I don't think we should stay there.

33.5
Example answers:
2. I think everybody should have enough food.
3. I think people should drive more carefully.
4. I don't think the police should carry guns.
5. I think I should get more exercise.

UNIT 34

34.1
2. have to take
3. has to read
4. have to speak
5. has to travel
6. have to hit

34.2
2. have to go
3. had to buy
4. have to change
5. had to answer
6. have to wake
7. have to take

34.3
2. did he have to wait
3. does she have to go
4. did you have to pay
5. do you have to do
6. did they have to leave early
7. does he have to go to Moscow

34.4
2. doesn't have to wait.
3. didn't have to get up early.
4. doesn't have to work (so) hard.
5. don't have to leave now.
6. didn't have to tell me something I already know

34.5
Example answers:
2. I have to go to work every day.
3. I had to go to the dentist yesterday.
4. I have to go shopping tomorrow.
5. I had to take the bus to work last week.
6. I had to go to bed at 9:00 when I was younger.

UNIT 35

35.1
2. Would you like an apple?
3. Would you like some coffee? / a cup of coffee?
4. Would you like some cheese? / a piece of cheese?
5. Would you like a sandwich?
6. Would you like some cake? / a piece of cake?

35.2

2. Would you like to play tennis tomorrow?
3. Would you like to come to a concert next week?
4. Would you like to borrow my umbrella?

35.3

2. Do you like
3. Would you like
4. would you like
5. Would you like
6. I like
7. would you like
8. Would you like
9. Do you like
10. I'd like
11. I'd like
12. do you like

UNIT 36

36.1

2. 'd rather read
3. I'd rather have
4. I'd rather wait

36.2

2. would you rather have/eat dinner
3. would you rather have/drink
4. would you rather watch
5. would you rather call him

36.3

2. take
3. to go
4. get/have/find
5. carry/do
6. see / call / talk to / speak to . . . to send / to write

36.4

2. I'd rather be a journalist / a school teacher.
3. I'd rather live in a big city / in a small town.
4. I'd rather have a small house / a big house.
5. I'd rather study electronics / philosophy.
6. I'd rather watch a soccer game / a movie.

UNIT 37

37.1

3. Don't buy
4. Smile
5. Don't sit
6. Have
7. Don't forget
8. Sleep
9. Be . . . Don't drop

37.2

2. let's take the bus
3. let's watch TV
4. let's go to a restaurant
5. let's wait a little

37.3

3. No, let's not go out.
4. No, don't close the window.
5. No, don't call me (tonight).
6. No, let's not wait for Andy.
7. No, don't turn on the light.
8. No, let's not take a taxi.

UNIT 38

38.1

3. There's / There is a hospital.
4. There isn't a swimming pool.
5. There are two movie theaters.
6. There isn't a university.
7. There aren't any big hotels.

38.2

Example answers:

3. There is a university in . . .
4. There are a lot of big shops.
5. There isn't an airport.
6. There aren't many factories.

38.3

2. There's / There is
3. is there
4. There are
5. are there
6. There isn't
7. Is there
8. Are there
9. There's / There is . . . There aren't

38.4

2.–6.
There are eight planets in the solar system.
There are five players on a basketball team.
There are twenty-six letters in the English alphabet.
There are thirty days in September.
There are fifty states in the United States.

38.5

2. It's
3. There's
4. There's . . . Is it
5. Is there . . . there's
6. It's
7. Is there

UNIT 39

39.1

2. There was a carpet
3. There were three pictures
4. There was a small table
5. There were some flowers
6. There were some books
7. There was an armchair
8. There was a sofa

39.2

3. There was
4. Was there
5. there weren't
6. There wasn't
7. Were there
8. There wasn't
9. There was
10. there weren't

39.3

2. There are
3. There was
4. There's / There is
5. There's been / There has been *or* There was
6. there was
7. there will be
8. there were . . . there are
9. There have been
10. there will be *or* there are

UNIT 40

40.1

2. It's cold.
3. It's windy.
4. It's sunny/clear. *or* It's a nice day.
5. It's snowing.
6. It's cloudy.

40.2

2. It's / It is
3. Is it
4. is it . . . it's / it is
5. It's / It is
6. Is it
7. is it

8. It's / It is
9. It's / It is

40.3

2. far is it from the hotel to the beach?
3. How far is it from New York to Washington?
4. How far is it from your house to the airport?

40.4

3. It
4. It . . . It
5. There
6. it
7. It . . . there
8. It

40.5

2. It's nice to see you again
3. It's impossible to work in this office
4. It's easy to make friends
5. It's interesting to visit different places
6. It's dangerous to go out alone

UNIT 41

41.1

2. is   5. will
3. can   6. was
4. has

41.2

2. 'm not   5. isn't
3. weren't   6. hasn't
4. haven't

41.3

3. doesn't   6. does
4. do   7. don't
5. did   8. didn't

41.4

Example answers:

2. I like sports, but my sister doesn't.
3. I don't eat meat, but Jenny does.
4. I'm American, but my husband isn't.
5. I haven't been to Japan, but Jenny has.

41.5

2. wasn't   7. has
3. is   8. do
4. does   9. hasn't
5. can't   10. will
6. did   11. might

41.6

2. Yes, I do.   *or*   No, I don't.
3. Yes, I do.   *or*   No, I don't.
4. Yes, it is.   *or*   No, it isn't.
5. Yes, I am.   *or*   No, I'm not.
6. Yes, I do.   *or*   No, I don't.
7. Yes, I will. *or*   No, I won't.
8. Yes, I have. *or*   No, I haven't.
9. Yes, I did.   *or*   No, I didn't.
10. Yes, I was. *or*   No, I wasn't.

UNIT 42

42.1

2. You do?   5. I do?
3. You didn't?   6. She did?
4. She doesn't?

42.2

3. You have?   8. You aren't?
4. She can't?   9. You did?
5. You were?   10. She does?
6. You didn't? 11. You won't?
7. There is?   12. It isn't?

42.3

2. aren't they   5. don't you
3. wasn't she   6. doesn't he
4. haven't you   7. won't you

42.4

2. are you   6. didn't she
3. isn't she   7. was it
4. can't you   8. doesn't she
5. do you   9. will you

UNIT 43

43.1

2. either   5. either
3. too   6. either
4. too   7. too

43.2

2. So am I.
3. So have I.
4. So do I.
5. So will I.
6. So was I.
7. Neither can I.
8. Neither did I.
9. Neither have I.
10. Neither am I.
11. Neither do I.

43.3

1. So am I.
2. So can I.   *or*   I can't.

3. Neither am I.   *or*   I am.
4. So do I.   *or*   I don't.
5. Neither do I.   *or*   I do.
6. So did I.   *or*   I didn't.
7. Neither have I. *or*   I have.
8. Neither do I.   *or*   I do.
9. So am I.   *or*   I'm not.
10. Neither was I. *or*   I was.
11. Neither did I. *or*   I did.
12. So do I.   *or*   I don't.

UNIT 44

44.1

2. They aren't / They're not married.
3. I haven't had dinner.
4. It isn't cold today.
5. We won't be late.
6. You shouldn't go.

44.2

2. I don't like cheese.
3. They didn't understand.
4. He doesn't live here.
5. Don't go away!
6. I didn't do the dishes.

44.3

2. They haven't arrived.
3. I didn't go to the bank.
4. He doesn't speak Japanese.
5. We weren't angry.
6. He won't be happy.
7. Don't call me tonight.
8. It didn't rain yesterday.
9. I couldn't hear them.
10. I don't believe you.

44.4

2. 'm not / am not
3. can't
4. doesn't
5. isn't / 's not
6. don't . . . haven't
7. Don't
8. didn't
9. haven't
10. won't
11. didn't
12. weren't
13. hasn't
14. shouldn't

44.5

3. He wasn't born in Los Angeles.
4. He doesn't like Los Angeles.
5. He'd like to live someplace else.

6. He can drive.
7. He hasn't traveled abroad.
8. He doesn't read the newspaper.
9. He isn't interested in politics.
10. He usually watches TV at night.
11. He didn't watch TV last night.
12. He went out last night.

UNIT 45

45.1
3. Were you late this morning?
4. Has Kate seen that movie?
5. Will you be here tomorrow?
6. Is Paul going out tonight?
7. Do you like your job?
8. Does Nicole live near here?
9. Did you enjoy the movie?
10. Did you have a good vacation?

45.2
2. Do you use . . . a lot?
3. Did you use it yesterday?
4. Do you enjoy driving?
5. Are you a good driver?
6. Have you ever had an accident?

45.3
3. What are the children doing?
4. How is cheese made?
5. Is your sister coming to the party?
6. Why don't you tell the truth?
7. Have your guests arrived yet?
8. What time does your plane leave?
9. Why didn't Jenny go to work?
10. Was your car damaged in the accident?

45.4
3. are you reading?
4. did she go to bed?
5. are they going (on vacation)?
6. did you see him?
7. can't you come (to the party)?
8. has she moved?
9. (money) do you need?
10. doesn't she like you?
11. does it rain?
12. did you do it? / the shopping?

UNIT 46

46.1
2. fell off the shelf?
3. Who wants to see

4. Who took your umbrella? / Who took it?
5. What made you sick?
6. Who's / Who is coming?

46.2
3. Who did you call?
4. What happened last night?
5. Who knows the answer?
6. Who did the dishes?
7. What did Jane/she do?
8. What woke you up?
9. Who saw the accident?
10. Who did you see?
11. Who has your pen / it?
12. What does this word / it mean?

46.3
2. called you? did she want?
3. Who did you ask? What did he say?
4. Who got married? Who told you?
5. Who did you meet? What did she tell you?
6. Who won? What did you do (after the game)?
7. Who gave you the book? What did Catherine give you?

UNIT 47

47.1
2. are . . . looking for?
3. Who did you go to the movies with?
4. What/Who was the movie about?
5. Who did you give the money to?
6. Who was the book written by?

47.2
2. are they looking at?
3. is he going to?
4. are they talking about?
5. is she listening to?
6. are they waiting for?

47.3
2. Which hotel did . . . stay at?
3. Which team does he belong to / play for?
4. Which school did you go to?

47.4
2. What is the food like?
3. What are the people like?
4. What is the weather like?

47.5
2. What was the movie like?
3. What were the classes like?
4. What was the hotel like?

UNIT 48

48.1
3. color is it?
4. What time did you
5. What type of music do you like?
6. What kind of car do you want (to buy)?

48.2
2. Which coat
3. Which movie/film
4. Which bus

48.3
3. Which	7. Which
4. What	8. Who
5. What	9. What
6. Which	10. Which

48.4
2. How far
3. How old
4. How often
5. How deep
6. How long

48.5
2. How heavy is this box?
3. How old are you?
4. How much did you spend?
5. How often do you watch TV?
6. How far is it from New York to Los Angeles?

UNIT 49

49.1
2. How long does it take to get from Houston to Mexico City by car?
3. How long does it take to get from Tokyo to Kyoto by train?
4. How long does it take to get from JFK Airport to Manhattan by bus?

49.2

Example answers:

2. It takes . . . hours to fly from . . . to Australia.
3. It takes . . . years to become a doctor in . . . .
4. It takes . . . to walk from my home to the nearest supermarket.
5. It takes . . . to get from my house to the nearest airport.

49.3

2. How long did it take you to walk to the station?
3. How long did it take him / Tom to paint the bathroom?
4. How long did it take you to learn to ski?
5. How long did it take them to repair the computer?

49.4

2. It took us 20 minutes to walk / get home.
3. It took me six months to learn to drive.
4. It took Mark/him three hours to drive / get to Houston.
5. It took Lisa/her a long time to find / get a job.
6. It took me . . . to . . .

UNIT 50

50.1

2. where she/Sue is.
3. I don't know how old it is.
4. I don't know when he'll / Paul will be here.
5. I don't know why he was angry.
6. I don't know how long she / Donna has lived here.

50.2

2. where she/Susan works
3. what he/Peter said
4. why he went home early
5. what time the meeting begins
6. how the accident happened

50.3

2. are you
3. they are
4. the museum is
5. do you want
6. elephants eat
7. it is

50.4

2. if/whether they are married?
3. Do you know if/whether Sue knows Bill?
4. Do you know if/whether Gary will be here tomorrow?
5. Do you know if/whether he passed his exam?

50.5

2. you know where Paula is?
3. Do you know if/whether she is / she's working today?
4. Do you know what time she starts work?
5. Do you know if/whether the banks are open tomorrow?
6. Do you know where Sarah and Tim live?
7. Do you know if/whether they went to Jane's party?

50.6

Example answers:

2. Do you know what time the bus leaves?
3. Excuse me, can you tell me where the station is?
4. I don't know what I'm going to do tonight.
5. Do you know if there's a restaurant near here?
6. Do you know how much it costs to rent a car?

UNIT 51

51.1

2. She said (that) she was very busy.
3. She said (that) she couldn't go to the party.
4. He said (that) he had to go out.
5. He said (that) he was learning Russian.
6. She said (that) she didn't feel very well.
7. They said (that) they'd / they would be home late.
8. She said (that) she'd / she had just gotten back from vacation.
9. She said (that) she was going to buy a new computer.
10. They said (that) they didn't have a key.

51.2

2. (that) she wasn't hungry
3. (that) he needed it

4. (that) she didn't want to go
5. (that) I could have it
6. (that) he'd / he would send me a postcard
7. (that) he'd / he had gone home
8. (that) he wanted to watch TV
9. (that) she was going to the movies

51.3

3.	said	7.	said
4.	told	8.	told
5.	tell	9.	tell
6.	say	10.	say

UNIT 52

52.1

3. call
4. call Paul
5. to call Paul
6. to call Paul
7. call Paul
8. to call Paul
9. call Paul
10. call Paul

52.2

3. get
4. going
5. watch
6. flying
7. listening
8. eat
9. waiting
10. wear
11. doing . . . staying

52.3

4. to go
5. rain
6. to leave
7. help
8. studying
9. to go
10. wearing
11. to stay
12. taking
13. to have
14. hear
15. go
16. listening
17. to make
18. to be . . . take
19. use

53.1
3. to see
4. to swim
5. cleaning
6. to ask
7. visiting
8. going
9. to be
10. waiting
11. to do
12. to speak
13. to go
14. crying / to cry
15. to work . . . talking

53.2
2. to help
3. to see
4. reading
5. to lose
6. to send
7. raining
8. to go
9. watching / to watch
10. to wait

53.3
2. going / to go to museums
3. to go
4. writing / to write e-mails
5. to go (there)
6. traveling by train
7. walking

53.4
Example answers:
1. I enjoy cooking.
2. I don't like driving / to drive.
3. If it's a nice day tomorrow, I'd like to have a picnic by the lake.
4. When I'm on vacation, I like to do / doing very little.
5. I don't mind traveling alone, but I prefer to travel with somebody.
6. I wouldn't like to live in a big city.

UNIT 54

54.1
2. you to listen carefully.
3. want you to be angry.
4. want me to wait for you?
5. I don't want you to call me tonight.
6. I want you to meet Sarah.

54.2
2. me to turn left after the bridge.
3. him to go to the doctor.
4. me to help her.
5. him to come back in 10 minutes.
6. me use his phone.
7. her not to call before 8:00.
8. her to play the piano.

54.3
2. to repeat
3. wait
4. to arrive
5. to get
6. go
7. borrow
8. to tell
9. to make/get
10. think

UNIT 55

55.1
2.–4.
to a coffee shop to meet a friend.
I went to the drugstore to get some medicine.
I went to the supermarket to buy some food.

55.2
2. to read the newspaper
3. to open this door
4. to get some fresh air
5. to wake him up
6. to see who it was

55.3
Example answers:
2. I don't have time to talk to you now.
3. I called Ann to tell her about the party.
4. I'm going out to do some shopping.
5. I borrowed some money to buy a car.

55.4
2. to	7. to
3. to	8. to
4. for	9. for
5. to	10. for
6. for	11. to . . . for

55.5
2. for the movie to begin
3. for it to arrive
4. for you to tell me

UNIT 56

56.1
3. to
4. to
5. – *(no preposition)*
6. for
7. to
8. on . . . to
9. for
10. on
11. to
12. – *(no preposition)*
13. on
14. for
15. on

56.2
2. went fishing
3. goes swimming
4. going skiing
5. go shopping
6. went jogging/running

56.3
2. to college
3. shopping
4. to bed
5. home
6. skiing
7. riding
8. for a walk
9. on vacation . . . to Hawaii

UNIT 57

57.1
2. get your jacket
3. get a doctor
4. get another one
5. gets the job
6. get some milk
7. get a ticket
8. gets a good salary
9. get a lot of rain
10. get a new computer

57.2
2. getting dark
3. getting married
4. getting ready
5. getting late

57.3

2. get wet
3. got married
4. gets angry
5. got lost
6. get old
7. got better

57.4

2. got to New York at 12:00.
3. I left the party at 11:15 and got home at midnight.
4. *(Example answer)* I left home at 8:30 and got to the airport at 10:00.

57.5

2. got off
3. got out of
4. got on

UNIT 58

58.1

2. do
3. make
4. made
5. did
6. do
7. done
8. make
9. making
10. do
11. doing

58.2

2. 're/are doing (their) homework.
3. 's/is doing the shopping *or* 's/is shopping.
4. They're / They are doing (their) laundry.
5. She's / She is making a phone call.
6. He's / He is making the/his bed.
7. She's / She is doing/washing the dishes.
8. He's / He is making a (shopping) list.
9. They're / They are making a movie.
10. He's / He is taking a picture / photograph.

58.3

2. make
3. do
4. done
5. made
6. did
7. do
8. make
9. do
10. making
11. made
12. make . . . do

UNIT 59

59.1

3. He doesn't have / hasn't got
4. Gary had
5. Do you have / Have you got
6. we didn't have
7. She doesn't have / hasn't got
8. Did you have

59.2

2. 's/is having a cup of tea.
3. 's/is having breakfast.
4. 're/are having fun.
5. They're / They are having dinner.
6. They're / They are having an argument.

59.3

3. Have a good/great trip!
4. Did you have a nice/good weekend?
5. Did you have a nice/good vacation?
6. Have a great/good time! *or* Have fun!
7. Are you going to have a (birthday) party?

59.4

2. have something to eat
3. had a glass of water
4. had a bad dream
5. had an accident
6. have a baby

UNIT 60

60.1

2. him
3. them
4. her
5. him
6. them
7. her

60.2

2. I . . . them
3. he . . . her
4. they . . . us
5. we . . . him
6. she . . . them
7. they . . . me
8. she . . . you

60.3

2. him
3. like it
4. you like it
5. don't like her
6. Do you like them

60.4

2. him
3. them
4. they
5. us
6. it
7. She
8. them
9. me
10. her
11. them
12. he . . . it

60.5

2. it to him
3. give them to her
4. give it to me
5. give it to them
6. give them to us

UNIT 61

61.1

2. her
3. our hands
4. his hands
5. their hands
6. your hands

61.2

2. their
3. our
4. with her
5. live with my
6. lives with his parents.
7. with your parents
8. live with their parents.

61.3

2. their
3. his
4. his
5. her
6. their
7. her
8. their

61.4

2. his
3. Their
4. our
5. her
6. my
7. your
8. her
9. their
10. my
11. Its
12. His . . . his

61.5

2. my key
3. Her husband
4. your coat
5. their homework
6. his name
7. Our house

UNIT 62

62.1
2. mine
3. ours
4. hers
5. theirs
6. yours
7. mine
8. his

62.2
2. yours
3. my . . . Mine
4. Yours . . . mine
5. her
6. My . . . hers
7. their
8. Ours

62.3
3. friend of hers
4. friends of ours
5. friend of mine
6. friend of his
7. friends of yours

62.4
2. Whose camera
   hers.
3. Whose gloves are
   're/are mine.
4. Whose hat is this?
   It's his.
5. Whose money is this?
   It's yours.
6. Whose books are these?
   They're / They are ours.

UNIT 63

63.1
2. her . . . her name.
3. know them . . . can't
   remember their
4. know you . . . I can't
   remember your name.

63.2
2. him
3. them at their
4. with me at my
5. with her at her
6. to stay with you at your

63.3
2. hers
3. him mine
4. our . . . us theirs
5. her . . . her his
6. your . . . you ours
7. their . . . them yours

63.4
2. them
3. him
4. our
5. yours
6. us
7. her
8. their
9. mine

UNIT 64

64.1
2. myself
3. herself
4. themselves
5. myself
6. himself
7. yourself
8. yourselves

64.2
2. was by himself.
3. go out by yourself.
4. went to the movies by myself.
5. lives by herself.
6. live by themselves.

64.3
2. see each other.
3. call each other a lot.
4. They don't know each other.
5. They're / They are sitting
   next to each other.
6. They gave each other presents /
   a present.

64.4
3. each other
4. yourselves
5. us
6. ourselves
7. each other
8. each other
9. them
10. themselves

UNIT 65

65.1
3. Pedro's
4. brother
5. Daniel's
6. Paul's
7. grandmother
8. sister
9. Julia's
10. father.
11. Alberto's

65.2
2. Andy's
3. Dave's
4. Jane's
5. Diane's
6. Alice's

65.3
3. OK
4. Simon's phone number
5. My brother's job
6. OK
7. OK
8. Paula's favorite color
9. your mother's birthday
10. My parents' house
11. OK
12. OK
13. Sylvia's party
14. OK

UNIT 66

66.1
2. a
3. a
4. an
5. a
6. an
7. a
8. an
9. an

66.2
2. a vegetable
3. a game
4. a tool
5. a mountain
6. a planet
7. a fruit
8. a river
9. a flower
10. a musical instrument

66.3
2. a sales clerk.
3. an architect.
4. He's a taxi driver.
5. He's an electrician.
6. She's a photographer.
7. She's a nurse.
8. a/an . . .

66.4
2.–8.
   Tom never wears a hat.
   I can't ride a bicycle.
   My brother is an artist.
   Rebecca works in an office.
   Jane wants to learn a
      foreign language.
   Mike lives in an old house.
   Tonight I'm going to a party.

UNIT 67

67.1
2. boats
3. women
4. cities

5. umbrellas
6. addresses
7. knives
8. sandwiches
9. families
10. feet
11. holidays
12. potatoes

67.2
2. teeth
3. people
4. children
5. fish
6. leaves

67.3
3. . . . with a lot of beautiful **trees**.
4. . . . with two **men**.
5. *OK*
6. . . . three **children**.
7. Most of my **friends** are **students**.
8. He put on his **pajamas** . . .
9. *OK*
10. Do you know many **people** . . .
11. I like your **pants**. Where did you get **them**?
12. . . . full of **tourists**.
13. *OK*
14. **These scissors aren't** . . .

67.4
2. are
3. don't
4. watch
5. were
6. live
7. Do
8. are
9. them
10. some

UNIT 68

68.1
3. a pitcher
4. water
5. toothpaste
6. a toothbrush
7. an egg
8. money
9. a wallet
10. sand
11. a bucket
12. an envelope

68.2
3. . . . **a** hat.
4. . . . **a** job?

5. *OK*
6. . . . **an** apple . . .
7. . . . **a** party . . .
8. . . . **a** wonderful thing.
9. . . . **an** island.
10. . . . **a** key.
11. *OK*
12. . . . **a** good idea.
13. . . . **a** car?
14. . . . **a** cup of coffee?
15. *OK*
16. . . . **a** coat.

68.3
2. a piece of wood
3. a glass of water
4. a bar of soap
5. a cup of tea
6. a piece of paper
7. a bowl of soup
8. a loaf of bread
9. a jar of honey

UNIT 69

69.1
2. a newspaper/paper, some flowers / a bunch of flowers, and a pen.
3. I bought some stamps, some postcards, and some bread / a loaf of bread.
4. I bought some toothpaste / a tube of toothpaste, some soap / a bar of soap, and a comb.

69.2
2. Would you like some coffee / a cup of coffee
3. Would you like some cookies / a cookie
4. Would you like some bread? (*or* . . . a piece of bread? / a slice of bread?)
5. Would you like a sandwich?
6. Would you like some cake / a piece / slice of cake

69.3
2. some . . . some
3. some
4. a . . . some
5. an . . . some
6. a . . . a . . . some
7. some
8. some
9. some . . . a

69.4
2. eyes
3. hair
4. information
5. chairs
6. furniture
7. job
8. wonderful weather

UNIT 70

70.1
3. a
4. the
5. an
6. the . . . the
7. a . . . a
8. a . . . a
9. . . . **a** student . . . **a** journalist . . . **an** apartment near **the** college . . . **The** apartment is . . .
10. . . . two children, **a** boy and **a** girl. **The** boy is seven years old, and **the** girl is three . . . in **a** factory . . . doesn't have **a** job . . .

70.2
2. **the** airport
3. **a** cup
4. **a** nice picture
5. **the** dictionary
6. **the** floor

70.3
2. . . . send me **a** postcard.
3. What is **the** name of . . .
4. . . . **a** very big country.
5. What is **the** largest . . .
6. . . . **the** color of **the** carpet.
7. . . . **a** headache.
8. . . . **an** old house near **the** station.
9. . . . **the** name of **the** director of **the** movie . . .

UNIT 71

71.1
3. . . . **the** second floor.
4. . . . **the** moon?
5. . . . **the** best hotel in this town?
6. *OK*
7. . . . **the** football stadium?
8. . . . **the** end of May.
9. *OK*
10. . . . **the** first time I met her.

11. *OK*
12. **The** Internet is a good place to get information.
13. *OK*
14. . . . on **the** top shelf on **the** right.
15. . . . in **the** country about 10 miles from **the** nearest town.

71.2
2. the same time
3. the same age
4. the same color
5. the same problem

71.3
2. **the** guitar
3. breakfast
4. television/TV
5. **the** ocean
6. **the** bottom

71.4
2. **the** name
3. **The** sky
4. television
5. **The** police
6. **the** capital
7. lunch
8. **the** middle

UNIT 72

72.1
2. **the** movies
3. **the** hospital
4. **the** airport
5. home
6. jail/prison

72.2
3. school
4. **the** station
5. home
6. bed
7. **the** post office

72.3
2. **the** movies
3. go to bed
4. go to jail/prison
5. go to **the** dentist
6. go to college
7. go to **the** hospital / are taken to **the** hospital

72.4
3. **the** doctor
4. *OK*
5. *OK*
6. *OK*
7. **the** bank
8. *OK*
9. *OK*
10. *OK*
11. **the** station
12. *OK*
13. **the** hospital
14. *OK*
15. **the** theater

UNIT 73

73.1
Example answers:
2. I don't like dogs.
3. I hate museums.
4. I love big cities.
5. Tennis is all right.
6. I love chocolate.
7. I don't like computer games.
8. I hate parties.

73.2
Example answers:
2. I'm not interested in politics.
3. I know a lot about sports.
4. I don't know much about art.
5. I don't know anything about astronomy.
6. I know a little about economics.

73.3
3. friends
4. parties
5. **The** stores
6. **the** milk
7. milk
8. basketball
9. computers
10. **The** water
11. cold water
12. **the** salt
13. **the** people
14. Vegetables
15. **The** houses
16. **the** words
17. pictures
18. **the** pictures
19. English . . . international business
20. Money . . . happiness

UNIT 74

74.1
3. Sweden
4. **The** Amazon
5. Asia
6. **The** Pacific
7. **The** Rhine
8. Kenya
9. **The** United States
10. **The** Andes
11. Bangkok
12. **The** Alps
13. **The** Red Sea
14. Jamaica
15. **The** Bahamas

74.2
3. *OK*
4. **the** Philippines
5. **the** south of France
6. **the** Washington Monument
7. *OK*
8. **the** Museum of Art
9. *OK*
10. Belgium is smaller than **the** Netherlands.
11. **the** Mississippi . . . **the** Nile
12. **the** National Gallery
13. **the** Park Hotel near Central Park
14. *OK*
15. **The** Rocky Mountains are in North America.
16. *OK*
17. **the** United Kingdom
18. **the** west of Ireland
19. **the** University of Michigan
20. **The** Panama Canal joins **the** Atlantic Ocean and **the** Pacific Ocean.

UNIT 75

75.1
2. that house
3. these postcards
4. those birds
5. this seat
6. These dishes

75.2
2. Is that your umbrella?
3. Is this your book?
4. Are those your books?
5. Is that your bicycle/bike?
6. Are these your keys?
7. Are those your keys?

8. Is this your watch?
9. Are those your glasses?
10. Are these your gloves?

75.3
2. that's
3. This is
4. That's
5. that
6. this is
7. That's
8. that's

UNIT 76

76.1
2. need one
3. I'm going to get one
4. I don't have one
5. I just had one
6. there's one on First Avenue

76.2
2. a new one
3. a better one
4. an old one
5. a big one
6. a different one

76.3
2. ones?
   green ones.
3. Which one?
   The one . . . a/the red door.
4. Which ones?
   The ones on the top shelf.
5. Which one?
   The black one.
6. Which one?
   The one on the wall.
7. Which one?
   The tall one with long hair.
8. Which ones?
   The yellow ones.
9. Which one?
   The one . . . a/the mustache
   and glasses.
10. Which ones?
   The ones I took at the party
   last week.

UNIT 77

77.1
2. some
3. any
4. any
5. any
6. some
7. any

8. some
9. some
10. any . . . any
11. some . . . any
12. some

77.2
2. some questions
3. any pictures
4. any . . . languages
5. some friends
6. some milk
7. any batteries
8. some . . . air
9. some fruit
10. any help

77.3
3. I have some
4. I don't have any
5. I didn't buy any
6. I bought some
7. I didn't make any

77.4
2. something
3. anything
4. anything
5. Somebody/Someone
6. anything
7. anybody/anyone
8. something
9. anything
10. anybody/anyone

UNIT 78

78.1
2. no stores near here.
3. Carla has no free time.
4. There is no light in this room.
6. There isn't any milk in the
   fridge.
7. There aren't any buses today.
8. Tom doesn't have any brothers
   or sisters.

78.2
2. any   8. no
3. any   9. any
4. no   10. no
5. any   11. None
6. no   12. any
7. any

78.3
2. no money
3. any questions
4. no friends

5. no difference
6. any furniture
7. no answer
8. any air conditioning
9. no line

78.4
Example answers:
2. Three.
3. Two cups.
4. None.
5. None.

UNIT 79

79.1
2. nobody in the office.
3. have nothing to do.
4. There's nothing on TV.
5. There was no one at home.
6. We found nothing.

79.2
2. anybody on the bus.
3. I don't have anything to read.
4. I don't have anyone to
   help me.
5. She didn't hear anything.
6. We don't have anything
   for dinner.

79.3
3a. Nothing.
4a. Nobody. / No one.
5a. Nobody. / No one.
6a. Nothing.
7a. Nothing.
8a. Nobody. / No one.
3b. want anything.
4b. didn't meet anybody /
   anyone. *or* met nobody /
   no one.
5b. Nobody / No one knows
6b. I didn't buy anything. *or* I
   bought nothing.
7b. Nothing happened.
8b. Nobody / No one was late.

79.4
3. anything
4. Nobody / No one
5. Nothing
6. anything
7. anybody/anyone
8. nothing
9. anything
10. anything
11. nobody / no one

12. anything
13. Nothing
14. Nobody / No one . . .
    anybody/anyone

UNIT 80

80.1
2. something
3. somewhere
4. somebody/someone

80.2
2a. Nowhere.
3a. Nothing.
4a. Nobody. / No one.
2b. going anywhere.
3b. I don't want anything.
4b. I'm not looking for anybody /
    anyone.

80.3
3. anything
4. anything
5. somebody/someone
6. something
7. anybody/anyone . . . nobody /
   no one
8. anything
9. Nobody / No one
10. anybody/anyone
11. Nothing
12. anywhere
13. somewhere
14. anything
15. anybody/anyone

80.4
2. anything to eat
3. nothing to do
4. anywhere to sit
5. something to drink
6. nowhere to park
7. something to read
8. somewhere to stay

UNIT 81

81.1
2. Every day
3. every time
4. Every room
5. every word

81.2
2. every day
3. all day
4. every day

5. all day
6. all day
7. every day

81.3
2. every   6. all
3. all   7. every
4. all   8. all
5. Every   9. every

81.4
2. everything
3. Everybody/Everyone
4. everything
5. everywhere
6. Everybody/Everyone
7. everywhere
8. Everything

81.5
2. is
3. has
4. likes
5. has *or* is
6. was
7. makes
8. Is . . . Does

UNIT 82

82.1
3. Some
4. Most of
5. most
6. any of
7. all *or* all of
8. None of
9. any of
10. Most
11. most of
12. Some
13. All *or* All of
14. some of
15. most of

82.2
2. All of them.
3. Some of them.
4. None of them.
5. Most of them.
6. None of it.

82.3
3. Some people . . .
4. Some of **the** questions . . . *or*
   Some questions . . .
5. OK
6. All insects . . .

7. OK (*or* . . . all **of** these books)
8. Most of **the** students . . . *or*
   Most students . . .
9. OK
10. . . . most of **the** night

UNIT 83

83.1
3. Both   9. Neither
4. Neither   10. either of
5. Neither   11. Both
6. both   12. neither of
7. Either   13. Both
8. neither of   14. either of

83.2
2. Both windows
3. Neither man is *or* Neither
   of them is . . .
4. Both men have (got) *or*
   Both of them have . . .
5. Both buses / Both of the buses
   go *or* . . . are going
6. Neither answer / Neither of
   the answers is

83.3
3. Both of them are
4. Neither of them has
5. Both of them live in Boston.
6. Both of them like to cook.
7. Neither of them can play
   the piano.
8. Both of them read the
   newspaper.
9. Neither of them is interested
   in sports.

UNIT 84

84.1
2. many   8. many
3. much   9. How many
4. many   10. How much
5. many   11. How much
6. much   12. How many
7. much

84.2
2. much time
3. many countries
4. many people
5. much luggage
6. many times

84.3
2. a lot of interesting things
3. a lot of accidents

4. a lot of fun
5. a lot of traffic

84.4
3. a lot of snow
4. *OK*
5. a lot of money
6. *OK*
7. *OK*
8. a lot

84.5
3. plays tennis a lot.
4. doesn't use his car much.
   (*or* . . . a lot.)
5. He doesn't go out much.
   (*or* . . . a lot.)
6. She travels a lot.

UNIT 85

85.1
2. a few
3. a little
4. a few
5. a little
6. a few

85.2
2. a little milk
3. A few days
4. a little Russian
5. a few friends
6. a few times
7. a few chairs
8. a little fresh air

85.3
2. very little coffee
3. very little rain
4. very few hotels
5. very little time
6. Very few people
7. very little work

85.4
2. A few   5. few
3. a little   6. a little
4. little   7. little

85.5
2. . . . **a** little luck
3. . . . **a** few things
4. *OK*
5. . . . **a** few questions
6. . . . **few** people
7. *OK*

UNIT 86

86.1
2. like that green jacket.
3. you like classical music?
4. I had a wonderful trip.
5. We went to a Japanese
   restaurant.

86.2
2. dark clouds
3. long vacation
4. hot water
5. fresh air
6. sharp knife
7. dangerous job

86.3
2. looks new.
3. feel sick.
4. look surprised.
5. smell nice.
6. tastes terrible.

86.4
2. look new.
3. don't sound American.
4. don't feel cold.
5. don't look heavy.
6. doesn't taste good.

UNIT 87

87.1
2. badly   5. fast
3. quietly   6. dangerously
4. angrily

87.2
2. work hard
3. sleep well
4. win easily
5. Think carefully
6. know her very well
7. explain things clearly/well
8. Come quickly

87.3
2. angry   8. quiet
3. slowly   9. badly
4. slow   10. nice (*See*
5. careful   *Unit 86C.*)
6. hard   11. quickly
7. suddenly

87.4
2. well   5. well
3. good   6. good . . . good
4. well

UNIT 88

88.1
2. bigger
3. slower
4. more expensive
5. higher
6. more dangerous

88.2
2. stronger
3. happier
4. more modern
5. more important
6. better
7. larger
8. more serious
9. prettier
10. more crowded

88.3
2. hotter/warmer
3. more expensive
4. worse
5. farther
6. more difficult   *or*   harder

88.4
3. taller
4. harder
5. more comfortable
6. better
7. nicer
8. heavier
9. more interested
10. warmer
11. better
12. bigger
13. more beautiful
14. sharper
15. more polite
16. worse

UNIT 89

89.1
3. taller than Ben.
4. work earlier than
5. works harder than Liz.
6. more money than Liz.
7. better driver than Ben.
8. is more patient than Liz.
9. is a better dancer than Liz. /
   dances better than Liz.
10. is more intelligent than Ben.

11. speaks Spanish better than Ben. / speaks better Spanish than Ben. / 's Spanish is better than Ben's.

12. goes to the movies more than Liz. / more often than Liz.

89.2

2. older than her. / than she is.

3. harder than me. / than I do.

4. watch TV more than him. / than he does.

5. 're/are a better cook than me. / than I am. *or* cook better than me. / than I do.

6. know more people than us. / than we do.

7. have more money than them. / than they do.

8. run faster than me. / than I can.

9. 've/have been here longer than her. / than she has.

10. got up earlier than them. / than they did.

11. were more surprised than him. / than he was.

89.3

2. is much younger than his father.

3. cost a little more than yours. / than your camera. *or* was a little more expensive than . . .

4. much better today than yesterday. / than I did yesterday. / than I felt yesterday.

5. a little warmer today than yesterday. / than it was yesterday.

6. is a much better volleyball player than me. / than I am. *or* is much better at volleyball than me. / than I am. *or* plays volleyball much better than me. / than I do.

UNIT 90

90.1

2. longer than . . . as long as

3. heavier than . . . not as heavy as B.

4. older than C . . . not as old as B.

5. more money than C but not as much as A. *or* . . . but less (money) than A.

6. harder than A but not as hard as B.

90.2

2. as big as mine. / as my room.

3. get up as early as you. / as you did.

4. didn't play as well as us. / as we did.

5. haven't been here as long as me. / as I have.

6. isn't as nervous as her. / as she is.

90.3

2. as
3. than
4. than
5. as
6. than
7. as
8. than

90.4

2. on the same street as Laura.

3. at the same time as Andy.

4. car is the same color as Laura's.

UNIT 91

91.1

2. longer than
   the longest.
   the shortest.

3. is younger than C.
   C is the oldest.
   B is the youngest.

4. D is more expensive than A.
   C is the most expensive.
   A is the cheapest.

5. A is better than C.
   A is the best.
   D is the worst.

91.2

2. the happiest day

3. the best movie

4. the most popular singer

5. the worst mistake

6. the prettiest city

7. the coldest day

8. the most boring person

91.3

2. is the highest mountain in the world.

3.–6.
   Brazil is the largest country in South America.
   Alaska is the largest state in the United States.
   The Nile is the longest river in Africa. / in the world.
   Jupiter is the largest planet in the solar system.

UNIT 92

92.1

2. enough chairs

3. enough paint

4. enough wind

92.2

2. isn't big enough.

3. long enough.

4. isn't strong enough.

92.3

3. old enough

4. enough time

5. big enough

6. eat enough

7. enough space

8. tired enough

9. practice enough

92.4

2. sharp enough to cut

3. warm enough to go

4. enough bread to make

5. well enough to win

6. enough time to read

UNIT 93

93.1

2. too heavy

3. too low

4. too fast

5. too big

6. too crowded

93.2

3. enough

4. too many

5. too

6. enough

7. too much

8. enough

9. too

10. too many

11. too much

93.3

3. too far.

4. 's/is too expensive.

5. 's not / isn't big enough.

6. was too difficult.

7. 's not / isn't good enough.
8. 'm/am too busy.
9. was too long.

93.4
2. too early to go to bed.
3. too young to get married.
4. too dangerous to go out at night.
5. too late to call Sue (now).
6. too surprised to say anything.

UNIT 94

94.1
3. I like this picture very much.
4. Tom started his new job last week.
5. *OK*
6. Jane bought a present for her friend.   *or*   Jane bought her friend a present.
7. I drink three cups of coffee every day.
8. *OK*
9. I borrowed 50 dollars from my brother.

94.2
2. bought a new computer last week.
3. Paul finished his work quickly.
4. Emily doesn't speak French very well.
5. I did a lot of shopping yesterday.
6. Do you know New York well?
7. We enjoyed the party very much.
8. I explained the problem carefully.
9. We met some friends at the airport.
10. Did you buy that jacket in Canada?
11. We do the same thing every day.
12. I don't like football very much.

94.3
2. arrived at the hotel early.
3. goes to Puerto Rico every year.
4. have lived here since 2002.
5. was born in Florida in 1984.
6. didn't go to work yesterday.
7. went to a wedding last weekend.
8. had my breakfast in bed this morning.

9. is going to college in September.
10. saw a beautiful bird in the garden this morning.
11. parents have been to Tokyo many times.
12. left my umbrella in the restaurant last night.
13. you going to the movies tomorrow night?
14. took the children to school this morning.

UNIT 95

95.1
2. always gets up early.
3. 's/is never late for work.
4. He sometimes gets angry.
5. He rarely goes swimming.
6. He's / He is usually at home in the evenings.

95.2
2. is always polite.
3. usually finish work at 5:00.
4. has just started a new job.
5. I rarely go to bed before midnight.
6. The bus isn't usually late.
7. I don't often eat fish.
8. I will never forget what you said.
9. Have you ever lost your passport?
10. Do you still work in the same place?
11. They always stay at the same hotel.
12. Jane doesn't usually work on Saturdays.
13. Is Tina already here?
14. What do you usually have for breakfast?
15. I can never remember his name.

95.3
2. also speak French.
3. I'm also hungry.
4. and I've also been to Guatemala.
5. Yes, and I also bought some books.

95.4
1. both play
   They're / They are both
   They've both got / They both have

2. 're/are all
   were all born in
   They all live in Miami.

UNIT 96

96.1
2. still have an old car?
3. you still a student?
4. Are you still studying Japanese?
5. Do you still go to the movies a lot?
6. Do you still want to be a teacher?

96.2
2. looking for a job.
   's/is still looking (for a job).
   He hasn't found a job
3. was
   She's / She is still asleep.
   She hasn't woken up yet. /
   She isn't awake yet.   *or*
   She hasn't gotten up yet. /
   She isn't up yet.
4. were having dinner. / were eating (dinner).
   They're / They are still having dinner. / . . . still eating (dinner).
   They haven't finished (dinner) yet. / They haven't finished eating (dinner) yet.

96.3
2. Is . . . here yet?   *or*   Has . . . arrived/come yet?
3. Have . . . gotten the results of your blood test yet? /
   Have . . . received the . . . /
   Do . . . have the . . .
4. Have you decided where to go (for vacation) yet? / Do you know where you're going (for vacation) yet?

96.4
3. 's/has already gone/left.
4. already have one.   *or*   've/have already got one.
5. 've/have already paid it.   *or*   already paid it.
6. already knows.

UNIT 97

97.1
2. it to Gary.
3. gave them to Sarah.

4. He gave it to his sister.

5. He gave them to Robert.

6. He gave it to a neighbor.

97.2

2. Joanna a plant.

3. gave Richard a tie.

4. I gave Emma some chocolates / a box of chocolates.

5. I gave Rachel some flowers / a bouquet of flowers.

6. I gave Kevin a pen.

97.3

2. lend me an umbrella?

3. you give me . . . address?

4. Can you lend me 20 dollars?

5. Can you send me some information?

6. Can you show me the letter?

7. Can you get me some stamps?

97.4

2. lend you some money

3. send the letter to me

4. buy you a present

5. pass me the sugar

6. give it to her

7. showed the police officer my driver's license

UNIT 98

98.1

3.–7.

went to the window and (I) looked out.

I wanted to call you, but I didn't have your number.

I jumped into the river and (I) swam to the other side.

I usually drive to work, but I took the bus this morning.

Do you want me to come with you, or should I wait here?

98.2

Example answers:

2. because it was raining. / because the weather was bad.

3. but it was closed.

4. so he didn't eat anything. / so he didn't want anything to eat.

5. because there was a lot of traffic. / because the traffic was bad.

6. goodbye, got into her car, and drove off/away.

98.3

Example answers:

3. I went to the movies, but the movie wasn't very good.

4. I went to a coffee shop and met some friends of mine.

5. There was a movie on television, so I watched it.

6. I got up in the middle of the night because I couldn't sleep.

UNIT 99

99.1

2. When I'm tired, I like to watch TV.

3. When I called her, there was no answer.

4. When I go on vacation, I always go to the same place.

5. When the program ended, I turned off the TV.

6. When I got to the hotel, there were no rooms.

99.2

2. when they heard the news.

3. they went to live in France.

4. while they were away.

5. before they came here

6. somebody broke into the house.

7. they didn't believe me.

99.3

2. I finish

3. it's

4. I'll be . . . she leaves

5. stops

6. We'll come . . . we're

7. I come . . . I'll bring

8. I'm

9. I'll give . . . I go

10. I'll tell . . . I'm

99.4

Example answers:

2. you finish your work

3. I'm going to buy a motorcycle

4. you get ready

5. I won't have much free time

6. I come back

UNIT 100

100.1

2. the driving test, you'll get your license.

3. you fail the driving test, you can take it again.

4. If you don't want this magazine, I'll throw it away.

5. If you want those pictures, you can have them.

6. If you're busy now, we can talk later.

7. If you're hungry, we can have lunch now.

8. If you need money, I can lend you some.

100.2

2. I give

3. is

4. I'll call

5. I'll be . . . get

6. Will you go . . . they invite

100.3

Example answers:

3. you're busy.

4. you'll feel better in the morning.

5. you're not watching it.

6. she doesn't practice.

7. I'll go and see Chris.

8. the weather is good.

9. it rains today.

100.4

2. When

3. If

4. If

5. if

6. When

7. if

8. when . . . if

UNIT 101

101.1

3. wanted

4. had

5. were/was

6. didn't enjoy

7. could

8. tried

9. didn't have

101.2

3. I'd go / I would go

4. she knew

5. we had

6. you won

7. I wouldn't / would not stay

8. we lived

9. It would be

10. the salary was/were

11. I wouldn't / would not know

12. would you change

101.3

2. I'd watch it / I would watch it

3. we had some pictures on the wall

4. the air would be cleaner

5. every day was/were the same

6. I'd be bored / I would be bored

7. we had a bigger house / we bought a bigger house

8. we would/could buy a bigger house

101.4

Example answers:

2. If I could go anywhere in the world, I'd go to Antarctica.

3. I wouldn't be very happy if I didn't have any friends.

4. I'd buy a house if I had enough money.

5. If I saw an accident in the street, I'd try and help.

6. The world would be a better place if there were no guns.

UNIT 102

102.1

2. who sells meat.

3. is a person who plays a musical instrument.

4. A patient is a person who is sick in the hospital.

5. A dentist is a person who takes care of your teeth.

6. A fool is a person who does stupid things.

7. A genius is a person who is very intelligent.

8. A liar is a person who doesn't tell the truth.

102.2

2. who opened the door was wearing

3. who took the test passed (it).

4. police officer who stopped our car wasn't very friendly.

102.3

2. who

3. which

4. which

5. who

6. which

7. who

8. who

9. which

That *is also correct in all these sentences.*

102.4

3. . . . a machine that/which makes coffee.

4. *OK* (which *is also correct*)

5. . . . people who/that never stop talking.

6. *OK* (who *is also correct*)

7. *OK* (that *is also correct*)

8. . . . the sentences that/which are wrong.

9. . . . a car that/which cost $60,000.

UNIT 103

103.1

2. pen you gave me.

3. jacket Sue is wearing.

4. flowers I gave you?

5. didn't believe the story he told us.

6. much were the oranges you bought?

103.2

2. meal you cooked was excellent.

3. I'm wearing aren't very comfortable.

4. people we invited to dinner didn't come.

103.3

2. you were talking to?

3. the keys you were looking for?

4. party you're going to?

5. the movie you were talking about?

6. music you're listening to?

7. the e-mail you were waiting for?

103.4

2. where you had dinner?

3. town where you live?

4. the factory where you work?

UNIT 104

104.1

2. at   7. at

3. in   8. in

4. at   9. at

5. in   10. in . . . at

6. in

104.2

3. at   11. at

4. on   12. in

5. in   13. on

6. in   14. on

7. on   15. at

8. on   16. at

9. at   17. on

10. on   18. in

104.3

3. B   8. B

4. A   9. both

5. both   10. both

6. A   11. B

7. B   12. both

104.4

2. call you in three

3. exam is in two weeks. / . . . in 14 days.

4. will be here in half an hour. / . . . in 30 minutes.

104.5

3. in

4. – *(already complete)*

5. – *(already complete)*

6. in

7. on

8. – *(already complete)*

9. – *(already complete)*

10. – *(already complete)*

11. in

12. at

UNIT 105

105.1

2. until 2003.

3. since 2003.

4. South Korea until 2007.

5. Australia since 2007.

6. in a hotel from . . . to 2005.

7. in a restaurant since 2005.

8. from 1996 to 2002.

9. a journalist since 2002.

11. for _____ years.

12. lived in Australia for ____ years.
13. in a hotel for three years.
14. has worked in a restaurant for ____ years.
15. was a teacher for six years.
16. has been a journalist for ____ years.

105.2
2. until
3. for
4. since
5. Until
6. for
7. for
8. until
9. since
10. until
11. for
12. until
13. Since
14. for

UNIT 106

106.1
2. after lunch
3. before the end
4. during the course
5. before they went to Mexico
6. during the night
7. while you're waiting
8. after the concert

106.2
3. while
4. for
5. while
6. during
7. while
8. for
9. during
10. while

106.3
2. eating
3. answering
4. taking
5. finishing/doing
6. going/traveling

106.4
2. in a bookstore for two years after finishing high school.
3. going to sleep, I read for a few minutes.
4. walking for three hours, we were very tired.
5. have a cup of coffee before going out.

UNIT 107

107.1
2. In the box.
3. On the box.
4. On the wall.
5. At the bus stop.
6. In the field.
7. On the balcony.
8. In the pool.
9. At the window.
10. On the ceiling.
11. On the table.
12. At the table.

107.2
2. in
3. on
4. in
5. on
6. at
7. in
8. in
9. at
10. at
11. in
12. at
13. on
14. at
15. on the wall in the living room

UNIT 108

108.1
2. At the airport.
3. In bed.
4. On a ship.
5. In the sky.
6. At a party.
7. At the doctor's.
8. On the second floor.
9. At work.
10. On a plane.
11. In a taxi.
12. At a wedding.

108.2
2. in
3. in
4. at
5. at
6. in
7. in
8. at
9. in
10. in
11. on
12. on
13. at
14. in
15. on
16. at

UNIT 109

109.1
2. to
3. in
4. to
5. in
6. to
7. to
8. in

109.2
3. to
4. to
5. (at) home . . . to work
6. at
7. – (already complete)
8. to
9. at
10. at a restaurant . . . to the hotel

109.3
2. to
3. to
4. in
5. to
6. to
7. at
8. to
9. to
10. at
11. at
12. to Maria's house . . . (at) home
13. – (already complete)
14. meet at the party . . . go to the party

109.4
1. to
2. – (already complete)
3. at
4. in
5. to
6. – (already complete)

109.5
Example answers:
2. Yesterday I went to work.
3. At 11:00 yesterday morning I was at work.
4. One day I'd like to go to Alaska.
5. I don't like going to parties.
6. At 9:00 last night I was at a friend's house.

UNIT 110

110.1
2. next to / by
3. in front of
4. between

5. next to / by
6. in front of
7. behind
8. on the
9. in the

110.2
2. behind
3. above
4. in front of
5. on
6. by / next to
7. below / under
8. above
9. under
10. by / next to
11. across from
12. on

110.3
2. fountain is . . . the theater.
3. The bank/bookstore is across from the theater. *or* Paul's office is across from the theater. *or* The theater is across from . . .
4. The bank/supermarket is next to the bookstore. *or* The bookstore is next to the . . .
5. Paul's office is above the bookstore.
6. The bookstore is between the bank and the supermarket.

UNIT 111

111.1
2. under
3. Go up
4. Go down
5. Go along
6. Go into the hotel.
7. Go past the hotel.
8. Go out of the hotel.
9. Go over the bridge.
10. Go through the park.

111.2
2. off
3. over
4. out of
5. across
6. around
7. through
8. on
9. around
10. into . . . through

111.3
1. out of
2. around
3. in
4. from . . . to
5. around
6. on/over
7. over
8. out of

UNIT 112

112.1
2. on time
3. on vacation
4. on the phone
5. on television

112.2
2. by
3. with
4. about
5. on
6. by
7. at
8. on
9. with
10. about . . . by

112.3
1. with
2. without
3. by
4. about
5. at
6. by
7. on
8. with
9. at
10. by
11. about
12. by
13. on
14. with
15. by
16. by

UNIT 113

113.1
2. in
3. to
4. at
5. with
6. of

113.2
2. at
3. to
4. about
5. of
6. of
7. from
8. in
9. for
10. about
11. of
12. at

113.3
2. interested in going
3. good at getting
4. fed up with waiting
5. sorry for/about waking
6. Thank you for waiting.

113.4
2. past me without speaking.
3. do anything without asking me first.
4. went out without locking the door.

113.5
Example answers:
2. afraid of the dark.
3. very good at drawing.
4. I'm not interested in cars.
5. I'm fed up with living here.

UNIT 114

114.1
2. to
3. for
4. to
5. at
6. for

114.2
2. to
3. of
4. to
5. for
6. for
7. of/about
8. for
9. on
10. to
11. at
12. for

13. to
14. – *(already complete)*
15. to
16. on
17. – *(already complete)* . . . (to)
18. of/about
19. at
20. of
21. for
22. – *(already complete)*

114.3
Example answers:
3. on the program.
4. depends (on) what it is.
5. It depends on the weather.
6. It depends (on) how much you want.

UNIT 115

115.1
2. went in
3. looked up
4. rode off/away
5. turned around
6. got off
7. sat down
8. got out

115.2
2. away
3. around

4. out . . . back
5. down
6. over
7. back
8. in
9. up
10. away . . . back

115.3
2. Hold on
3. slowed down
4. takes off
5. get along
6. speak up
7. broken down
8. fall over / fall down
9. work out
10. gave up
11. went off

UNIT 116

116.1
2. took off her hat. *or* took her hat off.
3. put down his bag. *or* put his bag down.
4. picked up the magazine. *or* picked the magazine up.
5. put on his sunglasses. *or* put his sunglasses on.
6. turned off the faucet. *or* turned the faucet off.

116.2
2. put his jacket on.
   put it on.
3. took off her glasses.
   She took them off.
4. I picked the phone up.
   I picked it up.
5. They gave the key back.
   They gave it back.
6. We turned off the lights.
   We turned them off.

116.3
2. take it back
3. picked them up
4. turned it off
5. bring them back

116.4
3. knocked over
4. look it up
5. throw them away
6. tried on
7. showed me around
8. gave it up *or* gave up
9. fill it out
10. put your cigarette out

Answer Key to Additional Exercises

(see page 244)

1

3. is a doctor.
4. The children are asleep.
5. Gary isn't hungry.
6. The books aren't on the table.
7. The hotel is near the station.
8. The bus isn't full.

2

3. she's / she is
4. Where are
5. Is he
6. It's / It is
7. I'm / I am   *or*   No, I'm not. I'm
8. What color is
9. Is it
10. Are you
11. How much are they?

3

3. He's / He is taking a shower.
4. Are the children playing?
5. Is it raining?
6. They're / They are coming now.
7. Why are you standing here? I'm / I am waiting for somebody.

4

4. Sam doesn't want
5. Do you want
6. Does Helen live
7. Sarah knows
8. I don't travel
9. do you usually get up
10. They don't go out
11. Tom always leaves
12. does Julia do . . . She works

5

3. She's / She is a student.
4. She doesn't have a car.
5. She goes out a lot.
6. She has / She's got a lot of friends.
7. She doesn't like Houston.
8. She likes to dance.
9. She isn't / She's not interested in sports.

6

1. Are you
   do you live
   Do you have
   old is she
2. How old are you
   What do you do / Where do you work / What's your job
   Do you like/enjoy
   Do you have
   Do you (usually) go
3. What's his name
   What does he do / What's his job
   Does he live/work in

7

4. is 32 years old.
5. I have / I've got two sisters.
6. We often watch TV at night.
7. Jane never wears a hat.
8. My car has a flat tire.   *or*   My car's got / has got a flat tire.
9. These flowers are beautiful.
10. Mary speaks German very well.

8

3. are you cooking
4. plays
5. I'm leaving
6. It's raining
7. I don't watch
8. we're looking
9. do you pronounce

9

2. we go
3. shining
4. are you going
5. do you take
6. She writes
7. I never read
8. They're watching
9. She's talking
10. do you usually have
11. He's visiting
12. I don't drink

10

2. went
3. found
4. was
5. had/took
6. told
7. gave
8. were
9. thought
10. invited/asked

11

3. was good at sports.
4. He played soccer.
5. He didn't work hard at school.
6. He had a lot of friends.
7. He didn't have a bicycle.
8. He wasn't a quiet child.

12

3. How long were you / How long did you stay
4. Did you like/enjoy
5. Where did you stay?
6. Was the weather
7. When did you get/come

13

3. I forgot
4. did you get
5. I didn't speak
6. Did you have
7. he didn't go
8. she arrived
9. did Robert live
10. The meal didn't cost

14

2. were working
3. opened
4. rang . . . was cooking
5. heard . . . looked
6. was looking . . . happened
7. wasn't reading . . . was watching
8. didn't read
9. finished . . . paid . . . left
10. saw . . . was walking . . . was waiting

15

3. is playing
4. gave
5. doesn't like
6. did your parents go
7. saw . . . was driving
8. Do you watch
9. were you doing
10. goes
11. 'm/am trying
12. didn't sleep

16

2. haven't read / 've never read
3. Have you seen
4. 've / have had
5. Have you (ever) been
6. have you lived / have you been living / have you been
7. 've / have known
8. 's / has been raining *or* has rained *or* has been horrible/bad

17

3. 's/has been
4. for
5. since
6. has he lived / has he been
7. for
8. 've/have been

18

Example answers:

3. I've just started this exercise.
4. I've met Julia a few times.
5. I haven't had dinner yet.
6. I've never been to Australia.
7. I've lived here since I was born.
8. I've lived here for three years.

19

3. bought / got
4. went
5. 've/have seen *or* saw
6. haven't started (it) (yet)
7. was
8. didn't see
9. finished *or* graduated from
10. 's/has been
11. was
12. 've/have never made

20

3. 's/has lived there since last May. or 's been living . . .
4. she left at 4:00.
5. How many times have you been there?
6. I've / I have been tired all day.
7. It was on the table last night.
8. I've eaten there a few times.
9. What time did they get here?

21

1. was / did you go (there) / were you there
2. have you had bought/got
3. have you lived / have you been living / have you been we lived / we were did you live / were you
4. have you worked / have you been working did you do was / worked as

22

Example answers:

2. I didn't go out last night.
3. I was at work yesterday afternoon.
4. I went to a party a few days ago.
5. It was my birthday last week.
6. I went to South America last year.

23

2. B   9. C
3. D   10. D
4. A   11. A
5. A   12. C
6. D   13. B
7. C   14. C
8. B   15. A

24

1. was damaged . . . be torn down
2. was built . . . is used . . . is being painted
3. is called . . . be called . . . was changed
4. have been made . . . are produced

25

2. is visited
3. were damaged
4. be built
5. is being cleaned
6. be forgotten
7. has been repaired
8. be kept
9. Have you ever been bitten
10. was stolen

26

2. was stolen last week.
3. 're/are wanted on the phone.
4. bananas have been eaten.
5. machine will be repaired.
6. 're/are being watched.
7. housework has to be done.

27

3. pushed
4. was pushed
5. has taken *or* took
6. is being repaired
7. invented
8. was the camera invented
9. 've/have been washed *or* were washed
10. 've/have washed them. *or* washed them.
11. did they send
12. be sent

28

2. B   8. B
3. A   9. B
4. C   10. A
5. B   11. B
6. C   12. C
7. C

29

1. *B:* I stayed
   A: did you do
   B: I watched
   A: Are you going
   B: I'm going
   A: are you going to see
   B: I don't know. I haven't decided

2. *A:* have you been
   B: We arrived
   A: are you staying / are you going to stay
   A: do you like
   B: we're having

3. *A:* I've just remembered / I just remembered – Karen called
   B: She always calls *or* She's always calling . . . Did she leave
   A: she wants
   B: I'll call . . . Do you know
   A: I'll get

4. *A:* I'm going . . . Do you want
   B: are you going
   A: Have you ever eaten
   B: I've been . . . I went

5. *A:* I've lost / I lost . . . Have you seen
   B: You were wearing . . . I came
   A: I'm not wearing
   B: Have you looked / Did you look
   A: I'll go

30

1. we met
2. we sat / we were sitting
3. We didn't know
4. we became
5. we liked
6. we spent
7. We finished
8. we meet
9. has been
10. she's working
11. She's coming
12. she comes
13. we'll have / we're going to have
14. It will be

31

2. we're staying
3. we enjoyed
4. We watched
5. slept
6. I don't sleep
7. we're not doing / we're not going to do
8. we're going
9. to see

10. We haven't decided
11. wants
12. to go
13. I'll send
14. you're having
15. are studying / have been studying
16. he had
17. he needs
18. We've been
19. We got
20. seeing
21. I liked
22. we went
23. we left
24. had
25. he wasn't injured
26. was damaged
27. We've changed / We changed
28. we're leaving
29. We're staying / We're going to stay / We'll stay
30. flying
31. That will be / That's going to be
32. finished
33. I'll let
34. we get
35. are looking
36. We're going
37. we'll send

32

2. A	11. B
3. B	12. A
4. C	13. C
5. B	14. B
6. C	15. C
7. B	16. A
8. A	17. C
9. C	18. B
10 A	

33

2. a car
3. the fridge / the refrigerator
4. a teacher
5. school
6. the movies
7. a taxi
8. the piano
9. computers
10. the same

34

4. a horse
5. The sky
6. a tourist
7. for lunch (−)
8. the . . . the
9. a watch
10. remember names (−)
11. the next train
12. sends e-mails (−)
13. the backyard
14. the Majestic Hotel
15. sick last week (−) . . . to work (−)
16. the . . . the
17. to the radio . . . having breakfast (−)
18. like sports (−) . . . is basketball (−)
19. a . . . an
20. the . . . the . . . the . . . the
21. After dinner (−) . . . watched TV (−)
22. northern Mexico (−) . . . the south

35

2. in	11. for
3. on	12. at
4. at	13. in
5. on	14. at
6. in	15. on
7. since	16. by
8. on	17. for . . . on
9. by	18. to . . . in
10. in	19. at . . . in

Answer Key to Study Guide

(see page 263)

Present

1.1	B
1.2	A
1.3	C
1.4	A
1.5	C, D
1.6	B
1.7	D
1.8	C
1.9	C
1.10	A
1.11	C
1.12	A
1.13	D
1.14	C
1.15	A
1.16	D
1.17	C, D
1.18	A, D

Past

2.1	B
2.2	E
2.3	D
2.4	B
2.5	A
2.6	D
2.7	A
2.8	C
2.9	C
2.10	E

Present perfect

3.1	B, E
3.2	D
3.3	B
3.4	D
3.5	E
3.6	B
3.7	A
3.8	C
3.9	D
3.10	E

Passive

4.1	D
4.2	C
4.3	E
4.4	A
4.5	A

Verb forms

5.1	D
5.2	B

Future

6.1	A
6.2	A
6.3	C
6.4	A, B
6.5	B
6.6	C
6.7	D
6.8	C
6.9	B, C

Modals, imperative, etc.

7.1	C, D
7.2	A, C
7.3	A
7.4	D
7.5	B
7.6	C
7.7	B, D
7.8	C
7.9	C
7.10	C
7.11	B, D
7.12	A
7.13	B

There and *It*

8.1	B
8.2	E
8.3	A
8.4	A
8.5	B

Auxiliary verbs

9.1	D
9.2	A
9.3	C
9.4	B
9.5	B
9.6	C
9.7	D

Questions

10.1	D
10.2	D
10.3	A
10.4	A
10.5	B
10.6	D
10.7	B
10.8	A
10.9	C, E
10.10	C
10.11	A
10.12	A, C

Reported speech

11.1	E
11.2	A, B, D

-ing and *to . . .*

12.1	B
12.2	D
12.3	B
12.4	C
12.5	B, C
12.6	C
12.7	A
12.8	D

Go, get, do, make, and *have*

13.1	A, D
13.2	C
13.3	C, D
13.4	A, D
13.5	B
13.6	D

Pronouns and possessives

14.1	A
14.2	C
14.3	D
14.4	B
14.5	B, C
14.6	A
14.7	E
14.8	A
14.9	D
14.10	C

A and *the*

15.1	C
15.2	B
15.3	A, C
15.4	B
15.5	B
15.6	A
15.7	D
15.8	C

15.9   B
15.10 B
15.11 E
15.12 D
15.13 B
15.14 A

Determiners and pronouns

16.1   C
16.2   C
16.3   B
16.4   B
16.5   C
16.6   A, C
16.7   D
16.8   B, D
16.9   A
16.10 B
16.11 D
16.12 B, D
16.13 A
16.14 A, B
16.15 D
16.16 A, C
16.17 D
16.18 B
16.19 A

Adjectives and adverbs

17.1   A
17.2   C
17.3   C
17.4   D

17.5   B
17.6   B
17.7   A, C
17.8   E
17.9   A
17.10 B
17.11 D
17.12 A
17.13 D
17.14 C

Word order

18.1   B
18.2   C
18.3   B
18.4   A
18.5   A, D

Conjunctions and clauses

19.1   C
19.2   A
19.3   D
19.4   E
19.5   B, C
19.6   A, B
19.7   B, D
19.8   A

Prepositions

20.1   A, D
20.2   E
20.3   C, D
20.4   B
20.5   A, D

20.6   A
20.7   B
20.8   C
20.9   B
20.10 D
20.11 D
20.12 A
20.13 C
20.14 D
20.15 A
20.16 E
20.17 C
20.18 B
20.19 D
20.20 D

Phrasal verbs

21.1   C
21.2   A, B
21.3   B

Index
The numbers are unit numbers (not page numbers).

CD-ROM TERMS AND CONDITIONS OF USE

This is a legal agreement between you ("the customer") and Cambridge University Press ("the publisher") for *Basic Grammar in Use*, Third Edition, CD-ROM.

1. Limited license

(a) You are purchasing only the right to use the CD-ROM and are acquiring no rights, express or implied, to the software itself, or the enclosed copy, other than those rights granted in this limited license for educational use only.

(b) The publisher grants you the license to use one copy of this CD-ROM on your site and to install and use the software on this CD-ROM on a single computer. You may not install the software on this CD-ROM on a single secure network server for access from one site.

(c) You shall not: (i) copy or authorize copying of the CD-ROM, (ii) translate the CD-ROM, (iii) reverse-engineer, alter, adapt, disassemble, or decompile the CD-ROM, (iv) transfer, sell, lease, lend, profit from, assign, or otherwise convey all or any portion of the CD-ROM, or (v) operate the CD-ROM from a mainframe system.

2. Copyright

All titles and material contained within the CD-ROM are protected by copyright and all other applicable intellectual property laws and international treaties. Therefore, you may not copy the CD-ROM. You may not alter, remove, or destroy any copyright notice or other material placed on or with this CD-ROM.

3. Liability

The CD-ROM is supplied "as-is" with no express guarantee as to its suitability. To the extent permitted by applicable law, the publisher is not liable for costs of procurement of substitute products, damages, or losses of any kind whatsoever resulting from the use of this product, or errors or faults in the CD-ROM, and in every case the publisher's liability shall be limited to the suggested list price or the amount actually paid by the customer for the product, whichever is lower.

4. Termination

Without prejudice to any other rights, the publisher may terminate this license if you fail to comply with the terms and conditions of the license. In such event, you must destroy all copies of the CD-ROM.

5. Governing law

This agreement is governed by the laws of England, without regard to its conflict of laws provision, and each party irrevocably submits to the exclusive jurisdiction of the courts of England. The parties disclaim the application of the United Nations Convention on the International Sale of Goods.

SYSTEM REQUIREMENTS

WINDOWS

- Windows XP, Windows Vista, or Windows 7
- 800GHz or faster Intel/AMD (XP) or 1GHz Intel/AMD CPU (Vista and Windows 7)
- 256MB RAM or better (XP) or 1GB RAM or better (Vista and Windows 7)
- Resolution at least 1024 x 768 pixels
- Microphone
- Internet connection (for accessing Cambridge Dictionaries Online)

MAC

- Mac OS X 10.4+
- 500MHz G3/1GHz Core Solo
- 256MB RAM or better
- Resolution at least 1024 x 768 pixels
- Microphone
- Internet connection (for accessing Cambridge Dictionaries Online)